Analyzing Social Networks

Sara Miller McCune founded SAGE Publishing in 1965 to support the dissemination of usable knowledge and educate a global community. SAGE publishes more than 1000 journals and over 800 new books each year, spanning a wide range of subject areas. Our growing selection of library products includes archives, data, case studies and video. SAGE remains majority owned by our founder and after her lifetime will become owned by a charitable trust that secures the company's continued independence.

Los Angeles | London | New Delhi | Singapore | Washington DC | Melbourne

2nd Edition

Analyzing Social Networks

Stephen P Borgatti

Martin G Everett

Jeffrey C Johnson

Los Angeles | London | New Delhi
Singapore | Washington DC | Melbourne

Los Angeles | London | New Delhi
Singapore | Washington DC | Melbourne

SAGE Publications Ltd
1 Oliver's Yard
55 City Road
London EC1Y 1SP

SAGE Publications Inc.
2455 Teller Road
Thousand Oaks, California 91320

SAGE Publications India Pvt Ltd
B 1/I 1 Mohan Cooperative Industrial Area
Mathura Road
New Delhi 110 044

SAGE Publications Asia-Pacific Pte Ltd
3 Church Street
#10-04 Samsung Hub
Singapore 049483

First edition published April 2013. Reprinted 2013, 2015, 2016 (twice), and 2017.
This second edition first published 2018.

Editor: Jai Seaman
Assistant editor: Aly Owen
Production editor: Tom Bedford
Copyeditor: Christine Bitten
Proofreader: Audrey Scriven
Indexer: David Rudeforth
Marketing manager: Susheel Gokarakonda
Cover design: Shaun Mercier
Typeset by: C&M Digitals (P) Ltd, Chennai, India
Printed in the UK

Library of Congress Control Number: 2017941096

British Library Cataloguing in Publication data

A catalogue record for this book is available from the British Library

ISBN 978-1-5264-0409-1
ISBN 978-1-5264-0410-7 (pbk)

At SAGE we take sustainability seriously. Most of our products are printed in the UK using FSC papers and boards. When we print overseas we ensure sustainable papers are used as measured by the PREPS grading system. We undertake an annual audit to monitor our sustainability.

This book is for Lin Freeman, our mentor. Much of what is said in this book comes originally from Lin, either through classes or informal conversations.

Contents

Acknowledgements

We would like to acknowledge the considerable help of Bill Stevenson (Boston College), who wrote the original draft of the data collection chapter, as well as the guidance provided by the questions posed to us over the years from many workshop participants. We would also like to thank Michael Zurek for his help on the glossary.

Preface

Welcome to the world of social network analysis. This book is intended as a general introduction to doing network research. The focus is on methodology, from research design and data collection to data analysis. Of course, since methodology and theory are deeply intertwined, this book is also about network theory. What the book is not is a survey of empirical research on social networks.

The book is also meant to be relatively non-technical. We try not to simplify to the point of being inaccurate, but, when forced to make a choice, we have opted for intelligibility and transmitting the spirit of an idea. In each case, however, we provide pointers to the appropriate technical literature so that the reader can get a fuller picture if desired.

Doing network analysis implies using network analysis software. A number of packages exist, including UCINET (Borgatti et al., 2002) and Pajek (Batagelj and Mrvar, 1998). As two of the authors of UCINET are authors of this book, we use UCINET for most of our examples. However, we do *not* intend this book to be a tutorial on UCINET. This means we focus on generic data analysis issues and, in general, do not give detailed UCINET-specific instructions. For those interested, however, the book's website (https://study.sagepub.com/borgatti2e) gives detailed information on how all the UCINET examples are done. The one exception to all of this is Chapter 5, which is much more UCINET-focused than the rest of the book.

One of the issues we faced in writing this book was how to keep it down to a reasonable size and maintain an understandable flow. We wanted to write a guide rather than an encyclopedia. As a result, we had to leave some things out. In general, our approach to this was to include only methods and concepts that are in demand and tend to be useful in a variety of settings. For example, although the k-plex (Seidman and Foster, 1978) is one of our favorite network concepts, we left it out of the chapter on subgroups because, in general, other approaches tend to be more practical. Similarly, in the chapter on centrality, we successfully resisted the temptation to present even a small fraction of all the measures that are available in the literature.

Throughout the book, we use empirical examples to illustrate the material. Because social networks are studied in a variety of traditional academic disciplines, we draw our examples from a wide variety of fields, including anthropology, sociology, management and health care.

The book consists of 15 chapters that, in our minds at least, are logically grouped into four sections. The first section consists of an introduction (Chapter 1) and some mathematical foundations (Chapter 2). Chapter 1 lays out our perspective on the network research enterprise as a whole. It discusses the kinds of things we try to explain, along with the main approaches to explaining them. Chapter 2 reviews – in very simple terms – some of the basic concepts in graph theory and matrix algebra. A reader familiar with network analysis could skip these two chapters, but we think it advisable to familiarize yourself with our notation and terminology.

The next section has six chapters which are all about research methods. Chapter 3, on research design, is about the choices we make in setting up a study to investigate a given research question. Some of it applies to social science research in general, but much of it presents issues that are specific to social network analysis, such as the special challenges to respondent privacy. A key concept introduced here is the distinction between whole-network research designs and personal-network (aka egocentric) research designs. Chapter 4 discusses different options for the collection of network data, focusing specifically on survey methods for full network designs. Chapter 5 is about the data manipulations we often do to prepare network data for different analyses. Because it also discusses the importing and exporting of data, this chapter is more closely tied to UCINET than any other chapter. Chapter 6 is about fundamental exploratory multivariate techniques that are not specifically designed for social network analysis but are often used as part of the analysis process. Chapter 7 is about ways of visualizing network data in order to reveal patterns. Finally, Chapter 8 is about statistical techniques for testing hypotheses with network data. These are techniques specifically tailored for the special challenges of network data, such as non-independence of observations. The first part of the chapter is about using permutation-based versions of standard techniques such as correlation and regression. The second part is about exponential random graph and SIENA models. These techniques are not available in UCINET, and the statistical underpinnings of the models are far outside the scope of this book. However, we have included a brief introduction so that the reader is at least familiar in the broadest terms with these options and can then decide whether to explore them further.

The third section of the book is about the core concepts and measures of network analysis. Chapter 9 discusses measures at the whole-network level of analysis, such as the density of ties and the degree of clustering. Chapter 10 is about measures of node centrality, which can be seen as characterizing each node's position in a network. Chapter 11 is about definitions and methods of detecting groups (sometimes called 'clusters' or 'communities') within a network. Chapter 12 discusses ways of conceptualizing and measuring structural similarities in how nodes are connected in the network.

The final section of the book consists of three cross-cutting chapters organized around different kinds of data. Chapter 13 is about methods of analyzing affiliation-type data, as when we have persons' memberships in groups. Chapter 14 provides a set of heuristics useful in processing large networks, such as ways of breaking down the problem into a series of smaller ones, or changing the problem to analyze ties among clusters of nodes. Finally, Chapter 15 is concerned with designing, collecting and analyzing ego network data. We note that there is no chapter devoted to longitudinal data, but examples of longitudinal analyses can be found in many of the chapters in the network concepts section.

With certain exceptions, the chapters do not depend heavily on each other, so the book does not need to be read sequentially. One reviewer has suggested beginning with Chapters 1 and 2 for an introduction to networks, then Chapters 3–5, 15, 14 and 13 on study design and implementation, Chapters 9–12 on social network concepts and measures, and finally Chapters 6–8 on analyzing network data.

The second edition contains some new sections and additional material as well as some changes to the text in order to clarify and improve the flow. In addition, we have added some problems and exercises to each chapter.

We are grateful to our mentor, Lin Freeman, for teaching us social network analysis in the first place. It is his take on the field that this book presents. We also thank Roberta Chase for many painful hours editing our less-than-perfect prose, Adam Jonas for managing all the (constantly changing) figures and tables, Chris Cooper for managing the references, and Filip Agneessens and Eric Quintane for their close reading of Chapter 8. We also thank Bill Stevenson for writing the original draft of the data collection chapter. Finally, we acknowledge NSF, DTRA, ARO and DARPA, whose grants have supported portions of this work.

We hope you find the book useful and will send us gently-worded suggestions for improvement.

Steve, Martin and Jeff
December 2017

Online Resources

The second edition of *Analyzing Social Networks* is supported by a wealth of online resources for students to aid study and support revision, which are available at https://study.sagepub.com/borgatti2e.

- Glossary **flashcards** help you get to grips with key terms and revise for exams.
- A **UCINET Quick Start Guide** contains all your need-to-know information about getting started with the software.
- **Sample datasets for analysis** take your learning off the page and give you the opportunity to practice the techniques you have learned in small, manageable pieces.
- **Worked examples** show how to tackle common processes and techniques step-by-step.
- **Additional exercises** and **answers to in-text questions** test your knowledge and ensure you have retained the most important parts of each chapter.
- A **link to the authors' website** ensure you stay up to date with the latest UCINET and NetDraw developments.

1

Introduction

Learning Outcomes

1. Understand what constitutes a social network
2. Understand the differences between different kinds of ties
3. Identify and describe different levels of analysis
4. Formulate problems in terms of network variables

1.1 Why networks?

An obvious question to ask is why anyone would want to analyze social network data. The incontestable answer, of course, is because they want to. But what are some sensible-sounding reasons that a researcher could use in polite company? One is that much of culture and nature seems to be structured as networks – from brains (e.g., neural networks) and organisms (e.g., circulatory systems) to organizations (e.g., who reports to whom), economies (e.g., who sells to whom) and ecologies (e.g., who eats whom). Furthermore, a generic hypothesis of network theory is that an actor's position in a network determines in part the constraints and opportunities that he or she will encounter, and therefore identifying that position is important for predicting actor outcomes such as performance, behavior or beliefs. Similarly, there is an analogous generic hypothesis at the group level stating that what happens to a group of actors is in part a function of the structure of connections among them. For example, a sports team may consist of a number of talented individuals, but they need to collaborate well to make full use of that talent.

1.2 What are networks?

Networks are a way of thinking about social systems that focus our attention on the relationships among the entities that make up the system, which we call actors or nodes. The nodes have characteristics – typically called 'attributes' – that distinguish among them, and these can be categorical traits, such as being male, or continuous attributes, such as being 56 years of age. The relationships between nodes also have characteristics, and in network analysis we think of these as kinds of ties or links. Thus, the relationships between Bill (male, 47 years old) and Jane (female, 43 years old) may be characterized by being married, living together, co-owners of a business, having friends in common, and a multitude of other relational characteristics that we refer to as ties. These relational characteristics can also be continuously or ordinally valued, as in having known each other for 12.5 years and having fights 3–5 times a year.

Of special interest in network analysis is the fact that ties interlink through common nodes (e.g., the A→B link shares a node in common with the B→C link), which creates chains or paths of nodes and links whose endpoints are now connected indirectly by the path. This in turn creates the connected web that we think of as a network.[1] Part of the power of the network concept is that it provides a mechanism – namely, indirect connection – by which disparate parts of a system may affect each other.

The nodes in a network can be almost anything, although when we talk about *social* networks we normally expect the nodes to be active agents rather than, say, inanimate objects.[2] Most often, nodes are individuals, such as individual persons or chimpanzees. But they can also be collectivities, such as teams, firms, cities, countries or whole species.

Whether actors are collectivities or individuals should not be confused with levels of analysis. In network analysis, it is useful to distinguish between three levels of analysis: the dyad, the node and the network (see Table 1.1). At the dyad level of analysis, we study pairwise relations between actors and ask research questions like 'do pairs of actors with business ties tend to develop affective ties?'. The dyad level is the fundamental unit of network data collection, and is the unit with the greatest frequency (i.e., most disaggregate). In Table 1.1, the notation $O(n^2)$ indicates that the number of dyads in a network is

---

[1] However, it should be understood that we do not require a network to be connected, nor to have any ties at all. This is important when analyzing networks over time, as initially a set of actors (say, a new task force charged with investigating unethical behavior in an organization) may have no ties at all to each other, but will develop ties over time. If the data are collected over time, we may see the network become connected.

[2] But this gets more complicated in the case of two-mode networks. See Chapter 13 for more on this.

Table 1.1 Examples of research questions by level of analysis and type of node.

	Type of node	
Level of analysis	**Individuals**	**Collectivities**
Dyad level $O(n^2)$	Are employees whose offices are near each other more likely to develop friendships than employees whose offices are further apart?	Are firms with similar organizational cultures more likely to form joint ventures with each other?
Node level $O(n^1)$	Are employees who are more central in their organization's friendship network less likely to leave for another company?	Are firms with more diverse technology partners more likely to introduce innovative products into the market?
Group/Network level $O(n^0)$	When a network of employees is characterized by many redundant paths between all pairs of persons, is the network less disrupted by individuals leaving the firm?	When a network of firms is densely connected, does this place the network at greater risk of catastrophic failure (because of cascade effects)?

of order n^2, where n is the number of nodes in the network.[3] At the node level of analysis, we ask questions like 'do actors with more friends tend to have stronger immune systems?'. Most node-level network properties are aggregations of dyad-level measurements, as when we count the number of ties that a node has. The number of nodes in the network is, of course, of order n.

At the group or network level, we ask questions like 'do well-connected networks tend to diffuse ideas faster?'. The number of objects at this level of analysis is of order n^0, which is to say, 1. This means, for example, that if we have a friendship network, a variable at this level of analysis will consist of a single quantity that characterizes the network as a whole (e.g., how densely connected it is). Note that at each level of analysis, the nodes could be individuals or collectivities, as shown in Table 1.1.

It is worth noting that the 'micro' versus 'macro' terminology used in many of the social sciences can refer to either the rows or the columns of Table 1.1. For instance, in the management literature, micro refers to studies in which the cases are persons and macro refers to studies in which the cases are firms. But in economics, it is more common to use micro to refer to the study of actor-level behavior (whether the actors are individuals or firms) and macro to refer to studies of the economy as a whole (i.e., the network level of analysis). Another source of confusion is the use of 'levels' in multilevel or mixed models in statistics. Here we might calculate the centrality of students within grade-level networks

---

[3] The use of this notation to represent levels of analysis is due to David Krackhardt (personal communication).

in order to predict future success, but use a multilevel regression model that takes into account characteristics of the students' school and school district. At the same time, people who study personal networks often regard ties or alters (level 1 cases) as nested within egos (level 2 cases).

1.3 Types of relations

Relations among actors can be of many different kinds, and each type gives rise to a corresponding network. So, if we measure friendship ties, we have a friendship network, and if we also measure kinship ties among the same people, we have both a friendship network and a kinship network. In the analysis we may choose to combine the networks in various ways, but fundamentally we have two networks. Perhaps the most commonly studied ties for persons are friendship ties, advice- or other support-giving, communication and, the most basic of all, simple acquaintanceship (who knows whom). Acquaintanceship is especially important in large networks, such as a firm of 160,000 employees or society as a whole. The latter is the basis for the famous Milgram (1967) small world or 'six degrees of separation' study. The process of how individuals become acquainted has been the subject of considerable research, including Newcomb's (1961) seminal book, *The Acquaintance Process*.

Table 1.2 provides a useful taxonomy of types of ties among persons. Inspired by Atkin's (1977) distinction between backcloth and traffic, the principal division in the table is between the relational states (on the left) and the relational events (on the right). Relational states refer to continuously present relationships between nodes, such as being someone's brother or friend. 'Continuously persistent' does not mean that the relationship will never end, but rather that, while it does exist, it exists continuously over that time. This contrasts with relational events, such as selling a house. Although the process may take months to execute, the concept of a sale is a discrete event. (Of course, we can always define a relational state based on a relational event simply by casting it in a timeless way. For example, if Bill sells a house to Jim, it is an event, but the relation 'has ever received a house from' is a state.) Events that recur can also be counted, as in the number of emails that X sent to Y last month. We often use recurring relational events as evidence of an underlying relational state, as in assuming that a frequent lunch partner is a friend. We may also regard recurring events as antecedents of relational states, so that if we frequently have lunch together (perhaps for work-related reasons), we may develop a friendship. It is difficult to develop friendships without any interactions at all.

Within relational events, the table distinguishes between interactions and flows. Interactions are behaviors with respect to others and often observable by third parties. Flows are the outcomes of interactions, and interactions form the medium that enables things to flow. Flows may be intangibles, such as beliefs, attitudes, norms, and so on, that are passed from person to person. They can also consist of physical resources such as money or goods. In this book, we use flow in a relatively strict sense that doesn't include all types of causal chains. For example, if I tell you something that causes you to pick up a gun and shoot someone and then the police lock you up, we don't call that a flow. But if I tell you that grapefruit amplifies the effects of certain drugs, and you tell that to someone else who passes it on to someone else, we call it a flow. The difference is that in the second case it is the same state that is moving through the network. In the first case, it is something different in each person. But both cases involve a causal chain. Flows, then, are a special case of a more general category of causal cascades.

Within relational states, the table distinguishes between similarities, relational roles and relational cognition. Taking these in reverse order, relational cognition refers to thoughts and feelings that people have about each other. This includes acquaintance – who knows whom. Relational cognitions are essentially unobservable by other network members except as inferred from interactions. A highly consequential example of relational cognition is the trust relation, which can determine whether transactions will take place, and at what cost.

The relational roles category includes some of the most permanent of human relations, such as 'parent of' and 'sibling of'. Typically, the persons we have these relationships with are named or categorized by the relationship. Hence the person we have a friendship tie with is called a friend and is seen as enacting the friend role. When these relationships are asymmetric (such as 'mother of'), our culture typically provides us with named reciprocal roles. Hence we have parents and children, students and teachers, bosses and subordinates, and so on.

The similarities category refers to relational phenomena that are not quite social ties but can be treated as such methodologically, and which are often seen as both antecedents and consequences of social ties. For example, physical proximity (i.e., similarity in physical location) provides opportunities for face-to-face interactions.

Table 1.2 Taxonomy of types of relations.

Relational states							Relational events	
Similarities			Relational roles		Relational cognition			
Location	Participation	Attribute	Kinship	Other role	Affective	Perceptual	Interactions	Flows
Same spatial and temporal space	Same clubs, same events	Same gender, same attitude	Mother of, sibling of	Friend of, boss of, student of, competitor	Likes, hates	Knows, knows of, sees as happy	Sold to, talked to, helped, fought with	Information, beliefs, money

At the same time, certain social relations (e.g., romantic) often lead to radical increases in proximity (as in moving in together). Co-membership in groups (such as universities, gyms, teams, workplaces) provides many opportunities for interaction. Co-participation in events (such as attending the same conference or the same political rally) also provides opportunities for interaction. We can also define similarities in terms of attributes of nodes, such as gender and race. An enduring finding in social psychology is homophily – the tendency for people to like people who are similar to themselves on socially significant attributes.

One reason for pointing out the difference between relational states and relational events is that most of network analysis is built on relational states. For example, most centrality measures are best understood as generating predictions of the amount or timing of flow that is expected to arrive at a node as a function of its position in a network of relational states. The network is an observable system of roads. The centrality measures estimate the amount or timing of traffic that might flow to each node, given a set of assumptions about how things flow (e.g., whether they travel only along shortest paths). In most cases, if we were able to measure flow directly, we would not need to calculate centrality: we would simply use the observed flow instead.

It is worth pointing out that when nodes are collectivities, such as firms, there are two different kinds of ties possible. First, there are ties among the firms qua firms – that is, ties that are explicitly between the firms as single entities, such as a joint venture between two firms, an alliance, a purchase agreement, and so on. Second, there are ties between the individual members of the firms. Even though these are not 'official' ties between the organizations, they may serve all the same functions. For example, if the chief executive officers of two companies are friends, they may well share considerable information about each other's organization, constituting a flow of information between the firms. Table 1.3 provides examples of both kinds of ties among firms, cross-classified using the typology in Table 1.2.

Table 1.3 Relations among firms.

Type	Firms as entities	Via individuals
Similarities	Joint membership in trade association; co-located in Silicon Valley	CEO of organization A sits on same board as CEO of organization B
Relations	Joint ventures; alliances; distribution agreements; owns shares in; regards as competitor	Chief scientist of A is friends with chief scientist of B
Interactions	Sells product to; makes competitive move in response to	Representatives of A converse with representatives of B
Flows	Technology transfers; cash infusions	Employee of A leaks information to employee of B

1.4 Goals of analysis

Network analyses can be applied or basic.[4] By 'applied' we mean that the study consists of calculating a number of metrics to describe the structure of the network or capture aspects of individuals' positions in the network. The results are then interpreted and acted upon directly. For example, in an applied setting such as public health, we might use a centrality analysis of a network of drug addicts to detect good candidates for costly training in healthful practices, with the hope that these individuals would then diffuse the practices through the network. Or in management consulting, we might detect groups of employees from one organization in a merger situation who are not integrating well with the other company and create some kind of intervention with them. Applied studies are basically univariate in the sense that the variables measured are not correlated with each other. Rather, the correlations are assumed – because they have been observed or deduced in other, basic, research. For example, in the drug addict case, we choose to identify central players because previous research has suggested that getting central players to adopt a behavior will have add-on effects through diffusion to others. The causal relationships have been established, so we need only measure the predictor variables.

In contrast, basic research studies are multivariate and correlative – they try to describe the variance in certain variables as a function of others. The objective is to understand the dependent variables (i.e., outcomes) as the result of a causal process acting on a set of starting conditions. The independent variables serve to capture the initial conditions as well as traces of the theorized process. These are the kinds of studies we usually see in academic research. The function of network analysis in these studies is often to generate the variables that will be correlated, either as independent/explanatory variables or as dependent/outcome variables. As an example of the former, we might construct a measure of the centrality of each actor in a network, and use that to predict each actor's ability to get things done (i.e., their power). Studies of this type seek to create a network theory of _____, where we fill in the blank with the dependent variable, such as aggression or status attainment, yielding a 'network theory of aggression' or a 'network theory of status attainment'. As an example of using network variables as dependent variables, we might use the similarity of actors on attitudinal and behavioral variables (e.g., political views and smoking behavior) to predict who becomes friends with whom. Studies of this type seek to generate a _____ theory of networks, where we fill in the blank with a mechanism relating to the independent variables, such as a 'utility-maximization theory of network tie formation' or a 'balance theory perspective on network change'.

---

[4] Some might use 'descriptive' or 'explanatory', but explanation is theory and a theory is a description of how a system works.

Table 1.4   Types of network studies classified by direction of causality and level of analysis.

	Network variables as independent/ explanatory	Network variables as dependent/ outcomes
Dyad level	Friendship between pairs of farmers to predict which pairs of farmers make the same decision about going organic	Similarity of interests (e.g., sky diving) to predict who becomes friends with each other
Node level	Centrality in organizational trust network to predict who is chosen for promotion	Extraversion to predict who becomes central in friendship network
Network level	Shortness of paths in a group's communication network to predict group's ability to solve problems	Type of organizational culture (emphasizing either cooperation or competition) to predict structure of the trust network

Whether we use network variables as the independent variables in our analyses or as the dependent variables, they can be at any of the three levels of analysis discussed earlier. Table 1.4 gives examples of studies representing six possible combinations.[5]

1.5 Network variables as explanatory variables

When network variables are used as independent variables, the researcher is implicitly or explicitly using network theory to explain outcomes. These outcomes can be highly varied given that networks are studied in so many different fields – anything from individual weight gain to firm profitability. But because network processes are being used to explain these outcomes, there is a certain amount of unity in the logic that is used to predict the outcomes.

Most network theorizing is based on a view of ties as conduits through which things flow – material goods, ideas, instructions, diseases, and so on. Atkin (1977) referred to this as the backcloth and traffic model, where the backcloth is a medium, like a road system, that enables some kind of traffic to flow between locations. Within this basic conception, however, there are many different mechanisms that have been proposed to relate flows to outcomes. To discuss these, it is helpful to classify the outcomes being studied into a few broad categories. One basic category of outcomes consists of some sort of achievement, performance or benefit, either for individual nodes or for whole networks. Studies of this sort are known as social capital studies. An example is

---

[5] For simplicity, the table excludes cases where network variables are both the independent and dependent variables, as when friendship ties are used to predict business ties, or one kind of node centrality is used to predict another.

social resource theory (Lin, 2001), which argues that an actor's achievement is in part a function of the resources that their social ties enable them to access. Thus, an entrepreneur who is well connected to people who control a variety of important resources (e.g., money, power, knowledge) should be better positioned to succeed than one who has only her own resources to draw on. Thus, the key here is the inflow of resources that the entrepreneur's ties afford her.

Another perspective, which we refer to as *arbitrage* theory,[6] argues that a node B can benefit if it has ties to A and C, who are otherwise unconnected and who have achieved differing levels of progress toward a common goal. For example, if C has already solved something that A is still struggling with, B can make herself useful by bringing C's solution to A (for a price!). Here, the benefit is derived from the combination of an inflow and an outflow. Yet another network mechanism linking networks to achievement is *auctioning*. Here, if B has something that both A and C need, B can play them off against each other to bid up the price or extract favors from each. In this case, the benefit comes from the potential outflow from B to her contacts. In all of these cases, achievement is some sort of function of social ties. That is, the structure of the network and the position of individual nodes within it are crucial factors in predicting outcomes. This is very clear in the last two examples, in which a node B occupies a position between two others. But it is also true of the first case (social resource theory), because the resources of a node's connections may themselves be a function of their connections.

Another basic category of outcomes is what we might call 'style'. Unlike achievement, where one outcome is 'better' than another, style is about choices. Studies in this category look at things like political views, decisions to adopt an innovation, acquisition of practices and behaviors, and so on. These outcomes are often phrased in dyadic terms, so that what we are trying to explain is why, say, two firms have adopted similar internal structures, or why two people have made the same decision on the kind of smartphone to buy. The classic network explanation for these observed similarities is diffusion or influence. Through interactions, actors affect each other and come to hold similar views or become aware of similar bits of information. This is a perspective that clearly stems from a view of ties as conduits. But it is not necessarily the case that node A resembles node B because they influenced each other. It could be that a third party is tied to both of them and is influencing them both. It could also be something more subtle. For example, consider predicting employees' reaction to their phone ringing. Suppose some people cringe when it rings and others enjoy it. It could be that the people who cringe are those who are highly central in the advice network, meaning that lots of people are constantly calling to get their help and this gets annoying. Notice it is not that the central people are infecting each other with a bad attitude toward the phone, or even that third parties are

---

[6] Arbitrage is our term for one specific mechanism in Burt's (2004) discussion of brokerage.

infecting both of them with that attitude. It is a reaction that both have to the same situation, namely receiving so much flow. Essentially, the argument is that nodes are shaped by their social environments, hence nodes that have similar environments (such as both being central) will have similar outcomes.[7]

1.6 Network variables as outcome variables

It is often asserted that there is more research examining the consequences of network variables than the antecedents. This could be true, but it could also be a misperception due to the fact that the various factors that impinge on network variables come from a wide variety of different fields and will not have any particular theoretical unity. This is especially clear when you consider that the network properties being explained can be at different levels of analysis (i.e., the dyad, the node and the whole network), and that they may not be talked about using network terms. For example, there is a large and venerable literature on the acquaintance process (Newcomb, 1961) that never uses the term 'network'.

One of the oldest and most frequently replicated findings in social psychology is homophily – the tendency for people to have positive ties to those who are similar to themselves on socially significant attributes such as gender, race, religion, ethnicity and class. One way of thinking about these findings is in terms of a logistic regression in which the cases are dyads, the dependent variable is whether or not the nodes in the dyad have a positive tie, and the independent variables are things like *samegender* (a variable that is 1 if the nodes in the dyad are the same gender and 0 otherwise) and *agediff* (the absolute value of the difference between their ages).[8] In predicting most kinds of positive ties (but not marriage or other romantic relationships) we find a positive coefficient for *samegender* and a negative coefficient for *agediff*.

It is worth noting that having positive ties with people similar to oneself need not be solely the result of a preference. It could also reflect the availability of suitable partners. For example, if most people in an organization were women, we would expect most of these women's work friends to be women as well, simply because of availability. At the same time, we would expect most men to have quite a few women as friends, again because of availability. We would not want to conclude from such data that women are homophilous whereas men are heterophilous. One of the historical roots of social network analysis is in structuralist sociology, which, in the name of parsimony, urges us to seek answers in opportunities and constraints before turning to preferences.

---

[7] Note this is an example of a causal cascade that is not a flow, as discussed earlier.

[8] See Chapter 8 for a discussion of how to deal with issues of non-independence of observations that arise in an analysis of this type.

This suggests two basic types of factors in tie formation – opportunity and preference – and these are often intertwined. As an example of an opportunity-based mechanism, another well-known finding in the literature is that one tie leads to another. For example, business ties can lead to friendship ties, and vice versa. The presence of one tie sets up the opportunity for another kind of tie to form. More generally, as discussed in the third section of this chapter, we often expect relational states like friendship to lead to interactions (e.g., talking) through which things like information can flow, and which in turn can change the relationship (e.g., sharing intimacies deepens the relationship).

An example of a preference-based mechanism is balance theory (Festinger, 1957; Heider, 1958). In this theory, a person tries to be congruent with those she likes. So, if Jane likes Sally, and Sally likes Mary, it would cause Jane cognitive dissonance to dislike Mary. Based on balance theory, we would expect either that Jane's estimation of Mary would rise, or her estimation of Sally would decline. Note that an opportunity-based perspective would also predict the development of a positive tie between Jane and Mary because both of them are friends with Sally and Sally might well invite both to the same events, where they might interact and learn to like each other.

1.7 Summary

Network analysis is about structure and position. To this end, the field has developed an impressive array of concepts to characterize position and structure. In large part, the field has been able to express these concepts formally (i.e., in mathematical terms). This is a huge advantage because it means we can program computers to detect and measure these concepts in data, which in turn allows us to test hypotheses empirically. One downside, however, has been that some social scientists, unfamiliar with formal theorizing, have misconceived of the field as a methodology. It does indeed have a distinctive methodology that is born of its fundamentally relational view of social phenomena. But the theoretical concepts that are so emblematic of the field, such as centrality and structural equivalence, are just that: theoretical concepts that are part of a distinctive approach to explaining the social world (Borgatti and Halgin, 2011).

1.8 Problems and Exercises

1. There are three levels of analysis in the study of social networks: the dyadic level, node level and network level. For each of the research problems described below, what level of analysis is appropriate?

    a.   In a coeducational summer camp for teens, researchers want to know the extent to which attitudes about religion play a role in the formation of friendships within the first week of coming to camp.

    b.   An anthropologist is interested in studying the relationship between Canadian Inuit hunters' structural position in a hunting advice network, as measured by indegree centrality, and their hunting success.

    c.   A sports psychologist is interested in studying the relationship between basketball team cohesion off the court and number of regular season wins among a sample of 30 US universities.

    d.   A political scientist hypothesizes a relationship between the presence of international trade relations and the formation of bilateral defense agreements.

    e.   An agricultural extension researcher proposes that time of adoption of a new fertilizer among Iowa corn farmers is related to the structural centrality of farmers in a communication network.

    f.   An organizational sociologist hypothesizes that the more regional sales teams have a centralized information-sharing network the greater the team's overall sales.

    g.   An educational researcher is interested in how the political views of incoming freshmen at a large university affect the formation of friendship ties over the first semester.

    h.   A network researcher is interested in the relationship between astronaut knowledge of mission network structure and psychological well-being over the course of a 30-day simulated mission.

    i.   A management researcher advocates that highly centralized networks are more efficient at a variety of task settings than distributed networks, and designs an experiment to test this hypothesis.

2.   For each of the research problems identified in Problem 1, which is the explanatory variable, and is it a network or non-network variable?

3.   Based on the taxonomy of relations in Table 1.2, what type of relation best reflects each of the following? Explain your answer.

    a.   International trade

    b.   Financial transactions among banks

    c.   Preschool children's stated play preferences

    d.   College student attendance at university functions

    e.   Who one trusts in an organization

    f.   Advice-seeking among scientific research team members

    g.   Who one talks to about important matters

    h.   Money lending in a rural Indian community

    i.   Conflict among ethnic groups in South Sudan

    j.   Enjoys working with small project teams

    k.   Would want to work with future projects with others in a high-tech firm

    l.   Sexual relationships among IV drug users

    m.   Lab proximity of scientists in a research institute

    n.   Observed interactions at a company picnic

    o.   County commissioners and their votes on policy issues

Don't forget to visit the website at
https://study.sagepub.com/borgatti2e

2
Mathematical Foundations

Learning Outcomes

1. Represent networks in graph-theoretic language
2. Identify paths, walks, trails and components
3. Formulate networks in matrix terms
4. Compute and interpret multiplication of adjacency matrices

2.1 Introduction

As should be evident from Chapter 1, social network analysis is a social science. The actors we study are typically individuals (specifically humans, but also other social species such as apes and dolphins) or organizations (such as corporations). But networks are encountered in many other fields as well, including physics, ecology, chemistry, neurology, genetics and computer science. What these instances of network analysis have in common is an underpinning in a branch of discrete mathematics called graph theory. In this chapter we introduce the terminology and basic conceptual building blocks of graph theory. In addition, we present a short introduction to matrices, which can also be used to represent networks, and matrix algebra, which has proved very useful in network analysis.

2.2 Graphs

One way of conceptualizing networks mathematically is as *graphs*. The term 'graph' here does not refer to a diagram but rather a mathematical object (Harary, 1969). A graph $G(V, E)$ consists of a set of vertices V (also called nodes or points), and a set of edges E (or links or lines). The edges connect pairs of vertices. To express that an edge connecting vertices u and v exists in a graph G, we write $(u, v) \in E(G)$. If we think of G as a binary relation, then we could also write uGv. For example, if G represents the 'likes' relation, the uGv would indicate that u likes v. When two vertices are joined by an edge, we say the vertices are adjacent. So, adjacent just means 'has a tie'. If an edge connects A with B, and another edge connects A with C, we say that the two edges are incident upon A. The number of edges incident on a node is called the 'degree' of that node.

Graphs may be directed or undirected. In a directed graph, the edges are like arrows – they have direction. Edges in directed graphs are often referred to as arcs, and can be thought of as ordered pairs of vertices. For example, the graph depicted visually in Figure 2.1 consists of a set of vertices $V = \{A, B, C, D, E\}$, and a set of ordered pairs $E = \{(A, B), (B, C), (C, D), (D, A), (D, E)\}$. The (C, D) pair indicates that C sends a tie to D. If the tie is reciprocated, the pair (D, C) would also be a member of the set E (but, in the example, it is not). Directed graphs are used to represent relational phenomena that logically have a sense of direction – for example, 'is the parent of' and 'gives advice to'. Note that directed relations can be reciprocated. It could be, for example, that in a certain group of people, every time someone gives advice to someone else, they receive advice from that person as well.

In undirected graphs, the edges are unordered pairs. Undirected graphs are used for relations where direction does not make sense or logically must always be reciprocated, as in 'was seen with' or 'is kin to'.

Although not a mathematical necessity, in social network analysis we usually organize things such that every edge in a graph means the same thing – that is, represents the same social relation. So a given graph $G(V, E)$ contains only friendship ties, while another graph $H(V, A)$ contains only advice ties among the

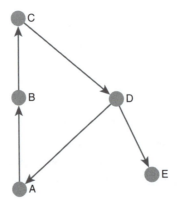

Figure 2.1 A simple directed graph.

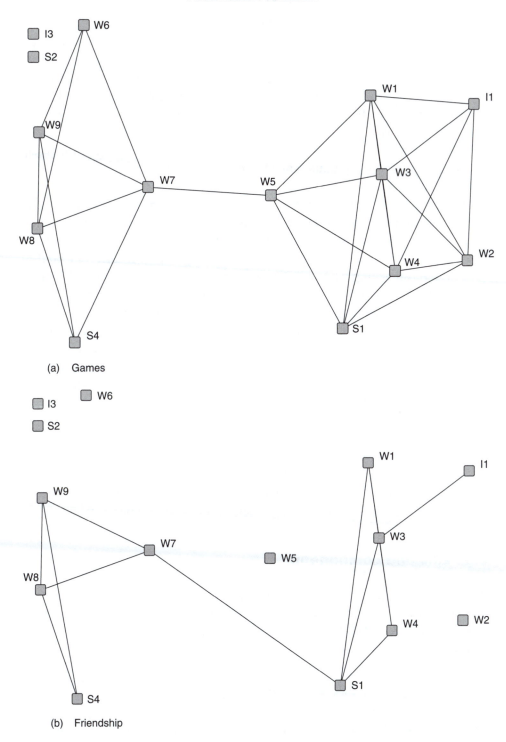

(a)   Games

(b)   Friendship

Figure 2.2   A multirelational network consisting of two relations: (a) who plays games with whom; (b) friendship ties.

same set of vertices. This means we think of the friendship and advice networks as different from each other and analyze them separately, though there are certainly exceptions to this.[1] In general, we expect each kind of social relation to have a different structure and to have different implications for the nodes involved. For example, being highly central in a friendship network might be very pleasant, while being central in a hatred network could be quite the opposite. Similarly, having many ties in a sexual network could imply a high risk of contracting a sexually transmitted disease, while having many ties in a gossip network implies an accumulation of (possibly incorrect!) information about one's social environment.

When we have more than one relation on the same set of vertices, we often refer to our data as a multirelational dataset, or (confusingly) as a network. Thus, the term 'network' in its largest graph-theoretic sense can refer to a collection of graphs in which each graph represents a different kind of social tie. As an example, Figure 2.2 shows some data from the Roethlisberger and Dickson bank wiring room dataset (Roethlisberger and Dickson, 1939). Figure 2.2a shows who plays games with whom, while Figure 2.2b shows friendship ties. As we can see, the two graphs have many points of similarity but are by no means identical. For example, in the games network, W5 and W7 are adjacent, whereas they are not in the friendship network. On the other hand, W3 and I1 are tied in both networks. When the relationship between two nodes includes multiple ties, the relationship is said to be 'multiplex'. We might even define a new network in which a tie exists between two nodes if their relationship is multiplex.

In the games network, there are two vertices that have no connections, I3 and S2. These are called 'isolates'. The friendship network has five isolates. We call the number of connections an actor has her 'degree'. Nodes with just one tie (i.e., degree 1) are called 'pendants'.[2] The friendship network has one pendant (I1).

2.3 Paths and components

A key concept in graph theory is the notion of a path. In the friendship network, vertices W1 and W7 do not have a tie, but information passed along between friends could reach W7 from W1 through the intermediary S1. A sequence of adjacent nodes forms a path. If the graph is directed, the sequence must respect

---

[1] For example, we might regard all ties between nodes as implying acquaintance, so we include all of them and call the resulting network the acquaintance network.

[2] Technically, a node is only a pendant if the one node it has a tie to has more than one tie.

the direction of the edges to be called a 'path'. Actually, the term 'path' refers to a particular kind of sequence, namely one which never revisits a vertex. For example, in the friendship graph, the sequence S4–W9–W8–W7 is a path, but W9–W8–S4–W9–W7 is not because it visits W9 twice. A sequence that revisits nodes but never revisits an edge is called a 'trail'. The sequence W9–W8–S4–W9–W7 is a trail, but W8–W7–W9–W8–W7–S1 is not because the line from W8 to W7 is used twice. Such a sequence is called a 'walk'. A walk is any sequence of adjacent nodes, without restriction. Obviously, every path is a trail, and every trail is a walk.

Paths, trails and walks matter because they correspond to different processes that we might want to model. Consider a coin changing hands as it moves through the economy. The coin does not know where it has been before, and neither do the people passing it along. As a result, the sequence it follows is completely unrestricted and is best described as a walk – perhaps even a random walk. In contrast, consider a juicy bit of gossip flowing through the network. Looking at the friendship graph in Figure 2.2b, does it seem likely that the gossip would follow the sequence W8–W7–W9–W8–W7–S1? Probably not. In most cases, W8 would remember having told W7 the story, and would not do it again anytime soon. Barring a few well-known exceptions (Alzheimer's cases; any family gathering) people do not tell the same stories again to the same people. So gossip probably does not traverse the network in an unrestricted way. One question, though, is whether it would revisit a node, as in the sequence W9–W8–S4–W9–W7. In many cases, the answer would be yes, because S4 does not know that W9 has already received this particular bit of information. Hence, an appropriate way of modeling the flow of gossip would be as trails. Finally, consider the case of a deadly virus that is spread by contact. In fact, let us suppose it is so virulent that it kills anyone it infects. To model the movement of this virus we would probably use paths because it never revisits a node. (Less gruesomely, we could imagine that it does not revisit nodes because once they get it, they become immune.)

The length of a walk (and therefore a trail and a path) is defined as the number of edges it has. The shortest path between two vertices is called a 'geodesic'. Geodesics are not necessarily unique as there could be multiple paths of equally short length between a given pair of vertices. In the friendship graph, W3–W4–S1 and W3–W1–S1 are both geodesics. The length of a geodesic path between two vertices is called the 'geodesic distance', or simply the 'distance'. If we assume that it takes a unit of time for something to traverse a link, the distance between two nodes indicates the fastest something could travel from one node to the other. A long geodesic distance implies that, even under the very best conditions, it would be a long time before something gets from one node to the other.

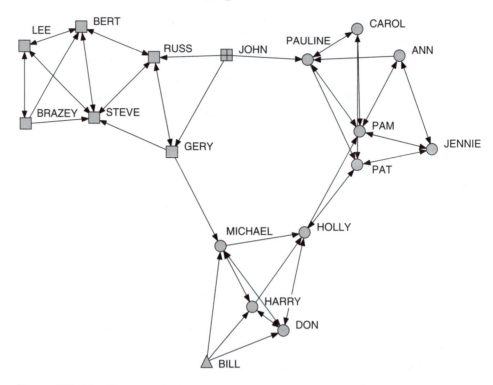

Figure 2.3 The Campnet dataset.

Some nodes cannot reach each other by any path. For example, consider the graph in Figure 2.3 (the standard UCINET Campnet dataset, which we describe in detail in Chapter 8). Try to find a path (respecting the direction of ties) from Holly to Brazey. There is no way to do it. The basic problem is that Michael and Pauline have no outgoing ties toward the left-hand side of the graph, and so there is no way for anyone on the right-hand side to reach anyone on the left-hand side. In this sense, the left- and right-hand sides belong to different components of the graph. A component is defined as a maximal set of nodes in which every node can reach every other by some path. The 'maximal' part means that if you can add a node to the set without violating the condition that everyone can reach everyone, you must do so. This means that the set {Lee, Bert, Brazey} is not a component, because we could add Steve and everyone could still reach each other. The component they are part of consists of Lee, Bert, Brazey, Steve, Russ and Gery. By this definition, there are four components in the graph: {Lee, Bert, Brazey, Steve, Russ, Gery}, {Michael, Harry, Don, Holly, Pam, Pat, Jennifer, Ann, Pauline, Carol}, {Bill}, and {John}. Bill and John form singleton components. These components are depicted by different node shapes in Figure 2.3.

In directed graphs like Figure 2.3, it is sometimes useful to consider 'weak components', which are the components you would find if you disregarded the directions of the edges. To distinguish weak components from the kind where we respect the direction of the edges, we can refer to the latter as 'strong components'. If the data are not directed, we just use the term 'components'.

The games network in Figure 2.2a has an interesting bowtie-like structure. It is worth noting the importance of the edge connecting W5 with W7. If this edge were not there, the group on the left would be separated from the group on the right. We call such edges 'bridges'. The friendship relation Figure 2.2b has two bridges: the one connecting S1 and W7 and the one connecting I1 with W3. Vertices with that same property are called 'cutpoints'. In the games relation W5 and W7 are cutpoints, and in the friendship relation S1, W7 and W3 are cutpoints. Note that I1 in the friendship relation is not a cutpoint since its removal does not separate any part of the network. In these examples the cutpoints are at the ends of bridges, but it is possible to have cutpoints that are not part of a bridge.

In many circumstances we have values associated with our edges. These may represent the strength of the tie, the frequency of interaction or even a probability. This applies to both directed and undirected network data. In our diagrams we can put the value on the edge, but for complex networks this is often not practical and we discuss other approaches in the chapter on visualization. Figure 2.4 gives a valued network where the values are 1, 2 or 3. If A sends a tie to B with a value of 2, the value is placed closer to the sending vertex. It can be seen that some ties are reciprocated but not always with the same value.

How socially close actors are to each other in a network is known as 'dyadic cohesion'. The simplest, most fundamental measure of dyadic cohesion is adjacency itself. If you and I have a tie (say, a trust tie) then we are more cohesive than if we did not have a tie. Of course, we have to be careful to think about what kind of relation is being measured. A graph in which every node has a 'hates' tie to every other node may be mathematically cohesive, but the sociological reality is that the network is maximally non-cohesive. If the data consist of valued ties (e.g., strengths or frequencies), so much the better, because then we have degrees of cohesion instead of simple presence or absence.

It is useful to note that some nodes that are not adjacent may still be indirectly related. All nodes that belong to the same component are far more cohesive than a pair of nodes that are in separate components. If a virus is spreading in one component, it will eventually reach every node in the component – but it cannot jump to another component. Naturally, if we are using the existence of a path from one node to another as a measure of cohesion, it is only a small stretch to consider counting the number of links in the shortest path between two nodes as an inverse measure of dyadic cohesion. However, one

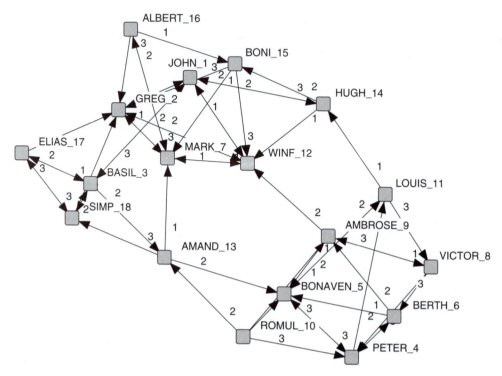

Figure 2.4   A valued network.

problem with geodesic distance is that the distance between nodes in separate components is technically undefined (or, popularly, infinite). A solution is to use the reciprocal of geodesic distance $(1/d_{ij})$ with the convention that if the distance is undefined, then the reciprocal is zero. This also has the advantage of making it so that larger values indicate more cohesion. We explore these ideas in more detail in Chapter 9.

2.4 Adjacency matrices

Another way to conceptualize networks mathematically is by using matrices. An adjacency matrix is a matrix in which the rows and columns represent nodes and an entry in row i and column j represents a tie from i to j. In other words, the adjacency matrix A of a non-valued graph is defined as a matrix in which $a_{ij} = 1$ if there is a tie from i to j, and $a_{ij} = 0$ otherwise. The direction is important and it must be remembered that, by convention, the direction goes from the rows to the columns. If the graph has valued edges, then we can simply use those values as the entries in the adjacency matrix. When the values are all positive, we often use the convention that a zero indicates no tie (alternatively, we can use a specially designated missing-value code to indicate no tie; this is a necessity when the matrix can include negative values). If the graph is reflexive – that is, vertices can have ties to themselves – then there can be values down the main diagonal. For most relations self-loops are not allowed, and in this case the diagonal is often filled with zeros (a convention we shall use), but it could be argued that the diagonal should be blank. If the graph is undirected, then the matrix will be symmetric, meaning that the top right half of the matrix (above the main diagonal) will be the mirror image of the bottom half of the matrix, and x_{ij} will always equal x_{ji}. If the graph is directed, x_{ij} need not equal x_{ji} (although it may). The adjacency matrix for the games relation in Figure 2.2 is given in Matrix 2.1.

We can also use matrices to represent derived connections between pairs of nodes such as geodesic distance. Given a graph then the geodesic distance matrix D has elements d_{ij} equal to the geodesic distance between i and j. When there is no possibility of confusion, we simply use the term 'distance matrix'.[3] The matrix D is in fact extremely similar to the adjacency matrix of a graph; where there are 1s in the adjacency matrix, there are 1s in the distance matrix. But where there are 0s in the adjacency matrix, there is a range of values in the

		1 I1	2 I3	3 W1	4 W2	5 W3	6 W4	7 W5	8 W6	9 W7	10 W8	11 W9	12 S1	13 S2	14 S4
1	I1	0	0	1	1	1	1	0	0	0	0	0	0	0	0
2	I3	0	0	0	0	0	0	0	0	0	0	0	0	0	0
3	W1	1	0	0	1	1	1	1	0	0	0	0	1	0	0
4	W2	1	0	1	0	1	1	0	0	0	0	0	1	0	0
5	W3	1	0	1	1	0	1	1	0	0	0	0	1	0	0
6	W4	1	0	1	1	1	0	1	0	0	0	0	1	0	0
7	W5	0	0	1	0	1	1	0	0	1	0	0	1	0	0
8	W6	0	0	0	0	0	0	0	0	1	1	1	0	0	0
9	W7	0	0	0	0	0	0	1	1	0	1	1	0	0	1
10	W8	0	0	0	0	0	0	0	1	1	0	1	0	0	1
11	W9	0	0	0	0	0	0	0	1	1	1	0	0	0	1
12	S1	0	0	1	1	1	1	1	0	0	0	0	0	0	0
13	S2	0	0	0	0	0	0	0	0	0	0	0	0	0	0
14	S4	0	0	0	0	0	0	0	0	1	1	1	0	0	0

Matrix 2.1 Adjacency matrix of relation 1 in Figure 2.2.

---

[3] More generally, elsewhere in the book we refer to 'proximity matrices', which is a general category of matrices – including distance matrices – that record the closeness or similarity (or farness or dissimilarity) of pairs of entities.

Analyzing Social Networks

		1	2	3	4	5	6	7	8	9	10	11	12	13	14	15	16	17	18
		H	B	C	P	P	J	P	A	M	B	L	D	J	H	G	S	B	R
1	HOLLY	0	2	1	1	2	2	2	2			1		2					
2	BRAZEY	5	0	7	6	6	7	7	7	4		1	5		5	3	1	1	2
3	CAROL	2		0	1	1	2	1	2	4			3		4				
4	PAM	3		2	0	2	1	1	1	5			4		5				
5	PAT	1		1	2	0	1	2	2	3			2		3				
6	JENNIE	2		2	1	1	0	2	1	4			3		4				
7	PAULINE	2		1	1	1	2	0	2	4			3		4				
8	ANN	3		2	1	2	1	1	0	5			4		5				
9	MICHAEL	1		3	2	2	3	3	3	0			1		1				
10	BILL	2		4	3	3	4	4	4	1	0		1		1				
11	LEE	5	1	7	6	6	7	7	7	4		0	5		5	3	1	1	2
12	DON	1		3	2	2	3	3	3	1			0		1				
13	JOHN	3	4	2	2	2	3	1	3	2		3	3	0	3	1	2	2	1
14	HARRY	1		3	2	2	3	3	3	1			1		0				
15	GERY	2	3	4	3	3	4	4	4	1		2	2		2	0	1	2	1
16	STEVE	4	2	6	5	5	6	6	6	3		1	4		4	2	0	1	1
17	BERT	4	2	6	5	5	6	6	6	3		1	4		4	2	1	0	1
18	RUSS	3	3	5	4	4	5	5	5	2		2	3		3	1	1	1	0

Matrix 2.2 Geodesic distance matrix for Campnet data.

distance matrix, providing a more nuanced account of lack of adjacency. The distance matrix must be symmetric for undirected data. Matrix 2.2 gives the geodesic matrix for the network in Figure 2.3. This was produced by running the geodesic distance routine in UCINET. We see that the distance from Brazey to Pam is 6, and there is no path from Brazey to Bill as this entry is blank. Note that in this case the zeros on the diagonal do have meaning.

2.5 Ways and modes

The adjacency matrix of a graph is always square: it has the same number of rows as columns. Moreover, it is a one-mode matrix, which means that the rows and columns both refer to the same single set of entities. In contrast, in a two-mode matrix the rows and columns refer to different sets of (non-interchangeable) nodes, and would only coincidentally be square. For example, the classic dataset collected by Davis et al. (1941) in their book, *Deep South*, is shown in Matrix 2.3. The 18 rows of the matrix correspond to

	E1	E2	E3	E4	E5	E6	E7	E8	E9	E10	E11	E12	E13	E14
EVELYN	1	1	1	1	1	1	0	1	1	0	0	0	0	0
LAURA	1	1	1	0	1	1	1	1	0	0	0	0	0	0
THERESA	0	1	1	1	1	1	1	1	1	0	0	0	0	0
BRENDA	1	0	1	1	1	1	1	1	0	0	0	0	0	0
CHARLOTTE	0	0	1	1	1	0	1	0	0	0	0	0	0	0
FRANCES	0	0	1	0	1	1	0	1	0	0	0	0	0	0
ELEANOR	0	0	0	0	1	1	1	1	0	0	0	0	0	0
PEARL	0	0	0	0	0	1	0	1	1	0	0	0	0	0
RUTH	0	0	0	0	1	0	1	1	1	0	0	0	0	0
VERNE	0	0	0	0	0	0	1	1	1	0	0	1	0	0
MYRNA	0	0	0	0	0	0	0	1	1	1	0	1	0	0
KATHERINE	0	0	0	0	0	0	0	1	1	1	0	1	1	1
SYLVIA	0	0	0	0	0	0	1	1	1	1	0	1	1	1
NORA	0	0	0	0	0	1	1	0	1	1	1	1	1	1
HELEN	0	0	0	0	0	0	1	1	0	1	1	1	0	0
DOROTHY	0	0	0	0	0	0	0	1	1	0	0	0	0	0
OLIVIA	0	0	0	0	0	0	0	0	1	0	1	0	0	0
FLORA	0	0	0	0	0	0	0	0	1	0	1	0	0	0

Matrix 2.3 Two-mode Southern women dataset.

women, and the 14 columns correspond to events the women attended. In the matrix, $x_{ij} = 1$ if woman i attended event j; this is sometimes called an 'affiliation matrix'.

More generally, matrices can be described as having ways and modes. The ways are the dimensions of the matrix – normally two, as when we have rows and columns – while the modes are the kinds of entities being represented. A three-way matrix has rows, columns and levels, as in a data cube. For example, suppose we have data indicating which persons attended which annual conferences in each year. This could be represented by a three-way, three-mode matrix. As an example of a three-way, one-mode matrix, consider the cognitive social structure data that David Krackhardt (1987) pioneered. He asked each member of a group to tell him which people in the group had friendship ties with which others. So, they were not just being asked about their own ties to others, but their perceptions of everyone else's ties to every-one else. The result is a person-by-person matrix for each person. Combining these into a single data matrix we get a three-way, one-mode matrix X in which $x_{ijk} = 1$ if person k perceives a tie from i to j. Note that x_{iji} is person i's perception of his or her own tie to j.

2.6 Matrix products

A cornerstone of matrix algebra is matrix multiplication, an operation that is defined as follows. If A and B are conformable matrices (which means that the number of columns in A equals the number of rows in B), then the product of A and B is written $C = AB$ and is calculated as follows:

$$C_{ij} = \sum_k a_{ik} b_{kj} \qquad (2.1)$$

We can use matrix multiplication to construct compound social relations. For example, if F is an adjacency matrix representing the 'friend of' relation and matrix E represents the 'enemy of' relation, then the product FE is a compound relation we might call 'enemy of a friend of'. If the (i, j) cell of FE is greater than 0, this indicates that i has at least one friend for whom j is an enemy. In other words, j is the enemy of i's friend. More generally, $FE(i, j)$ gives the number of i's friends who have j as an enemy.

It is worth remembering that matrix multiplication is not commutative, so that AB need not be the same as BA (and, because of lack of conformability, may not even be calculable). For example, if F is the friendship relation and B is the 'boss of' relation, then if I have an FB relationship with Jane, she is the boss of at least one of my friends. But if I have a BF relationship with Jane, she is a friend of my boss. These are very different relationships.

We can also compute products of matrices with themselves. For example, if F is the friendship matrix, then FF is the 'friend of friend' relation. When the (i, j) cell of FF is greater than 0, it indicates that i has at least one friend who considers j a friend. The magnitude of the (i, j) cell gives the number of times that i has a friend that has j as a friend, which is to say, it is the number of friends of i who have j as a friend. Another way to think of this is in terms of walks. The FF matrix, or F^2, gives the number of walks from i to j that are of length 2 – that is, walks with one intermediary. Multiplying the FF matrix again by F gives us F^3, whose entries give the number of walks of length 3 from any node to any other.

More generally, the matrix F^k gives the number of walks of length k that start at the row node and end at the column node. It is worth remembering that these are walks rather than simple paths, which means they can double back on themselves. For example, suppose $F^3(i, j) = 2$. This means that there are two walks of length 3 that start at i and end at j. One such walk might be i–k–i–j. Another walk might be i–k–m–j. Both are walks of length 3. An important application of matrix powers is given in Chapter 10, where we discuss Bonacich's (1987) beta centrality concept.

A useful application of matrix products is to express social theories in formal form. For example, the notion that 'the friend of my friend is my friend, the friend of my enemy is my enemy, the enemy of my friend is my enemy, and the enemy of my enemy is my friend' can be expressed compactly as four equations:

$$F = FF$$

$$E = FE$$

$$E = EF$$

$$F = EE$$

Of course, once these principles are expressed as equations, they can also be tested. Using methods covered in Chapter 8, we can count how often (i.e., for how many i, j pairs) it is true that, say, $E = EF$. For example, we could count how often $EF(i, j) = E(i, j)$ across all i and j, and test whether this quantity is larger than we would expect by chance.

2.7 Summary

Social networks can be represented mathematically as graphs – mathematical objects consisting of two sets: a set of vertices and a set of edges connecting the vertices. The edges may or may not have a direction associated with them and can also have values. Each graph represents a single relation, but we often have multirelational networks with different sets of edges from different relations on the same set of vertices. A path is a sequence of non-repeated vertices such that adjacent pairs form an edge. Sets of vertices that are mutually reachable form components, and if they take account of direction, they are known as strong components. The length of the shortest path between any two vertices is called the geodesic distance. An alternative representation is to use matrices, with the adjacency matrix being by far the most common way to do this. We can also use matrices to capture the distance between all pairs of vertices in a network. If the data have two modes, we can use a reduced form of the adjacency matrix called an affiliation matrix.

2.8 Problems and Exercises

1. For the types of relations listed in Problem 3 in Chapter 1, are the ties implied by these relations directed or undirected?
2. Re-express the simple graph below as an adjacency matrix.

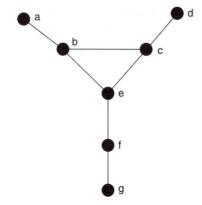

Figure 2.5

3. Re-express the graph in Problem 2 as a geodesic distance matrix. What do those distances mean?
4. For the graph in Problem 2 above, provide examples of each of the following:

    a. Paths
    b. Trails
    c. Walks

5. Re-express the directed valued graph below as a valued proximity matrix.

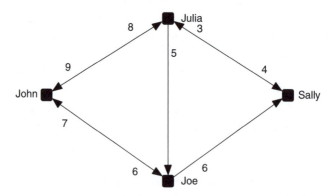

Figure 2.6

6. For the bank wiring room games graph in Figure 2.2a, if the edge between nodes W7 and W5 were removed, how many components would the graph now have? If we were to calculate geodesic distances for the new graph, what would be the distance between W9 and W3? Explain.
7. For each of the network examples in Chapter 1, Problem 3, are the associated matrices one-mode or two-mode?
8. Given a friendship relation and 'is the boss of' relation, use matrix multiplication to hand-calculate the 'is friends with the boss of' relation.

Friend of	A	B	C	D
A	0	1	1	0
B	1	0	0	0
C	1	0	0	1
D	0	0	1	0

X

Boss of	A	B	C	D
A	0	1	0	0
B	0	0	1	0
C	0	0	0	0
D	1	0	0	0

=

Friend of boss of	A	B	C	D
A				
B				
C				
D				

Matrix 2.4

Recall that if cell (A, C) has a value greater than zero in the 'is friends with the boss of' matrix, it means that A is friends with C's boss. From a power perspective, how would you view the row sums of the 'Friend of boss of' matrix?

Don't forget to visit the website at
https://study.sagepub.com/borgatti2e

3

Research Design

Learning Outcomes

1. Design effective and reliable network research projects
2. Identify sources and boundaries of network data
3. Understand and minimize the effects of data error

3.1 Introduction

This chapter is about designing network research. We try to lay out some of the issues that need to be considered when constructing a network study. In particular, we try to highlight the implications in terms of the interpretation, validity and feasibility of different combinations of design choices. The reader will recognize that many of the issues discussed here are common to all social science research and are not particular to social network analysis. For example, social networks can be studied via experiments, quasi-experiments, field studies and so on. They can be studied not only quantitatively but also ethnographically. The data collection can be cross-sectional or longitudinal. In addition, however, we also discuss some special design issues specific to social network analysis, such as the decision between whole-network and personal-network designs, as well as how to bound the network, what kinds of ties to measure, and so on.

It should be noted that this chapter touches on several topics that are discussed in greater depth in other chapters. In particular, the reader should consult Chapters 1, 4, 8 and 15.

3.2 Experiments and field studies

While most social network research has been carried out using field studies, typically survey-based, there is a well-known body of network research employing experimental designs of one form or another. True experiments are the gold standard for the study of causation. For a study to be a true experiment it must have a pre-post (i.e., variables measure before some intervention or treatment, and then again after) or post-only design, together with random assignment of units to treatment groups and manipulation of the independent variable (such as a social intervention) while controlling for all other factors, both known and unknown. The key element of a true experiment is the random assignment; in quasi-experimental research there is usually a pre-post design, along with manipulation of the independent variable, but the units of analysis are not randomly assigned to treatments (usually because it is technically not feasible or is unethical, such as assigning smoking to randomly chosen participants). Field studies, or observational studies, may be longitudinal but more often are cross-sectional and do not involve a manipulation of the independent variable. As one goes from true experiments to field designs, there is less control over various threats to the studies' reliability and validity.

Table 3.1 provides some examples of experiments and quasi-experiments in social network research. As we move from the Rand et al. (2011) study down to that of Soyez et al. (2006), researcher control over the various aspects of the study declines. In the Rand et al. (2011) experiment, subjects are randomly assigned to one of four conditions. In each of the conditions the links in the who-can-communicate-with-whom network are manipulated. The study objective is to examine the evolution of cooperation in each of the experimental conditions. In the Barr et al. (2009) field experiment, subjects were randomly chosen from Orma villages in Kenya and small industrial operations in Ghana and were assigned to one of two player conditions. The behavior of subjects in the two reflected either degrees of trust or trustworthiness on the part of the players. Although there was random assignment of subjects, there was no direct manipulation of one of the primary independent variables of interest, individual-level social capital. Instead, social capital was measured separately and used as one of several independent variables in attempts to account for individual-level variation in subjects' game-playing behaviors. Finally, the Soyez et al. (2006) study used a classic quasi-experimental design in which subjects from four different clinics or cohorts were assigned in sequence, and not randomly, to one of two experimental conditions. Subjects in the control condition received standard treatment for drug abuse while subjects in the experimental condition received standard treatment plus a social network intervention.

Table 3.1 Experimental and quasi-experimental designs in social network research.

Study	Design	Conditions and manipulation	Independent and dependent variables

Rand et al. (2011)	Experiment. Random assignment of 785 subjects to one of four conditions.
	
	A repeated cooperative dilemma game is played with other subjects in an artificial network.
		1 Random link condition
		2 Fixed link condition
		3 Strategic link condition
		  3a Viscous condition
		  3b Fluid condition
			The independent variable is the experimental network condition, and the dependent variable is the evolution of cooperation in an iterative game.

Barr et al. (2009)	Experiment. Assign players of the Trust Game to two player conditions, one reflecting trust and the other trustworthiness. Players were randomly selected from the community to play.	Two cultural settings (Orma of Kenya and workers in Accra, Ghana). Two player conditions in the Investment Game protocol.	The independent variable was social capital (betweenness centrality) and the dependent variables were player 1 and player 2 behaviors reflecting degrees of trust (player 1 behavior) and trustworthiness (player 2 behavior).
Soyez et al. (2006)	Quasi-experiment. Members of four cohorts were assigned to social network intervention involving three elements. Assignment to conditions was based on sequential program admission, not random assignment.	The first group was taken from the four cohorts admitted between 1 May 2000 and 30 April 2002 (N = 94) and received standard treatment (control group). The second group was taken from the four cohorts admitted between 1 January 2001 and 30 April 2002 and received standard treatment plus network intervention (experimental group).	Test how treatment factors predicted substance abuse treatment retention, where one of the treatment factors was social networks intervention (ego network).

Most research involving social networks employs field/observational designs of one form or another. Data can be collected at a single point in time (cross-sectional and lagged cross-sectional) or at multiple points in time (longitudinal). Collecting data at two or more points in time allows for the study of change. Examples of cross-sectional and longitudinal research in social networks are shown in Table 3.2. These examples were chosen to help illustrate not only basic elements of research design but also studies that examine both the causes and the consequences of social network structure. The study by Christakis and Fowler (2007) analyzed data repurposed from the Framingham Heart Study, which had a prospective (longitudinal) design. Christakis and Fowler used it to study the 'contagion' of obesity through social networks in a population.

Table 3.2 Examples of field studies in social network research.

Study	Design	Independent variable	Dependent variable
Christakis and Fowler's (2007) study of networks and obesity (Framingham data)	Prospective design; follow a cohort through time	Ties to obese actors at time t_i	Weight at time t_{i+1}
Burt (1995) structural holes	Cross-sectional design	Individual level social capital (e.g., constraint)	Performance evaluations; bonuses received
Casciaro (1998) study of personality and network accuracy	Cross-sectional design	Strong need for achievement	Social network accuracy
Johnson et al.'s (2003) study of group dynamics in polar research stations	Prospective, repeated measures design	Core–periphery structure	Morale and individual level psychological well-being
Padgett and Ansell's (1993) study of marriage among elite Renaissance Florentine families	Retrospective design; data gathered from historical records	Spanning structural holes in marriage relations	Financial gain and power

The advantage of this design is that network relations at one point in time can be used to predict outcomes such as obesity at some future time, providing some help in sorting out the direction of causation (even though it did not use a true experimental design, something that would be totally impractical in this case). They found evidence to suggest a contagion effect even for something that would appear on the surface not to be 'catchable' in the medical sense.

The cross-sectional studies by Burt (1995) and Casciaro (1998) both collected data via surveys at one point in time. However, Burt was interested in understanding how an actor's position in a network – the spanning of structural holes – influences outcomes such as evaluations of employee performance and sizes of bonuses received. Thus, some element of network structure is influencing some outcome of interest (e.g., performance). In contrast, Casciaro (1998), although also using a cross-sectional design, was interested in how personality influences an actor's accuracy in cognitive social structures. So here an attribute of an actor is influencing the ability of that actor to report accurately on the network relations of others. In other words, network accuracy is a consequence of personality.

In the Johnson et al. (2003) study a longitudinal repeated measures design was used. Although the table depicts a study about the role of core–periphery structure in influencing group morale, the premise of the research was more complex and illustrates a slight spin on the simple structural causes-and-consequences dichotomy.

Informal Role Characteristics of Crew   →   Group Structure   →   Group Morale

Figure 3.1   Relationship among variables for Johnson et al. (2003) study.

As shown in Figure 3.1, the study was more broadly focused on the relationship among three variables in which network structure was a mediating variable. The study focused on how the emergence of informal roles in the network (e.g., clown, expressive leader) affected the evolution of network structure. If certain roles emerged in certain combinations, it was expected that the network would form a core–periphery structure, and the more the network evolved a core–periphery structure, the higher the morale and individual-level psychological well-being (e.g., lower levels of depression). So, in a sense, this is an example of research that viewed structure as both a cause and a consequence.

Finally, the Padgett and Ansell (1993) study is not unlike the Burt example in that network structure is found to influence power among elite families in Renaissance Florence; here the network consists of connecting families by marriage that are not otherwise connected. This is an example of a retrospective case study where we are given an outcome – the rise of the Medici family in terms of power and wealth – and use historical data to speculate about why it happened.

3.3 Whole-network and personal-network research designs

There are two fundamental kinds of network research designs: 'whole-network' designs and 'personal-network' designs.[1] In general, when people talk about network analysis, they are referring to whole-network studies. In whole-network research, we study the set of ties among all pairs of nodes in a given set. For example, we might study who is friends with whom among all members of a given department in an organization. In whole-network studies, we can think of the relation being measured as a dyadic variable that has a value for every pair of nodes. For example, in the friendship case, every dyad might be assigned a 1 or a 0 indicating whether they are friends or not.

In personal-network studies, there is a set of focal nodes called 'egos' or 'index nodes', and their ties to others, called 'alters', are assessed, but the alters are not necessarily among the set of egos. An example of a personal-network

---

[1] In the literature, what we have called 'whole' network studies are known by a wide variety of names, such as 'socio-centric', 'complete' and 'full'. Studies using a personal-network research design are also known as 'ego-network studies' and 'ego-centered or egocentric studies'.

study is the General Social Survey of 1985, in which approximately 1500 egos were sampled using a probability sample from the population of Americans. Each was then asked for a list of up to five people with whom they discussed important matters. The aim was simply to understand something about the social environment of each of the egos, not to construct a network of ties among the 1500 (which would probably be completely empty), nor to connect the alters of one ego to the alters of any other ego (typically, the names of the alters are not even given in full).

In general, whole-network designs enable researchers to employ the full set of network concepts and techniques, which often assume that the entire network is available. This is particularly true of positional concepts such as betweenness centrality or regular equivalence. However, because the cost (to the researcher and the respondent) of whole-network designs increases quickly with network size, the richness of the data often suffers as the researcher has to scale back the number of questions he asks (see Chapter 4 for more information on this). In that sense, personal-network designs can yield richer, more detailed data about the network area local to the respondent, but at the cost of losing information on the global pattern of connections. Personal-network designs also have the advantage of simplifying issues of bounding the network, since there is no cost to allowing a respondent to mention any alter they like. Personal-network designs also have significant advantages with respect to confidentiality, as personal-network surveys can be entirely anonymous (with respect to the respondents), and when the respondents mention alters, they do not need to give the alters' real names. This can improve the quality of the data (because the respondent feels safer in giving these) and simplify the process of getting approval from human subject review boards.[2]

As we devote a separate chapter to personal-network designs, the rest of this chapter focuses on whole-network designs, although many of the points we make apply to personal-network designs as well.

3.4 Sources of network data

Network data can be collected from either primary or secondary sources. In primary data collection, we directly ask people questions or observe their behavior. What is asked or observed is determined by the objectives of the study, and the researcher has a lot of control over the types of relations studied and the types of actor attributes collected. In secondary data collection, we gather data that already exist somewhere, whether in paper records (e.g., fish exchange

---

[2] Institutional review boards or IRBs in the US.

records, historical marriage records), or electronic databases (e.g., Enron emails, social networking sites). Secondary data are often easier and quicker to collect but impose strong and arbitrary limits on the type of relations studied. Some of the computer-based data generated by social media such as Facebook and even email represent a transitional form between primary and secondary data. Although the data are collected directly, as in primary research, there are limitations on the types of relations available for study, as in secondary research.

Most published network research in the social sciences is based on primary data sources. Much of this is based on surveys, in which respondents are asked to report on their ties with others. However, there are also some well-known examples of direct observation. One of the stages of the well-known Hawthorne studies (Roethlisberger and Dickson, 1939) involved planting an observer at the back of the room where a set of employees constructed telephone wiring apparatuses. The observer was there for several months and recorded all kinds of interactions among the workers, including who played games with whom during breaks, who had conflicts with whom, who traded jobs with whom, and so on.

In recent years, we have seen a significant increase in the use of secondary sources. One reason for this is the increased availability of electronic records of all kinds, including bibliometric data (e.g., who cites whom), membership data (e.g., who is on what corporate board, who was in what movie) and of course social media (e.g., who follows whom on Twitter). Another reason is the increasing importance in the social science literature of longitudinal data, which are often only feasible to collect from secondary sources. However, not all secondary research is electronic. As previously mentioned, one of the best-known network analyses of archival data is the study by Padgett and Ansell (1993), who analyzed the pattern of marriages among Renaissance Florentine families.

3.5 Types of nodes and types of ties

As noted in Chapter 1 (see Table 1.2), there are many kinds of ties one could measure. Most network studies involve persons as the nodes and interpersonal relations as the ties. However, the nodes can be all kinds of entities – monkeys, firms, countries and so on. And the type of node obviously has a major impact on what kinds of ties are collected and how they are collected. These decisions – who to study, what ties to study, and where to obtain the data – are interlinked and must to some extent be considered together.

Table 3.3 reproduces in simplified form the typology of types of ties presented in Chapter 1. At the top left of the table are co-occurrences. One advantage of co-occurrence data is that they are relatively easy to collect. One reason is that membership-type data are often not thought of as particularly private or sensitive.

In addition, they are often available via archival sources. For example, we can look up the names of people serving on the boards of directors of firms. We can use the Internet Movie Database (IMDb) to find people who have served as cast or crew together on films. A frequently reanalyzed dataset in the network literature was collected by Davis et al. (1941) for their *Deep South* book. To obtain these data, they used the society pages of a local newspaper to learn which women attended which social events.

Next, we have true social relations – ties that have a continuous nature in the sense that they can be seen as relational states (such as being friends) rather than events (such as 'having sent an email to'). Many social relations have a quality of being institutionalized such that they have a degree of reality apart from the perceptions of the individuals involved. An example is marriage, where two people are married to one another even if they deny it. As such, information on such ties can be collected from sources other than the two people involved, such as others in the community, family members, archival records, and so on. Other types of social relations, such as affective and perceptual ties, have no independent existence or corroboration: short of inferring the tie based on some behavioral theory, such data have to be obtained by surveying the perceiver.

The third type of dyadic phenomenon, interactions, can be either directly observed or reported on by respondents. Who people talk to, watch movies with, hang out with, or communicate with via ham radio are all interactions, and are all, in principle, observable. Of course, there are always issues of interpretation. For example, if two people are verbally sparring, are they having a conflict or a friendly competition?

Table 3.3 Types of dyadic phenomena commonly studied.

Category	Varieties and examples
Co-occurrences	Co-membership in groups
	Co-participation in events
	Physical distances
	Similarities in attributes (e.g., political views)
Social relations	Kinship relations
	Affective relations (e.g., dislikes)
	Perceptual relations (e.g., knows)
Interactions	Transactions (e.g., 'sells to')
	Activities (e.g., 'sleeps with')
Flows	Ideas and information
	Goods
	Infections

In a network study of a fish camp, Johnson and Miller (1983) observed two Italian fishers engaged in what appeared to be a heated discussion. Johnson asked a younger Italian fisher, who was also observing, what the conflict was all about. The younger Italian explained that there was no conflict, but that the two men – who were brothers – were simply having a friendly discussion about a nephew. Johnson was interpreting that interaction from his cultural perspective rather than from the perspective of the two Italians engaged in the interaction.

It is worth noting here the difference between using a highly interpreted label such as 'friendly competition', versus a less interpreted label, such as 'verbal sparring', versus something even less interpreted, such as 'communicated face to face'. The higher the level of interpretation, the more theoretically useful the data are likely to be, but the greater the chance of being wrong. It is also worth noting that interactions are often collected as a proxy for unseen underlying social relations. For example, we might record who talks to whom outside of work and assume this means they are friends. Again, making these kinds of interpretations is often more powerful but may be quite unwarranted.

Electronic interactions are often available in archival form, as when we mine the email logs of a company's email server. Although convenient to collect, email interactions are particularly difficult to interpret with respect to inferring an underlying social relation. People email their friends, but they also email work colleagues, family members, acquaintances, and strangers, even on a corporate email account. Even when we have access to the content of the emails, it may be very difficult to determine what the underlying relationships are between the interactants.

Finally, the fourth type of dyadic phenomena, flows, can be seen as the outcomes of interactions. When two people interact, information is exchanged. Knowledge is transferred. Material goods can also be transferred, as in the sharing networks of subsistence hunters, where the catch is distributed among group members or traded for other commodities. In general, these kinds of data are rarely collected because they are difficult to obtain. More often, interactions are recorded, and flows are assumed. For example, many studies ask, 'Who do you seek advice from?', and the assumption is that the resulting data can be used as a proxy for the flow of information (from the alter to the ego). But, in fact, we don't know which bit of information actor A received from actor B. In a few cases, however, direct measures of flows are obtainable, as in tables of the dollar values of flows of raw materials and manufactured goods between countries. Similarly, personnel flows between companies, universities, football teams and the like are readily observable. In general, flows among collective actors like countries and organizations are easier to measure than flows between individuals, since they are public actors that are under observation by many.

3.6 Actor attributes

As noted in Chapter 1, the analysis of social networks involves more than networks. For example, node-level research normally combines network-derived variables, such as node centrality, with non-network attributes of the actors, such as demographic characteristics or personality characteristics. In some cases, the network-based variable will be among the independent variables (as when we predict performance based on centrality, controlling for competence), and sometimes it will be the dependent variable, as when we use personality characteristics to predict centrality. Either way, an important part of the research design will be to collect non-network data that will be combined in the analysis with network data.

A particularly important class of node attributes is the set of behaviors, attitudes, ideas, perceptions, beliefs, etc., that individuals have. Because these are changeable, they provide opportunities to study how networks influence individuals. Choices like what clothes to wear and what words to use are strongly influenced by the choices made by our friends, family and others in our personal networks. For some choices, the number of friends making the same choice is crucial, as in which chat system to use: it isn't useful to choose the better communication platform unless the people you want to communicate with also choose that platform.

3.7 Sampling and bounding

One of the most vexing problems for those just starting out in network research is the problem of bounding the network, although this is a bit of a misnomer. It is not the network that needs bounding, but the study. In some cases the decision seems easy and may even be made tacitly without conscious effort. Well-known examples include Sampson's (1969) study of a monastery, Zachary's (1977) study of a karate club, Bernard and Killworth's (1973) study of a research ship, Krackhardt's (1987) study of a company in Silicon Valley, and Johnson et al.'s (2003) study of a polar research station. All these involve groups that have obvious boundaries. In other cases, the problem seems nearly insurmountable. For example, if we are interested in studying social influences on consumer purchasing, we know we cannot study the entire network – all 7 billion living humans. For convenience, we might choose residents of the city in which we are located, or, more realistically, a small neighborhood. The problem is that no matter whom we choose, we can be sure that a large number of influencers of these people will be outside the sample.

Notice that the problem is not really the size of the network but rather the nature of the research question. If the research interest is social influence on decision-making, the studies we cited above as examples of easy boundary specification do not look so simple: while the monks may be fairly isolated, the employees of a company are not. The principal influencers of an employee's decisions (say, to leave the company) may well be outside the company, such as family members and members of competing companies.

To deal with this problem, we offer two suggestions. First, if your research question does not allow you to restrict the set of alters that a respondent could name, use a personal-network research design. You still have to decide who will be your respondents, but this could be as simple as a random sample from the population to which you wish to generalize. In a sense, the boundary specification problem involves two sets of actors that need bounding: the egos (in whose ties we are interested), and the alters (those with whom egos have ties). In the case of a whole-network study, these two sets of actors are the same. In personal-network studies, however, they are not, and this is quite liberating. It is also substantively interesting: in a very real sense, in a personal-network design each respondent has their own custom social world with its own boundary.

The second suggestion is to consider whether you are studying a sociological group or not. The realist school of network research design restricts itself to studying only groups, but the nominalist school sees no essential problem with studying networks that are not groups (Laumann et al., 1983). Groups are sociologically real – they are recognized by their members and, in principle at least, they have boundaries; part of the concept of a group is that there are members and non-members, even if in fact the boundaries are fuzzy and/or contested. If one is studying the internal network of a group, then getting the boundaries more or less right is important. One does not want to miss bona fide members of the group, nor does one want to include non-members. Both errors threaten the validity of the study, and the inclusion of non-members can also add considerably to the scope and complexity of the project.

If you are not studying natural groups, then the study boundaries are determined by the research question (see Table 3.4). For example, you might be interested in how the structure of the trust network in different classrooms affects the class's ability to successfully perform group projects. In this case, the network of trust ties within each classroom is assessed, and ties outside the class are not measured. This is not a problem; it does not imply that no ties to the outside world exist, nor that these ties are unimportant. It is just that the research is specifically about how the ties within a classroom affect classroom outcomes. Whether you think that is a fruitful research question is another matter. The point is that choosing an 'artificial' boundary (i.e., one that may not correspond to a sociological group) is not necessarily a threat to the validity of

Table 3.4 Sampling and bounding networks.

Type of sample	Nominalist/etic (researcher-defined networks)	Realist/emic ('natural' groups)
Random sample	Random sample of persons matching researcher's criteria.	Do ethnographic pre-study to determine group members, then sample from it.
Snowball sample	Interview any qualifying actor with a tie to any actor already selected, up to K waves or until quotas or cost limits reached.	Get starter set of group members. Select all group members with tie to previously selected member. Repeat until few new names appearing.
	E.g., ask each person who they inject drugs with, then interview those people. Repeat.	E.g., get self-identified members of gang. Ask them for other members. Repeat.
Census	All persons matching researcher criteria. E.g., all members of the Anthropology dept.	Get list of 'members' from somebody in group. E.g., locate gang member, obtain list of members, interview all/adjust on basis of subjective information.

the research design. And, as explained above, even if one is studying a natural group and knows what the boundaries are, the research objectives may necessitate studying group members' ties to people outside the group. Note that this does not mean that the choice of boundary is irrelevant. A well-known finding in the field is Brass's (1984) finding that an individual's centrality within their department was positively related to power and promotions, but their centrality within the organization as a whole was not.

Most groups have fuzzy boundaries. Even formal groups such as corporations which have membership lists have part-timers, virtual workers, temps, new hires, current applicants, retirees, consultants, etc. One basic approach to approximating the boundaries is snowball or other respondent-driven sampling methods (Johnson, 1990). In a study of communication networks in the king mackerel fishery in the southeastern United States, Maiolo and Johnson (1992) used key informant free-lists (see Borgatti, 1994, for a description of the technique) and commercial license lists to identify an initial set of seeds for a snowball sample. Although a commercial license list existed for commercial fishers and commercial dealers, there was no such list for sportfishers who targeted king mackerel, which is both an important commercial and sport species. In addition, the fact that someone was a commercial fisher did not mean they necessarily targeted king mackerel. Key informants known to target king mackerel in both the commercial and recreational sectors were asked to free-list fishers they knew who regularly targeted that species. This list provided a seed list from which to begin the snowball sample of actors 'who talked to each other about king mackerel fishing'. However, the problem was where to stop. During the course of the snowball sample, which was conducted by both phone and face-to-face interviews across North Carolina, South Carolina, Georgia and Florida, there were periods of time when there was considerable sample saturation or name redundancy in the elicitation of alters. This saturation represented fuzzy boundaries around the fisher community that were often related to geographical factors. Thus, boundaries were placed on the basis of tie intensity and redundancy in the course of the snowball sample. However, it should be noted that if the purpose of the study is to discover the nature of ties that connect various areas of high redundancy or density in social networks, then ties bridging these areas of high density need to be pursued, and the redundancy criteria may need to be applied across several waves of a snowball sample.

Many studies use a combination of nominalist (or etic) criteria and realist (or emic) criteria. An example of this is Johnson's (1986) study of the diffusion of innovations through a network of commercial fishers. Initially Johnson used the commercial license list obtained from the North Carolina Division of Marine Fisheries to identify commercial license holders in a small fishing community in North Carolina. He could have used the list as the boundary for the network, but the list included anyone who had purchased a commercial fishing license no matter how much they actually fished, and he wanted to weed out the people who really were unconnected to the local fishing world. His solution was to use the fishers' own perceptions to refine the sample. Using the licensing list, he wrote the names of each fisher on a card and asked fishers in the community to sort the names into piles according to how similar they perceived the fishers to be to one another (i.e., an unconstrained pile-sort task). Based on the pile-sort results, it was clear that there were perceived differences among the various license holders based on amount of income derived from commercial fishing. A multidimensional scaling plot (see Chapter 6) revealed two clear clusters that basically broke down by those perceived as full-time fishers as opposed to those viewed as part-time fishers. The final set of actors used for the network survey included only full-time fishers identified in the analysis. Thus, actors' perceptions were used in combination with a researcher-derived list to determine the final set of actors used in the study.

3.8 Sources of data reliability and validity issues

Errors in network data can arise from a multitude of sources. The way questions are framed, the manner in which network boundaries are specified, the willingness of respondents to answer questions, the manner in which data are aggregated, informant accuracy, the erroneous attribution of behaviors, etc., can all create error in terms of missing data or the presence of data that lack validity and may be misleading. Borgatti et al. (2006) examined the effect of data error on the measurement of centrality. They examined four kinds of error: omission of nodes, omission of ties, inclusion of false nodes and inclusion of false ties. They found that errors in various centrality measures resulting from the random exclusion and inclusion of edges in random graphs vary as a function of characteristics of the network itself (e.g., density, sparseness), and that the accuracy of measures declines predictably with the amount of error introduced. The latter is good news for network researchers, but it must be remembered that Borgatti et al. studied only artificial networks, not empirically collected networks. Moreover, their results are average values across thousands of trials. Even if the accuracy of a betweenness measurement declines an *average* of 10% when 10% error is introduced in the data, there can be individual cases where the introduction of 10% error causes a great deal more error in the measurement of centrality. For example, consider the network shown in Figure 3.2. A missing tie between nodes 4 and 5 in the top figure would completely hide the brokering importance of these two nodes. Conversely, the erroneous addition of a tie between nodes 3 and 8 would make node 3 look far more important than it really was. The lower graph in Figure 3.2 has the tie between 3 and 8 added and the changes to the betweenness scores are shown in the panel at the top right.

Johnson et al. (1989) used a Monte Carlo simulation approach to study error in networks derived from snowball samples employing a fixed-choice methodology. They found that degree centrality was relatively robust under different sampling conditions, a finding echoed by Costenbader and Valente (2003) and Wang et al. (2012).

Compared to the collection of other types of data in the social sciences (e.g., attribute-based survey data), the collection of social network data can be quite challenging. A major threat to validity in social network research stems from problems of missing data that are due to a number of different sources at a number of different stages in the research process. In addition, errors can arise from data (e.g., a network tie) that are erroneously included – what we have been referring to as 'commission errors'. These sources of error all can lead to model misspecification.

One major contributor to missing data is non-response in network surveys. This can happen if the network boundaries are not properly specified on theoretical or other grounds. Network surveys are extremely susceptible to non-response bias in that missing actors and their links can affect structural and analytical outcomes at both the network and individual levels. Respondents can refuse to participate in the survey at all or can refuse to answer some or all survey questions due to such things as interviewee burden or question sensitivity; they may drop out of a longitudinal study prematurely as a result.

The design of the study and subsequent sample or instrument design (e.g., types and forms of relational questions) for a given social network

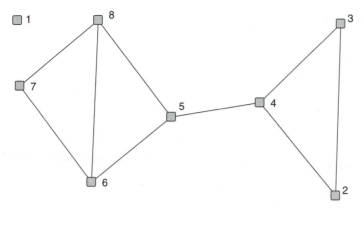

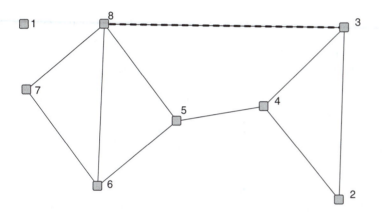

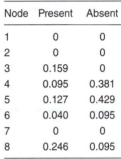

Betweenness Centrality

Node	Present	Absent
1	0	0
2	0	0
3	0.159	0
4	0.095	0.381
5	0.127	0.429
6	0.040	0.095
7	0	0
8	0.246	0.095

Figure 3.2 Effects of adding a tie on the betweenness centrality of nodes in a network.

problem and context can also be important in limiting threats to validity (and this can vary cross-culturally). Respondent unreliability and inaccuracy have been shown to produce error of various kinds (but the error is often well behaved, as discussed below). The following provides a summary of some types of error that are of concern, beginning with two that were discussed earlier in the chapter.

- **Omission errors**. Missing edges and nodes can have large impacts on errors in network variables, particularly for some centrality measures. Such missing data can make networks appear to be more disconnected than they really are or make other nodes and edges in the network appear to be more important than they really are (as evidenced by the missing of a single tie between nodes 4 and 5 in Figure 3.2). If data are being collected in surveys using open-ended format questions, omission errors are most frequently a result of the insufficient elicitation of respondent's alters (see Chapter 4 for more discussion).

- **Commission errors**. Like omission errors, the erroneous inclusion of nodes and edges can affect the ultimate determination of node-level measures and the identification of key nodes (as is clear in Figure 3.2).

- **Edge/node attribution errors**. These result from assigning a behavior or attributing something to either an edge or node incorrectly. Misassignment of a behavior to a node can yield attributed linkages in a network that in reality do not exist. Attribution error is a common problem in the interpretation of two-mode data that has been converted to one-mode. For example, two individuals in a university program may co-attend a large number of classes. We therefore assume a connection (either pre-existing or as a result of meeting in class). But it could easily be that one of the individuals is a non-traditional student who is older and married and does not hang out with other students in the program. Treating co-attendance as a tie is, in this case, a mistake. Collection of other relational data could help in determining whether an active tie actually exists in this case (e.g., triangulation).

- **Data collection and retrospective errors**. Care should likewise be taken when using network data collected from individuals where the network elicitation question deals with reports of behavior, particularly having to do with social interactions of a temporally discrete nature. For example, questions that are of the kind 'who are the people you interacted with yesterday in the plaza?' are notoriously prone to error. Bernard and Killworth (1977), Bernard et al. (1980, 1982), and Killworth and Bernard (1976, 1979) conducted a series of studies on informant accuracy in social networks involving fraternity members, ham radio operators, and deaf people communicating with teletype machines, to mention a few. They found that people were inaccurate in their reporting of interactions with others. For example, ham radio operators, who kept logs of radio conversations, made both omission and commission errors in their retrospective reporting of radio interactions. Bernard, Killworth and Sailer asked the operators to list all the people they talked to on the radio the day before; the researchers then checked the accuracy of the reported communications with the actual communications as recorded in the log books and found them to be woefully inaccurate. The overall conclusion of their studies was, in their words, that 'what people say, despite their presumed good intentions, bears no useful resemblance to their behavior' (Bernard et al., 1982: 63).

The Bernard et al. research led to a flurry of other studies on the topic. An important study by Freeman et al. (1987) and Freeman and Romney (1987) found that informants are more accurate in reporting long-term patterns of behavior than behaviors at some point in time. They observed the participants in a colloquium series at the University of California Irvine throughout the quarter. On the day after the last colloquium of the quarter, the people who attended were asked to list all the participants present at that last colloquium. There were inaccuracies, as expected, but these inaccuracies were patterned and predictable. Omission errors included people who normally did not attend the colloquium but happened to be at the last one, while commission errors included people who usually came to the colloquium but happened to not be there for the final one. Thus, individual informants were reporting more on what usually happened rather than on what happened during a specific colloquium. A better way to ask the question posed at the beginning of this section about plaza interactions would be 'who are the people you usually interact with in the plaza?' or 'who are the people you interacted with most in the plaza over the last two weeks?' These reports of long-term patterns of behavior are much less prone to error.

Research on ego biases in cognitive networks (Krackhardt, 1987, 1990; Kumbasar et al., 1994; Johnson and Orbach, 2002) has shown that some individuals in the network are more accurate about reporting linkages than others. They find that active, more powerful nodes tend to be more accurate. Johnson and Orbach (2002), for example, found that the more central an actor is in the political network, the more accurate their cognitive networks. These all have implications for methods for assessing and weighting the reliability and validity of network data and for potentially fixing missing data problems.

- **Data management/data entry**. Errors due to data entry, coding and transcription/ translation are well known in other analytical and modeling domains, but they can be even more problematic in the network context as they can have larger effects. Fischer (2006), for example, suggests that some of the contested results of the McPherson et al. (2006) research on the shrinking of Americans' social networks in a longitudinal study of the General Social Survey may be due in part to what Fischer refers to as random or technical errors (e.g., software problems, interview procedures, coding errors).
- **Data fusion/aggregation**. Decisions often have to be made on aggregating data on different temporal, relational and spatial scales. Such aggregations, if done improperly, can create errors at a variety of levels. For example, when aggregating longitudinal real-time or streaming data for analysis, important individual nodes and edges may be excluded because they have lost their importance in the network. As in the boundary specification problem, there should be some guiding principles, preferably of a theoretical nature, for making aggregation decisions (e.g., before and after a hypothesized important event).
- **Errors in secondary sources and data mining**. Various forms of secondary source data may have inherent biases which should be considered in any analysis. This type of data can be easier to collect than primary types of data (e.g., data scraped from the Web), but it can be fraught with errors at a variety of levels. Examples of important questions one should ask when using secondary source data include: if, instead of obtaining this tie from some records, we asked a survey question, what survey question would the tie correspond to? Are nodes really the same? For example, telephone records show ties between phones. But the phones may be used by multiple people, and a given person may have multiple phones. Does the observation of two individuals at the same event imply a tie? Are records temporally comparable, at the same scale, etc.? For further discussion of this issue, see Section 4.6 in Chapter 4.

- **Formatting errors**. In data mining or Web scraping there are errors that can be due to differences in document or website formatting. These errors can lead to the over- or under-representation of terms, actors, attributes, etc. in the data retrieval process. Care should be taken that any relations assigned among nodes are not an artifact of formatting errors. In addition, Web scraping and automated data mining methods should be scrutinized for consistency in the operationalization of important concepts. The bottom line is that the quality of a study is a function of the quality of the data: garbage in, garbage out.

3.9 Ethical considerations

Network research poses different ethical challenges from those of other kinds of social research, particularly in whole-network research designs. In whole network designs, it is impossible to collect the data anonymously. Personal-network research designs can be anonymous, both with respect to the respondent and the people they mention (e.g., they can use nicknames). But for all practical purposes, full network designs require that the respondent identify themselves, which means the researcher can only offer confidentiality. This makes it imperative that the researcher make it clear to the respondent who will see the raw data what can reasonably be predicted to happen to the respondent as a result of an accidental breach of confidentiality.

A related issue is that, unlike other research, non-participation by a respondent in a network study does not necessarily mean that they are not included in the study. Even if an actor chooses not to fill out the survey, other respondents may still list that person as a friend, enemy, etc. A person who does not wish to be embarrassed by their poor standing in the group will still be found to be the person most often named as difficult to work with. This can be remedied by eliminating all non-respondents from the dataset altogether. However, this may wreck the quality and representativeness of the data, which introduces its own ethical issues. This is particularly a problem in applied settings, where decisions will be based on the results of the study. The researcher can, of course, consider it enough to warn management of the problem, but realistically the researcher knows that the management is not going to fully appreciate the depth of the problem, especially since it may be difficult to explain just how the picture is misleading without revealing the very information that the researcher is trying to suppress.

The non-participation issue points to a more subtle underlying difference between network research (of all kinds) and conventional social science. Whereas in conventional studies the respondent usually reports only on herself, in network studies the respondent reports on other people, some of whom may not wish to be reported on. And if these people were not also intended to be respondents in the study, they will not have been contacted to sign consent forms. As a matter of general principle, this does not seem unethical, as the respondent owns her own perceptions. This needs to be considered on a case-by-case basis, however. For example, if the respondent reports seeing someone engage in illegal activities, there is a clear implication that the named party does in fact do illegal things; it is not 'just' a perception as in 'I think John respects me'. In general, the researcher needs to balance his research need against the dangers posed by revelation to both the alters and the respondents who tell on them. Also, an interesting aspect of many social ties, particularly those based on role relationships such as 'is a friend of', is that neither person owns the relationship exclusively; it is a joint creation, and so it is at least plausible to argue that neither party can ethically report on it without the consent of the other.

The issue of which ties it is acceptable to ask about is particularly important in organizational research, especially when the price of getting access to the organization is providing feedback to management. It is generally accepted that the behavior of employees of an organization is open to scrutiny by management. Supervisors base their evaluations of subordinates on all kinds of factors, both formal and informal. How employees relate to each other is something that is of legitimate interest to managers and, indeed, in the case of sexual harassment, an obligation. It is also generally accepted that some things are private; what employees do in the privacy of their own bedrooms with their spouses is none of the organization's business. But what of employee friendships? This is one of the most commonly asked questions in organizational network studies. As a general rule, the network researcher is far more interested in informal ties, including negative ties, than those dictated by the formal structure of the organization. It seems at least plausible to argue that these sorts of questions fall into a gray area between acceptable management scrutiny and invasion of privacy.

Another way in which network studies (of the full network type) differ from conventional social science studies is that missing data are exceptionally troublesome. If a few highly central players are missing, the resulting network could be quite different from what it would have been had those people responded. This creates unfortunate incentives for network researchers to discourage respondents from opting out of a study. As a result, they may not do a fully adequate job of outlining the risks to respondents. In organizational settings, they will also be sorely tempted to get the boss to send a clear message to employees that they should participate in the survey. This might not be coercive from a workplace legality standpoint, but many academic human subject review boards (institutional review boards in the US) would disagree.

Another issue that is special to full network research has to do with data visualization. In most social science research it is variables, not respondents, that are the focus of interest. Respondents are merely anonymous replications – the more the better. Fundamentally, they are treated as bundles of attribute values. Consequently, it is rarely useful to express the results of quantitative research by providing displays of individual data.[3] But in network analysis it is extremely common to present a network diagram that shows who is connected to whom. Such diagrams are not highly digested outputs of analysis, but rather low-level displays that represent the raw data; the outgoing arrows from any node have a one-to-one correspondence with that person's filled-out questionnaire, compactly revealing each person's responses. The obvious solution, of course, is to suppress the node labels or identify nodes only categorically, such as by department or gender. But the level of risk to respondents here is much higher than most con- sent forms would suggest, because organizational members can often deduce the identity of one person (e.g., the only high-ranking woman in the Boston office), and once that person has been identified, their known associates can sometimes be deduced as well, eventually unraveling the whole network. At the very least, participants can often identify themselves (e.g., when they remember listing exactly seven friends and no other node in the graph has exactly seven ties).

A final point of difference is not fundamental to the field but has to do with the fact that most potential respondents do not know much about social network analysis. Most people today have a great deal of experience filling out survey questionnaires in a variety of contexts from political polls to marketing research to job applications. Although new media like Facebook present some new chal- lenges, when it comes to simple questionnaires we would argue that people have an intuitive feel for the potential consequences of disclosing personal informa- tion. Coupled with explicit consent forms that outline some of the risks, most researchers would agree that respondents' common sense provides adequate protection. Network surveys, on the other hand, are a whole new ballgame. Most respondents in a network study will not have participated in one before, and, in organizational contexts, managers receiving network information will not have done so either. As a result, there is a greater burden on researchers to be clear about the risks. Even if a consent form were to clearly state that the data would *not* be kept confidential and would be reported back to the group, many respondents would not be able to fully imagine how it would feel to be identified in the analysis as, say, a peripheral player whom nobody really likes.

In short, the design of a network study generally requires more attention to ethical issues than ordinary studies, particularly in organizational settings. We advise using an expanded consent form that explains more about the outputs of network analysis than is customary in other types of research. For more sugges- tions, see the papers by Borgatti and Molina (2003, 2005).

---

[3] This is not true of qualitative research, however, where it is common to provide direct quotations (albeit anonymously) from individual respondents.

3.10 Summary

Network studies need to be carefully designed to take account of the particular features inherent in social networks. Personal-network research designs, in which information is gathered from a random sample of actors who give information on their connections, pose fewer data collection problems than whole-network designs. However, the downside is that ego-network studies fail to capture the full structural properties of the whole network. Determining which actors to include in a study can be challenging, and network boundaries are not always clear. Even when formal groups are considered, there is often a degree of ambiguity about membership. When the boundary is not clear, snowball or respondent-driven sampling can be used to determine a population. Errors in network data can occur from a variety of sources, and any study needs to take steps to try and reduce these errors as much as possible. The nature of network data and subsequent analysis and visualization give rise to a number of ethical considerations which are particular to network studies, and these need to be clearly thought through before data collection begins.

3.11 Problems and Exercises

1. For each of the research problems in Chapter 1, Problem 1, what are the independent and dependent variables? Based on the designs outlined in Tables 3.1 and 3.2, what type of research design does each of the research problems suggest?

2. For each of the research questions below, discuss whether a whole or personal network approach is more appropriate.

   a. How do social relations in a university sports club influence members' attitudes towards university sports policies?

   b. To what extent is smoking behavior among adolescents affected by their social networks?

   c. How much do voting patterns in a state legislature conform to political party affiliation?

   d. How do immigrants' social networks affect cultural assimilation?

   e. Does the network structural position of a manager in a financial firm impact that manager's performance?

   f. To what extent is toothpaste brand selection affected by consumers' social networks?

   g. To what extent is the social network structure at a commercial fish camp in Canada influenced by ethnicity?

   h. What factors influence the development of cooperative social relations among activists in an environmental social movement?

3. Produce a hypothetical social network study example for each of the three major types of research designs: experimental, quasi-experimental and observational. For each example, identify the independent and dependent variables.

4. For the hypothetical observational design presented in Problem 3 above, is the design cross-sectional, retrospective, or prospective? What are the advantages and disadvantages of each in the study of social networks?

5. Bounding the network in whole social network studies can be challenging and is important in designing valid research. For each of the social network examples below, provide a discussion for how the networks might be bounded in the design of a whole network study.

    a. A study of fraternities at a medium-sized Midwestern university
    b. The study of an informal gay group in an urban neighborhood
    c. The network relations among active hunters in a small village in the Amazon
    d. Relationships among NGOs involving a dam project in West Africa
    e. Food-sharing networks in a village in Central Asia
    f. The political network of community activists in a moderate-sized city

6. Nonresponse in social network surveys can be a major threat to the validity of a social network study. What are some of the ways researchers can minimize survey nonresponse?

7. What are some of the key ethical concerns in social network research as opposed to other types of more traditional research, such as classical social surveys?

Don't forget to visit the website at
https://study.sagepub.com/borgatti2e

4

Data Collection

Learning Outcomes

1. Identify sources of network data
2. Design effective network questionnaires
3. Mine archival and electronic sources for network data

4.1 Introduction

On the surface, asking network questions might seem pretty straightforward. For example, we just ask 'Please tell me the names of all your friends'. But there is a lot more to it than that. First, how will respondents interpret the term 'friend'? Can we expect 'friend' to have the same meaning for all respondents no matter what their ethnic, regional, educational or social class? Second, do we ask the question in an open-ended format, or do we provide the respondent with a roster of names to choose from (i.e., a closed-ended format)? If we use an open-ended question, respondents may forget to list people, and if we use a list or aided format we need to know all the names of network members in advance. Third, do we just want to know whether or not a tie exists between two people, or do we want to know the strength of that tie? And if we want to know something about its strength, do we use an absolute or relative scale? Finally, do we use pen and paper or some type of electronic format for collecting the data? The answers to these questions will ultimately depend on characteristics of the population, the type of social relations being studied and, above all, the research objectives.

In this chapter we discuss a variety of issues relating to the collection of primary network data in full network research designs. This includes working around respondent sensitivities and selecting the right question formats, including closed-ended versus open-ended rosters, use of rating scales, multi-item batteries, electronic surveys, and so on. Many of the issues we discuss apply to personal-network research designs as well, but we note that there is a chapter (Chapter 15) devoted entirely to personal-network designs. We close the chapter with a discussion of collecting archival and electronic data.

4.2 Network questions

In principle, we can study networks of all kinds of entities and all kinds of relations. Our research objectives, for example, may call for us to study trust ties among terrorists over time. Unfortunately, that may not be possible. There are always practical considerations that get in the way. Even if we can get respondents to talk to us, we will rarely have carte blanche with respect to what we ask, and how much we ask. Depending on the context, some types of relational questions are more sensitive than others, and this respondent sensitivity can impact interviewees' willingness to answer questions or, worse, answer honestly and competently. Further, such sensitivity can vary by cultural context (e.g., economic relations may be more sensitive in some cultures than others), can vary over time (e.g., some relational questions may be of a more sensitive nature at the beginning of a longitudinal study than toward the end), and can vary as a function of the data collection methods employed (e.g., face-to-face versus online interviews).

The proper selection of the network questions and formats is critical to the success of any network study. The structure of network questions greatly influences the validity and reliability of respondent answers due to such things as question clarity, burden, sensitivity, and cognitive demand. Many of the issues concerning standard survey and questionnaire development and design apply equally to the study of social networks. However, social network questions are somewhat unique in that we are not simply asking about some attribute of the respondent or ego (e.g., age); we are asking them about their web of social relations that may evoke emotional responses or tax their abilities to recall aspects of their network relations and/or network behaviors.

A short case study illustrates the point. Johnson et al. (2003) studied the network dynamics at polar research stations. At the beginning of the four-year study, the researchers were initially interested in the formation of friendships and the ability of individuals to assess potential friendships one day following the initial contact. One of the researchers attended the first training exercise of the first winter-over crew preparing to deploy to the South Pole station. During a break in training, the crew members were given a questionnaire asking them to rank the other members of the crew from 1 to $n - 1$ with respect to how likely they were to form a friendship with each one over the coming winter. The exact request was as follows:

> Please rank the following members of the winter-over crew in order of their friendship or potential friendship to you from 1 to 20. The member you feel closest to should be ranked '1' while the individual you feel most distant from should be ranked 20. We realize this task is difficult because of the short amount of time you have known other members of the group; your judgments may be based more on your sense of the potential for friendship than on any current relationship. Whatever the difficulty it is important you fill the form out completely. Thank you!

Immediately, several of the crew began to grumble and protest and one crew member threw down his pencil and walked out of the room. One respondent wrote on the survey form 'I would really like to do my best to cooperate and help but *please* [respondent's emphasis] no more rankings', while yet another put '1' next to each crew member's name. This resistance to the administered network question was related to two primary problems. First, it was discovered that the initial period of group formation was filled with great optimism (i.e., a utopian stage), where there was a general perception that everyone would get along and be friends over the course of the austral winter. The task of having people rank-order one another in terms of potential friendship created quite a negative emotional response on the part of crew members, since they believed at this point in the group formation process that 'everyone' would be friends and ranking people meant that some people would be ranked near the bottom of people's list, therefore implying a possible lack of friendship. Thus, both the type of relation and how it was measured (i.e., rank-order) were problematic in practice. The mix of a rank-order collection method and actors' judgments as to expectations of friendship fostered a 'perfect storm' in terms of sensitivity and interviewee burden. Eventually the researcher met with the crew at an 'all-hands meeting'. They all discussed the survey, and agreed on a compromise: the survey would ask the crew about 'who one interacts with socially' rather than 'friendship' and would measure it on an 11-point Likert scale (from 0 to 10) anchored with words from never (0) to most often (10), as shown in Figure 4.1. Thus, the relational question and the method of measurement were ultimately determined in concert with those being studied. A beneficial side-effect of this process was that it created a sense of investment in the design of the study on the part of the crew and helped foster an extremely high and sustained response rate over the winter and in subsequent years.

It is worth noting that while respondents were initially very sensitive about discussing their feelings about each other, they had fewer problems doing so

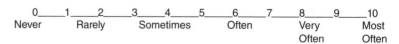

Figure 4.1 Relative interaction scale developed in cooperation with the South Pole winter-over crew.

later, and were even willing to answer questions about their negative feelings toward others. This reflects a temporal component in question sensitivity and its ultimate impact on potential non-response bias. Thus, the maturity and other characteristics (e.g., cultural context) of the group itself may have an impact on the level of emotional reaction to one or a given set of network questions. This variability means that network surveys have to be pre-tested and in some cases co-developed with the research subjects. This is particularly true in management consulting settings where the reason for collecting the network data is that there is some kind of political or interpersonal problem. Under those conditions, people become very wary of researchers asking sensitive questions like 'who do you trust?' and 'who don't you get along with?'

It is essential to do some ethnographic background research to explore the types of network relations and labels or terms that are appropriate for a study and to discover the best way to word the questions. Once the questions are developed they should be pre-tested to make sure respondents are clear about what they mean. The greater the heterogeneity of the backgrounds of the members of the group, the more critical this becomes.

It is also very useful to do some ethnographic work at the back end of a study. Patterns found in the analysis can often be quickly explained quite readily by the members of the group themselves. It is also useful to test the results – which could be spurious – against their insider knowledge to see if they have validity from a native's point of view. We refer to the practice of doing ethnography at either end of a quantitative study as 'the ethnographic sandwich'.

4.3 Question formats

A fundamental issue in the design of network questions is whether to use an open- or closed-ended format. Figure 4.2 provides examples of the types of questions used in each. With a closed-ended question format, the set of nodes comprising the network are chosen in advance and a roster created; respondents are then asked about each person on the roster. The main advantage of using rosters (besides guaranteeing that the set of respondents matches the set of actors being asked about) is that respondents are less subject to recall error. All they have to do is respond to each name they are asked about. Some may think this recall problem in open-ended question formats is overblown, but a simple empirical example provides some insight. In the South Pole study discussed extensively throughout this book, winter-over crews were debriefed by the researchers at the end of each winter. The crew sizes across three separate years were quite small, ranging from 22 to 28 people. The crews in each station had been together for well over a year and spent 8.5 months together in total isolation over the austral winter. If asked about any randomly chosen crewmate, crew members could fill books of information about them. But when asked in the debriefing interviews to list all their crewmates, it was found that they would commonly forget about up to 25% of their fellows. So, recall error is a significant issue.

Another advantage of the roster is that it limits potential biases affecting the probability of an actor being selected by a respondent. Imagine someone in an organization who works in the basement in a physically isolated part of the building. If actors in the organization were asked in an open-ended format to list 'people that they don't know but would like to get to know', this person may systematically be left out because of the limitations of human recall. The lack of selection of these physically isolated people may not have anything to do with who they are as human beings or as potential friends; it may just be a matter of people forgetting about them because of their location. The disadvantages of the roster method are that (a) it requires deciding ahead of time which nodes will be asked about, and (b) it can be cumbersome and intimidating when the list of potential alters gets large – say, more than 500 names. The latter problem can be ameliorated by the use of hierarchically organized rosters (especially in online surveys), such as having the respondent first select an organizational unit, then respond to each of the names in that unit. The same can be done with lists organized alphabetically.

In comparison, unaided or open-ended question formats require no prior decisions about who to obtain information about. So, in cases where the list of potentially relevant alters is large (e.g., the population of American consumers), and/or insufficient ethnographic work has been done to have a clear idea of who to ask about, the open-ended approach may be the only way to ask questions. In this case respondents are asked to list people that they, for example, 'talk to' or 'share needles with'. Besides recall issues, open-ended questions have a number of potential disadvantages in a full network research context. The biggest issue is identifying the actor whom a respondent names. If they mention 'Bob Smith', is that the same as the 'Bobby Smith' whom someone else mentioned? And is it the same as another respondent in the study whom the researchers know as 'Robert Smith'? This is particularly a problem in populations where full or even real names are rarely known, such as drug injectors on the streets of Hartford, CT (Weeks et al., 2002). In personal-network research designs, this is not a problem because we do not need to draw connections across different respondents.

Closed-ended (aided)	Example
• Boundaries are known and all actors listed • Becomes cumbersome as networks grow in size • Fewer concerns about respondent recall and accuracy • Each actor has approximately an equal chance of being selected	Who would you converse with if you met on the street? (check as many as apply) Felicia Hardy ☐ Steve Rogers ☐ Sam Wilson ☐ Patsy Walker ☐ Bruce Banner ☐ Ted Salis ☐ Kitty Pride ☐
Open-ended (unaided)	Example
• Much more subject to recall error • Can use a fixed-choice method limiting the number of actors elicited • Each actor in the network does not have an equal chance of being chosen given recall and free-listing issues • Better for face-to-face interviews where probing can be used	If you wanted to learn more about what goes on in the Avengers organization, who would you talk to? (Please list as many relevant names as you can in the spaces provided) _____ _____ _____ _____

Figure 4.2   Examples of closed- and open-ended network question formats.

Another potential problem with the open-ended format concerns the size of respondent lists. For example, in an unlimited choice format, if respondent A lists 30 alters while respondent B lists 15 alters, can we conclude that respondent A has a larger network than respondent B? That might be the case, but it might not. Perhaps A is very energetic and really thinks long and hard about the question, while B is tired and bored with the survey and just wants to get it over with. One way to deal with this is to limit the number of names people can provide. Unfortunately, this has problems as well because people use varying heuristics for recalling names (Brewer, 1995a, 1995b). In the South Pole debriefing, it was apparent that some respondents were mentally walking through the station to remember names. They moved from the garage through the carpenter shop to the generator room into the bar then the galley, and so on, as they recalled fellow crew members. Others recalled names based on social groupings. All of this is to say that limiting names to a certain number can systematically bias the resulting networks.

The recall problem in open-ended elicitation can be somewhat ameliorated with the use of different types of interview probes (Brewer, 2000). For instance, in the free-list example above, if the interviewer had verbally repeated the names listed by each respondent and simply asked 'So you have listed John, Susie, ... and Sarah: are there any other crew not listed that wintered-over with you?', possibly followed by 'Can you think of anyone else?', there is a good

Repeated roster	Multigrid

Q1. Please indicate with which of the following you would converse if you met them on the street.

Felicia Hardy	☐
Steve Rogers	☐
Sam Wilson	☐
Patsy Walker	☐
Bruce Banner	☐
Ted Salis	☐
Kitty Pryde	☐

Q2. Please indicate with which of the following people you work.

Felicia Hardy	☐
Steve Rogers	☐
Sam Wilson	☐
Patsy Walker	☐
Bruce Banner	☐
Ted Salis	☐
Kitty Pryde	☐

Q1. In the grid below, please indicate those people you would converse with if you met them on the street.

Q2. In the grid below, please check off the names of the people you work with.

Q3. In the grid below, please check off the names of a selected set of people whom you don't know but would like to know, based on things you've heard, or their interests, etc.

	Q1 Converse with	Q2 Work with	Q3 Want to Know
Felicia Hardy	☐	☐	☐
Steve Rogers	☐	☐	☐
Sam Wilson	☐	☐	☐
Patsy Walker	☐	☐	☐
Bruce Banner	☐	☐	☐
Ted Salis	☐	☐	☐
Kitty Pryde	☐	☐	☐

Figure 4.3 Repeated roster versus multigrid formats.

chance that the respondent would have noticed the missing crew member(s) and provided the additional name(s). Of course, the use of probes can be readily done in face-to-face interviews but would be much more difficult in other types of self-administered survey formats. In some settings, such as organizations, it is possible to use visual aids to help stimulate recall, such as providing office maps or unit-level organizational charts.

If a roster format is chosen, there are a number of further decisions to make about how the questions and lists should be structured. The two primary formats for closed-ended questions are repeated rosters and multigrids. Figure 4.3 provides examples of each type of format. In repeated rosters the same list of network members is repeated following each network question. Respondents can then circle or check the appropriate names in response to each of the questions. The multigrid format places the lists in a series of columns with each column associated with a relational question. Again, respondents can check or circle the appropriate answers. The two are similar in terms of potential reliability and validity, but the multigrid is a more compact format; if one is using pencil-and-paper collection, the latter format can help reduce the number of pages in the survey. Sometimes this has a beneficial psychological effect on respondents in that it makes the survey appear shorter than it would using the repeated roster. There is probably nothing more daunting to a potential respondent than when a researcher pulls out a one-inch thick survey and places it on the table in front of them.

The roster examples in Figure 4.3 involve respondents making simple yes/no decisions about a given tie: either there was a tie or there was not. This checklist method has an advantage in that it is less cognitively demanding on respondents. Moreover, it is quick and easy to administer. However, one drawback is that it provides no discrimination with respect to a tie's value such as tie frequency or strength. For that, we need to use some kind of ratings approach that allows for the assessment of the frequency of contacts or the strength of relationships. We can elicit tie values by using either an absolute or a relative scale. Figure 4.4 shows types of questions in the two approaches. With absolute scales, we are attempting to assign to each person on the list that is given to respondents or listed by respondents the degree of interaction within a specified period of time. So we might ask 'Do you seek advice from _____ once a year, once a month, once a week?' When using absolute scales, it is important to do sufficient preliminary research to determine the appropriate time intervals, or risk getting no variance (e.g., all respondents choose 'every day' because in that setting everyone interacts multiple times a day). Another issue with absolute scales is that people are not particularly good at them. Given two alters, respondents probably have a good idea which one they interact with more often, but they may be inaccurate about whether it is once a week, once every couple of weeks, or once a month.

Some researchers use questions that are more explicitly ordinal and generic, such as an *n*-point Likert scale anchored with words such as 'very infrequently', 'somewhat infrequently', 'neither infrequently nor frequently', 'somewhat frequently' and 'very frequently'. Such questions are easier to write, since the researcher does not have to know what range of frequencies to ask about. However, such scales are also quite vulnerable to response sets. Some respondents are very liberal and rate everyone as somewhat or very frequent, while others are more conservative, rarely venturing above the middle point. Others are conservative in another way: they rarely venture far from the middle point in either direction. We can try to mitigate this problem by using a relative scale such as 'much less than average', 'less than average', 'about average', 'more than average' and 'much more than average'. A thoughtful respondent should see this as an invitation to use all ends of the scale. Unfortunately, there is also less information in this scale than in an absolute scale. Greater than average interaction for one person might be interacting once a day but for another

Tie frequency	Format of question	Comments
Absolute	'How often do you talk to _____, on average?' – Once a year or less – Every few months – Every few weeks – Once a week – Every day	Need to do pre-testing to determine appropriate time scale Danger of getting no variance Assumes a lot from respondents
Relative	'How often do you speak to each person on the list below?' – Very infrequently – Somewhat infrequently – About average – Somewhat frequently – Very frequently	Assumes less of respondents; easier task Is automatically normalized within respondent • Removes response set issues • Makes it hard to compare values in different rows

Figure 4.4 Question formats for assessing frequency of contact.

person it might be once every two weeks, and there is no way to distinguish them. A value of '4' for one person may refer to wildly different levels of inter-action than a '4' for someone else.

The same kinds of trade-offs are seen in full ranking data. In the full ranking task, the respondent is asked to rank everyone, except themselves, from 1 to $n - 1$. Ranking has the advantage of asking for only ordinal judgments (is A more than B?). These are more natural than rating scales, which ask the respondent to assign a number between, say, 1 and 7 to represent their feelings about each other person. However, as the list of names gets longer, respondents find full rankings increasingly difficult to do and find ratings much easier and faster to do.

One other technique that is worth mentioning is the idea of breaking a single complicated question into more numerous but simpler questions. Rating every individual on a list on a 1–5 scale is a slow process compared to checking names off. So, one possibility is to convert the rating question into multiple check-off tasks. For example, instead of asking 'How often do you see each of the follow-ing people?' using a scale of 1 = once a year, 2 = once a month, and 3 = once a week, we can instead ask three separate questions: 'who are the people on this list you see at least once a year?', 'who are the people on this list you see at least once a month?', and 'who are the people on this list you see at least once a week?'. It may seem counterintuitive, but it is often faster and easier this way. This is especially true if electronic surveys are used because the second question only has to list the names that were selected in the first question, and the third question only has to list the names checked off in the second question. The task then becomes lightning fast.

4.4 Interviewee burden

Sometimes the size and particular boundaries for a network are dictated by the methods employed. Some data collection methods are labor-intensive and burdensome, where such burden varies as a function of network size. Two examples of this are personal-network studies and cognitive social structure studies, where respondents are asked to report on the network connections of all other actors in the network (Krackhardt, 1987; Kumbasar et al., 1994; Johnson and Orbach, 2002). In these types of studies, the number of data points needed from a respondent increases with the square of the number of alters, rapidly increasing the burden on the respondent.

In a study by Johnson and Orbach (2002) on political networks and the passing of a piece of environmental legislation, there were potentially over 400 actors in the political network involving legislators, staff, resource managers, lobbyists and private citizens. The researchers were interested in the relationship between knowledge of the political landscape and political power. However, the respondents were very high-status people (e.g., the President Pro Tem of the North Carolina Senate, cabinet-level secretaries, legislative committee chairs and co-chairs, etc.), who will not grant a researcher a 3-hour interview. To deal with this, the study began by asking 10 politically knowledgeable key informants (Johnson, 1990) to free-list actors who were seen as 'important' in the development and passing of a particular piece of environmental legislation. The top 45 names most frequently listed by the key informants were used to bound the network. This is like the data-driven, emic or realist strategy for bounding a network discussed in Chapter 3, except that in the legislative case described here methodological realities were partially driving boundary specifications.

In addition, for the cognitive network data collection, the respondents were asked to name only three people on the list whom they thought each of the political actors talked to most about a given piece of environmental legislation over a period of time. This reduced the task to approximately 135 reported dyads, which was much more reasonable, although still daunting, given the research population. As we shall see in the chapter on personal networks, this is also a very important consideration in designing personal-network surveys.

Interviewee burden, more generally, can lead to various kinds of non-response on the part of actors. There is plenty of literature discussing these issues in survey research (Dillman, 1977; Church, 2001) and this is also a real concern in personal-network approaches. However, unlike typical survey research where researchers are willing to accept at least some level of missing data and non-response bias, in whole-network surveys such levels are unacceptable and pose real threats to the validity of any study (as discussed in Chapter 3). As we have seen from earlier examples, the goal is to minimize respondent anger and frustration. One potential source of respondent displeasure, which can result in non-response or early withdrawal from the interview, is the length of the interview itself. A major reason people state for their unwillingness to participate in surveys is being 'too busy' or having lack of motivation (Sosdian and Sharp, 1980). It is important to keep in mind that network interviews and the complexity of certain social network methods can place huge temporal and cognitive demands on respondents.

There are no hard-and-fast rules about what makes an interview too long or too demanding. However, the shorter the network survey instrument, the better, particularly if one is engaged in a longitudinal study where sustained participation is crucial. One rule of thumb for achieving an optimally sized network survey instrument is to include only those questions that are theoretically critical for the study at hand – no more and no less. If you are uncertain about the theoretical relevance of a network question, you should conduct exploratory or ethnographic research to find out. Conducting ethnographic work prior to a full network survey can help in assuring the reliability and validity of network questions and in understanding the capacity of respondents to answer instruments of a given size (e.g., chief executives of companies and fishers in Cuba may face different time constraints and different levels of enthusiasm).

One final note is that the placement of network questions in any survey may impact outcomes. As discussed earlier, network questions are often cognitively demanding. If such questions are placed at the end of an already extensive survey, there are chances that respondents may be less thorough in their responses or may even refuse to answer. It is to issues of cognitive demand and interviewee burden that we now turn.

4.5 Data collection and reliability

As discussed in Chapter 3, whole network approaches can be sensitive to missing data (Borgatti et al., 2006). This is particularly true for smaller networks, where the absence of actors or ties can have relatively large effects. The manner in which we collect network data can have a profound impact on actor participation and on the reliability and validity of the social network data sought.

Table 4.1 shows some of the ways in which researchers have typically collected network data. The columns in the table represent a few of the trade-offs one should consider in the course of choosing a data collection method for a network study. As we have seen from the polar research station network earlier in this chapter, some network questions may be more emotionally sensitive than others. Self-administered network surveys, including mail-out and online surveys, may minimize the degree of self-consciousness on the part of respondents. In addition, they do not suffer from reactions to the interviewer, and they are very convenient for the researcher. On the other hand, self-administered surveys that are not hand-delivered typically have much lower response rates.

An important means for reducing non-response on the part of actors is the building of rapport with respondents before administering the survey (Johnson, 1990). This is particularly a problem with self-administered mail-out and online surveys, where there is limited opportunity to establish contact and create a relationship. Dillman (1977) provides suggestions for overcoming some of the disadvantages of mail-out and phone surveys in terms of increasing response rates. However, face-to-face data collection provides the greatest opportunity for establishing rapport with respondents. Additionally, it facilitates the use of elicitation interviewing techniques for the collection of network data, such as various probing techniques to improve respondent recall (Brewer, 2000; Johnson and Weller, 2002). Network elicitation is difficult to do in a less inter-active context and limited in phone and group interview formats. Mail-out surveys are particularly at a disadvantage when using network questions that are open-ended.

Some studies have argued that low response rates in surveys are due less to potential respondents' resistance to participation and more to the researcher's inability to simply find and interview respondents (Sosdian and Sharp, 1980). These issues have become increasingly problematic for methods such as phone surveys, where people may have been overwhelmed by telemarketers, donation solicitations and political canvassing. In addition, the use of mobile phones is creating new challenges to the valid use of phone interviews and surveys. With technologies such as caller ID, people can now monitor calls and choose not to answer the phone. Johnson (1990), for example, found that using respondents to

Table 4.1 Features of different survey types.

Type of data collection	Issues of sensitivity	Interviewer response effects	Data handling errors	Cost of administering	Ability to establish rapport	Ability to maximize elicitation
Face-to-face	High	High	Moderate	High	High	High
Self-administered	Low	Low	Moderate	Moderate	Low	Low
Mail-out	Low	Low	Moderate	Low	Low	Low
Electronic	Low	Low	Low	Low	Low	Low
Phone	Moderate	Moderate	Moderate	Moderate	Moderate	Moderate
Group setting	High	Moderate	Moderate	High	Moderate	Moderate

call ahead to their listed alters (who would be more likely to answer phone calls from friends) in a snowball sample limited this problem, particularly in a population of older adults in a small Midwestern town who were suspicious of strangers (Johnson and Griffith, 2010a).

Comparative research has shown that the different survey approaches vary in response or return rates. Such studies have also found that differences in response rates can vary depending on the social, organizational or cultural context. For example, in a comparison of different survey approaches, whereas mail-out surveys win out in one context, they may just as readily lose out to other methods, such as online surveys, in another. The point here is that the data collection method you choose should be sensitive to the given cultural and social context in which you plan to work (Church, 2001). In addition, we advocate making as much contact with potential respondents as possible independent of the type of data collection approach. In fact, the more you can engage in ethnographic on-the-ground efforts, the better your chances for maximizing response rates in network surveys. In the polar research example (Johnson et al., 2003), two of the investigators spent months training and deploying with winter-over crews. This enabled them to build rapport so as to maximize the chances of study participation over the austral winter, a period when members of the research team were not present and monthly questionnaires were distributed by the station physician.

4.6 Archival data collection

In order for data collected from archival sources to be of use in the study of social networks, it must contain information on social relations that are amenable to either a one-mode or two-mode network format. Some archival sources are inherently relational and very structured, such as church marriage records, records of business partnerships, legislative voting records, ledger sheets, and accounts of trades. In such cases, ties may be readily determined among and between social entities such as individuals, firms, families, tribes, and businesses (one-mode). Or they can be inferred indirectly through co-occurrences, such as overlaps in voting behavior among members of Parliament at the start of World War II, the co-occurrence of patrons among seventeenth-century scientists in Italy, or co-attendance at early twentieth-century political rallies or events in New York (two-mode). Additionally, the nature and structure of the archival data frames just which network relations a study can use. If you are interested in economic exchange among villagers in Tuscany in the sixteenth century, but all that exists are marriage records, then the relational data available are not suitable for your research problem.

Relational data in archival sources can also be extracted from less structured historical sources. Many accessible historical records may not be as well structured as in the examples above and may be freer flowing, as in the form of a narrative. If these narratives – such as letters between luminaries of some historical period – mention names, events, locations, etc., then it is possible to build a social network database by coding the narratives. For example, in a series of letters from Galileo's daughter, Maria Celeste, to her father, there are many mentions of people and places that can be used to piece together social relations among actors of the time. In the following excerpt from Maria's letter of 10 August 1623, there is clear reference to an exchange of letters between Galileo and the new Pope:[1]

> The happiness I derived from the gift of the letters you sent me, Sire, written to you by that most distinguished Cardinal, now elevated to the exalted position of Supreme Pontiff, was ineffable, for his letters so clearly express the affection he has for you, and also show how highly he values your abilities. I have read and reread them, savoring them in private, and I return them to you, as you insist, without having shown them to anyone else except Suor Arcangela, who has joined me in drawing the utmost joy from seeing how much our father is favored by persons of such caliber. May it please the Lord to grant you the robust health you will need to fulfill your desire to visit His Holiness, so that you can be even more greatly esteemed by him; and, seeing how many promises he makes you in his letters, we can entertain the hope that the Pope will readily grant you some sort of assistance for our brother.

This excerpt clearly reveals relationships among Galileo's family as well as other relationships, even providing information on the possible strength of Galileo's relationship to the Pope. The coding of relations from the 124 letters Maria wrote to her father might describe much about aspects of Galileo's familial and political networks from the period 1623–1633.

Another example comes from the same Galileo Project database. Relations among scientists and the structure of the scientific community of Galileo's time can be derived using archival sources that include scientists' university attendance, scientific disciplinary training, patronage (often a major source of support for an academic of the time), correspondence among scientists, and membership in scientific societies. From these sources, two-mode data can be constructed from patronage (scientist-by-patron), university attendance (scientist-by-university) and scientific societies (scientist-by-scientific societies). One-mode data can be derived from the correspondence among scientists – the equivalent of emails today. This can be coupled with attribute data in records and narratives, such as

---

[1] Galileo Project: http://galileo.rice.edu/fam/letters/10aug1623.html.

date of birth and death, father's status and occupation, nationality, aspects of education, religion, and means of support (e.g., inherited wealth), to test any number of hypotheses about power or the dominance of scientific thought in Galileo's time.[2]

There are a number of classic studies that have extracted social network data from archival sources. In a study of social change, Bearman (1993) looked at local elite social networks in Norfolk, England, between 1540 and 1640. The network data for the study were derived from various archival records on kinship relations over that time period and were related to various attributes such as status (i.e., class of gentry), occupation and religion. Similarly, Padgett and Ansell (1993) coded data from a major historical work on social dynamics in fifteenth-century Florence, with a particular focus on the rise of the Medici (Kent, 1978), to build a multiplex network dataset (intermarriage ties, business ties, joint ownerships, partnerships, bank employment, real estate ties, patronage, personal loans, friendships, and what they call 'surety ties' – actors who put up bond for someone in exile). Attribute data were also coded from the various historical accounts and included economic wealth obtained from tax records (*catasto*), a family status measure based on 'date of first Prior (a monastic superior)', neighborhood residence, and tax assessments for the 600 richest households in Florence in 1403. In these two examples the authors were able to build datasets that included dynamic networks involving multiple relations and modes (both one- and two-mode) and a variety of attributes that could be used to test hypotheses.

One of the real advantages of archival sources for the study of social networks is that archival data are often longitudinal in nature. This allows for the study of network dynamics and evolution and facilitates the study of social change. Longitudinal research that involves the collection of primary data must use a prospective design in which data are collected periodically over some time period. This can be very costly and time-consuming. Imagine having to prospectively collect network data over a 100-year period as in the Bearman example above (1540–1640).

It is important to make one final comment about the validity of archival sources. As discussed in the chapter on research design, secondary or archival sources can suffer from a number of reliability and validity issues. Archival records can document non-events (e.g., Congressional Record) or represent a reconstruction of the past or an event to meet some agenda where narratives or numbers are constructed to make a group or a single actor look good in light of poor outcomes. Often these records include elements of scapegoating and false attribution. Thus, records may

---

[2] http://galileo.rice.edu/Catalog/Docs/categories.html.

be biased in that they are constructed to fit some agenda or reflect actor biases (e.g., state-owned newspaper reports). For example, in the South Pole research Johnson reviewed 15 years of managers' end-of-year reports and found them to contain inaccuracies (he compared ethnographic historical interviews with the reports). This was understandable in that these reports were an attempt to put a more positive spin on the winter events to make the station manager look good and to place the blame for any problems on others. Had these reports been used to construct some valid historical account of the social dynamics and life at the stations, any resulting conclusions drawn from an analysis would have had some likelihood of being wrong. It is always best to use triangulation of multiple independent sources so that the data can be verified and validated.

4.7 Data from electronic sources

The collection of data from electronic sources is very similar to the collection of network data in archival or historical research. Many sites on the Internet contain information that is inherently network-oriented. There is a large amount of existing data on – or data that can be mined from – email communications, social networking sites, movie, music and book databases, scientific citation databases, wikis, Web pages, digital news sources, and so on. Many of these already have information available in a one-mode or two-mode network format, while others require the writing of programs for data mining in order to put it into data formats that can be more readily analyzed. Twitter readily affords network data in the form of follower and followee ties, while social networking sites, such as Facebook, consist of literally millions of ego networks. Electronic sources offer almost endless opportunities to collect and analyze network data of one kind or another.

An example of a useful electronic data source is the Internet Movie Database (IMDb) which has a tremendous amount of data on virtually every movie ever made. For example, it has – in machine-readable form – the cast and crew, storyline and plot summaries, news articles about the movie, trivia, quotes, references, movies that reference a given movie, company credits, technical specs and so on. Some of this information can be used to construct two-mode data matrices, such as actor-by-movie, movie-by-keyword, movie-by-news article and so on, which can then be converted into one-mode networks (see Chapters 5 and 13 on this). As an illustration of the use of IMDb data, we examined the following research question: do conservatives and liberals in Hollywood work together on films? We obtained a list of the top 20 most liberal and the top 20 most conservative actors in Hollywood from a (now defunct) website called celepolitics.com. Looking at

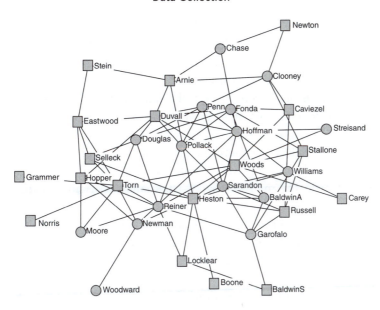

Figure 4.5 Collaboration ties among Hollywood actors. Squares are conservatives and circles are liberals.

only movies involving these 40 actors yielded a 40 × 96 two-mode network. Figure 4.5 shows the affiliation network for the 40 actors. Despite having different ideologies, at first glance it appears that conservative and liberal actors do in fact work together in Hollywood. In looking at the network visualization, however, there appears to be some segregation by ideological stance, with conservatives co-occurring more to the left and liberals more to the right of the graph.

The above analysis is just a simple example but does show how an online database can be studied from a network perspective. However, like archival data, electronic sources of data can have reliability and validity problems. The Web of Science database, for example, provides some important lessons on potential errors in electronic sources. This source contains data on citations between scientific papers which can be analyzed in terms of networks among scientists. One obvious problem with many databases of this kind is that some of the data are copied from original sources by hand or via optical character recognition software, and therefore contain errors. In addition, the sources themselves may contain errors: the authors might use different initials than in other papers, and they may misspell the names of the authors they cite. Electronic data need to be cleaned and checked just like primary data. These databases are sometimes so large that the data cleaning task can be daunting, but it is an important one nevertheless.

Although electronic sources afford almost unlimited opportunities for the collection of network data, caution should be exercised in inferring the meaning of social ties in such sources. Although Facebook ties are called 'friends', these need not correspond to the usual meaning of friends and can in fact include a wide variety of types and strengths. On the other hand, with sufficient creativity, effort and access to data it is possible to add quite a bit of richness to Facebook data. For example, we might declare a tie from A to B to be strong to the extent that A tags B in A's pictures. This can also be used to establish directionality, which is otherwise absent in the Facebook friend tie.

The same is true for micro-blogging sites such as Twitter. Although clear directed ties exist between followers and the followed, there is no direct indicator of strength of tie, and it is difficult to know what the followership ties entail. We can be sure that information is flowing from the followed to follower, at least in the case where the follower retweets a message, but can we infer an emotional bond between follower and followed? Should we expect structural hole theory to apply to the follower relation?

4.7.1 Social media

Probably the largest source of network data in recent years has been from social media sites. Unfortunately access to these data is controlled by the social media companies and they are able to determine the level of access for any researcher. As an example, Facebook until relatively recently allowed members to download a network of all their friends including ties between friends. This ceased in 2014 but a number of Facebook networks are still publicly available and can be found on the web. In addition, Facebook does still allow some access for example to Fan Page networks. Some providers such as Snapchat have never allowed access whereas sites such as Reddit and even YouTube do allow data access. It would not be possible in this chapter to discuss all the potential sites that allow access so we restrict our discussion to Twitter as an example.

There are essentially three ways to get Twitter data. All these methods use an API (Application Programming Interface) that is a means by which a developer can access the Twitter data by writing a computer program using the open source APIs provided by Twitter. As this is a highly technical means to get data we shall discuss a simple-to-use program, NodeXL (available at http://www.smrfoundation.org/nodexl/), which allows the non-expert access to two of these. NodeXL is an add-on to Excel and can be downloaded and allows some functionality for free. These two methods provide access to two different sorts of data. The first is the search API. This gives potential access to all Tweets that have occurred based on a search criterion. This criterion can be a hashtag, username, location, etc. However, Twitter limits the amount of data that can be accessed in a number of ways.

For an individual user, you can only have access to the last 3,200 Tweets over the last week. For a keyword, the limit is 5,000. But the biggest restriction is that you can only make 180 queries in any 15-minute period. Hence if you wish to build a network of any size this has to be done over a period of time.

The second API in NodeXL is the streaming API. In this instance Tweets are collected in real time. In essence, rather than pulling the data down these are pushed to the researcher. Again, this is restricted by Twitter and the percentage of data received is dependent upon the volume of activity. This has been estimated at between 1% and 40% and is compounded by the fact that the sampling strategy is not published.

To obtain data simply download NodeXL and then click on the import button. Some Twitter data can be imported directly using the free basic edition but the Pro addition allows the user to download some Facebook data, Flickr and YouTube. Once in NodeXL it provides a number of features to analyze and draw the network or it can be exported for use in other network analysis packages. A good introduction to using NodeXL for social media data collection and analysis is the book by Hansen et al. (2010).

As a simple example Figure 4.6 shows the Twitter network for just 100 Tweets using the search term Brexit on 4 April 2017. The relation is 'replies to' or 'mentions' and the isolates have been deleted. Clearly this is a very fragmented network but it represents a very small sample of Tweets which used that term over the previous week.

It is possible to get all Tweets that satisfy a specified criterion in real time by using the Twitter Firehose API. Access to the Firehose is controlled by two commercial companies – GNIP and Datasift – and to gain access requires payment.

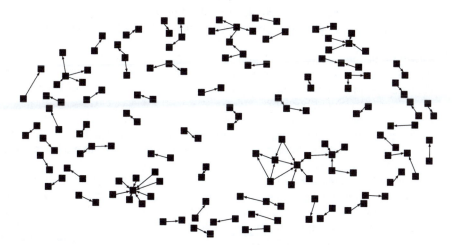

Figure 4.6 The Twitter network of just 100 tweets using the search term "Brexit" on 4 April 2017. The edges are 'replies to' or 'mentions'.

4.8 Summary

The collection of primary social network data via questionnaires or interviews is very different from that of standard survey data. Problems of recall make it difficult for a respondent to name others in their network on an unaided basis, so the free-list method should only be used when it is not possible to use a roster. It is important to use precise terms when asking respondents about any association. For example, a question such as 'who did you socialize with last month?' is preferable to a vaguer one such as 'who is your friend?'. Likert scales are less demanding on the respondent than absolute scales and therefore are often the preferred method for collecting valued data. However, they do have the drawback that different respondents can interpret the questions differently. These effects can be lessened by normalization, but they cannot be eliminated. Pre-testing questions and using ethnographic methods to help develop questions and scales will help ensure question relevance and validity. Historical sources rarely contain social network data, so associations between actors usually have to be deduced from attendance at events or meetings or inferred indirectly from narratives. Data from electronic sources do not usually suffer from these issues, since they are often already in network form. However, sources such as Twitter or Facebook present challenges of interpretation, since the connections made do not always reflect those in the offline world.

4.9 Problems and Exercises

1. For the network boundary problem (Problem 5) in Chapter 3, provide examples of questions that a researcher might ask to collect network data. In addition, discuss the advantages and disadvantages for open- versus closed-ended question formats in each case.
2. Network data can be extracted from both archival and electronic data sources. Provide an example of social network data that can be collected from each source.
3. When designing a social network survey instrument, what are some of the ways you can reduce respondent burden?
4. John, a social network researcher, is interested in the relationship between people's frequency of recreational interactions and their political attitudes. Provide examples of the kinds of questions John might ask, using both an absolute and relative format for eliciting tie frequency.
5. Jennifer studies organizational behavior and is interested in understanding the relationship between frequency of interaction among employees in a corporate headquarters with 355 employees and their attitudes about corporate culture. She wants to use a closed-ended multigrid question format in her study. Discuss the advantages and disadvantages of this approach in this case, and provide some suggestions of ways to reduce respondent burden.

Don't forget to visit the website at
https://study.sagepub.com/borgatti2e

5
Data Management

Learning Outcomes

1. Configure network and attribute data for standard software packages
2. Apply elementary transformations to matrix data
3. Extract and reconfigure network and attribute data

5.1 Introduction

In this chapter we discuss how to format network data for import into a network analysis software package, how to transform network data to make it suitable for different analyses, and how to export network data and results for use in other programs, such as statistical packages. For obvious reasons, this chapter is a little more specific to the UCINET program than most chapters of the book. The data import section discusses the various choices available for formatting network data in electronic files. We also make suggestions for checking and cleaning newly imported data. The section on data transformation focuses on common adjustments made to network data, such as imputing missing values, symmetrizing, dichotomizing, aggregating and subsetting network data. We do not discuss converting two-mode data to one-mode data, as we devote a separate chapter to that topic (see Chapter 13). The data export section discusses ways of transferring data and results to statistical programs as well as to spreadsheet and word-processing software.

5.2 Data import

One of the most important steps in any network analysis is formatting the data for import into a network analysis software package. Familiarizing yourself with standard data formats *before* entering or downloading data can save a great deal of time because it can be very costly to reformat the data after they are entered.

Regardless of how data are obtained, eventually they must be held in an electronic file, such as a spreadsheet, database, or text file. For large datasets, a proper database such as Microsoft Access or MySQL is useful, but since few network analysis programs can read database files directly, they entail an extra step of converting to something the programs can read. For most users, we recommend using Microsoft Excel as a sort of universal translator. Current versions of Excel can handle large datasets, and the fact that each datum is stored in its own spreadsheet cell solves the parsing issues that arise when programs have to read text files, such as having to decide whether 'Pitney Bowes' refers to two nodes or one, and whether '7,100' represents seven thousand one hundred, or seven and one tenth, or a pair of numbers seven and one hundred. In the case of UCINET, Excel files can be imported directly or simply cut and pasted into the DL Editor. Other programs require text files, but it is relatively easy to convert Excel files to text as needed. Several network analysis programs read text files written in the DL (Data Language) data description language. We give some examples later in this chapter.

The issue of which type of file to use for storing data is not as important as the format of the data. The UCINET program can read a wide variety of formats (such as matrix formats and list formats), allowing the user to choose one that is convenient for their situation (e.g., typed in from paper surveys, saved from electronic surveys, downloaded from archival sources). We begin by discussing matrix formats.

5.2.1 Matrix formats

A conceptually straightforward data format is the full matrix format. Figure 5.1 shows a screenshot of a network in full matrix format held in a Microsoft Excel file. The example shows a standard one-mode dataset, meaning that the rows and columns are the same. Note that the first row and column are used for node labels, and these particular labels happen to contain spaces. It is also possible to use numeric labels, or no labels at all (in which case nodes will be assigned the ordinal numbers from 1 to N as labels). Note also that these matrix entries are tie strengths, meaning there are values other than simple 1s and 0s. The matrix can be easily transferred to UCINET by cutting and pasting into the UCINET DL Editor. A screenshot of the DL Editor is shown in Figure 5.2, using a different dataset.

In general, matrix formats are best used with dense networks. If the network is very sparse, as most networks are, the adjacency matrix will consist mostly of

	United States of America	Sao Tome and Principe	North Korea	Myanmar	Tuvalu	Canada	Guinea-Bissau	Bahamas	Grenada	St. Kitts and Nevis	Nicaragua	Guyana	Suriname	Paraguay
United States of America	0	0	0	0	0	307823	0.5	475.4	4.8	57.1	1580.3	140.7	171.6	68
Sao Tome and Principe	0	0	0	0	0	0.24	0	0	0	0	0	0	0	
North Korea	0	0	0	39.1	0	0.08	0	0.36	0	0.58	0	13.87	7.83	24.
Myanmar	0	0	39.1	0	0	8.17	0	0	0	0	0	0	0	0.
Tuvalu	0	0	0	0	0	0	0	0	0	0	0	0	0	
Canada	307823	0.24	0.08	8.17	0	0	0	22.26	0.93	8.64	66.94	123	209.9	13.
Guinea-Bissau	0.5	0	0	0	0	0	0	0	0	0	0	0	0	
Bahamas	475.4	0	0.36	0	0	22.26	0	0	0	0	0	0	0	
Grenada	4.8	0	0	0	0	0.93	0	0	0	0.3	0	6.66	0.17	
St. Kitts and Nevis	57.1	0	0.58	0	0	8.64	0	0	0.3	0	0	0.4	0	
Nicaragua	1580.3	0	0	0	0	66.94	0	0	0	0	0	0	0	(
Guyana	140.7	0	13.87	0	0	123	0	0	6.66	0.4	0	0	17.6	
Suriname	171.6	0	7.83	0	0	209.9	0	0	0.17	0	0	17.6	0	
Paraguay	68.3	0	24.88	0.03	0	13.54	0	0	0	0	0.3	0	0	
Macedonia	44.9	0.01	1.32	0.07	0.01	3.25	0	0	0	0	0	0	0	
Slovenia	505.9	0	0.08	0.44	0	66.71	0	0	0	0	0	0.25	0.03	0.
Moldova	39.2	0	0.05	0.03	0	23.11	0	0	0	0	0	0	0	
Belarus	584.8	0	1.93	0.06	0	27.87	0	0	0	0.46	1.08	0	0	
Georgia	117.6	0	0.35	0	0	54.02	0	0	0	0	0	0.01	0	
Azerbaijan	741.5	0	47.08	0	0	1.64	0	0	0	0.58	0	0	0	

Figure 5.1 Full matrix format.

zeros, in which case it is more economical to use a format where non-ties are not entered, such as the list formats. Many-valued datasets, such as one giving the physical distances between pairs of nodes, are completely dense, since there is a value for every pair of nodes. For these kinds of data, matrix formats do a good job.

The matrix format is also useful for importing attribute data, where each column in the matrix is an attribute. For example, Figure 5.2 shows a screenshot

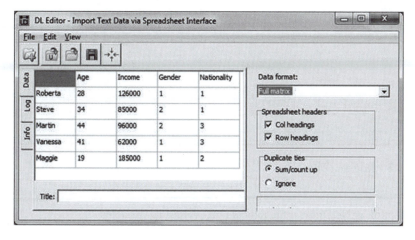

Figure 5.2 Attribute data formatted as a full matrix in UCINET's DL Editor.

of the UCINET DL Editor with four attributes pertaining to a network of five nodes. Unfortunately, most network analysis programs require attributes to have numeric values, so a codebook must be kept in order to know whether a '1' under 'gender' means male or female.[1] We include a fuller discussion of working with attributes later in the chapter.

5.2.2 List formats

When the number of links that exist in a network is much smaller than the number that could exist, the most economical thing to do is store only the ties and leave out the non-ties. There are a number of formats that do this, including the nodelist and edgelist formats.

Nodelists

The nodelist format is the simplest and most economical of all the formats. It is used only for binary data (i.e., presence/absence of ties; no tie strengths). Figure 5.3 shows a screenshot of the UCINET DL Editor spreadsheet with data in a nodelist format representing a five-node undirected network. The first name in each row gives the node that is 'sending' a tie – the ego. The names that follow in the same row are the nodes receiving each tie – the alters. Hence, the first row

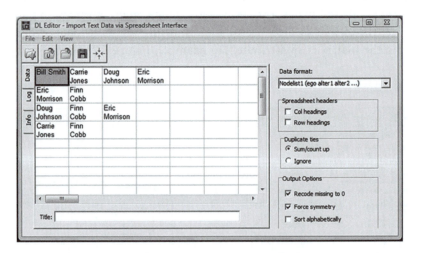

Figure 5.3 Nodelist data.

---

[1] An exception is NetDraw, which allows text values in variables.

	Bill Smith	Carrie Jones	Doug Johnson	Eric Morrison	Finn Cobb
Bill Smith	0	1	1	1	0
Carrie Jones	1	0	0	0	1
Doug Johnson	1	0	0	1	1
Eric Morrison	1	0	1	0	1
Finn Cobb	0	1	1	1	0

Matrix 5.1   Matrix generated from a nodelist.

with 'Bill Smith', 'Carrie Jones', 'Doug Johnson' and 'Eric Morrison' states that there is a tie from 'Bill Smith' to 'Carrie Jones', and from 'Bill Smith' to 'Doug Johnson', and so on. In addition, because the 'force symmetry' option is on, the program automatically supplies a tie from 'Carrie Jones' to 'Bill Smith', from 'Doug Johnson' to 'Bill Smith', and so on for all the others. From these data, the program constructs an adjacency matrix (see Matrix 5.1). The order of rows and columns in the adjacency matrix is determined by the order in which the program encounters the names of the nodes. (This order is overridden if 'sort alphabetically' is checked.) A visualization of this network is given in Figure 5.4.

In any list format, the node identifiers can be numbers instead of names. Using numbers can be more economical than typing long names over and over again, and the labels for the nodes can be added later. One thing to note, if using labels directly, is to make sure you always spell the names exactly the same way and use the same case each time. Programs like UCINET are case-sensitive and will regard 'Bill' as a different label from 'bill'. Another thing to watch out for, particularly in larger studies, is different individuals who happen to have the same name.

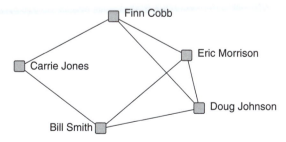

Figure 5.4   Network constructed using nodelist format.

Figure 5.5 shows the same data as Figure 5.3 placed in a text file using the DL data description language mentioned at the beginning of the chapter. The 'dl' at the beginning tells the software to expect the DL syntax. The 'n=5' gives the number of actors, while 'format=nodelist1' tells the program to expect a one-mode nodelist format, and 'symmetric=yes' states that this is symmetric data, so that every link should be treated as reciprocated, and 'data:' indicates the end of information about the data and the beginning of the data themselves. Note that node labels are surrounded by full quotation marks. If this were not done, the program reading the data would interpret Bill as one node and Smith as another.

```
dl n=5
format=nodelist1
symmetric=yes
labels embedded
data:
"Bill Smith" "Carrie Jones" "Doug Johnson" "Eric Morrison"
"Eric Morrison" "Finn Cobb"
"Doug Johnson" "Finn Cobb" "Eric Morrison"
"Carrie Jones" "Finn Cobb"
```

Figure 5.5   Data from Figure 5.3 in a text file using the DL data description language.

When dealing with two-mode data, we need to indicate both the number of rows and columns. For example, the data file in Figure 5.6 describes a person-by-activity matrix. This time we have to take stock of both the number of actors ('nr=3'), which will be the rows in the matrix, and the number of events ('nc=5'), which will be the columns in the matrix. No quotes were used around labels because none contained any punctuation marks like spaces or commas, although it never hurts to include the quotes.

```
dl nr=3, nc=5
format = nodelist2
row labels embedded
column labels embedded
data:
George, Darts, Pool, Dancing
Sue, Dancing, Volleyball
Sally, Dancing, Darts, Basketball
```

Figure 5.6   Two-mode nodelist data in a text file using the DL syntax.

Edgelists

The edgelist format consists of a set of rows in which each row represents a tie in the network. Each row has two columns indicating the pair of nodes that have the tie. Optionally, a third column can be included which gives the strength of the tie. When network data are stored in databases, they are frequently organized in this way (recall the IMDb example in Chapter 4). Figure 5.7 shows a screenshot of the UCINET DL Editor spreadsheet with data in a simple edgelist format representing a five-node undirected network. This type of format is also applicable to two-mode data (in which case it is referred to as edgelist2).

Most network studies collect multiple relations on the same set of nodes. For example, a researcher might ask respondents about their friendships, their professional relationships, family ties, and so on. One way of entering multi-relational data is to use a variation on the edgelist called the edgelist23 format. This consists of node–node–relation triples, as shown in Figure 5.8. The data are from

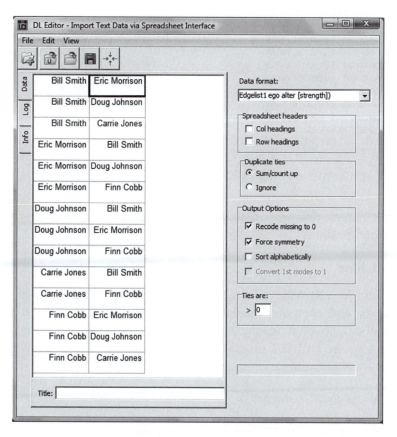

Figure 5.7 Edgelist format for the same data as in Figure 5.3.

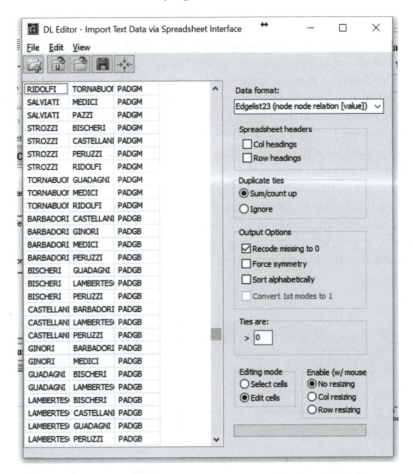

Figure 5.8 Padgett data in edgelist23 format.

UCINET's Padgett dataset, which contains two different kinds of social ties –
marriage and business.

5.2.3 XML files

XML is short for eXtensible Markup Language. XML files are text files that are
both human and computer readable. A particular variant used in network
analysis is GML (graph modeling language). An abbreviated example is provided
in Figure 5.9. The UCINET program can read GML files through its command
line interface (CLI), using a command like this:

```
->lesmis = loadgml("lesmis.gml")
```

The result is a new UCINET dataset called "lemsis".

```
Creator "Mark Newman on Fri Jul 21 12:44:53 2006"
graph
[
  node
  [
    id 0
    label "Myriel"
  ]
  node
  [
    id 1
    label "Napoleon"
  ]
...
edge
  [
    source 1
    target 0
    value 1
  ]
  edge
  [
    source 2
    target 0
    value 8
  ]
  edge
  [
    source 3
    target 0
    value 10
  ]
```

Figure 5.9   Excerpt from a GML data file.

5.3 Cleaning network data

Once the data are imported, it is advisable to examine them in some detail. There are usually a number of problems, and if these are detected early, you can avoid repeating analyses on the flawed data. One kind of problem to look for is repeated nodes. This occurs when an actor has been entered twice, or more commonly when there are slight differences in how the node's name was typed. Another common problem is missing actors. This could be because of non-response or an error in entering or copying the data. The non-response issue is a serious problem to which we return later.

It is always worth thinking about whether the data should logically have certain characteristics and then checking that those are in fact present. For example, many relations, such as 'had lunch with', are supposed to be symmetric, so you should make sure that is true. If it is not, you need to determine whether this is due to some mistake in the process of entering and importing the data, or whether it simply reflects what the respondents said (due to recall problems or problems with the way the questionnaire was worded).

Another thing to look for is isolates. In some data collection designs a node cannot be in the study unless it has ties, so any isolates you find suggest a problem with the data.

In many studies, the researcher will have some ethnographic feel for the data. For example, you might have a pretty good idea of which nodes should be central and which ones not. Running a quick centrality analysis early on will let you check the data against your intuition.

In many cases, one of the most useful things you can do is construct a picture of the network (see Chapter 7). Often you can tell at a glance that something is very wrong. For example, you might see that the network is divided into a number of unconnected fragments, which might not make any sense given how you collected the data.

5.4 Data transformation

Here we discuss a small sample of the myriad transformations that are often applied to data in the course of an analysis. These include transposing matrices, symmetrizing, dichotomizing, imputing missing values, combining relations, combining nodes, extracting subgraphs, and many more.

5.4.1 Transposing

To transpose a matrix is to interchange its rows with its columns (see Figure 5.10). When applied to a non-symmetric adjacency matrix, this has the effect of reversing the direction of all the arcs (see Figure 5.11). This can be helpful in maintaining a consistent interpretation of the ties in a network. When we construct adjacency matrices from surveys, we generally do it in such a way that the rows correspond to respondents (egos) and the columns correspond to the people mentioned by ego (alters). However, it is also convenient to think of the row node as sending to the column node, as in sending information or resources. These two conventions can be in conflict. For example, suppose the survey asks, 'who do you seek advice from?' A '1' in cell (3, 7) means that person 3 says they seek advice from person 7. But in which direction does advice flow? Advice is flowing from person 7 to person 3. In this case, it might be useful to transpose the matrix and think of it as who gives advice to whom. A similar situation

	A	B	C	D	E	F	G	H	I	J	K	L	M	N	O	P	Q	R
A	0	1	1	0	1	0	0	0	0	0	0	0	0	0	1	0	0	0
B	0	0	1	0	1	1	0	0	0	0	0	0	0	0	0	0	0	0
C	0	1	0	0	0	0	1	1	0	0	0	0	0	0	0	0	0	0
D	0	1	1	0	1	0	0	0	0	0	0	0	0	0	0	0	0	0
E	0	1	0	1	0	1	0	0	0	0	0	0	0	0	0	0	0	0
F	0	1	0	0	0	0	1	0	0	0	1	0	0	0	0	0	0	0
G	0	0	1	1	1	0	0	0	0	0	0	0	0	0	0	0	0	0
H	0	0	0	0	0	0	0	0	1	1	0	0	1	0	0	0	0	0
I	0	0	0	0	0	0	0	1	0	0	1	0	0	0	0	1	0	0
J	0	0	0	0	0	0	0	1	1	0	0	0	1	0	0	0	0	0
K	0	0	0	0	0	0	0	1	1	0	0	1	0	0	0	0	0	0
L	0	0	0	0	0	0	0	1	0	1	0	0	1	0	0	0	0	0
M	0	0	0	0	0	0	0	1	0	1	0	0	0	1	0	0	0	0
N	0	0	0	0	0	0	0	0	0	1	0	1	1	0	0	0	0	0
O	0	1	0	0	0	0	0	0	0	0	0	0	1	0	0	0	0	1
P	0	0	0	0	0	0	0	0	1	0	0	0	0	0	1	0	1	1
Q	0	0	0	0	0	0	0	0	0	1	0	0	0	0	0	1	0	1
R	0	0	0	0	0	0	0	0	0	1	0	0	0	0	0	1	1	0

(a)

	A	B	C	D	E	F	G	H	I	J	K	L	M	N	O	P	Q	R
A	0	0	0	0	0	0	0	0	0	0	0	0	0	0	0	0	0	0
B	1	0	1	1	1	1	0	0	0	0	0	0	0	0	1	0	0	0
C	1	1	0	1	0	0	1	0	0	0	0	0	0	0	0	0	0	0
D	0	0	0	0	1	0	1	0	0	0	0	0	0	0	0	0	0	0
E	1	1	0	1	0	0	1	0	0	0	0	0	0	0	0	0	0	0
F	0	1	0	0	1	0	0	0	0	0	0	0	0	0	0	0	0	0
G	0	0	1	0	0	1	0	0	0	0	0	0	0	0	0	0	0	0
H	0	0	1	0	0	0	0	0	1	1	1	1	1	0	0	0	0	0
I	0	0	0	0	0	0	0	1	0	1	1	0	0	0	0	1	0	0
J	0	0	0	0	0	0	0	1	0	0	0	1	1	1	0	0	1	1
K	0	0	0	0	0	1	0	0	1	0	0	0	0	0	0	0	0	0
L	0	0	0	0	0	0	0	0	0	0	1	0	0	1	0	0	0	0
M	0	0	0	0	0	0	0	1	0	1	0	1	0	1	1	0	0	0
N	0	0	0	0	0	0	0	0	0	0	0	0	1	0	0	0	0	0
O	1	0	0	0	0	0	0	0	0	0	0	0	0	0	0	1	0	0
P	0	0	0	0	0	0	0	0	1	0	0	0	0	0	0	0	1	1
Q	0	0	0	0	0	0	0	0	0	0	0	0	0	0	0	1	0	1
R	0	0	0	0	0	0	0	0	0	0	0	0	0	0	1	1	1	0

(b)

Figure 5.10 A matrix and its transpose: (a) who likes whom; (b) who is liked by whom.

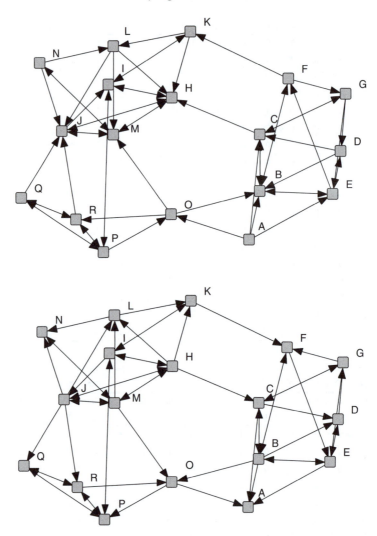

Figure 5.11 Transposing an adjacency matrix is equivalent to reversing the direction of the arrows.

occurs with food webs, where we have data on which species eat which other species. Ecologists like to reverse the direction of the arrows because they think in terms of the direction of energy flow through the ecosystem (e.g., carbon flowing from the prey to the predator).

So far we have only considered transposing two-dimensional matrices. Stacked datasets can be seen as three-dimensional matrices consisting of rows, columns and layers or slices. In these matrices, three different transpositions can be done: interchanging rows with columns, rows with layers, and columns with layers. The column–layer transposition is particularly useful. Suppose, for example, we have run a centrality analysis on UCINET's Padgett dataset, which we encountered earlier. This dataset contains two matrices corresponding to marriage and business ties among Florentine families during the Renaissance. When we run centrality on it, the result is a new three-dimensional dataset consisting of two person-by-centrality measure layers, one for each type of tie, as shown in Matrix 5.2. This way of organizing the results lends itself to answering a question like 'how does the Medici's centrality vary depending on how we measure centrality?' but is not as helpful for answering 'how does the Medici's centrality in the marriage network compare with their centrality in the business network?'. For that, we would rather have the results for the two networks side by side and have the measures correspond to the different matrices, as shown in Matrix 5.3. We can accomplish this transposition easily in UCINET's command line interface (CLI, previously known as the matrix algebra facility). Assuming the centrality results are in a dataset called PADGETT-CENT, we would type:

```
-->display transpose(padgett-cent col layer)
```

5.4.2 Imputing missing data

Missing data can be a problem in full network research designs. The most common kind of missing data is where a respondent has chosen not to fill out the survey. This creates a row of missing values in the network adjacency matrix. For some analyses, such as the QAP regressions that are discussed in Chapter 8, this is not a big problem. Many graph-theoretic procedures, however, such as centrality measures, will treat the missing values as non-ties, which is simply incorrect.

An obvious solution is to eliminate that node from the analysis altogether (deleting both their row and their corresponding column in the adjacency matrix). The trouble with this is that the remaining network is a little misleading. If the missing node is the most important in the network – and it is not unusual for important people to be unwilling to fill out a survey – the picture we get will be very different from what we should have had. Moreover, since the other nodes made responses about that node, removing them means wasting a lot of good data. It would seem worthwhile, then, to search for ways to retain the problematic node.

Marriage	Degree	BonPwr	2Step	ARD	Eigen	Bet
ACCIAIUOL	1.0	301.3	6.0	5.9	0.1	0.0
ALBIZZI	3.0	557.4	10.0	7.8	0.2	19.3
BARBADORI	2.0	482.7	9.0	7.1	0.2	8.5
BISCHERI	3.0	644.6	8.0	7.2	0.3	9.5
CASTELLAN	3.0	590.4	6.0	6.9	0.3	5.0
GINORI	1.0	171.3	3.0	5.3	0.1	0.0
GUADAGNI	4.0	660.3	9.0	8.1	0.3	23.2
LAMBERTES	1.0	202.8	4.0	5.4	0.1	0.0
MEDICI	6.0	982.7	11.0	9.5	0.4	47.5
PAZZI	1.0	103.0	2.0	4.8	0.0	0.0
PERUZZI	3.0	628.3	6.0	6.8	0.3	2.0
PUCCI	0.0	0.0	0.0	0.0	0.0	0.0
RIDOLFI	3.0	778.2	11.0	8.0	0.3	10.3
SALVIATI	2.0	333.8	7.0	6.6	0.1	13.0
STROZZI	4.0	811.2	8.0	7.8	0.4	9.3
TORNABUON	3.0	742.9	10.0	7.8	0.3	8.3

Business	Degree	BonPwr	2Step	ARD	Eigen	Bet
ACCIAIUOL	0.0	0.0	0.0	0.0	0.0	0.0
ALBIZZI	0.0	0.0	0.0	0.0	0.0	0.0
BARBADORI	4.0	756.2	9.0	6.8	0.4	25.0
BISCHERI	3.0	663.5	5.0	5.4	0.3	2.5
CASTELLAN	3.0	754.5	7.0	6.0	0.4	5.0
GINORI	2.0	370.7	7.0	5.4	0.2	0.0
GUADAGNI	2.0	452.9	4.0	4.4	0.2	0.0
LAMBERTES	4.0	838.5	5.0	5.9	0.4	6.0
MEDICI	5.0	471.8	7.0	6.9	0.2	24.0
PAZZI	1.0	142.7	5.0	4.4	0.1	0.0
PERUZZI	4.0	908.5	7.0	6.5	0.5	13.5
PUCCI	0.0	0.0	0.0	0.0	0.0	0.0
RIDOLFI	0.0	0.0	0.0	0.0	0.0	0.0
SALVIATI	1.0	142.7	5.0	4.4	0.1	0.0
STROZZI	0.0	0.0	0.0	0.0	0.0	0.0
TORNABUON	1.0	142.7	5.0	4.4	0.1	0.0

Matrix 5.2   Three-dimensional matrix containing centrality measures computed on the Padgett dataset.

	Degree		Beta Centrality		Betweenness	
	PADGM	PADGB	PADGM	PADGB	PADGM	PADGB
ACCIAUOLI	1	0	301.3	0.0	0.0	0.0
ALBIZZI	3	0	557.4	0.0	19.3	0.0
BARBADORI	2	4	482.7	756.2	8.5	25.0
BISCHERI	3	3	644.6	663.5	9.5	2.5
CASTELLANI	3	3	590.4	754.5	5.0	5.0
GINORI	1	2	171.3	370.7	0.0	0.0
GUADAGNI	4	2	660.3	452.9	23.2	0.0
LAMBERTESCHI	1	4	202.8	838.5	0.0	6.0
MEDICI	6	5	982.7	471.8	47.5	24.0
PAZZI	1	1	103.0	142.7	0.0	0.0
PERUZZI	3	4	628.3	908.5	2.0	13.5
PUCCI	0	0	0.0	0.0	0.0	0.0
RIDOLFI	3	0	778.2	0.0	10.3	0.0
SALVIATI	2	1	333.8	142.7	13.0	0.0
STROZZI	4	0	811.2	0.0	9.3	0.0
TORNABUONI	3	1	742.9	142.7	8.3	0.0

Matrix 5.3   Centrality measures after transposing columns and layers of Matrix 5.2 (some measures omitted for brevity).

In the case of symmetric or undirected relations, a simple cure is to fill in any missing rows with the data found in the corresponding column. The assumption is that, if the respondent had been able to answer, they would have listed all the actors that mentioned them. This may not be exactly right, but it will be more accurate than treating the missing values as zeros.[2] UCINET has a command called REPLACENA within the CLI to do this. For example, given a matrix called MARRIAGE with a couple of rows of missing data, you would type:

```
-->cleanedmarriage = replacena(marriage transpose(marriage))
```

This tells the program to construct a transposed version of the MARRIAGE matrix (in which the columns become the rows and vice versa), then replace all missing values in the MARRIAGE matrix with the corresponding value in the transposed matrix. This effectively replaces the missing rows

---

[2] Of course, one should not do this when calculating reciprocity rates, as it will artificially inflate those values.

in MARRIAGE with the corresponding columns, yielding a new file called 'cleanedmarriage'.

For non-symmetric relations, such as 'seeks advice from', this technique would not make sense. However, if you were wise enough to have asked your respondents both 'who do you seek advice from?' and 'who seeks advice from you?', you could use the transpose of the second matrix to fill in the missing rows in the first, and vice versa. In other words, you assume that if someone says Bill seeks advice from them, then if Bill had been able to answer the survey, he would have said he seeks advice from that person.

For more sophisticated ways of imputing missing values, the reader is advised to consult the relevant literature. For example, Butts (2003) presents a Bayesian approach intended for cognitive social structure data. For general matrices, Candès and Recht (2012) present ingenious methods for recovering missing cells. In general, it is a good idea to run the analyses separately using different ways of handling missing values (including simply removing nodes with missing data), to see if the results are robust. If they are not, there is the danger that any findings are an artifact of the method used to handle missing values.

5.4.3 Symmetrizing

Symmetrizing refers to creating a new dataset in which all ties are reciprocated (and perhaps regarded as undirected). There are many reasons to symmetrize data. One very practical reason is that some analytical techniques, such as multidimensional scaling, assume symmetric data. In other cases, symmetrizing is part of data cleaning. For example, when we ask respondents to name their friends using an open-ended questionnaire item, we often find unintended asymmetry because respondents simply forget to mention people, as noted in the previous chapter. In these cases, we often create a new, symmetric adjacency, using the rule that if either person mentioned the other, then there is a tie. We call this the OR, or union, rule. Alternatively, if we suspect name-dropping, we might adopt a stricter rule, namely that only if both people mention each other will we consider it a tie. This is called the AND, or intersection, rule. Obviously, the union rule creates networks denser than the original, while the intersection rule makes them sparser. As discussed in Chapter 14, the latter can be helpful when dealing with large networks.

In other cases, we symmetrize in order to study an underlying symmetric relationship that is not quite the same thing as the observed tie. For example, suppose we have asked respondents who they receive advice from. In seeking advice, we know that an actor reveals the problem they are trying to solve. In this sense, there is an exchange of information. It may be that this exchange of information is the social relation we are really interested in studying, perhaps because we see it as a proxy for a certain level of collaboration or intimacy. In this case, we symmetrize using the rule that if either gives advice to the other, we say there is an exchange tie.

From the point of view of a matrix representing a network, when we symmetrize we are comparing an (i, j) entry with the corresponding (j, i) entry and, if needed, making them the same. The union rule corresponds to taking the larger of the two entries. The intersection rule takes the smaller of the two. Many other options are possible as well. For valued data we might consider taking the average of the two entries. For example, if i estimates having had lunch with j eight times in a month, but j estimates having lunched with i ten times, we can view these as two measurements of the same underlying quantity, and use the average as the best available estimate of that quantity.

5.4.4 Dichotomizing

Another common data transformation is dichotomizing, which refers to converting valued data to binary data. In this case, we take a valued adjacency matrix and set all cells with a value greater than (or less than, or exactly equal to) a certain threshold to 1, and set all the remaining cells to 0 (see Matrices 5.4 and 5.5). The usual reason for doing this is again very practical: some methods, especially graph-theoretic methods, are only applicable to binary data. Also, dichotomizing with a high cut-off can serve to reduce the density of the network, which is useful in handling large networks (see Chapter 14).

When dichotomizing for these very practical reasons, it is usually advisable to dichotomize at different levels and run the analyses on each of the

	1	2	3	4	5	6	7	8	9	10	11	12	13	14	15
1	0	2	1	0	2	0	0	2	2	2	2	1	1	1	0
2	2	0	3	3	1	4	2	0	2	1	1	2	0	2	0
3	1	3	0	6	1	2	2	1	2	0	2	2	1	1	0
4	0	3	6	0	2	2	1	0	0	0	4	3	1	0	0
5	2	1	1	2	0	1	1	2	1	1	2	1	1	0	0
6	0	4	2	2	1	0	1	2	2	0	2	0	1	0	0
7	0	2	2	1	1	1	0	1	1	0	1	0	2	1	0
8	2	0	1	0	2	2	1	0	2	1	2	0	2	0	0
9	2	2	2	0	1	2	1	2	0	3	3	0	1	1	0
10	2	1	0	0	1	0	0	1	3	0	3	1	0	1	0
11	2	1	2	4	2	2	1	2	3	3	0	0	1	0	0
12	1	2	2	3	1	0	0	0	0	1	0	0	0	0	0
13	1	0	1	1	1	1	2	2	1	0	1	0	0	1	0
14	1	2	1	0	0	0	1	0	1	1	0	0	1	0	0
15	0	0	0	0	0	0	0	0	0	0	0	0	0	0	0

Matrix 5.4 Original valued data.

```
                                  1 1 1 1 1 1
                1 2 3 4 5 6 7 8 9 0 1 2 3 4 5
                - - - - - - - - - - - - - - -
         1      0 1 0 0 1 0 0 1 1 1 1 0 0 0 0
         2      1 0 1 1 0 1 1 0 1 0 0 1 0 1 0
         3      0 1 0 1 0 1 1 0 1 0 1 1 0 0 0
         4      0 1 1 0 1 1 0 0 0 0 1 1 0 0 0
         5      1 0 0 1 0 0 0 1 0 0 1 0 0 0 0
         6      0 1 1 1 0 0 0 1 1 0 1 0 0 0 0
         7      0 1 1 0 0 0 0 0 0 0 0 0 1 0 0
         8      1 0 0 0 1 1 0 0 1 0 1 0 1 0 0
         9      1 1 1 0 0 1 0 1 0 1 1 0 0 0 0
        10      1 0 0 0 0 0 0 0 1 0 1 0 0 0 0
        11      1 0 1 1 1 1 0 1 1 1 0 0 0 0 0
        12      0 1 1 1 0 0 0 0 0 0 0 0 0 0 0
        13      0 0 0 0 0 0 1 1 0 0 0 0 0 0 0
        14      0 1 0 0 0 0 0 0 0 0 0 0 0 0 0
        15      0 0 0 0 0 0 0 0 0 0 0 0 0 0 0
```

Matrix 5.5   Dichotomized data.

resulting datasets. This approach retains the richness of the data and can reveal insights into the network structure that would not be easy to deduce from techniques designed to deal with valued data directly. It also gives you an idea of the extent to which your findings are robust across different definitions of ties. Unless theoretically motivated, you do not want results that hinge on a particular, perhaps arbitrary, choice of dichotomization thresholds.[3]

In other cases we dichotomize because different research questions call for different kinds of ties. For example, we might have measured ties using a scale like this: 0 = don't know, 1 = acquaintance, 2 = friend, 3 = best friend. With respect to estimating the chance of hearing some random bit of information, perhaps we would dichotomize at anything greater than 0. But with respect to estimating a person's feeling of having emotional support, we might count only friendships, and dichotomize at larger than 1.

5.4.5 Combining relations

As noted in the discussion of edgelist23 data formats, most network studies collect multiple relations on the same set of nodes. For some analyses, however, we

---

[3] UCINET includes a routine which seeks a 'natural' dichotomization threshold. Essentially, it searches for a cut-off such that the gap between the average value above the cut-off and the average value below the cut-off is as large as possible. This is similar to finding a large drop in a scree plot. Another way to look at this same process is to find the cut-off that maximizes the correlation of the dichotomized matrix with the original matrix. In other words, choosing that cut-off that leads to the least loss of information.

will combine some of these separate relations into one. For example, we might take three separate network questions, such as 'who do you attend sports events with?', 'who do you go to the theater with?', and 'who do you go out to dinner with?' and combine them into a more general, analytically defined, relation, such as 'who socialized with whom'. More broadly, we might take several relations involving friendship, support, liking and so on and combine them to create a category of relations that we might call 'expressive ties'. Similarly, we might take a number of network questions about coordinating at work, getting work advice from, and so on, and build an instrumental tie matrix.

To construct the adjacency matrix for an aggregated relation we can use tools like UCINET's Boolean Combination procedure, or simply sum the individual adjacency matrices. For example, in UCINET we might use the CLI to add a set of matrices corresponding to positive relations. The following command creates a new relation called 'positive' from all the relations in the Sampson dataset (Sampson, 1969) that we deem to be positive:

```
-->positive = add(samplk1 samplk2 samplk3 sampes sampin samppr)
```

If desired, we can then dichotomize the matrix so that a tie in any of these relations constitutes a tie in the new relation. Otherwise, we could use the raw numbers as an indication of the strength of the positive tie.

	Factor 1	Factor 2
SAMPLK3	0.864	−0.088
SAMPIN	0.858	−0.088
SAMPES	0.852	−0.115
SAMPLK2	0.844	−0.089
SAMPLK1	0.745	−0.046
SAMPPR	0.739	−0.099
SAMNPR	−0.046	0.624
SAMPDLK	−0.078	0.818
SAMPDES	−0.102	0.889
SAMPNIN	−0.113	0.804

Matrix 5.6 Rotated factor loadings for relations in the Sampson monastery dataset.

Alternatively, we can take an empirical approach and try to discover which relations are highly correlated. In UCINET we can do this by using the Tools|Similarities procedure to compute Pearson correlations between all pairs of adjacency matrices, and then running Tools|Scaling|Factor Analysis on the correlation matrix to obtain varimax-rotated factor loadings. When we do this with the Sampson data, we find two factors, corresponding to positive and negative ties (see Matrix 5.6). It is worth noting that the positive and negative relations form two separate and orthogonal factors rather than two poles of the same factor. The results suggest it would be sensible to sum the positive matrices and, separately, the negative matrices to obtain two final networks for analysis.

5.4.6 Combining nodes

Sometimes we collect data at an individual level but want to analyze it at a higher level. For example, we collect data on who collaborates with whom in an organization, but what we are really interested in is the pattern of ties between departments (see Figure 5.12). As a result, we want to aggregate the nodes into departments such that a tie between any two nodes becomes a tie between their departments. The inter-departmental ties could be defined as a simple count of the individual-level ties, or we could normalize the count to account for the number of people in each department. One normalization is to divide the count of ties between department A and department B by the number possible, which is simply the size of department A multiplied by the size of department B.[4]

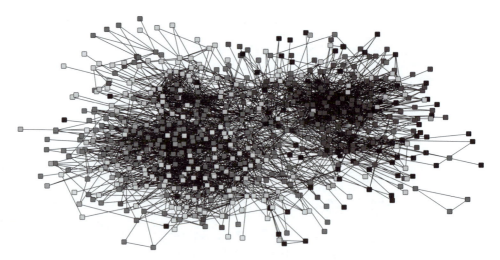

Figure 5.12 Collaboration ties among 960 scientists, shaded by department.

---

[4] When A and B refer to the same department and the network is non-reflexive, we use $n(n - 1)$, which accounts for the impossibility of self-loops.

These are called densities, and the valued adjacency matrix thus created is called a density table.

Another normalization is to divide the values in each row by the total number of outgoing ties for members of the department corresponding to that row. The resulting matrix gives the proportion of a department's ties that are going to each department (including itself). This tells you how the department members are

	BHS	CCG	DCL	ES	HEW	IS	MS	SRG	STAT	TAS
BHS	2.01	1.21	0.89	0.16	0.71	0.20	0.15	3.35	2.62	1.28
CCG	1.21	1.80	0.67	0.30	0.72	0.43	0.40	2.31	2.95	0.80
DCL	0.89	0.67	1.88	0.27	0.63	0.42	0.77	1.87	3.03	0.74
ES	0.16	0.30	0.27	2.79	0.45	1.15	1.80	0.30	1.49	0.30
HEW	0.71	0.72	0.63	0.45	1.47	0.95	0.83	2.03	2.23	0.62
IS	0.20	0.43	0.42	1.15	0.95	3.27	1.32	0.70	2.33	0.24
MS	0.15	0.40	0.77	1.80	0.83	1.32	2.67	0.46	2.01	0.34
SRG	3.35	2.31	1.87	0.30	2.03	0.70	0.46	7.13	4.00	2.53
STAT	2.62	2.95	3.03	1.49	2.23	2.33	2.01	4.00	7.86	2.10
TAS	1.28	0.80	0.74	0.30	0.62	0.24	0.34	2.53	2.10	1.55

Matrix 5.7 Ties between departments. Values are observed counts divided by expected.

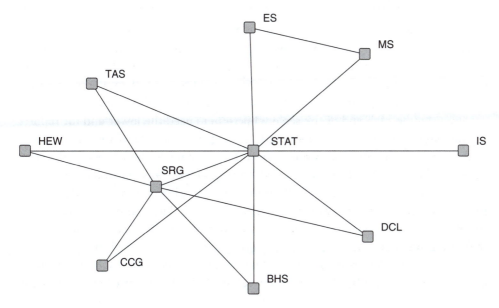

Figure 5.13 Ties between departments based on Matrix 5.7.

allocating their 'relational energy' across departments. Still another normalization is to divide the number of ties between departments by the expected value, given a model of independence – that is, a model in which nodes make ties without regard for what department they are in. These are the values shown in Matrix 5.7. Regardless of the choice of method to normalize, the valued matrix can also be dichotomized. The result is a new network – in which the nodes are departments – which can be analyzed in all the usual ways, such as running a subgroup analysis to find out which departments cluster together. Figure 5.13 shows the network of ties based on a dichotomized version of Matrix 5.7.

5.4.7 Subgraphs

Finally, it may be the case that we do not want to analyze the whole network. We may wish to delete some nodes from the network. This may be because they are outliers in some respect, or because we need to match the data to another dataset where some but not all the same nodes are present. Or we may wish to combine nodes to form one node that is connected to the same nodes as the individuals were. One reason for combining nodes may be that the data were collected at too fine a level and we need to conduct a coarser-grained analysis. Combining nodes in the same departments would be an example of moving up from the individual level to the department level.

5.5 Normalization

There may be times when we want to re-express, standardize or normalize network data to ensure we are making fair comparisons across rows, columns or entire matrices. In Chapter 4 we discussed the concern that in the use of ratings scales for collecting strength-of-tie data there could be a problem due to respondents' use and interpretations of the scales. Some respondents may have more readily used the high end of the scale while others used the lower end for reporting on essentially the same tie strength. In another example, if respondents are asked to assess the physical distance from their homes to the homes of all other actors in the network, it may be that some respondents answer in feet, others in yards, and others in meters. In both of these cases, it is necessary to reduce each row to a common denominator in order to make the data comparable. One way to get around these different scale issues is to normalize the data. A classic normalization procedure is to compute z-scores for each row so each has a mean of 0 and a standard deviation of 1 (excluding the main diagonal). Another approach is to divide each row by the maximum value. Both of these procedures assume that the rows are the respondents and therefore the measuring devices that need to be made comparable. There is a range of procedures: one can normalize with respect to means, marginals, standard deviations, means and standard deviations together, Euclidean norms, and maximums. Each type of normalization can be performed on each row separately, on each column separately, on each row *and* each column (iteratively), and on the matrix as a whole.

5.6 Cognitive social structure data

As introduced in Chapter 2, cognitive social structure data (Krackhardt, 1987) are data collected from each actor in a network on the respondent's perception of who is tied to whom. We can think of this as N adjacency matrices, each $N \times N$ in size. If the relation in question is who likes whom, we can also think of these data as comprising a single three-dimensional matrix LIKE in which $LIKE(k, i, j) = 1$ if person k perceives that person i has a tie to person j. Note that, depending on how we collected the data, the perceived ties may be directed so that $LIKE(k, i, j)$ need not equal $LIKE(k, j, i)$.

Typically, one of the reasons for collecting data of this type is to investigate the accuracy of people's perception of the network. For example, Krackhardt (1987) found that managers who had more accurate views of the network had more power in the organization. However, measuring accuracy entails defining a right answer – the 'true' network. There are several approaches to doing this (Krackhardt, 1987: 116). Perhaps the most commonly used is what Krackhardt calls the 'row-dominated locally aggregated structure' (RLAS). In the RLAS, we assume that the person sending a tie (such as trust) to another is the authority on that tie, and we take their word for it. This means that to construct the RLAS matrix, we simply define $RLAS(i, j)$ to be equal to $LIKE(i, i, j)$. The RLAS is the matrix you would have obtained had you simply collected ordinary network data. The RLAS is especially suitable for mental relations because the respondent herself is probably the best judge of how she feels about someone else.

Another way to construct the true matrix is the intersection method. Here the idea is that a tie exists from i to j if i says they have a tie to j, and j perceives an incoming tie from i. This is not reciprocity, which would be that i says they lent money to j and j says they lent money back to i. Rather, it is agreement: i says they lent money to j, and j says that *they borrowed money from i*. This matrix can be defined as $ILAS(i, j) = 1$ if $LENT(i, i, j) = 1$ and $LENT(j, i, j) = 1$. The logic of the intersection approach is that you have more confidence in a tie if both people involved report that tie. The ILAS is particularly appropriate for ties that have a sense of inter-subjective reality, such as interactions.

An alternative approach is a consensus method that takes into account the perceptions not just of the two people involved in a tie, but everyone else's as well. For example, we could use a threshold model that declares a tie from *i* to *j* if at least a certain percentage of people (say, 50%) see it that way. There are a number of more sophisticated versions of this approach as well (Romney et al., 1986; Butts, 2003). The consensus approach is particularly appropriate for observable relations that the participants themselves might prefer to keep hidden. For example, two co-workers having an affair may seek to downplay their relationship, but the rest of the office may still see them as very close.

Once a 'true' network is constructed, we can then evaluate the similarity between each person's individual perceived network and the true network. This is simply a matter of measuring the similarity between each person's perceived matrix and the adjacency matrix of the true network.

5.7 Matching attributes and networks

A quirk of network analysis programs such as Pajek and UCINET (but not NetDraw) is that they identify nodes by position in the data file rather than using unique identifiers. They allow node labels, such as 'John Smith' and '101–2', but the way they identify nodes internally is simply by their ordinal position in the list of nodes. As a result, if you delete node 15, what used to be node 16 will now be seen as node 15 in the program.

Among other things, this means that to combine network and attribute data in a single analysis, you must be careful to ensure that the nodes are in the same

```
                                          1
                        1 2 3 4 5 6 7 8 9 0
                        S J M V R C A A J F
                        - - - - - - - - - -
         1     Steve    0 0 1 0 0 0 0 0 0 1
         2      Jeff    1 0 1 0 0 0 0 0 0 0
         3    Martin    0 1 0 0 0 0 1 1 0 0
         4   Vanessa    0 0 0 0 0 1 0 0 0 0
         5   Roberta    0 0 0 0 0 0 0 0 1 1
         6     Chris    0 0 0 0 0 0 0 0 0 0
         7       Ann    0 0 0 0 0 0 0 0 0 0
         8      Adam    1 1 1 1 0 1 0 1 0 0
         9     James    1 1 0 0 0 0 1 0 0 1
        10     Fiona    0 0 0 0 0 0 0 0 0 0
```

Matrix 5.8 A directed network.

		Age	Gender	Income
1	Adam	19	1	489
2	Ann	22	2	121
3	Chris	61	2	239
4	Fiona	37	2	3125
5	James	20	1	1421
6	Jeff	16	1	1030
7	Martin	44	1	1453
8	Roberta	26	2	3412
9	Steve	43	1	2050
10	Vanessa	35	2	245

Matrix 5.9 Attribute matrix of Matrix 5.8 in alphabetical order.

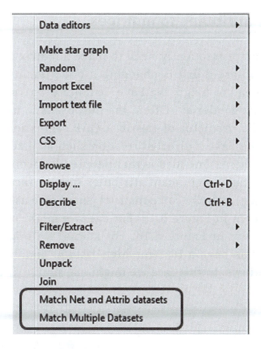

Figure 5.14 Data menu in UCINET.

order in the two files. For example, if the data consist of Matrices 5.8 (a network) and 5.9 (an attribute matrix), an analysis that uses the network and the attribute data together (incorrectly) assumes that the person in the second row of the network matrix (Jeff) is female, because the second person in the attribute

matrix is female. Similarly, if you have attribute data on 1000 people but collected network ties only among a subset of 50 people, a network analysis
program like UCINET (unlike NetDraw) will not know how to look up the values of the 50 people in the larger attribute dataset.

As a result, the researcher needs to take steps to ensure their attribute datasets are properly matched to their network datasets. If one has different matrices
for different social relations, such as a friend network and an advice network,
these need to be matched as well. An easy way to do this in UCINET is to run
"Match Net and Attrib datasets" or "Match Multiple Datasets", as shown in
Figure 5.14. This generates new versions of all the input datasets, whether
attribute or network, that are matched by node labels. Extra nodes found in
some files but not others are ignored.

5.8 Converting attributes to matrices

In network analysis we frequently need to make a matrix out of an attribute.
In general, what we are doing is changing a node quality into a relational
quality, so that instead of height we have 'is taller than', and instead of gender we have 'is same gender as'. Often, the purpose is to use the 'matricized'
attribute as a dyadic predictor of ties in a QAP regression (Chapter 8). For
example, suppose we have a directed relation such as 'likes' and we want to
predict who likes whom. One idea is that people like people who are similar
to themselves on socially significant attributes such as race, gender, age, and
status. For race and gender we can construct 'same race as' and 'same gender
as' matrices, as shown in Figure 5.15. For age, we might use absolute difference in age, as shown in Figure 5.16. For status, we might anticipate that
low-status individuals have a bias for higher-status individuals and against
lower-status individuals. In this case we might use simple difference in status,

Actor	Gender			A	B	C	D	E	F
A	1		A	1	0	0	1	1	0
B	2		B	0	1	1	0	0	1
C	2		C	0	1	1	0	0	1
D	1		D	1	0	0	1	1	0
E	1		E	1	0	0	1	1	0
F	2		F	0	1	1	0	0	1

Figure 5.15   Converting gender into 'same gender as'.

as shown in Figure 5.17. Alternatively, we might argue that the probability of liking someone increases with their status, even if that status is still lower than one's own. In that case what we want to do is to create a matrix in which the values in each column equal the status of the node corresponding to that column. Effectively, it is like writing the status vector as a row vector and then copying it $n - 1$ times. This is shown in Figure 5.18.

Actor	Age
A	14
B	67
C	34
D	33
E	56
F	45

	A	B	C	D	E	F
A	0	53	20	19	42	31
B	53	0	33	34	11	22
C	20	33	0	1	22	11
D	19	34	1	0	23	12
E	42	11	22	23	0	11
F	31	22	11	12	11	0

Figure 5.16 Converting age into 'difference in age'.

Actor	Status
A	6
B	10
C	3
D	5
E	9
F	4

	A	B	C	D	E	F
A	0	-4	3	1	-3	2
B	4	0	7	5	1	6
C	-3	-7	0	-2	-6	-1
D	-1	-5	2	0	-4	1
E	3	-1	6	4	0	5
F	-2	-6	1	-1	-5	0

Figure 5.17 Converting status into relative status using a simple difference.

Actor	Status
A	6
B	10
C	3
D	5
E	9
F	4

	A	B	C	D	E	F
A	6	10	3	5	9	4
B	6	10	3	5	9	4
C	6	10	3	5	9	4
D	6	10	3	5	9	4
E	6	10	3	5	9	4
F	6	10	3	5	9	4

Figure 5.18 Converting status into 'status of alter'.

5.9 Data export

Data analysis can be seen as a series of transformations where the output of one analysis becomes the input to another. In analyzing social network data, for example, we might start with an Excel file, convert it to a UCINET system file, dichotomize it, symmetrize the dichotomized matrix, run centrality on the symmetrized and dichotomized matrix, factor-analyze the centrality measures, and regress some outcome variable on the resultant principal factor. Anywhere along the line, we might want to output data to another software package (such as a statistical package) or create a table or figure for a presentation or paper.

As with data import, we usually recommend using Excel as an intermediary that can communicate with many kinds of software. Programs like UCINET typically produce two kinds of output: an output log file which is a text file meant for humans to peruse and a data file that is not. While it is possible to cut and paste the contents of a log file into Excel (and use Excel's text-to-columns feature), it is a cumbersome and needlessly complicated way to transfer data. A better approach is to open in the UCINET spreadsheet the data file that was created by any analysis, and then cut and paste it into Excel. This spreadsheet-to-spreadsheet transfer is much more efficient.

Sometimes we want to reformat the data before transferring it to another program. For example, suppose we are analyzing longitudinal network data, such as friendships among 17 college men measured at 15 points in time (this is the Newfrat dataset in UCINET). The data are stored in a single 'stacked' UCINET dataset consisting of 15 person-by-person matrices that can be thought of as layers or slices in a three-dimensional data object. If we run, say, centrality on a dichotomized version of this dataset, the program will produce a new stacked dataset containing the centrality scores for each person on each centrality measure for each time point, arranged as 15 person-by-measure matrices. To analyze this using, say, a random effects regression in Stata, we execute the following series of steps.

First, join all the matrices together 'vertically' to create a new matrix that has 255 rows and as many columns as there are centrality measures (say, six columns). The rows are person–time pairs which are appropriate for longitudinal analyses. We can do this in UCINET's CLI by typing the following:

```
-->newmat = appendasrows('newmat-cent')
```

The result is a new matrix called newmat, which can be opened in the UCINET spreadsheet pasted into Excel, and then transferred to Stata. Before transferring to Stata, however, it is useful to open another matrix – automatically created by APPENDASROWS and named newmat-id – in the UCINET spreadsheet, and cut and paste the contents into the Excel file. The newmat-id matrix consists of two variables that give the person-ID and the time-period-ID for each of the 255 cases.

5.10 Summary

Network data need to be in specific formats in order to efficiently enter them into computer programs. Most networks are sparse, so list formats are one of the most efficient ways to enter data. Binary data can be formatted as nodelists, whereas valued data require edgelists. We normally have attribute information on the nodes of a network. This information is in the form of full matrices or vectors and can be imported using spreadsheet formats. Once imported, data should be examined and cleaned, if necessary, to make sure they are as accurate as possible. Then various transformations such as symmetrizing, dichotomizing, normalizing and transposing can be applied. Note that if the transformations have fundamentally changed the nature of the relation, this must be taken into account when interpreting the output obtained from any analysis. For example, if an advice network has been symmetrized via the maximum method, we can no longer interpret x_{ij} as indicating that node i gives advice to node j. However, we can reasonably regard x_{ij} as indicating that i and j are involved in an exchange of information.

5.11 Problems and Exercises

(Note: Problems in the chapters to follow will be using UCINET and E-Net for the problems and exercises. Exercise datasets and help with using UCINET can be found at https://study.sagepub.com/borgatti2e)

1. Below are social network data collected from members of a book club at a university on who talks to whom about school-related matters. Format the data in each of the following ways:

    a. A text file using the DL description language in a nodelist1 format. Import the DL text file into UCINET using Data|Import text file|DL.
    b. Enter the data in the UCINET DL Editor in edgelist1 format and save as a UCINET data file (in the DL Editor save using the "Edgelist1 ego alter" in the "Data format" menu).
    c. Enter the data in a nodelist1 format in Excel and import the data into UCINET using the DL Editor (in the DL editor open the Excel file and save the file as a UCINET data file using the "Nodelist2 (woman event1 event2 ...)" in the "Data format" menu).

Data:

> Mark reports he talks to Gene, Silvia, and Sarah
> Gene reports he talks to Tim
> Silvia reports she talks to Tim and Sarah
> Sarah reports she talks to Tim
> Tim reports he talks to Sarah

2. In addition to the one-mode social network data above, two-mode data were also collected on what university events each had attended over the last six months. Format the data in each of the following ways:

   a. A text file using the DL description language in a nodelist2 format. Import the DL text file into UCINET using Data|Import text file|DL.

   b. Enter the data in a nodelist2 format in Excel and import the data into UCINET using the DL Editor (in the DL editor open the Excel file and save the file as a UCINET data file using the "Nodelist1 (ego alter1 alter2 ...)" in the "Data format" menu).

Data:

> Mark went to Hawking's Lecture
> Gene went to Hawking's Lecture and Spring Concert
> Silvia went to Hawking's Lecture, Halloween Event, and Fall Dance
> Sarah went to Hawking's Lecture, Halloween Event, Spring Concert, and Fall Dance
> Tim went to Halloween Event, Spring Concert, and Fall Dance

3. Demographic and attribute data were also collected. Data include age, gender and attitude towards premarital sex on a Likert scale from 1 to 5 (ranging from 1 being against and 5 for). Enter the data in a matrix format in Excel and import the data into UCINET using the DL Editor (in the DL editor open the Excel file and save the file as a UCINET data file using the "Full Matrix" in the "Data format" menu).

Data:

	Age	Gender (1=male,2=female)	Attitude
Mark	18	1	4
Gene	25	1	2
Silvia	19	2	2
Sarah	21	2	5
Tim	22	1	1

4. Finally, the students were asked to rate 'how much they interacted socially' with the other students over the last two weeks on a 5-point Likert scale with 1 being very

little and 5 being a great deal. Enter the data in a matrix format in Excel and import the data into UCINET using the DL Editor (in the DL editor open the Excel file and save the file as a UCINET data file using the "Edgelist1 ego alter [value])" in the "Data format" menu).

Data:

Mark	Gene	5
Mark	Silvia	4
Mark	Sarah	4
Mark	Tim	2
Gene	Mark	2
Gene	Silvia	2
Gene	Sarah	3
Gene	Tim	4
Silvia	Mark	2
Silvia	Gene	2
Silvia	Sarah	4
Silvia	Tim	4
Sarah	Mark	2
Sarah	Gene	1
Sarah	Silvia	2
Sarah	Tim	4
Tim	Mark	1
Tim	Gene	3
Tim	Silvia	2
Tim	Sarah	4

5. Often the direction of ties needs to be reversed for conceptual or other reasons. Advice relations are one clear example. In asking who goes to whom for advice the direction of the tie is from ego to an alter. But we might care about the flow of advice in a network and would therefore want to reverse the direction of the tie. For Krackhardt's advice network (KRACKAD.##h) transpose the matrix. In UCINET go to Transform|Transpose and input the data file and click on OK. Conceptually, what do the direction of the ties now represent?

6. Many types of network measures and procedures require that the data be symmetrical. For the Krackhadt advice network in Problem 5 above, symmetrize the adjacency network using both the minimum and maximum method. Go to Trannsform|Symmetrize and upload "KRACKAD.##h". Run once using the "Maximum" and once the "Minimum" symmetrizing method. What is the difference between the two methods in terms of the observed ties in each of the symmetrized matrices?

7. Similar to Problem 6 above, many types of network measures and analyses require the data to be in the form of adjacency matrices involving 1s and 0s. The file "Beginning_Winter_Valued.##h" is a proximity matrix containing South Pole crew members' reports of social interaction on a scale from 0 to 10 at the beginning of the winter, with 0 being not at all and 10 very frequently. The data need to be dichotomized. Dichotomize the matrix at three different levels of tie strength. Go to Transform|Dichotomize and input the proximity matrix. Under the dichotomization rule produce one dichotomized adjacency matrix at a weak tie strength, one at a moderate tie strength and one at a strong tie strength. In a comparison of the three adjacency matrices, how do the number of observed ties differ among the three networks?

Don't forget to visit the website at
https://study.sagepub.com/borgatti2e

6

Multivariate Techniques Used in Network Analysis

Learning Outcomes

1. Represent one- and two-mode data in a two-dimensional map
2. Cluster data into groups using hierarchical clustering
3. Correctly interpret the information contained in the clusters and maps

6.1 Introduction

In this chapter we briefly introduce the reader to a number of data analysis techniques that are not specific to network analysis, but are often used as an integral part of network analysis procedures. We use these throughout the book. For the most part, they consist of exploratory multivariate statistics, such as multidimensional scaling, correspondence analysis and hierarchical clustering.

6.2 Multidimensional scaling

The purpose of multidimensional scaling (MDS) is to provide a visual representation of the pattern of proximities among a set of objects. By proximities we mean any symmetric, one-mode matrix of similarities, tie strengths, dissimilarities, distances, etc. among a set of objects. MDS places points (corresponding to our objects) in space such that the distances between the points correspond in a predetermined way to the proximities among objects in the data. For example,

	BOSTON	NY	DC	MIAMI	CHICAGO	SEATTLE	SF	LA	DENVER
BOSTON	0	206	429	1504	963	2976	3095	2979	1949
NY	206	0	233	1308	802	2815	2934	2786	1771
DC	429	233	0	1075	671	2684	2799	2631	1616
MIAMI	1504	1308	1075	0	1329	3273	3053	2687	2037
CHICAGO	963	802	671	1329	0	2013	2142	2054	996
SEATTLE	2976	2815	2684	3273	2013	0	808	1131	1307
SF	3095	2934	2799	3053	2142	808	0	379	1235
LA	2979	2786	2631	2687	2054	1131	379	0	1059
DENVER	1949	1771	1616	2037	996	1307	1235	1059	0

Matrix 6.1   Distances between cities in the USA.

Figure 6.1   Cities MDS output.

if the input data are physical distances between US cities, what MDS will do is to draw a map of the USA. Matrix 6.1 gives an example of driving distances between nine US cities. An MDS map based on those data is shown in Figure 6.1.

When running an MDS analysis, the user must specify whether their proximity data are to be regarded as distances or similarities. If distances, the program tries to place objects A and B near each other when the input value $X(A, B)$ is small, and far apart when the input value is large. If similarities, the program puts pairs of objects with the largest values near each other on the map.

MDS can draw maps in any number of dimensions, but for the purposes of visualizing data on a screen or sheet of paper we use just one or two dimensions. Of course, limiting the dimensionality may force the map to be distorted. If the input data consist of distances between cities all over the world, it will be impossible to draw a map in just two dimensions without introducing significant distortion. The amount of distortion in a map is known as 'stress', and the objective of MDS algorithms is to minimize stress.

In metric MDS, stress is evaluated on the basis of a linear relationship between the input proximities and the resulting map distances, very much like the least squares criterion of ordinary regression. As a rule of thumb, we consider stress values of less than 0.2 to be acceptable when using metric MDS. In non-metric MDS (Kruskal, 1964), stress is evaluated based on a monotonic (ordinal) relationship such that stress is zero if the rank order of input proximities matches the rank order of map distances. By convention, we consider stress values of less than 0.12 acceptable for non-metric scaling. The map shown in Figure 6.1 was drawn using metric MDS and the stress was 0.014, which is nearly perfect.

When stress is high, caution must be used in interpreting the map, since some distances will not be right. The distortions may be spread out over all pairwise relationships, or concentrated in just a few egregiously distorted pairs. In general, however, because most MDS algorithms minimize *squared* residuals, longer distances tend to be more accurate than shorter distances, so larger patterns are still visible even when stress is high.

There are two important things to realize about an MDS map. The first is that the axes are, in themselves, meaningless, and the second is that the orientation of the picture is arbitrary. Thus, an MDS representation of distances between US cities need not be oriented such that north is up and east is right. In fact, north might be diagonally down to the left and east diagonally up to the left. All that matters in an MDS map is which point is close to which others.

There are two things to look for in interpreting an MDS picture: clusters and dimensions. Clusters are groups of items that are closer to each other than to other items. For example, in an MDS map of perceived similarities among animals, it is typical to find that the barnyard animals such as chicken, cow, horse, and pig are all very near each other, forming a cluster. Similarly, the 'zoo' animals such as lion, tiger, antelope, monkey, elephant and giraffe form a cluster.

Dimensions are item attributes that seem to order the items in the map along a continuum. For example, an MDS of perceived similarities among breeds of dogs may show a distinct ordering of dogs by size. The ordering might go from right to left, top to bottom, or move diagonally at any angle across the map. At the same time, an independent ordering of dogs according to viciousness might be observed. This ordering might be perpendicular to the size dimension, or it might cut a sharper angle.

6.3 Correspondence analysis

Correspondence analysis refers to a collection of closely related techniques, including optimal scaling and biplot analysis, which are used for a variety of purposes. In this book, we use correspondence analysis primarily as a visualization technique, very much like MDS, but applied to two-mode data. Ideally, correspondence analysis is applied to frequency tables, such as Greenacre's (1984) example of the number of doctorates awarded by field and year (see Table 6.1).

The output of correspondence analysis is a set of coordinates in multidimensional space for both the row items and the column items, which can then be plotted. Figure 6.2 shows a correspondence analysis plot in two dimensions. The row items – the disciplines – are located in space such that two disciplines with similar profiles across time are placed near each other. For example, sociology and psychology both have rising profiles and are right next to each other. Similarly, the column items – the years – are placed so that years with the same profiles across disciplines are near each other. Since things take time to change, we typically see adjacent years near each other, as in the sequence 1970, 1971, 1972 and 1973. In addition (although there is some controversy about this), the disciplines are located near the years where they are relatively strong, and vice versa.

The term 'relatively strong' here means that the data value is large relative to the row and column averages. The way correspondence analysis is computed is based on a singular value decomposition (SVD) of a normalized version of the data matrix, where the data matrix is normalized by dividing each value by the square root of the product of the corresponding row and column sums. We do not discuss SVD here, but the interested reader can look this up in a standard book on matrices. In essence, it decomposes the matrix into factors which can be interpreted rather like factoring a number as a product of primes. The normalization removes the influence of rows and columns with particularly large

Table 6.1 Number of doctorates by year and field of study.

	1960	1965	1970	1971	1972	1973	1974	1975
Engineering	794	2073	3432	3495	3475	3338	3144	2959
Mathematics	291	685	1222	1236	1281	1222	1196	1149
Physics	530	1046	1655	1740	1635	1590	134	1293
Chemistry	1078	1444	2234	2204	2011	1849	1792	1762
Earth Sciences	253	375	511	550	580	577	570	556
Biology	1245	1963	3360	3633	3580	3636	3473	3498
Agriculture	414	576	803	900	855	853	830	904
Psychology	772	954	1888	2116	2262	2444	2587	2749
Sociology	162	239	504	583	638	599	645	680
Economics	341	538	826	791	863	907	833	867
Anthropology	69	82	217	240	260	324	381	385
Others	314	502	1079	1392	1500	1609	1531	1550

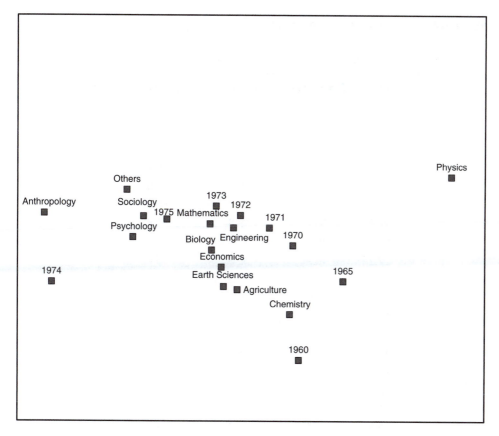

Figure 6.2 Correspondence analysis.

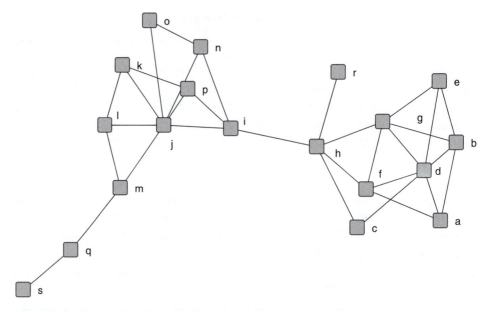

Figure 6.3 Example of a symmetric network.

Table 6.2 Centrality scores of network in Figure 6.3.

Node	Degree	Closeness	Betweenness	Eigenvector
a	16.7	29.0	0.2	40.5
b	22.2	29.5	0.5	50.9
c	11.1	34.6	2.6	25.7
d	33.3	30.5	3.7	65.7
e	16.7	29.0	0.0	43.0
f	22.2	36.0	10.7	50.2
g	27.8	36.7	18.8	60.6
h	27.8	45.0	57.5	40.0
i	22.2	46.2	53.3	18.8
j	38.9	42.9	43.5	16.6
k	16.7	31.6	0.3	8.4
l	16.7	32.7	1.0	7.6
m	16.7	33.3	20.9	6.3
n	16.7	37.5	3.3	10.1
o	11.1	31.0	0.0	6.5
p	16.7	37.5	3.3	10.6
q	11.1	26.1	11.1	1.6
r	5.6	31.6	0.0	9.7
s	5.6	20.9	0.0	0.4

values across the board. The SVD of this matrix then delivers row and column scores that are defined in terms of each other – that is, the score of a given row is proportional to the sum of the values in the row, weighted by the column scores. As a result, a row item's position is something like the centroid of the cloud of column items surrounding it. Similarly, the score of a given column is proportional to the sum of the values in the column, weighted by the row scores.

One way we use correspondence analysis in network analysis is to help find patterns in a collection of measures. For example, suppose we compute four well-known centrality measures (see Chapter 10) on the network shown in Figure 6.3. The resulting scores are shown in Table 6.2. A quick way to get an overview of the results is to run a correspondence analysis on Table 6.2, as shown in Figure 6.4. We can easily see which nodes scored high on eigenvector centrality (bottom left), or closeness (top left) or betweenness (bottom right). Note that degree centrality shows up in the center of the graph, indicating that it is highly related to all the other measures.

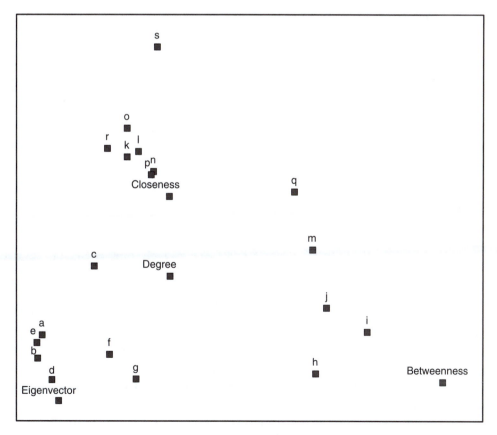

Figure 6.4 Correspondence analysis plot of centrality scores in Table 6.2.

6.4 Hierarchical clustering

Cluster analysis is a set of techniques for assigning items into groups or classes based on the similarities or distances between them. Typically, these groups are mutually exclusive, forming a partition. Johnson's (1967) hierarchical clustering produces a series of successive partitions that are nested within each other in the sense that you can get from the partition with fewer (but larger) classes to the partition with more (smaller) classes by subdividing one or more of the larger classes. Johnson's is an agglomerative method, which means that it starts with the partition that places each item in its own cluster and then joins two of the clusters to form the next partition, continuing this joining process until all items are in a single cluster.

Given a set of N actors to be clustered, and an $N \times N$ distance matrix, the basic process of Johnson's (1967) hierarchical clustering is this:

1. Start by assigning each item to its own cluster, so that if you have N items, you now have N clusters, each containing just one item. Let the distances between the clusters equal the distances between the items they contain.
2. Find the closest pair of clusters and merge them into a single cluster, so that now you have one less cluster.
3. Compute distances between the new cluster and each of the old clusters.
4. Repeat steps 2 and 3 until all items are clustered into a single cluster of size N.

Step 3 can be done in different ways, which is what distinguishes single-link from complete-link and average-link clustering. In single-link clustering (also called the nearest neighbor, the connectedness method and the minimum method), we consider the distance between one cluster and another cluster to be equal to the *shortest* distance from any member of one cluster to any member of the other cluster. In complete-link clustering (also called the diameter or maximum method), we consider the distance between one cluster and another cluster to be equal to the *longest* distance from any member of one cluster to any member of the other cluster. In average-link clustering, we consider the distance between one cluster and another cluster to be equal to the *average* distance from any member of one cluster to any member of the other cluster. More recently, Newman (2004) has introduced another criterion, which joins the pair of clusters that would maximize Q modularity, a measure of clustering quality (see Section 14.3.1 for a discussion of Q).

Example. The following example traces the first steps of a hierarchical clustering of distances in miles between US cities, shown in Matrix 6.2. The method of clustering is single-link.

The nearest pair of cities is Boston and NY, at distance 206. These are merged into a single cluster called 'Boston/NY'.

	BOSTON	NY	DC	MIAMI	CHICAGO	SEATTLE	SF	LA	DENVER
BOSTON	0	206	429	1504	963	2976	3095	2979	1949
NY	206	0	233	1308	802	2815	2934	2786	1771
DC	429	233	0	1075	671	2684	2799	2631	1616
MIAMI	1504	1308	1075	0	1329	3273	3053	2687	2037
CHICAGO	963	802	671	1329	0	2013	2142	2054	996
SEATTLE	2976	2815	2684	3273	2013	0	808	1131	1307
SF	3095	2934	2799	3053	2142	808	0	379	1235
LA	2979	2786	2631	2687	2054	1131	379	0	1059
DENVER	1949	1771	1616	2037	996	1307	1235	1059	0

Matrix 6.2 Input distance matrix.

Then the distance from this new compound object to all other objects is computed. In single-link clustering the rule is that the distance from the compound object to another object is equal to the shortest distance from any member of the cluster to the outside object. So the distance from 'Boston/NY' to DC is chosen to be 233, which is the distance from NY to DC (Matrix 6.3). Similarly, the distance from 'Boston/NY' to Denver is chosen to be 1771.

	BOSTON/NY	DC	MIAMI	CHICAGO	SEATTLE	SF	LA	DENVER
BOSTON/NY	0	233	1308	802	2815	2934	2786	1771
DC	233	0	1075	671	2684	2799	2631	1616
MIAMI	1308	1075	0	1329	3273	3053	2687	2037
CHICAGO	802	671	1329	0	2013	2142	2054	996
SEATTLE	2815	2684	3273	2013	0	808	1131	1307
SF	2934	2799	3053	2142	808	0	379	1235
LA	2786	2631	2687	2054	1131	379	0	1059
DENVER	1771	1616	2037	996	1307	1235	1059	0

Matrix 6.3 After merging Boston with NY.

The nearest pair of objects is Boston/NY and DC, at distance 233. These are merged into a single cluster called 'Boston/NY/DC'. Then we compute the distance from this new cluster to all other clusters, to get a new distance matrix (Matrix 6.4).

Now, the nearest pair of objects is SF and LA, at distance 379. These are merged into a single cluster called 'SF/LA'. Then we compute the distance from this new cluster to all other objects, to get a new distance matrix (Matrix 6.5).

This is then continued until we obtain in the penultimate merger the distance matrix shown in Matrix 6.6. Here we see the clusters have been merged so that we have two clusters, one consisting of Miami and one of all the other cities.

Analyzing Social Networks

	BOSTON/NY/DC	MIAMI	CHICAGO	SEATTLE	SF	LA	DENVER
BOSTON/NY/DC	0	1075	671	2684	2799	2631	1616
MIAMI	1075	0	1329	3273	3053	2687	2037
CHICAGO	671	1329	0	2013	2142	2054	996
SEATTLE	2684	3273	2013	0	808	1131	1307
SF	2799	3053	2142	808	0	379	1235
LA	2631	2687	2054	1131	379	0	1059
DENVER	1616	2037	996	1307	1235	1059	0

Matrix 6.4 After merging DC with Boston/NY.

	BOSTON/NY/DC	MIAMI	CHICAGO	SEATTLE	SF/LA	DENVER
BOSTON/NY/DC	0	1075	671	2684	2631	1616
MIAMI	1075	0	1329	3273	2687	2037
CHICAGO	671	1329	0	2013	2054	996
SEATTLE	2684	3273	2013	0	808	1307
SF/LA	2631	2687	2054	808	0	1059
DENVER	1616	2037	996	1307	1059	0

Matrix 6.5 After merging SF with LA.

The whole process is summarized in UCINET by the cluster diagram as shown in Figure 6.5. In the diagram, the columns are associated with the items and the rows are associated with levels (stages) of clustering. An 'X' is placed between two columns in a given row if the corresponding items are merged at that stage in the clustering. Hence, we can see at level 808 the clusters are (Miami), (Seattle, SF, LA), (Boston, NY, DC, Chicago) and (Denver). We see a clear split between the east coast and the west coast and so the clusters make sense. Unfortunately, not every dataset is as clearly structured and it has to be remembered that, regardless of whether distinct groups exist, the method will always start with everyone in a separate cluster and finish with everyone together, so care is needed in interpreting the results.

	BOSTON/NY/DC/CHICAGO/ DENVER/SF/LA/SEATTLE	MIAMI
BOSTON/NY/DC/CHICAGO/ DENVER/SF/LA/SEATTLE	0	1075
MIAMI	1075	0

Matrix 6.6 Penultimate distance matrix merger.

```
          S                   C
          E         B         H  D
    M     A         O         I  E
    I     T         S         C  N
    A     T         T         A  V
    M  L  S  L  O  N  D  G  E
    I  E  F  A  N  Y  C  O  R

Level   4  6  7  8  1  2  3  5  9
-----   -  -  -  -  -  -  -  -  -
  206   .  .  .  .  XXX   .  .  .
  233   .  .  .  .  XXXXX    .  .
  379   .  .  XXX   XXXXX    .  .
  671   .  .  XXX   XXXXXXX     .
  808   .  XXXXX    XXXXXXX     .
  996   .  XXXXX    XXXXXXXXX
 1059   .  XXXXXXXXXXXXXXX
 1075   XXXXXXXXXXXXXXXXX
```

Figure 6.5 Output of clustering of US cities.

6.5 Summary

We can represent square symmetric non-binary matrices as n-dimensional maps, with the distances between points equating to the values in the matrix, by a process known as multidimensional scaling. For visualization purposes, we are usually interested in two-dimensional maps. The accuracy of the map is measured by a stress coefficient. In metric multidimensional scaling, stress measures the extent to which the distances in the map correspond in a linear way to the input proximities. In non-metric multidimensional scaling, stress measures the extent to which the rank order of distances corresponds to the rank of input proximities. We can produce similar maps for non-square matrices using correspondence analysis. Both multidimensional scaling and correspondence analysis maps are often used to subjectively identify clusters of points. However, we can also use clustering algorithms to detect groups in proximity data. Hierarchical clustering is a clustering approach that yields a series of nested partitions of the points into groups. Each partition in the series is a refinement of the one above it.

6.6 Problems and Exercises

1. Create a UCINET data file for the adjacency matrix for the graph in Chapter 2, Problem 2. Using UCINET, produce a proximity matrix of geodesic distances (go to Network|Cohesion|Geodesic Distances and upload the adjacency matrix and hit OK). We want to visualize this dissimilarity data using non-metric multidimensional scaling (MDS). To visualize the data using non-metric MDS in UCINET go to Tools|Scaling/ Decomposition|Non-Metric MDS and enter the name of the data file (note: make certain the 'Similarities and Dissimilarities' is designated properly). Press OK to run. How would you characterize the spatial proximity among the nodes?

2. The data below came from a study of the social networks of Alaskan salmon fishers in a multi-ethnic fish camp (Johnson and Griffith, 1998). Selected members of the network were given cameras and asked to take pictures of anything that was of interest to them. The resulting pictures were then coded by theme and compared. The table shows the number of photos by each actor involving pictures of groups, pictures of single individuals, pictures of people working, and aesthetic pictures such as animals and sunsets. This table compares the pictures of two Italian fishers with three non-ethnic fishers (Lower48).

   a. Enter the data in a matrix format in Excel and import the data into UCINET using the DL Editor (in the DL editor open the Excel file and save the file as a UCINET data file using the "Matrix (incl. attributes, 2-mode, etc.)" in the "Data format" menu.) Save the file as "CA_ethnicicty_example".
   b. We want to explore the relationship between ethnicity and the thematic content of pictures. To do this we want to visualize the relationship between and among themes and the ethnicity of the fishers. For this we want to run a correspondence analysis. Under "Tools" in UCINET select Tools|Scaling/Decomposition|Correspondence and enter the name of the data file (CA_ethnicicty_example.##h). Press OK to run.
   c. Based on the correspondence analysis what might you conclude about the differences and similarities in the thematic content of the pictures between Italians and non-Italians?

	Groups	Single	Work	Aesthetic
Older_Italian	11	4	7	0
Younger_Italian	11	2	14	7
Lower48-1	2	12	11	14
Lower48-2	8	7	9	15
Lower48-3	9	6	6	12

3. For this problem we will use the network "Science_Collaboration.##h". This is a matrix containing the number of grants researchers in a university shared in common as principle investigators, co-principle investigators and/or co-investigators. The number in the cell of the matrix reflects the number of research grants two researchers have in common. We want to visualize these similarity data using non-metric multidimensional scaling (MDS). To visualize the data using non-metric MDS in UCINET go to Tools|Scaling/Decomposition|Non-Metric MDS and enter the name of the data file. Press OK to run.

   a. How might you interpret the MDS in terms of the structure of collaboration among the researchers?
   b. What is the stress coefficient for this MDS and what does it mean?

4. For the same proximity matrix used in the MDS example above, run a hierarchical cluster analysis (HCL). To run the HCL go to Tools|Cluster Analysis|Hierarchical and input the name of the data file (make sure to use "Similarities"). For the purposes of this example use the default method "WTD_AVERAGE (average between all pairs)". Similar to the MDS example above, how would you characterize the subgroupings of the research collaborations?

7

Visualization

Learning Outcomes

1. Visualize networks with or without node attributes in a meaningful way
2. Embed edge characteristics in network diagrams
3. Represent network change over time graphically

7.1 Introduction

One of the first things most people want to do with network data is construct a visual representation of these – in short, draw a picture. Seeing the network can provide a qualitative understanding that is hard to obtain quantitatively. A network diagram consists of a set of points representing nodes and a set of lines representing ties. Various characteristics of the points and lines, such as color, size, and shape, can be used to communicate information about the nodes and the relationships among them.

This chapter discusses the ins and outs of visualizing social networks. In the discussion to follow, note that we distinguish carefully between network elements and their graphical representation – that is, between nodes and the points that represent them, and between ties and the lines that represent them. In the sections that follow we examine aspects of the graphical representation of structural and compositional information using the capabilities of UCINET's NetDraw.[1] The first part of this chapter discusses methods for the spatial orientation of nodes and

---

[1] Other programs specializing in network visualization are Visone (http://visone.info/html/about.html) and Gephi (http://gephi.org/). In addition, a number of other network analysis programs include powerful visualization capabilities, such as Pajek and NodeXL.

things that are considered important in visualizing properties and attributes of nodes and edges or ties in network graphs. This is followed by a series of examples illustrating some possible ways to address these visualization issues and to reduce network complexity, particularly in large networks.

7.2 Layout

The layout of a network diagram refers to the position of the points in the diagram. It is the most important aspect of network visualization. A badly laid-out network diagram communicates very little information or can lead to errors in the interpretation of a given graph (McGrath et al., 1997). As an example, consider the diagram in Figure 7.1. In this figure, the actors from the bank wiring room dataset introduced in Chapter 2 (see Figure 2.2a) are laid out at random and their ties shown. It is hard to see from this graph the structure of the network in terms of any clustering or grouping, something that would be important to know. However, the nodes can be rearranged in such a way that the inherent clustering or grouping in the network is revealed, as can be seen in Figure 7.2.

There are three basic approaches to laying out networks: attribute-based scatter plotting, ordination (in particular, multidimensional scaling or MDS), and graph layout algorithms. We discuss each of these in turn.

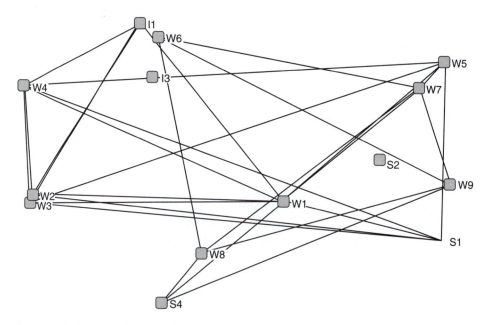

Figure 7.1 Random layout of the games relation in the bank wiring room dataset.

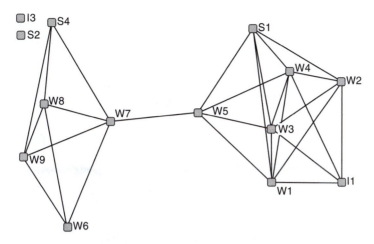

Figure 7.2 Games relation rearranged to reveal structure.

7.2.1 Attribute-based scatter plots

In this approach, we position points based on attributes of the nodes. For example, we can plot the points based on the age and income of the corresponding nodes. We then draw lines between the points to represent ties. These kinds of displays are useful when we are interested in visualizing how attributes of the nodes affect who is connected to whom. Scatter plots are most successful when both attributes are continuous (i.e., not categorical like gender or department), and when the attributes in fact do affect who is tied with whom.

Figure 7.3 shows a graph of trade in minerals among 24 countries in 1981 (Smith and White, 1992). In this graph, the nodes are placed in the space according to rates of secondary school enrollment ratio (X-axis) and energy consumption per capita (Y-axis). If we thought that the relationship between school enrollment and energy consumption was theoretically important for understanding the structure of trade relations, this would be a reasonable way to position the nodes in a two-dimensional space. Spatial information among the countries, such as GIS coordinates, could also be used to position the nodes in space where the latitude and longitude correspond to the X and Y attributes in this example.

7.2.2 Ordination

In this approach, we locate points based on multivariate statistics techniques such as principal components, correspondence analysis and MDS. Typically, the inputs to these procedures are valued proximity matrices, such as a matrix of distances between cities, or a matrix of correlations among variables.

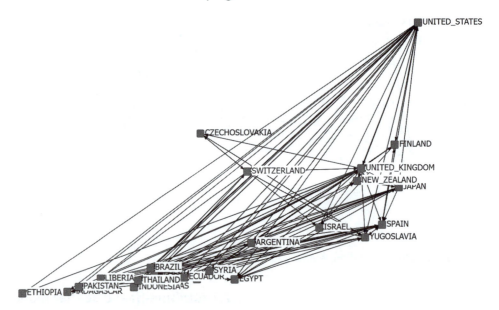

Figure 7.3 Trade in minerals among 24 countries with countries positioned in a scatter plot by school enrollment ratios (*X*) and energy consumption (*Y*) in 1981.

In these layouts, the distances between points are meaningful in the sense that there is a known mathematical relationship between the distances and the social proximities of the nodes. For example, in metric MDS, if the data contain information on the strength of ties between nodes, the resulting layout positions the points so that the points near each other are the ones that are strongly connected to each other, and the nodes that are far apart are the ones that are only weakly connected.

When no strengths of tie data are available (i.e., binary data), the standard thing to do is compute geodesic distances between nodes. As discussed in Chapter 2, by 'geodesic distance' we mean the number of links in the shortest path between a pair of nodes. The ordination algorithm would then lay out the points such that nodes with high geodesic distance between them would be far apart in the diagram, and the points corresponding to nodes with short geodesic distance would be close together.

Ordinations based on geodesic distance typically work very well in the sense that the resulting diagrams are relatively uncluttered, cohesive subgroups are clearly visible, and points corresponding to the more central nodes tend to be found in the center of the diagram. In addition, they have the advantage of interpretability – we know exactly why some nodes are further apart than others. Figure 7.4 is an MDS of the geodesic distances for the trade

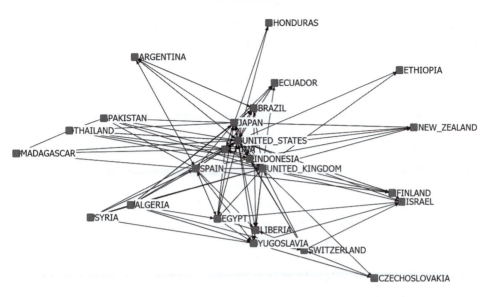

Figure 7.4 MDS of the geodesic distances for the trade in minerals for 24 countries.

in minerals for the 24 countries discussed above (ties were dichotomized for any trade in minerals between two countries that was greater than 0). In this graph the more central countries, such as the United States, are in the center of the graph while less central countries are on the periphery. Additionally, there appears to be some geographical dimensionality as one moves from the lower left to the upper right.

7.2.3 Graph layout algorithms

A wide variety of graph layout algorithms exist. Some are best-regarded as heuristic algorithms that are well defined in terms of the steps one takes to arrive at a layout, but it may be difficult to characterize the resulting output. Other graph layout algorithms consist of a function optimization algorithm that is used to maximize a specific mathematical function. The choice of optimization algorithms may vary – what defines the layout is the function being optimized. This is the approach taken in UCINET's NetDraw procedure (activated via the 'lightning bolt button'). The function optimized has three terms that capture three criteria that are optimized simultaneously. The first criterion – the correspondence between point distance and path distance between nodes – is the same as in the multidimensional approach described above. The second criterion is that nodes should not appear too close to each other so as to obscure one another. In MDS, if two nodes are the same distance from all third parties, they will be located on top of each other. The third criterion implements a preference for equal-length lines. This gives the pictured networks a kind of boxy appearance that makes it easier to spot symmetries. The result of trying to optimize all three criteria is a layout that tends be more readable and aesthetically pleasing than one based on ordination or node attributes. The disadvantage, however, is that distances between points in the diagram no longer correspond in a one-to-one way to path distances between nodes. Thus, we give up a measure of interpretability, in the mathematical sense, in order to get cleaner diagrams that are easier to read.

It is important to realize that the information in graph layouts is contained in the pattern of which nodes are connected to which others. The locations of the points do not necessarily reflect any mathematical or sociological properties – they are chosen based on essentially aesthetic criteria. As such, one must not attach too much meaning to the exact location of a node since the algorithm is not explicitly trying to identify cliques or place central nodes in the center.

Ultimately, any arrangement of nodes in space is equally valid as long as no ties are added or dropped. In other words, if we drag a node out of the center and put it on the periphery (dragging all its ties along with it), the resulting diagram is no less valid than the original. This is not true of attribute-based scatter plots and ordinations, in which the physical distances between the points have meanings which would be violated if the points were moved arbitrarily.

Figure 7.5 Network diagram using a graph layout algorithm.

Figure 7.5 is a graph with the countries arranged in space using NetDraw's graph layout algorithm. The structure is similar to Figure 7.4 in many ways but the graph is much easier to read and the nodes are distributed more evenly across the space.

7.3 Embedding node attributes

In generating network diagrams, we often want to embed additional information, such as attributes of the nodes. For example, in the trade data, we might want to indicate the continent that each country is located on, or the total amount of trade done by each country. Typically, we do this by mapping these node attributes to visual properties of the points. For example, continuous variables such as a country's wealth can be nicely represented by the size of the point corresponding to a country. Color gradients, such as light to dark, can also be used. The values of categorical variables can be nicely represented by colors or shapes of the points.

In programs like NetDraw, points have a number of visual properties that can be used to communicate information about the nodes they represent. For example, points can be many different shapes, sizes and colors. The shapes

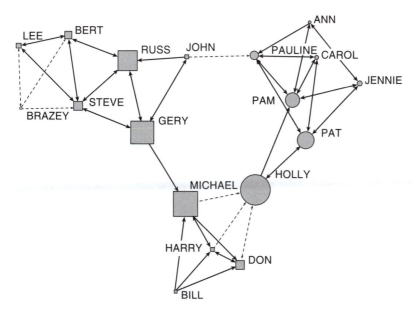

Figure 7.6 Campnet dataset. Circle shapes indicate women and square shapes indicate men. Size corresponds to each node's betweenness centrality. Solid lines are used for same-gender ties, dotted lines for cross-gender ties.

can be drawn with rims of different sizes and colors. Points can have textual labels attached, which can vary in terms of size, color and type of font. Taken all together, a very large number of node attributes can be simultaneously represented in a single network diagram. However, in our experience, using more than two or three properties at a time can be more distracting than informative.[2]

An example is given in Figure 7.6, which depicts the Campnet dataset we briefly encountered in Chapter 2 (Figure 2.3). In this visualization, the size of the nodes is used to represent the betweenness centrality of each node (see Chapter 10), while the shape of nodes is used to represent gender.

7.4 Node filtering

It is often useful to see what a network looks like when certain classes of nodes are removed. Sometimes this is done to remove nodes that are peripheral to a given research interest. Other times, it is to gauge the importance of the selected

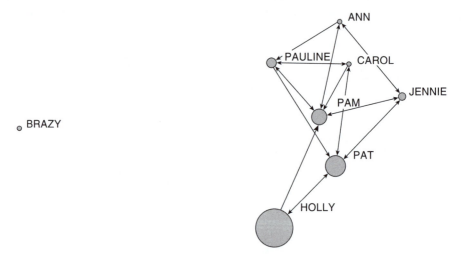

Figure 7.7 Network graph of strong ties among members of a methods camp showing ties among women only and selecting out men from the network.

---

[2] Some research has suggested that no more than six colors should be used in any network diagram (Derefeldt and Marmolin, 1981) although others have suggested the maximum may be more like nine (Smallman and Boynton, 1990). Much of this will depend on the size of the network, both in terms of the number of nodes and the number of ties.

set of nodes in connecting others. Programs like NetDraw make it easy to click points on and off. Look again at Figure 7.6 (of the Campnet dataset) where the squares are men and the circles are women. We see that even with a relatively small network like this it is still difficult to see possible relationships of interest. For this we may want to remove edges or nodes, particularly nodes with certain attributes. If one were interested in the ties among women in the current graph, in this case one can easily see how the women are connected to one another, although there may be some important nuances that are not evident. Figure 7.7 shows the Campnet network with the points corresponding to men clicked off. This emphasizes the isolation of one of the women. This of course was a simple graph, but in more complex graphs the ability to turn attributes on and off can be very helpful in discovering both structural and compositional properties of the network.

7.5 Ego networks

Filtering is also used to visualize the ego networks of particular nodes. By 'ego networks' we mean the set of nodes directly connected to a given node (whom we call ego), together with all ties among them. This is particularly useful when used to compare the structures around two different egos. For example, Figures 7.8 and 7.9 show the acquaintanceship networks of two drug injectors in the city of Hartford, CT (based on data from Weeks et al., 2002).

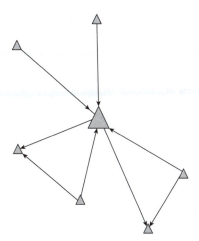

Figure 7.8 Relatively open ego network of Puerto Rican drug injector. Large node is ego. Triangles represent Puerto Ricans.

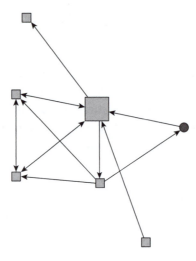

Figure 7.9 Relatively closed ego network of African-American drug injector. Squares represent African-Americans, while circles represent Native Americans.

As in the previous examples, data on the attributes of an ego's alters can be used to search for any organizing principles in the ego's network. In the two figures, one can see both the structural properties of the two networks in terms of being more or less open or closed and aspects of the qualitative properties of an ego's alters. In this case the two networks display high levels of homophily in that egos tend to be acquainted with alters that are of the same ethnicity.

Some personal or ego network studies collect data on large numbers of alters, in some cases up to 50 alters, and the resulting ego network graphs can become rather complex and difficult to visualize (McCarty et al., 2007). Figure 7.10 shows the ego network for actor 1 in the Zachary (1977) karate club dataset. Included are attributes of the actors on relationships to different factions as determined by Zachary. If we were to remove ego, since ego is obviously connected to all alters, it often helps reveal important properties of an ego's network. Figure 7.11 is a network graph with ego removed. From this graph, we can more clearly see that the ego's network consists of four components, where two of the larger components differ in terms of the homogeneity of alter characteristics. There will be a much more detailed discussion of compositional and structural attributes typically important in ego network studies in the chapter on ego networks.

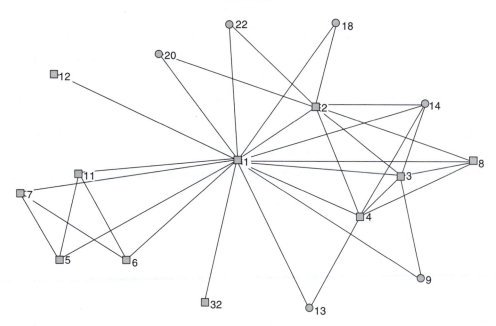

Figure 7.10 Ego network for actor 1 in the Zachary karate club dataset with strength of relationships outside the group as an attribute.

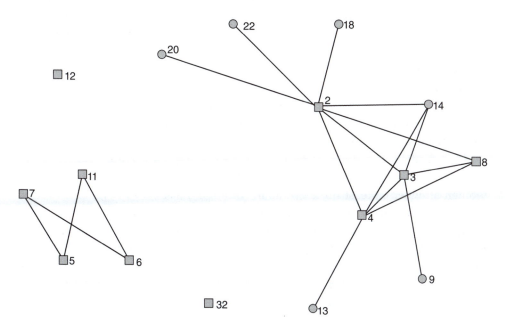

Figure 7.11 Ego network for actor 1 in the Zachary karate club dataset with ego removed.

7.6 Embedding tie characteristics

Like points, lines have a number of visual properties that can be mapped to network information. For example, the thickness of a line can be used to indicate the strength of a tie. Line style (solid, dashed, dot-dashed, etc.) can be used to represent different types of ties, such as solid for positive ties and dashed for negative ties. Line color is also used to indicate type of tie. It can also be used to reinforce node attribute information, as when we use, say, blue lines to indicate ties from women to women, and red lines to indicate ties between women and men. An arrowhead on a line can be used to indicate the direction of a tie, as in who is asking whom for advice. The arrowheads themselves can be differentiated by color, size and shape. Thus, one could use arrowhead size to indicate the amount of trade flowing from one country to another, or the extent to which person A likes person B.

7.6.1 Tie strength

There are several ways to communicate strength of tie. One way is to use the layout itself to represent tie strengths. For example, in the MDS approach discussed above, the distance between two points corresponds, inversely, to the strength of the tie between them. To illustrate this, we use a valued, one-mode dataset derived from the Davis et al. (1941) women-by-events data described in Chapter 2 (see Matrix 2.3). The data were transformed using the Affiliations procedure in UCINET to create a woman-by-woman matrix in which the cells indicate the number of events that each pair of women attended in common. Figure 7.12 shows a metric MDS of these data. A line is shown between two points if the corresponding women attended at least one social event in common.

We can make this diagram easier to read by suppressing lines representing weaker ties. For example, we might show a line between points only if the women attended at least three events in common. As shown in Figure 7.13, this approach makes the two-group structure of the data very evident.

Another approach to displaying strength of tie information is to make the thickness of lines proportional to the tie strength. An example is shown in Figure 7.14, in which the position of the nodes is determined by ordination. This diagram uses both physical distance and line thickness to communicate social proximity. One can see that the thicker lines tend to be within the groups and not between them.

When we want to visualize tie strength in asymmetrical relations, such as in economic exchange relations, making the tie proportional to tie strength will not work since the amount given from person A to person B may not be the same

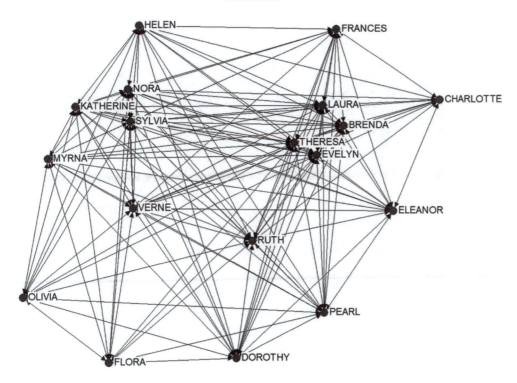

Figure 7.12 Ordination plot. Distance is inversely proportional to strength of tie.

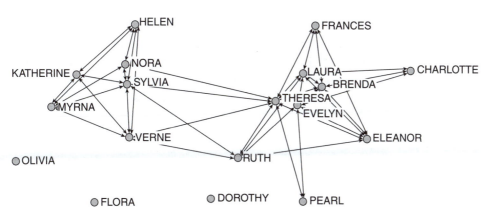

Figure 7.13 Ordination plot with weak ties suppressed.

as the amount given from person B to A. Since these relations are directional we can use the arrowheads to convey the relative amounts of flows back and forth between two nodes. Figure 7.15 is a graph of an exchange network of fish among salmon fishers in Alaska (Johnson and Miller, 1983). The labels have been

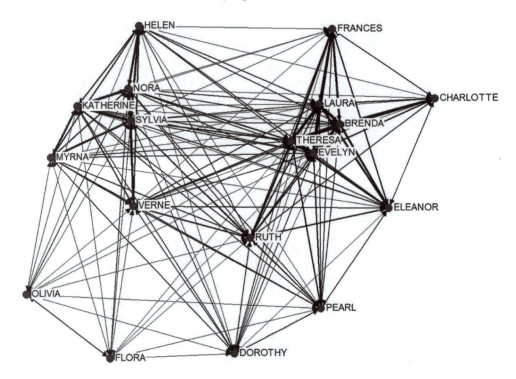

Figure 7.14 Ordination plus thickness. Both physical distance and thickness of line are used to represent strength of ties among women.

removed to make the graph more readable. The size of the arrowheads is proportional to the amount of fish given from one fisher to another. It is obvious that the central fisher in the component on the right has transferred large amounts of fish to four of the six fishers with whom he has exchange ties.

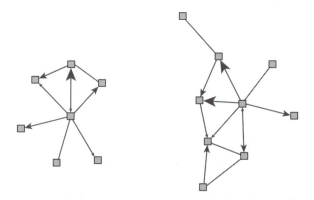

Figure 7.15 Fish exchanges among salmon fishers in Alaska with amounts transferred proportional to the size of the arrowheads.

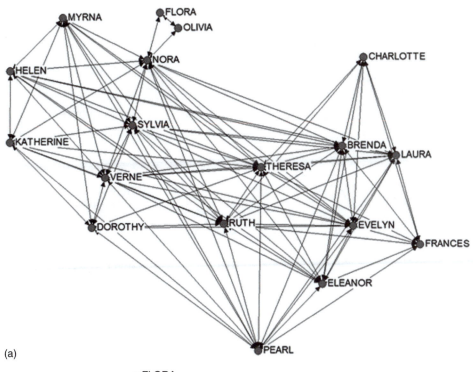

(a)

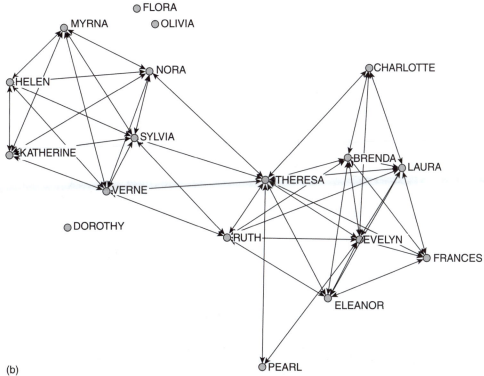

(b)

(Continued)

Figure 7.16 (Continued)

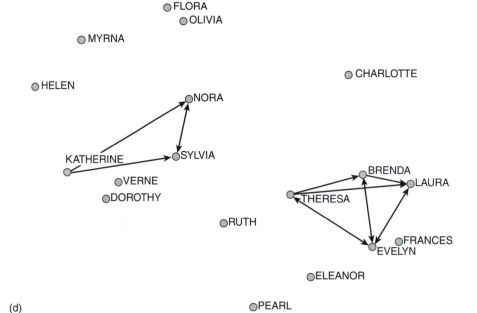

(c)

(d)

Figure 7.16 Graph-theoretic layout portraying increasingly strong ties: (a) Ties of strength 1 or greater; (b) Ties of strength 2 or greater; (c) Ties of strength 3 or greater; (d) Ties of strength 4 or greater.

A different approach is to abandon ordination in favor of graph-theoretic layouts, in combination with dichotomizing the data so that only strong ties are considered. By systematically increasing the cut-off value for dichotomization, one can create a series of diagrams that portray increasingly strong ties (see Figure 7.16).[3] In each successive network the criterion for what constitutes a tie increases by 1. In this case at a value of tie strength of 2 or greater (two more events in common), the structure of the networks becomes clearer. As we move through the successive graphs the core membership of the two factions becomes evident.

7.6.2 Type of tie

In most studies, we measure several different social relations on the same set of nodes. Programs like NetDraw make it easy to switch between relations while maintaining nodes in the same positions. For example, the bank wiring room dataset we first saw in Chapter 2 and visualized in Figure 7.2 was collected by a researcher observing interactions among a set of employees in one room over a period of months, recording a number of social interactions such as playing games during breaks or having conflicts over such things as whether the room's windows should be open or closed. Figure 7.17 shows game-playing ties among

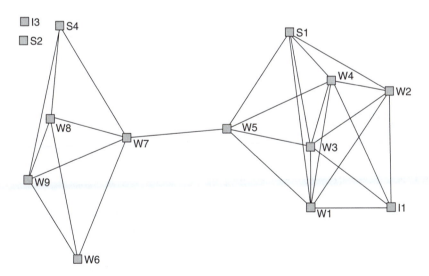

Figure 7.17 Game-playing relation among bank wiring room employees.

---

[3] To reproduce these diagrams using UCINET, open the Affiliations matrix in NetDraw, then use the Ties window to raise the cut-off level by 1 unit. Then press the layout button (a lightning bolt with an equals sign). Repeat several times until no more ties are visible.

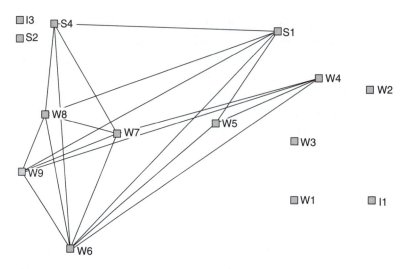

Figure 7.18 Conflict relation among bank wiring room employees.

the men we saw before, while Figure 7.18 shows conflict ties. Since the nodes remain fixed in the same positions and we have drawn the networks next to each other, it is easy to see that game-playing interactions occur within each of the two subgroups, but rarely between, and conflict interactions occur mostly between the two subgroups but also within the left-hand subgroup. Thus, it appears that while two groups exist, the right-hand group is in less conflict and is possibly more cohesive.

7.7 Visualizing network change

If network data are collected at multiple points in time, we can just treat each time point as a different relation and use all the techniques described above. We can also create a kind of meta-display by showing relationships between the time points rather than actors. For example, Burkhardt and Brass (1990) collected advice-giving relations among employees of a government agency at five points in time. We can correlate the adjacency matrices corresponding to each time period. Matrix 7.1 shows the correlation matrix obtained for the Burkhardt and Brass data.

As you might expect, the correlations with time 1 (first row) decrease from left to right, indicating that the social structure is increasingly different with each passing time period. In addition, the largest correlations for any time

	T1	T2	T3	T4	T5
T1	1.000	0.684	0.483	0.440	0.300
T2	0.684	1.000	0.582	0.543	0.335
T3	0.483	0.582	1.000	0.613	0.341
T4	0.440	0.543	0.613	1.000	0.371
T5	0.300	0.335	0.341	0.371	1.000

Matrix 7.1 Intercorrelations among the networks at each time period for the Burkhardt and Brass data.

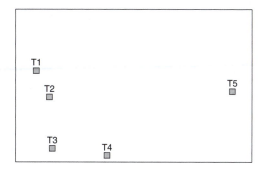

Figure 7.19 Correlations among time periods for the Burkhardt and Brass data, represented via metric MDS.

period are usually with the two periods on either side of it, indicating a kind of orderly change from period to period. However, the change is not linear. A metric MDS of this correlation matrix (Figure 7.19) shows a gap between time 2 and time 3, and another gap between time 4 and time 5, suggesting periods of incremental change punctuated by instances of more radical change.

To see how the network changed from time 1 to time 5, we can simply draw the two networks. Figures 7.20 and 7.21 present the networks at each time point using a graph layout algorithm and showing only strong ties. As we can see, at time 1 the network shows evidence of three groups (left, bottom right and top right). At time 5, the left and bottom right groups are still separate from each other, but the top left group seems to be in the process of being adopted by the other two groups. In addition, we can see individual changes in position. For example, node R53 is a central figure in the bottom right group at time 1, but becomes an isolate by time 5.

Figure 7.20   Friendship ties at time 1 for the Burkhardt and Brass data.

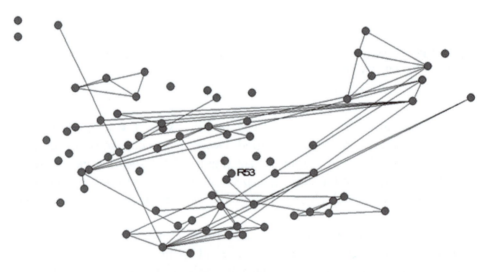

Figure 7.21   Friendship ties at time 5 for the Burkhardt and Brass data.

Another way to visualize change over time is to focus on the change in an actor's position in the network over some period instead of concentrating on changes in the overall structure over time. This can be readily accomplished by stacking the network matrices on top of one another and then subjecting this stacked matrix to correspondence analysis. Figure 7.22 shows how the matrices for two time periods can be stacked on top of one another (this can be very easily done using the 'Time Stack' utility in UCINET under the Transform menu). The data consist of ratings of reported interactions (on a scale from 0 to 10) at the beginning and end for people attending a workshop.

The stacked matrix can be analyzed using correspondence analysis (see Chapter 6) in order to visualize changes in the structural position of each of the actors in the network across multiple time periods. Figure 7.23 shows the changes in position for two time periods for reports of interaction for the workshop group. The figure reveals a tendency for members of the group to move closer to one another over time. The group appears to be becoming more cohesive and in fact density does increase between time 1 (5.90) and time 2 (6.13). Both Richard and Lisa, in particular, make a movement from the group's periphery to its core, followed to a smaller extent by Lynn.

		1	2	3	4	5	6	7	8	9	10	11	12	13	14	15	16	17
1	SUE	0	5	6	6	5	8	8	10	7	5	6	7	9	6	8	9	7
2	MARY	6	0	8	5	10	9	7	7	6	5	9	10	8	8	8	8	6
3	JOHN	8	3	0	8	8	8	5	9	9	5	9	6	9	5	9	6	9
4	BRYN	8	3	8	0	9	10	5	10	10	2	6	8	10	3	9	4	6
5	JEFF	3	9	7	5	0	9	4	4	4	3	8	5	4	2	4	2	3
6	STEVE	10	10	7	10	10	0	8	9	10	5	8	8	10	7	9	8	9
7	CHRISTINE	7	6	3	4	4	3	0	6	6	2	7	2	3	4	7	3	5
8	MARTIN	9	5	5	8	6	8	7	0	8	2	6	6	9	4	8	5	3
9	RICHARD	6	1	6	9	4	9	3	9	0	1	3	5	9	1	7	1	5
10	JEAN	2	1	2	2	2	1	2	2	2	0	2	2	2	1	2	2	1
11	ABBI	5	7	6	9	8	6	9	6	7	4	0	6	6	8	7	7	6
12	LISA	7	8	2	5	5	3	3	4	3	1	3	0	3	3	7	7	7
13	DAVID	9	10	10	10	10	10	8	10	8	1	8	8	0	6	9	5	6
14	LYNN	6	8	3	3	2	2	7	2	2	2	2	4	2	0	9	8	10
15	PETE	7	5	9	4	3	5	6	7	7	2	4	6	6	9	0	6	4
16	DELORES	7	5	7	5	5	6	4	5	6	2	6	8	6	5	8	0	4
17	SASHA	5	3	7	5	4	7	8	5	8	2	6	7	6	9	9	8	0
18	SUE2	0	6	8	8	8	10	8	10	9	5	7	9	10	9	10	9	9
19	MARY2	7	0	7	7	10	9	8	7	6	5	9	10	9	9	9	8	6
20	JOHN2	8	5	0	8	9	9	7	8	8	5	8	7	9	5	9	5	8
21	BRYN2	7	4	8	0	8	10	4	10	10	2	6	8	10	6	8	6	4
22	JEFF2	5	10	10	8	0	10	4	8	7	3	9	6	10	3	6	4	5
23	STEVE2	9	8	8	10	9	0	7	10	9	0	6	8	10	6	7	7	7
24	CHRISTINE2	1	6	1	4	4	3	0	4	4	0	6	2	3	6	2	2	3
25	MARTIN2	10	6	6	9	8	9	8	0	9	2	6	8	10	4	8	6	4
26	RICHARD2	10	4	10	9	7	10	4	10	0	2	7	10	10	5	9	7	9
27	JEAN2	0	0	0	0	0	0	0	0	0	0	0	0	0	0	0	0	0
28	ABBI2	5	7	6	7	7	5	7	5	6	2	0	6	5	6	5	5	5
29	LISA2	8	8	8	5	8	8	5	8	8	1	5	0	7	1	8	5	5
30	DAVID2	7	8	8	9	8	10	6	9	9	1	6	7	0	2	8	5	5
31	LYNN2	3	10	5	4	3	4	8	5	3	2	9	5	3	0	9	10	10
32	PETE2	8	3	8	2	4	4	4	8	2	2	8	5	5		0	6	4
33	DELORES2	6	6	6	6	6	6	4	6	6	4	5	6	6	5	6	0	5
34	SASHA2	7	5	7	6	7	7	6	6	8	0	7	7	6	9	8	9	0

Figure 7.22 Matrices *(n × n)* for two time periods for a workshop group stacked on top of one another to form an *n × 2n* matrix. The ratings of interaction for time 1 are not shaded while the ratings of interaction for time 2 are shaded.

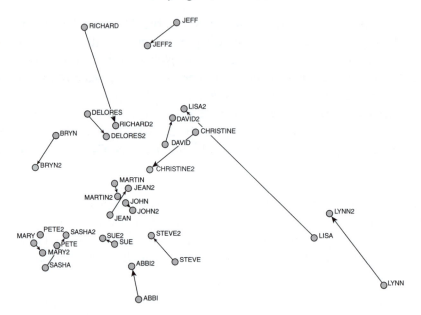

Figure 7.23 A graph of the changes in network position between two time periods using correspondence analysis.

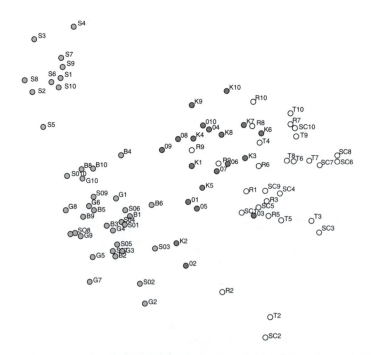

Figure 7.24 Stacked correspondence analysis of the co-occurrence matrices for the 10 years of voting behavior among the Supreme Court justices.

Multiple time points can also be visualized in that multiple matrices representing time periods or interview waves can be stacked and then visualized using correspondence analysis. Figure 7.24 is a graph showing decision co-occurrences for Supreme Court justices by year over a 10-year period. The graph shows the spatial location of each of the justices in each of the years. Figure 7.25 shows the spatial movement for Rehnquist over the course of the 10 years. What this graph clearly reveals is that Rehnquist himself has often entered what one might think of as swing vote spatial territory in the course of his decision behavior. In Figure 7.26 decision blocks (i.e., conservative, swing, liberal), as identified by media sources, are encompassed by convex hulls. Here the extreme edges of each of the blocks can be easily determined. For example, Scalia (SC1–10) over the 10-year period consistently defines the extremes of the conservatives, while Stevens (S1–10) consistently defines the extremes of the liberals. Although Kennedy (K1–10) and O'Connor (O1–10) were considered swing justices, there is a definite bias toward the conservative side of the graph, revealing that although they may be involved in swing decisions more frequently than other justices, they still tended to lean in a more conservative direction across the 10 years of decisions.

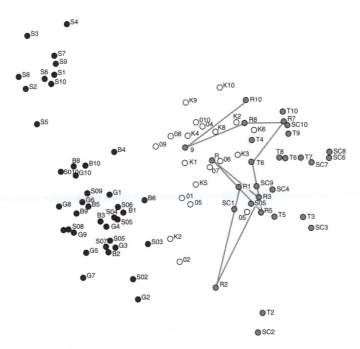

Figure 7.25 Stacked correspondence analysis of the co-occurrence matrices for the 10 years of voting behavior among the Supreme Court justices with Rehnquist's spatial movements connected over time.

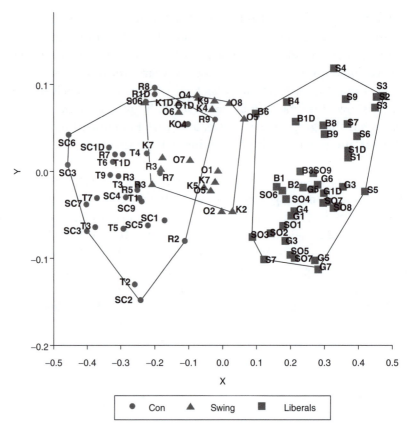

Figure 7.26 Stacked correspondence analysis of all time periods with conservative, swing and liberal justices identified as determined from media sources with members encompassed by convex hulls.

7.8 Exporting visualizations

Most network visualization programs have the ability to copy visualizations to the Clipboard, which can then be pasted into other applications. In NetDraw, pressing Ctrl-C will do it. In addition, all network visualization programs provide a means of saving the finished visualization as a graphics file. In NetDraw, one can save diagrams in a variety of formats including jpeg (.jpg), bitmap (.bmp) and metafile (.emf). Jpegs are a common choice because they are fairly good quality and are highly compressed, using up very little disk space. They are the format most commonly used in digital cameras, and can be opened in virtually all graphics programs. However, because of the lossy compression scheme they use, jpeg files do not have perfect fidelity, and do not resize well. The metafile format is a vector graphics format (like SVG) which stores instructions for creating a picture rather than a picture itself. As a result, it can be redrawn at any resolution/size. Not all graphics programs can read metafiles, but all Microsoft Office applications can.

In addition to saving a graphics file, NetDraw allows the user to save the data to a text file using a format called 'VNA' (short for 'Visual Network Analysis'). The VNA format allows you to save both network and attribute information together, and also visual information such as the color and size of nodes and lines. This is handy because it means the next time you start up NetDraw, you can open a previously saved VNA file and have everything look exactly as you left it in your last session. This can save a lot of time.

7.9 Closing comments

One of the most important constraints on the valid graphical representation of social networks concerns human limitations of perception. There has been a great deal of work on this topic, and an in-depth discussion was beyond the scope of this chapter. For a good review of issues concerning human color perception and the communication of network graphical information see Krempel (2002), or for a more general review see Munzner (2000). For further reading on the history of network visualization a good source is Freeman (2000). In this chapter we discussed a number of ways in which network structural and compositional information can be communicated in network graphs through the visual manipulation of the various properties of nodes and edges and their spatial relations. In addition, we examined various means for reducing the complexity of network structures through methods for reducing the graphical complexity of networks using such mechanisms as turning on and off nodes, ties, clusters, subgroups or components in order to reveal potentially hidden structural properties. More on this can be found in Chapter 14, which discusses strategies for dealing with large networks.

7.10 Summary

The ability to visualize a social network is one of the attractive features of social network analysis. When done correctly, visualization allows the researcher to obtain a simple qualitative understanding of the network structure. The use of good layouts to emphasize properties of the network is key, and graph layout algorithms are highly effective and widely used. In addition, the use of shape, size and color to capture nodal attribute properties can further enhance the effectiveness of any visualization. In a similar way, color, thickness and line style can be used to emphasize properties of edges. We do not always want to view the whole network (particularly if it is large or complex), so we often filter nodes or edges to reveal portions of the network which are of particular interest. Changes over time provide additional challenges, but these can be addressed by using techniques such as stacked correspondence analysis.

7.11 Problems and Exercises

1. We have already looked at ordination methods such as MDS in the preceding chapter. But there are other ways to orient the nodes in a graph. The chapter discusses the use of graph layout algorithms, as well as ordination methods, to orient the nodes of the network in a two- or three-dimensional space. For the scientific collaboration proximity matrix in the last chapter, use the spring embedder for placing the nodes in space. In NetDraw go to File|Open|UCINET Dataset|Network and open "Science_Collaboration.##h" (the default orientation of the nodes is a spring embedder). How does this spatial representation of the network compare to that produced by the MDS?

2. We often want to convey information on the graphs that reflect the attributes of the nodes and the edges such as gender, age, strength of ties, etc. To convey such information, we can vary nodal size and shape and for valued networks the size of the edges.

   a. Using the "Science_Collaboration.##h" data, visualize the network using the procedure as outlined in Problem 1 above. After visualizing the network in NetDraw we need to bring in a data file containing attributes of the nodes. To bring in the attribute file you go to File|Open|UCINET Dataset|Attribute data and load "Science_Attributes_All.##h". The data file contains three nodal attributes: Affiliation (academic discipline), Gender, and Sum (a measure of centrality for valued data discussed more in Chapter 10). Although you can't see the attribute data, they are in the background and ready for use. First we want to color the nodes by the academic discipline of the researchers. Go to Properties|Nodes|Symbols| Colors|Attribute-based. Click on the Select Attribute pull down menu and select Affiliation and click on the green check mark. The nodes are now colored by academic discipline. Do researchers collaborate mostly with researchers of the same discipline?

   b. The shape of the nodes can be varied to reflect a qualitative attribute of the node such as gender. Go to Properties|Nodes|Symbols|Shape|Attribute-based. Click on the Select Attribute pull down menu and select Gender and click on the green check mark. There are five women researchers in the network. Do women researchers tend to collaborate with one another?

   c. The science collaboration network is a proximity matrix. The edge value between two nodes reflects the number of research grants they have in common. Therefore we can visualize the strength of these collaborations between pairs of actors by making the size of the edges proportional to tie strength. Go to Properties|Lines|Size|Tie Strength. Click on the Select relation pull down menu and select Science_Collaboration and click on Apply. How might you characterize the distribution of strong collaborations in this network?

3. Often data are collected on more than one type of relation and it would be important to visualize two or more kinds of ties at the same time. Using the Padgett dataset (PADGETT.##h) in NetDraw, open the data file. In the "Rels" tab to the upper right, check both PADGM (marriage ties) and PADGB (business ties). Now go to Properties|Lines|Color|Relation and make the multiplex ties black, the marriage ties green, and the business ties blue. By multiplex, we mean that both kinds of ties are present at the same time. Now show only the multiplex relationships. To do this, in the Rels tab check PADGM and uncheck PADGB. Now click the AND radio button. Now check PADGB. You should see lines only for pairs of nodes tied by both kind of ties – just the black ones. Next save this as a new relation by clicking "Save as New Relation" at the bottom right. Call it "MPX". Then use the Dn button (bottom right) to show (a) nodes tied by marriage (and possibly business), (b) nodes tied by business (and possible marriage), and (c) nodes tied by both business and marriage. What would you conclude about the multiplexity of relations across the different types of relations?

8

Testing Hypotheses

Learning Outcomes

1. Comprehend the reasons for using, and principles of, permutation tests
2. Formulate testable hypotheses at the dyadic, monadic and whole-network level
3. Understand when SIENA and exponential random graph models may be appropriate

8.1 Introduction

Padgett and Ansell (1993) collected data on the relations between Florentine families during the Renaissance. One social relation they recorded was marriage ties between families. Another one was business ties among the same set of families. An obvious hypothesis for an economic sociologist might be that economic transactions are embedded in social relations, so that those families doing business with each other will also tend to have marriage ties with one another. One might even speculate that families of this time strategically intermarried in order to facilitate future business ties (not to mention political coordination).

How would we test this? Essentially, we have two adjacency matrices, one for marriage ties and one for business ties, and we would like to correlate them. We cannot do this in a standard statistical package for two reasons. First, programs like SPSS and Stata are set up to correlate vectors, not matrices. This is not too serious a problem, however, since we could just reshape the matrices so that all the values in each matrix were lined up in a single column with $N \times N$ values.[1] We could then

---

[1] Of course, we might ignore the diagonal values, yielding vectors of length N(N − 1), and for undirected data we might ignore the redundant top half of each adjacency matrix, yielding N(N − 1)/2 values per variable.

correlate the columns corresponding to each matrix. Second – and this is a serious problem – the significance tests used in standard statistical packages make a number of assumptions about the data which are violated by network data. For example, standard inferential tests assume that the observations are statistically independent, which, in the case of adjacency matrices, they are not. To see this, consider that all the values along one row of an adjacency matrix pertain to a single node. If that node has a special quality, such as being very anti-social, it will affect all their relations with others, introducing a lack of independence among all those cells in the row. Another typical assumption of classical tests is that the variables are drawn from a population with a particular distribution, such as a normal distribution. Often in network data, the distribution of the population variables is not normal or is simply unknown. Moreover, the data are probably not a random sample, and may not be a sample at all, but rather a population (e.g., you are studying the pattern of collaboration among all film studios in the world).

So we need special methods. One approach is to develop statistical models specifically designed for studying the distribution of ties in a network. This is the approach taken by those working on exponential random graph models (ERGMs) and stochastic actor-oriented longitudinal models (SAOMs), as exemplified by the rSIENA software package. A key feature of this approach is that the sources of non-independence in the data are explicitly modelled and accounted for. The downside of this is that the user must know which dependencies to include in the model. The upside, however, is that the model will quantify the relative importance of these different dependencies, which may be of primary theoretical interest. These models are complex subjects in their own right and a detailed discussion is beyond the scope of this book. However, we will provide a highly simplified introduction to give a flavor of what is involved.

An alternative approach is to use the generic methodology of randomization tests (also called permutation tests) to modify standard methods like regression. These methods are easy to use and interpret, and can be customized for different research questions. A key feature of this approach is that it effortlessly controls for *all* sources of dependencies. The downside of this is that there is no way to discover which kinds of dependencies were actually present and to what extent. The upside is that we don't need to specify in advance what kinds of dependencies might be present. UCINET provides a number of techniques of this type, and we begin our discussion with them.

8.2 Permutation tests

Classical significance tests are based on sampling theory and have the following logic. You measure a set of variables (say, two variables) on a sample of cases drawn via a probability sample from a population. You are interested in the relationship between the variables (in the population), as measured, say, by a correlation coefficient. So you correlate the variables using your sample data, and get a value like 0.384. The classical significance test then tells you the probability of obtaining a correlation that large given that in the population the variables are actually independent (correlation zero). When this probability is really low (less than 0.05), we call it significant and are willing to claim that the variables are actually related in the population, and not just an accident of sampling. When the probability is higher, we feel we cannot reject the null hypothesis that the variables are independent in the population and just happen to be correlated in the sample. Note that if you have a biased sample, or you do not have a sample at all, it does not make sense to use the classical test.

The logic of randomization tests is different and does not involve samples, at least not in the ordinary sense. Suppose you believe that tall kids are favored by your particular math teacher and as a result they learn more math than short kids. So you think height and math scores in this teacher's class will be correlated. You have the teacher give all the kids a math test, measure their height, and then correlate the two variables. You get a correlation of 0.384. Hypothesis confirmed? In the world of classical statistics we would say yes, because you have a population, and the correlation is not zero, which is what you wanted to know. But let us think about this a little more. Just for fun, instead of actually giving the math test, suppose you write down a set of math scores on slips of paper, and then have each kid select his or her math score by drawing blindly from a hat. Now, you know that in this experiment a kid's math score and height are totally independent because it was completely arbitrary who got what score. And yet, could it not happen, by chance alone, that all the high scores went to the tall people? It might be unlikely, but it could happen. In fact, there are lots of ways (permutations) that scores could be matched to kids, by chance alone, such that the correlation between height and score was positive (and just as many such that the correlation was negative). The question is, what proportion of all the ways the scores could have come out would result in a correlation as large as the one we actually observed (the 0.384)? In short, what are the chances of observing such a large correlation even when the values of the variables are assigned independently of each other? If the proportion is high, say, 20%, we probably do not want to conclude that the teacher is biased toward tall kids. Thus, even in a population, we still want a statistical test in order to guard against spurious correlations. The general logic is that one wants to compare the observed correlation against the distribution of correlations that one could obtain if the two variables were in fact independent of each other.

The permutation test essentially calculates all the ways that the experiment could have come out given that scores were actually independent of height, and counts the proportion of all assignments yielding a correlation as large as the one actually observed. This is the 'p-value' or significance of the test. In practice, however, there is a problem. The number of permutations of N objects grows very quickly with N. Indeed, the number of permutations of just 20 scores is greater than the number of seconds the universe has been in existence. So we cannot enumerate all possible permutations. Instead, we sample uniformly from the space of all permutations. Typically, we use very large samples, such as 20,000 permutations.

In the following sections we consider how randomization tests can be used to test a variety of network hypotheses. Before we start, however, it is important to remember that we may be interested in testing hypotheses at various levels of analysis. For example, one kind of hypothesis is the node-level or monadic hypothesis, such as the hypothesis that more central people tend to be happier. This kind of hypothesis closely resembles the hypotheses one encounters in non-network data analysis. The cases are single nodes (e.g., persons), and basically you have one characteristic of each node (e.g., centrality) and another characteristic of each node (e.g., test score), and you want to correlate them. That is just a matter of correlating two vectors – two columns of data – which seems simple enough, but as we will explain, there are a few subtleties involved.

Another kind of hypothesis is the dyadic one that we opened the chapter with. Here, you are hypothesizing that if a pair of persons (or, in the example, families) has a certain kind of relationship, it is more likely they will also have another kind of relationship. For instance, you might expect that the shorter the distance between people's offices in a building, the more they communicate over time (Allen, 1977). So the cases are pairs of persons (hence the label 'dyadic'), with the two variables normally organized as a pair of $N \times N$ matrices, and you want to correlate the two matrices. Clearly, this is not something you would ordinarily do in a traditional statistics package.

We may also want to test a hypothesis in which one variable is dyadic, such as friendship, and the other is monadic, such as gender. The research question being asked might be something like 'does the gender of each person affect who is friends with whom?'. In this question, the monadic variable is on the independent side and the dyadic variable is on the dependent side. Another research question might be 'are people's attitudes affected by who they interact with?'. Here it is the independent variable that is dyadic and it is the dependent variable that is monadic. As we shall see, we typically test these kinds of hypotheses by rephrasing them as purely dyadic hypotheses.

Finally, another kind of hypothesis is a group- or network-level hypothesis. For instance, suppose you have asked 100 different teams to solve a problem and you have measured how long it takes them to solve it. Time-to-solution is the dependent variable. The independent variable is a measure of some aspect of the social structure of each team, such as the density of trust ties among team members. The data file looks just like the data file for node-level hypotheses, except the cases here are entire networks rather than individual nodes.

We now consider how to test each of the four kinds of hypotheses, starting with the one involving the most numerous and least aggregate cases (dyadic) and ending with the one involving the least numerous and most aggregate cases (whole networks).

8.3 Dyadic hypotheses

Network analysis packages such as UCINET provide a technique called QAP correlation that is designed to correlate whole matrices. The QAP technique correlates the two matrices by effectively reshaping them into two long columns as described above and calculating an ordinary measure of statistical association such as Pearson's r. We call this the 'observed' correlation. To calculate the significance of the observed correlation, the method compares the observed correlation to a reference set of thousands of correlations between thousands of pairs of matrices that are just like the data matrices, but are known to be independent of each other. To construct a p-value, it simply counts the proportion of these correlations among independent matrices that were as large as the observed correlation. As elsewhere, we typically consider a p-value of less than 5% to be significant (i.e., supporting the hypothesis that the two matrices are related).

To generate pairs of matrices that are just like our data matrices and yet known to be independent of each other, we use a simple trick. We take one of the data matrices and randomly rearrange its rows (and matching columns). Because this is done randomly, we know that the resulting matrix is independent of the data matrix it came from. And because the new matrix is just a rearrangement of the old, it has all the same properties of the original: the same mean, the same standard deviation, the same number of 2s, the same number of cliques, etc. In addition, because we are rearranging whole rows and columns rather than individual cells, more subtle properties of the matrices are also preserved. For example, suppose one of the matrices records the physical distance between people's homes. A property of physical distance is that if the distance from i to j is 7, and the distance from j to k is 10, then the distance from i to k is constrained to lie between 3 and 17. That means that in the matrix, the (i, j), (j, k) and (i, k) cells are not independent of each other. Given the values of any two of them, the value of the third cell cannot be just anything. When we permute the rows and columns of such a matrix, these kinds of dependencies (or autocorrelation) are preserved, so when we compare

```
QAP CORRELATION
--------------------------------------------------------------------------------

Data Matrices:                          padgm
                                        padgb
# of Permutations:                      50000
Random seed:                            24322
Method:                                 Detailed (missing values ok)


QAP results for padgb * padgm (50000 permutations)

                            1         2         3         4         5         6         7         8
                       Obs Value Significa  Average   Std Dev   Minimum   Maximum Prop >= 0 Prop <= 0
                       --------- --------- --------- --------- --------- --------- --------- ---------
     1    Pearson Correlation   0.3719    0.0007    0.0002    0.0924   -0.1690    0.5071    0.0007    0.9999
     2     Euclidean Distance   4.3589    0.0007    5.4709    0.2529    3.8730    5.9161    0.9999    0.0007
     3      Hamming Distance    0.1583    0.0007    0.2500    0.0228    0.1250    0.2917    0.9999    0.0007
     4            Match Coef    0.8417    0.0007    0.7500    0.0228    0.7083    0.8750    0.0007    0.9999
     5          Jaccard Coef    0.2963    0.0007    0.0790    0.0464    0.0000    0.4000    0.0007    0.9999
     6 Goodman-Kruskal Gamma    0.7971    0.0007   -0.0690    0.3845   -1.0000    0.9000    0.0007    0.9999
     7          Hubert Gamma    8.0000    0.0007    2.5025    1.3668    0.0000   13.0000    0.0007    0.9999


NOTE: When you have missing data, the significance of Hubert's Gamma and Euclidean Distance will differ from
that of Pearson Correlation. Otherwise, they should be the same (unless the correlation is negative).


QAP Correlations

              1     2
           padgm padgb
           ----- -----
  1 padgm  1.000 0.372
  2 padgb  0.372 1.000


QAP P-Values

              1     2
           padgm padgb
           ----- -----
  1 padgm  0.000 0.001
  2 padgb  0.001 0.000

QAP statistics saved as datafile QAP Correlation Results
```

Figure 8.1 Results of QAP correlation.

the observed correlation against our distribution of correlations we can be sure we are comparing apples with apples.

To illustrate QAP correlation, we run it on the Padgett and Ansell data described in the introduction. As shown in Figure 8.1, the correlation between the network of marriage ties and the network of business ties is 0.372, and it is highly significant ($p = 0.0007$). The results support the hypothesis that the two kinds of ties are related.

One thing to note in the output is that 50,000 permutations were used in this run. It is important to run a large number like this in order to stabilize the p-value. Since the permutations are random, if we only used a handful of them, each time we ran the program we would get a slightly different p-value (but the correlation would always be the same). The larger the sample of permutations, the less the variability in p-values.

8.3.1 QAP regression

The relationship between QAP regression (also known as MR-QAP) and QAP correlation is the same as between their analogues in ordinary statistics. QAP regression allows you to model the values of a dyadic dependent variable (such as business ties) using multiple independent variables (such as marriage ties and some other dyadic variable, such as friendship ties or physical proximity of homes).

For example, suppose we are interested in advice-seeking within organizations. We can imagine that a person does not seek advice randomly from others. One factor that may influence who one seeks advice from is the existence of prior friendly relations – one is less likely to ask advice from those one does not know or does not like. Another factor might be structural position – whether they are in a position to know the answer. For example, we might predict that employees will often seek advice from those to whom they report. Krackhardt (1987) collected advice, friendship and reporting relationships among a set of managers in a high-tech organization, and these data are available in UCINET, allowing us to test our hypotheses.

To do this, we run one of the QAP multiple regression routines in UCINET. The result is shown in Figure 8.2. The R-square value of 6.3% suggests that neither who one reports to nor friendship is a major factor in determining who a person decides to seek advice from. In other words, there are other more important variables that we have not measured, perhaps including the amount of expertise that the other person has relative to the person looking for advice. Still, the 'reports to' relation is significant ($p < 0.001$), so it seems that it is at least a piece of the puzzle. Friendship is interestingly not significant: this is not quite in line with Casciaro and Lobo's (2005) finding that people prefer to seek advice from people they like even when there are more qualified – but less nice – people available.

It should be noted that, in our example, the dependent variable is binary. Using ordinary regression to regress a binary variable is known as the linear probability model and is unusual today, especially if we were not using permutation methods to calculate significance. Since we are, though, the p-values on each coefficient are valid and interpretable. But it is important to keep in mind that the regression coefficients mean the same thing they do in ordinary least squares regression: they have not been magically transformed into, say, odds, such that you could say that an increase in one unit of the X variable is associated with a

```
MULTIPLE REGRESSION QAP VIA DOUBLE DEKKER SEMI-PARTIALLING
----------------------------------------------------------------------------

# of permutations:          10000
Diagonal valid?:            NO
Random seed:                824
Dependent variable:         ADVICE
Partition variable (if any):
Predicted values:           ADVICE-mrpred (C:\Users\Martin\Documents\datafiles\ADVICE-mrpred
Residual values:            ADVICE-mrResid (C:\Users\Martin\Documents\datafiles\ADVICE-mrResid
Model fit stats:            ADVICE-mrfit (C:\Users\Martin\Documents\datafiles\ADVICE-mrfit
Model coefficients:         ADVICE-mrcoef (C:\Users\Martin\Documents\datafiles\ADVICE-mrcoef
Independent variables:      REPORTS_TO
                            FRIENDSHIP


MODEL FIT


            R-Square    Adj R-Sqr         Obs         Perms
         ------------ ------------ ------------ ------------
  Model     0.06319      0.05870    420.00000  10000.00000



REGRESSION COEFFICIENTS


             Un-Stdized Stdized Coef  P-value  As Large  As Small As Extreme Perm Avg  Std Err
             ---------- ------------ --------- --------- --------- ---------- -------- --------
  REPORTS_TO    0.47157     0.20177   0.00010   0.00010   1.00000    0.00010  0.00179  0.12429
  FRIENDSHIP    0.13582     0.11701   0.05239   0.05239   0.94771    0.10909 -0.00152  0.08450
  Intercept     0.39694     0.00000   0.00000   0.00000   0.00000    0.00000  0.00000  0.00000
```

Figure 8.2 Results of MR-QAP regression.

certain increase in the odds of that case being a 1 on the dependent variable. To have this interpretation, we would need to have run a logistic regression QAP (LR-QAP).[2] This can also be done in UCINET, although it is more time-consuming than MR-QAP.

---

[2] As an aside, we can interpret the coefficients from MR-QAP on binary data as follows. In our output, the 0.472 value for the 'reports to' coefficient means that when the X variable is one unit higher, the dependent variable will, on average, be 0.472 units higher. This does not mean each case is 0.472 units higher, but that in any batch of 1000 dyads where i reports to j, we expect to see about 472 more cases of advice-seeking than when i does not report to j. This is not too difficult to understand. The trouble comes when we consider dyads in which i does not report to j (X = 0) but does seek advice from j (Y = 1), and compare these with dyads in which i does report to j (X is a unit higher). Y is already at its maximum value, so for this batch of dyads, the expectation that Y will be an additional 0.472 units higher does not make sense.

As another example of how QAP regression can be used, we examine the Newcomb (1961) fraternity data in UCINET. This dataset consists of 15 matrices recording weekly sociometric preference rankings among 17 men attending the University of Michigan in the fall of 1956. The men were recruited to live in off-campus (fraternity) housing, rented for them as part of the Michigan Group Study Project supervised by Theodore Newcomb from 1953 to 1956. All were incoming transfer students with no prior acquaintance. We shall examine the first two time periods to study reciprocity and transitivity. We are interested to know if new friendship ties formed in Week 1 are a result of reciprocity and/or transitivity of ties formed in Week 0. One way to do this is to construct the dependent variable as the cell-by-cell difference between the matrix for Week 1 (called NEWC1) and Week 0 (called NEWC0). Alternatively, we can simply predict NEWC1 and include NEWC0 as a control variable. In order to illustrate the LR-QAP procedure, we choose the second approach and also dichotomize the matrices so that the (i, j) entry for each matrix equals 1 if person i ranked person j among their top three choices and 0 otherwise. We refer to the dichotomized matrices as NEWC0D and NEWC1D.

We now form two further matrices from NEWC0D. The first is simply the transpose of NEWC0D which, for ease of interpretation later, we shall call NEWC0D-Reciprocity. A value of 1 for cell (i, j) of the transpose of NEWC0D indicates that in Week 0, i received a nomination from person j. To the extent that people tend to reciprocate incoming ties, we should see that a 1 in NEWC0D-Reciprocity is matched by a 1 in the corresponding cell of NEWC1D.

Our second matrix will be the friends of friends matrix that has a 1 in the (i, j) entry if actor j is 2 steps or less away from actor i by the shortest path. We name this matrix NEWC0D-Transitivity. To the extent that one tends to become friends with one's friends' friends, we should see that a 1 in the (i, j) cell of NEWC0D-Transitivity should be matched to a 1 in the (i, j) cell of NEWC1D. The transitivity matrix also has direct ties, but these are accounted for by including NEWC0D in the regression.

We then run a QAP-based logistic regression using NEWC1D as the dependent variable, and NEWC0D, NEWC0D-Reciprocity, and NEWC0D-Transitivity as the independent variables. The results are shown in Figure 8.3. We can see from the p-values in the output (in the column labeled 'Sig') that NEWC0D is significant, which is what we would expect since it would be surprising if the social structure at time T was wholly unrelated to the social structure a week earlier. The reciprocity parameter is positive and significant ($p = 0.008$), indicating a greater-than-chance tendency to reciprocate ties, but the transitivity parameter

```
Dependent variable:                     newc1d

Overall fit of the logistic regression model

                      1          2          3          4          5
                     LL       R-Sqr        Sig        Obs      Perms
                  ---------- ---------- ---------- ---------- ----------
  1 Statistics:   -100.906      0.259      0.001        272       1000



LR Coefficients & Permutation Results (T-stats used in permutations)

                               1        2        3        4        5        6        7        8
                            Coef  OddsRat        T      Sig      Avg      Min      Max       SD
                            -------- -------- ------ -------- -------- -------- ------- ------
  1              Intercept   -2.614    0.073  -8.807
  2                 newc0d    2.290    9.880   5.921    0.001   -0.014   -1.998    2.290    0.439
  3     newc0d-Reciprocity    0.818    2.267   1.975    0.013   -0.001   -1.714    1.135    0.373
  4 newc0d-Transitivity (Closure)  0.598    1.818   1.634    0.089   -0.008   -1.358    1.086    0.382
```

Figure 8.3   Logistic regression results.

is not significant ($p = 0.071$), indicating no particular tendency to become friends with friends of friends.

8.4 Mixed dyadic–monadic hypotheses

In this section we consider ways of relating node attributes to relational data. For example, when we look at the diagram in Figure 8.4, in which gender is indicated by the shape of the node, it is hard to avoid the conclusion that the pattern of ties is related to gender. Specifically, there are more ties between members of the same gender than you would expect by chance. It would appear that actors have a tendency to interact with people of the same gender as themselves, a phenomenon known as 'homophily'. Homophily is an instance of a larger class of frequently hypothesized social processes known as 'selection', in which actors choose other actors based on attributes of those actors.

Another common type of hypothesis that links dyadic data with monadic attributes is the diffusion or influence hypothesis. Diffusion is the idea that people's beliefs, attitudes and practices come about in part because of interaction with others who already have those beliefs. So the fact that I own an iPhone may be in part due to the fact that my friend has one. I am more likely to have conservative political beliefs if everyone around me has conservative beliefs.

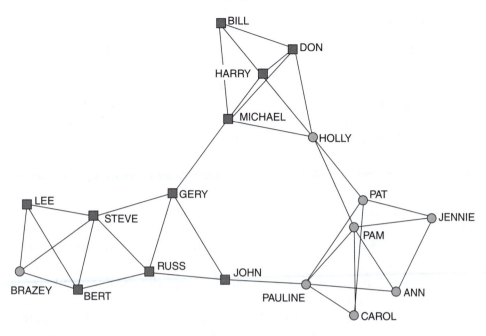

Figure 8.4 Campnet dataset showing top three choices among a set of men and women.

Both diffusion and selection hypotheses relate a dyadic variable (the network) with a monadic variable (the node attribute). The difference between diffusion/ influence and selection hypotheses is just the direction of causality. In diffusion, the dyadic variable causes the monadic variable, and in the selection the monadic variable causes the dyadic variable. We should note that, if the data are cross-sectional rather than longitudinal, we will not normally be able to distinguish empirically between influence and selection, although in the case of Figure 8.4 we tend to be confident that it is a case of people selecting friends based on gender rather than gender diffusion.

The standard approach to testing the association between a node attribute and a dyadic relation is to convert the problem into a purely dyadic hypothesis by constructing a dyadic variable from the node attribute. This is an age-old approach that was first dealt with statistically by geographers dealing with spatial (aka network) autocorrelation. Measures like Moran's I and Geary's C are used to test whether the distribution of a node attribute is independent of spatial proximity or adjacency (Cliff and Ord, 1973). Different techniques are needed depending on whether the attribute is categorical, such as gender or department, or continuous, such as age or wealth.

8.4.1 Continuous attributes

In traditional bureaucracies, we expect employees to have predictable career trajectories in which they move to higher and higher levels over time. As such, we expect managers to be older than the people who report to them. In modern high-tech organizations, however, we might expect more fluid career trajectories based more on competence than age. Hence, in this kind of organization we do not necessarily expect employees to be younger than their bosses.

One way to test this idea in the organization studied by Krackhardt (1987) would be to construct a node-by-node matrix of differences in age, and then use QAP correlation to correlate this matrix with the 'reports to' matrix. As discussed in Chapter 5, in UCINET we can construct a node-by-node matrix of differences in age using the Data|Attribute-to-Matrix procedure. This creates a matrix in which the (i, j) cell gives the age of node j subtracted from the age of node i – that is, it is the row node's value minus the column node's value. Matrix 8.1 shows the node-level age variable, along with the dyadic difference in age matrix computed by UCINET.

The 'reports to' matrix is arranged such that a 1 in the (i, j) cell indicates that the row person reports to the column person. Hence, if the organization were a traditional bureaucracy, we would expect a negative correlation between this matrix and the age-difference matrix, since the row person should be younger than the column person. But since the organization is a modern high-tech company, we are in fact actually expecting no correlation. The result is shown in

Age		1	2	3	4	5	6	7	8	9	10	11	12	13	14	15	16	17	18	19	20	21
33	1	0	-9	-7	0	1	-26	-22	-1	-29	-4	-13	-1	-15	-10	-7	6	3	0	1	-5	-3
42	2	9	0	2	9	10	-17	-13	8	-20	5	-4	8	-6	-1	2	15	12	9	10	4	6
40	3	7	-2	0	7	8	-19	-15	6	-22	3	-6	6	-8	-3	0	13	10	7	8	2	4
33	4	0	-9	-7	0	1	-26	-22	-1	-29	-4	-13	1	-15	-10	-7	6	3	0	1	-5	-3
32	5	-1	-10	-8	-1	0	-27	-23	-2	-30	-5	-14	-2	-16	-11	-8	5	2	-1	0	-6	-4
59	6	26	17	19	26	27	0	4	25	-3	22	13	25	11	16	19	32	29	26	27	21	23
55	7	22	13	15	22	23	-4	0	21	-7	18	9	21	7	12	15	28	25	22	23	17	19
34	8	1	-8	-6	1	2	-25	-21	0	-28	-3	-12	0	-14	-9	-6	7	4	1	2	-4	-2
62	9	29	20	22	29	30	3	7	28	0	25	16	28	14	19	22	35	32	29	30	24	26
37	10	4	-5	-3	4	5	-22	-18	3	-25	0	-9	3	-11	-6	-3	10	7	4	5	-1	1
46	11	13	4	6	13	14	-13	-9	12	-16	9	0	12	-2	3	6	19	16	13	14	8	10
34	12	1	-8	-6	1	2	-25	-21	0	-28	-3	-12	0	-14	-9	-6	7	4	1	2	-4	-2
48	13	15	6	8	15	16	-11	-7	14	-14	11	2	14	0	5	8	21	18	15	16	10	12
43	14	10	1	3	10	11	-16	-12	9	-19	6	-3	9	-5	0	3	16	13	10	11	5	7
40	15	7	-2	0	7	8	-19	-15	6	-22	3	-6	6	-8	-3	0	13	10	7	8	2	4
27	16	-6	-15	-13	-6	-5	-32	-28	-7	-35	-10	-19	-7	-21	-16	-13	0	-3	-6	-5	-11	-9
30	17	-3	-12	-10	-3	-2	-29	-25	-4	-32	-7	-16	-4	-18	-13	-10	3	0	-3	-2	-8	-6
33	18	0	-9	-7	0	1	-26	-22	-1	-29	-4	-13	-1	-15	-10	-7	6	3	0	1	-5	-3
32	19	-1	-10	-8	-1	0	-27	-23	-2	-30	-5	-14	-2	-16	-11	-8	5	2	-1	0	-6	-4
38	20	5	-4	-2	5	6	-21	-17	4	-24	1	-8	4	-10	-5	-2	11	8	5	6	0	2
36	21	3	-6	-4	3	4	-23	-19	2	-26	-1	-10	2	-12	-7	-4	9	6	3	4	-2	0

Matrix 8.1 Age of each node (left) and differences in ages between all pairs of nodes (right).

Figure 8.5. The correlation is negative, but it is not significant ($r = -0.0645$), just as we expected.

However, there are a couple of problems with our analysis. First of all, it is always difficult to test a hypothesis of no relationship, because if you do observe no relationship it could be simply because your statistical test lacks power (e.g., your sample size is too small). Second, our test implicitly assumes that every person could potentially report to anyone older than themselves. But our common-sense knowledge of the 'reports to' relation tells us that each person only reports to one manager. This creates a lot of cases where A is younger than B, but A fails to report to them. A better test would examine just pairs of nodes in which one reports to the other, and then test whether age difference is correlated with who reports to whom. We can do this by placing missing values for all cells in which neither party reports to the other. When we do this and rerun the analysis, we get a stronger correlation of -0.320, but it is still not significant: the p-value is 0.147. In this company, who you report to is simply not a function of relative age.

Another way to relate attributes to relations is in terms of sender and receiver effects. Suppose we are trying to predict who goes to whom for advice. An obvious hypothesis, given that we have just been working with age difference as a variable, is that people seek advice from those who are older than themselves. However, just to change things up a bit, let us formulate a slightly different hypothesis: the older people are, the more likely others are to seek advice from them, regardless of the age of the seeker. This is known as a receiver effect, which means there is a quality about certain nodes that attracts ties (physical attractiveness would be another example). To test this in a QAP context, we would use UCINET's Data|Attribute to Matrix function and choose the "duplicate rows (receiver effect)" option, which creates the matrix shown in Matrix 8.2. As you can see column 9 is all 62s, the age of node 9. Column 16 is all 27s, the age of node 16. If there is a positive correlation with 'seeks advice from', the advice matrix will have a lot of 1s in column 9, and very few 1s in column 16. We can test this by simply correlating the two matrices. As it turns out, the correlation is not significant. On a hunch, we constructed an additional matrix D in which $D(i, j) = 1$ if node i and node j were in the same department, and $D(i, j) = 0$ otherwise, and added this as a control variable in a regression using the receiver age effect to predict advice. The age effect was still not significant.

QAP results for High-Tec-Attributes-diffAGE2 * REPORTS_TO (5000 permutations)

	1	2	3	4	5	6	7	8
	Obs Value	Significa	Average	Std Dev	Minimum	Maximum	Prop >= 0	Prop <= 0
Pearson Correlation	-0.0645	0.1842	0.0018	0.0712	-0.2598	0.1572	0.8180	0.1842

Figure 8.5 QAP correlation between age difference and who reports to whom.

	1	2	3	4	5	6	7	8	9	10	11	12	13	14	15	16	17	18	19	20	21
1	33	42	40	33	32	59	55	34	62	37	46	34	48	43	40	27	30	33	32	38	36
2	33	42	40	33	32	59	55	34	62	37	46	34	48	43	40	27	30	33	32	38	36
3	33	42	40	33	32	59	55	34	62	37	46	34	48	43	40	27	30	33	32	38	36
4	33	42	40	33	32	59	55	34	62	37	46	34	48	43	40	27	30	33	32	38	36
5	33	42	40	33	32	59	55	34	62	37	46	34	48	43	40	27	30	33	32	38	36
6	33	42	40	33	32	59	55	34	62	37	46	34	48	43	40	27	30	33	32	38	36
7	33	42	40	33	32	59	55	34	62	37	46	34	48	43	40	27	30	33	32	38	36
8	33	42	40	33	32	59	55	34	62	37	46	34	48	43	40	27	30	33	32	38	36
9	33	42	40	33	32	59	55	34	62	37	46	34	48	43	40	27	30	33	32	38	36
10	33	42	40	33	32	59	55	34	62	37	46	34	48	43	40	27	30	33	32	38	36
11	33	42	40	33	32	59	55	34	62	37	46	34	48	43	40	27	30	33	32	38	36
12	33	42	40	33	32	59	55	34	62	37	46	34	48	43	40	27	30	33	32	38	36
13	33	42	40	33	32	59	55	34	62	37	46	34	48	43	40	27	30	33	32	38	36
14	33	42	40	33	32	59	55	34	62	37	46	34	48	43	40	27	30	33	32	38	36
15	33	42	40	33	32	59	55	34	62	37	46	34	48	43	40	27	30	33	32	38	36
16	33	42	40	33	32	59	55	34	62	37	46	34	48	43	40	27	30	33	32	38	36
17	33	42	40	33	32	59	55	34	62	37	46	34	48	43	40	27	30	33	32	38	36
18	33	42	40	33	32	59	55	34	62	37	46	34	48	43	40	27	30	33	32	38	36
19	33	42	40	33	32	59	55	34	62	37	46	34	48	43	40	27	30	33	32	38	36
20	33	42	40	33	32	59	55	34	62	37	46	34	48	43	40	27	30	33	32	38	36
21	33	42	40	33	32	59	55	34	62	37	46	34	48	43	40	27	30	33	32	38	36

Matrix 8.2   Matrix used to test age effect.

8.4.2 Categorical attributes

Borgatti et al. (2012) collected ties among participants in a three-week workshop. As noted earlier, a visual display of the Campnet dataset seems to suggest that gender affects who interacts with whom (see Figure 8.4). However, the human brain is notorious for seeing patterns and focusing on confirmatory evidence while ignoring contradictory data. Therefore, we would like to statistically test this homophily hypothesis.

An approach that is closely parallel to the way we handled age earlier is to construct a node-by-node matrix in which the (i, j) cell is 1 if nodes i and j belong to the same gender, and 0 if they belong to different genders. In UCINET this is done using the same Data|Attribute-to-Matrix procedure we used for continuous attributes, but selecting the 'Exact matches' option instead of 'Difference'. We can then use QAP correlation to correlate the matrix of actual network ties with the 'is the same gender' matrix. The result (not shown) is a strong correlation of 0.33 with a p-value of 0.0006, indicating support for the homophily hypothesis.

We should note, though, that we got a little lucky in this example. The independent variable, 'same gender', is a symmetric matrix – if I am the same gender as you, you must be the same gender as me. Yet the dependent variable is not symmetric. These data are of the forced choice type in which each person lists the top three people they interact with. This tends to force asymmetry because a popular person will be listed by many more than three others, yet the respondent is only allowed to reciprocate three of these. Further, there is

```
QAP results for campnet-sym * samegender (5000 permutations)

                              1          2          3          4          5          6
                      Obs Value  Significa    Average    Std Dev    Minimum    Maximum
                      ---------  ---------  ---------  ---------  ---------  ---------
     Pearson Correlation  0.3521     0.0008    -0.0013     0.0846    -0.2399     0.3521
```

Figure 8.6   QAP correlation with symmetrized Campnet data.

no way for a symmetric independent variable to perfectly predict a non-symmetric dependent variable (this is handled by the QAP significance test, but the R-square value may be misleadingly low). In this case, it might make more sense to symmetrize the Campnet matrix via the maximum method, which means that a tie is said to exist between two nodes if either lists the other as one of their top three interactors. If we take this approach and rerun the correlation, we obtain a correlation that is a little bit higher at 0.352, and of course still significant.

8.5 Node-level hypotheses

A node-level hypothesis is one in which the variables are characteristics of individual nodes, such as persons. For example, we might investigate whether the number of top management friends a person has predicts the size of her bonus at the end of the year. In some ways, this is an easy one: just run an ordinary regression. Indeed, this is the way most hypotheses of this type are tested in the literature. But suppose our research site is a small company of, say, 20 individuals and we have surveyed all of them. If we are being careful, we might note that the sample size is small and, while small sizes can be conservative (in the sense that if the results are significant on a small sample size it must be a pretty strong effect), if they get too small the assumptions of the classical significance test will no longer hold. We might also realize that we do not have an actual sample. We have the entire population of organization members, and the organization itself is a sample of one chosen non-randomly from the population of firms. This also is not a situation that the classical significance test for regression coefficients is meant to handle.

The safer thing to do is run a randomization test. For example, we could run ordinary least squares as usual to obtain the regression coefficients, but then use the permutation technique to construct the p-values. Figure 8.6 shows the results of testing a simple hypothesis that men will have more friends who are not friends of other friends. In other words, the hypothesis is that there will be fewer connections among men's friends than among women's friends. To test this, we constructed the dependent variable by running UCINET's Egonet density

```
p-values are 2-tailed

Overall Regression Fit Statistics (p-value for F is classical test)

                             Value
                             -------
                  Nobs          18
             R-Square        0.090
        Adj R-square        -0.031
            F(0,0)           0.744
            Prob > F         0.492

Regression Coefficients.

                        1        2        3        4        5
                     Coef       SE        T    c.Sig    p.sig
                   ------   ------   ------   ------   ------
        1  Intercept  0.463    0.214    2.165    0.046    0.519
        2     Gender  0.139    0.133    1.043    0.313    0.311
        3       Role -0.168    0.159   -1.055    0.307    0.303
```

Figure 8.7 Regressing ego-net density on gender and role. Column "c.Sig" gives p-values based on classical test, while "p.sig" gives p-values based on permutation test.

procedure, which gave us the proportion of each node's friends that were friends with each other. The independent variable was simply gender (coded 1 = women, 2 = men) and we also controlled for the individual's role (1 = participant, 2 = instructor). We then ran UCINET's node-level regression to produce Figure 8.7. As you can see, the hypothesis was not supported. Whatever determines the degree of connection among one's friends, it is not one's gender, nor one's role in the organization.

8.6 Whole-network hypotheses

A whole-network hypothesis is one in which the cases are collectivities such as teams, firms or countries, and the variables are characteristics of the network of ties within the units. For instance, Athanassiou and Nigh (2000) studied a sample of 37 firms, and looked at how a firm's degree of internationalization affected the density of advice ties among members of its top management team.

Assuming the firms are obtained via a random sample, to test a hypothesis like this we can just run a normal regression in a standard statistical package such as SPSS. The classical significance test would be perfectly valid. Of course, if we did use a randomization test, the results would also be perfectly valid, but would take more time to compute and require the use of a network analysis software package such as UCINET, or a specialized statistical package such as

StatXact. On the other hand, if the data were not collected via a random sample, it would be wise to use a randomization test.

Randomization tests provide an elegant and powerful way to deal with some of the special issues posed by social network data. A key advantage is that, if one has programming capability, one can construct a suitable significance test for any test statistic, including new ones developed specifically for the research at hand. One thing to remember, however, is that while a randomization test will allow you to test for significance even when you have a non-random sample or population, it does not magically create generalizability. A significant result relating X to Y in Mrs Smith's third-grade classroom tells you that, in that classroom, X and Y are probably not independent, but it does not make up for the fact that you did not randomly sample children from all over the world, nor did you sample from the set of all classrooms. Generalizability comes from your research design, not from significance statistics.

8.7 Exponential random graph models

QAP regressions are about comparing two (or more) networks using a modified general linear models framework. QAP deals with the violations of assumptions like independence of observations by using a permutation technique that controls for the dependencies among the observations. Occasionally, we can also use QAP to assess certain kinds of interdependencies, such as tendencies toward reciprocity or transitivity. We do this by constructing a hypothetical structure matrix that embodies the tendency, and then regressing the observed network on the structure matrices. Exponential random graph models (ERGMs, also known as p* models) are, in a very loose sense, the opposite of QAP models. They are primarily designed to model a network as an accumulation of micro-configurations (such as reciprocated dyads or open/closed triads) that are thought to represent social processes (such as honoring norms of reciprocity and the avoidance of cognitive dissonance). Thus, ERGMs can be used to characterize networks as outcomes of various micro-forces working together to produce the observed network. Because one can also specify a dyadic covariate, ERGMs can also be used to evaluate the association between two networks, just like QAP.[3] The difference here is that whereas QAP regards the myriad dependencies among ties in the networks as nuisances to be controlled away, ERGM explicitly models and interprets them.

As these models are not in UCINET, our discussion is more about getting a general idea of what they are and what they can be used for. More complete

---

[3] However, ERGM cannot specify a multivariate linear model of matrices of the form Y = b0+b1X1+b2X2 + ... , as QAP can.

descriptions can be found in Robins et al. (2007), Robins (2011) and Lusher et al. (2013). The models are related to the general linear models of standard statistics but have important modifications to deal with the fact that we cannot assume independence of observations – in our case the edges. A key concept is the notion of conditional dependence. If two edges share a common vertex then they are dependent, conditional on the rest of the graph. Models based on this type of conditional dependence are known as 'Markov random graph models' and are a special class of ERGMs. The models describe how a network is built up from smaller constituent parts called 'configurations'. These configurations are objects such as stars and triangles, and are selected by the researcher (from a set of possible configurations) on the basis of a particular hypothesis.

The result for a given network and a given set of configurations will be a set of parameter values, one for each of the chosen configurations, together with a standard error. Large positive parameters show that the corresponding configuration occurred more frequently than we would expect given the other configurations we have in the model. For example, a large transitivity parameter tells us there are more closed triads than we would expect given the density of the network and the propensity for open triangles. Large negative values would show that these configurations occurred less frequently than expected given the other configurations. By convention, parameter estimates that are more than twice as large as their standard error are regarded as significant. The parameters can be estimated by using Markov Chain Monte Carlo (MCMC) maximum likelihood estimation. In essence, the parameters are provisionally estimated and thousands of graphs are simulated based on the provisional model. For each one, the graph statistics corresponding to each parameter are calculated. The means of the graph statistics are compared to the corresponding statistics in the observed data, and the parameters are then adjusted to try to get the means closer to the observed data. When they are close enough the process is deemed to have converged. To assess closeness for each parameter, we compute the difference between the observed statistic associated with it and the simulation mean, and divide by the standard deviation. Ratios smaller than 0.1 are deemed to have achieved convergence.

However, convergence is not sufficient in an ERGM. A second step is needed to ensure that the model is an accurate representation of the observed data: goodness of fit. In the goodness of fit procedure, millions of graphs are simulated using the parameter estimate values of the fitted parameters in the model. A sample of these graphs is taken randomly and the average and standard deviation of a series of network statistics for these simulated graphs are compared to their values in the observed data. If the values are close enough (absolute value of a t-ratio below 2 for non-fitted parameters and below 0.1 for fitted parameters), then the model is assumed to be a good representation of the observed data. The issue for the researcher is what set of configurations should

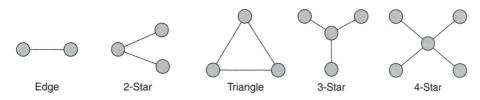

| Edge | 2-Star | Triangle | 3-Star | 4-Star |

Figure 8.8 Configurations for Markov random graph models.

be selected. Certain configurations are associated with assumptions about the data. It can be shown (though we do not provide any details here) that the configurations that are important for undirected graphs in this instance are edges, k-stars and triangles (typically, at least one parameter for density, one for degree distribution and one for clustering). Examples of these are shown in Figure 8.8. If we have directed data then more configurations are possible. These can include out-stars, in-stars and triangles – the latter can be cycles or transitive triads. In addition, we can include attribute effects such as homophily or popularity for both directed and undirected graphs.

Historically, Markov random graph models have had difficulties with estimation. Simulation studies have shown that the distributions of graphs associated with particular parameter combinations can be near degenerate, meaning that only a tiny handful of graphs have any meaningful probability under the model. Moreover, the distributions are bimodal with only very sparse or very dense graphs having any frequency. Snijders et al. (2006) introduced the use of higher order configurations (i.e., ones with more than three nodes) to stabilize the estimation. Some of these higher order configurations relax the assumption of conditional dependence in Markov random graph models to partial conditional dependence using 'social circuit' configurations which include edges that do not necessarily share a node, but are dependent in the sense that the probability of tie between A and B affects the probability of a tie between C and D. These give rise to new configurations such as 4-cycles which we use in combination with the Markov model configurations shown in Figure 8.8.

It is not just cycles of length 4 that can be added, but two important new classes of configurations called k-2-paths and k-triangles. A k-2-path is a configuration which has k independent paths of length 2 connecting two non-adjacent vertices. A k-triangle is similar except the two vertices are adjacent. These configurations are shown in Figure 8.9. These can also be extended to directed graphs where the k-triangles extend to a set of configurations called 'closure configurations' and the k-2-paths extend to connectivity configurations. We do not list all these configurations here.

ERGMs are also able to include actor attributes in a variety of ways. The simplest are effects used to test social selection hypotheses, such as parameters for

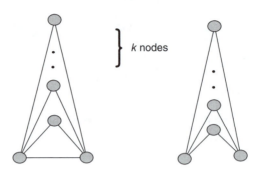

Figure 8.9 Configurations for undirected social circuit model k-triangle and k-2-path.

status-seeking and homophily. To include these, we simply represent them as configurations. For example, to test for homophily, we include in our configurations an edge between two female nodes to represent homophily among the women and an edge between two male nodes to represent homophily among the men. Effects can be specified for both categorical and continuous attributes.

In all statistical modeling there is the important issue of goodness of fit, and for iterative algorithms such as used in ERGMs, there is also the matter of convergence. As discussed earlier, we can measure the fit for any given statistic, including the fitted parameters, by taking the difference between the value in the observed graph (say, the number of reciprocated ties) and the mean of a sample of graphs simulated from the parameter estimates, and dividing by the simulation standard deviation. We call this metric a t-ratio. For statistics corresponding to fitted parameters, this t-ratio measures not only goodness of fit but convergence. As a rule of thumb, all the t-values (absolute values of) should be less than 0.1 for fitted parameters and less than 2 for other parameters. The trick is to find a small set of configurations which capture the properties we are interested in and which yield reasonable parameter values that converge. This can be a frustrating and time-consuming process and is more of an art than a science, but there are some standard approaches taught in workshops to help guide the researcher.

Since ERGMs are not part of the UCINET package, anyone wishing to use these models needs to use specialized software. Well-known packages include MPNet and Statnet, both of which are freely available on the Web. The examples we give here were done using MPNet, but we do not present any software-specific details. We first examine the Zachary (1977) karate club data available in UCINET and mentioned in Chapter 7. We have fitted a social circuit model using edges, k-stars, k-triangles and k-2-paths. The results are shown in Table 8.1.

Examining the results, we can see that the model converged, as all the t-ratios (last column of Table 8.1) are less than 0.1 in absolute value. The edge parameter represents the tendency for edges to occur on their own, given all the other parameters in the model, and is not normally interpreted. The k-stars parameter is not significant, indicating that the degree distribution is not significantly different from what would be expected at random (again, given all the other parameters). On the other hand, we see that the k-triangles and the k-2-paths are both significant and have a positive parameter estimate. The k-triangles show that the data have more closure than we would expect by chance, indicating a tendency toward clustering. The positive 2-path parameter suggests that there is also a tendency towards 2-paths (i.e., 2-paths that are not transitive). This suggests that there are also a number of actors that are surrounded by a large number of structural holes – perhaps playing bridging roles between network clusters. To feel certain about this interpretation, a good idea here would be to simulate a number of networks from the model to see what they look like. The ability to do this is a key advantage of ERG models.

Table 8.1 ERGM parameter estimates for the Zachary data. The asterisk indicates a value that is significant at the 0.05 level.

Parameter	Estimate	Standard error	Convergence
Edge	−1.949347	1.40466	−0.02120
k-stars	−0.515209	0.40709	−0.03146
k-triangles	0.617050*	0.23146	−0.05435
k-2-paths	0.129776*	0.02240	0.07138

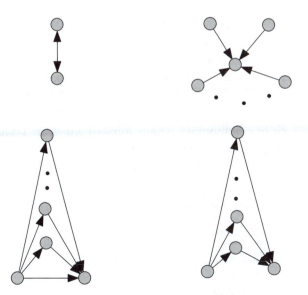

Figure 8.10 Configurations for Newcomb data (clockwise from top left): reciprocity, AinS, A2P-T paths and AT-T paths.

For our second example, we use the Newcomb fraternity data that we analyzed using QAP regression. The QAP regression was about network evolution and showed that changes in the network from Week 0 to Week 1 could be attributed in part to reciprocity but not to transitivity. In contrast, our ERGM analysis is cross-sectional and is intended to characterize the network at a single point in time, namely Week 1. We examine the top three choices for each actor in Week 1. Since we have artificially fixed the number of choices per actor, we do not select 'arc' as one of the configurations in the model (but we need to make sure that the outdegree is fixed at 3 in our simulations). We do select reciprocity, in-stars and the directed transitive versions of the k-triangle and the k-2-path. In MPNet the latter two are known as AT-T and A2P-T, respectively. The complete set of configurations is shown in Figure 8.10. The results are presented in Table 8.2.

The results in Table 8.2 show that reciprocity is significant and strongly positive, indicating that, overall, ties tend to be reciprocated. We also see a strong result for the in-stars, indicating significant variance in the degree distribution – some actors are very popular and are getting more nominations than we would have expected by chance. The non-transitive 2-paths parameter is not significant, but we do have a significant result for AT-T showing that the network has more transitivity than we would expect by chance. If we repeat the same analysis for the data in Week 0, we find that reciprocity and transitivity are significant but the in-stars are not. Hence, we can see that reciprocity and transitivity effects are important at both time periods, but the popularity effect only comes in at the second time period.

Our next example brings in actor attributes. In this example we examine the Freeman EIES data (Freeman and Freeman, 1979) also available in UCINET. We look at the friends network at time period 1 of the study, that is, friends and close friends among 32 academics. Also recorded are the four discipline areas of sociology, anthropology, mathematics/statistics and other. We fitted an ERGM with the same configurations as the Newcomb data example but we added arc, out-stars and discipline homophily. The results are given in Table 8.3.

As we would expect in friendship networks, there is a lot of reciprocity. Neither the in-stars effect nor the out-stars effect is significant, hence we do not

Table 8.2 ERGM for Newcomb fraternity data Week 1.

Parameter	Estimate	Standard error	Convergence
Reciprocity	2.291311*	0.63415	0.09943
AinS	0.814274*	0.36696	−0.07762
AT-T	0.416767*	0.20155	0.07639
A2P-T	−0.045393	0.26048	−0.03969

Table 8.3 ERGM for Freeman EIES data.

Parameter	Estimate	Standard error	Convergence
Arc	−1.526891*	0.59539	0.00427
Reciprocity	1.825968*	0.31221	0.01168
AinS	−0.449871	0.30209	0.00379
AoutS	−0.342527	0.29379	0.00328
AT-T	0.873116*	0.13446	0.00072
A2P-T	−0.162721*	0.03312	0.02098
Discipline homophily	0.272437*	0.07856	−0.05568

have individuals that are exceptionally popular nor claim to have a surprising number of friends. The positive and significant AT-T parameter shows that transitivity is prevalent, and the negative and significant A2P-T shows that there is a lack of 2-paths that do not have transitive closure. Finally, we see that friends tend to come from the same discipline. In summary, these data show all the classic structure of friendship, namely that it is reciprocated, that the friends of your friends are your friends, and that friends share common interests.

For our final example, we show how to examine the effects of a dyadic covariate, allowing a direct comparison with QAP regression. To do this, we return to the Padgett data discussed at the beginning of Section 8.3. In this case, we will take marriage ties as our dependent variable, business ties as our dyadic covariate, and wealth of each family as a node-level covariate. Using the ERGM command in the Statnet package in R (Handcock et al., 2017), we fit the following model:

```
> mymodel <- ergm(flomarriage~edges+nodecov('wealth')+edgecov(flobusiness))
> summary(mymodel)
```

The results are shown in Table 8.4.

The "nodecov('wealth')" term essentially creates a matrix W in which $W(i, j) = \text{wealth}(i) + \text{wealth}(j)$. To run a similar model using MR-QAP, we use UCINET's Data|Attribute to Matrix function to create the W matrix and then

Table 8.4 Monte Carlo MLE results.

	Estimate	Std. Error	p-value	
edges	−3.05205	0.622987	< 1e-04	***
nodecov.wealth	0.010668	0.005121	0.0394	*
edgecov.flobusiness	2.141349	0.613808	0.0007	***

Table 8.5 QAP Regression results.

	Un-Stdized	Stdized Coef	P-value
Intercept	0.00186	0	
sumWEALTH	0.00135	0.17683	0.0312
padgb	0.39845	0.35359	0.0004

regress marriage ties on both the W matrix and the business ties matrix. The results are given in Table 8.5.

The coefficients cannot be compared to the ERGM coefficients, but it is interesting to note that the p-values tell the same story.

8.8 Stochastic actor-oriented models (SAOMs)

In this section we give a highly simplified non-technical introduction to the stochastic actor-oriented models used in the R software package rSIENA (Snijders, 2001). SAOMs are used to analyze network panel data, that is, network data on a group of actors collected repeatedly over a period of time, the Newcomb fraternity data already discussed in this chapter being a classic example. The underlying model is a continuous-time Markov process and assumes that at a given moment only one change can occur in the network. That is, at a given moment only one tie can change by either being created or removed. To accommodate this assumption, the changes from one observation to the next are decomposed into a series of micro-steps, with only one change being permissible in any micro-step. How often this can happen is specified in the model by a rate function. This model therefore assumes that the actors in the network control their outgoing ties. As with all Markov processes, the model has no memory, which means that if there are a number of observations at different time points, the change from one point in time to the next only depends on the current state and not on the entire history. This has implications for the spacing of the time points and the interpretation of the results. It cannot, for example, consider reciprocating a tie that existed several time points prior and was subsequently dropped.

Also in the model is an evaluation function which tries to capture the overall advantage of an actor *i* dropping an existing tie or making a new tie. This function is in effect specified by the researcher but based on a number of well-known network criteria. In this respect this is very similar to the ERGMs where we combine network structure effects (e.g., reciprocity, transitivity and popularity) with attribute effects (e.g., homophily or the propensity of sending ties). One small difference is that in rSIENA we must take care that our choices are consistent with the actor having control over their outgoing ties, as this is an actor-oriented model. The rSIENA software package has all of these built in and the user is able to select them from a comprehensive list of possible effects relating to network structure and continuous and discrete actor attributes. The evaluation function is set up in terms of probabilities and so should not be seen as an entirely deterministic process: it captures the probability that an actor will make or break a tie (or do nothing). If the value of the function increases by an actor making a certain change then the probability that the actor makes this change also increases. The function (rather like the ERGM) has a number of parameters that need to be fitted to the data, and this is done by simulation and encompasses an approximation to the maximum likelihood values.

One advantage of these models over ERGMs is that they incorporate the choices actors make over time and so have a starting structure. This makes them more robust and easier to fit, providing the starting structure was relatively patterned. If, for example, we collected data in which we asked people to randomly select friends by simply drawing lots before they met and then followed this up by asking with whom they were friends after a number of social events, our data would not be suitable for this type of analysis, as our starting data were random.

We present a highly simplified example which was explored in more detail by Snijders et al. (2010), and the interested reader should consult that article for additional details. The data, reported by Knecht (2008), consist of 26 school children (17 girls and 9 boys) who listed whom they considered to be friends at four time periods.

It is well known that friendship among children in this age group has a tendency towards reciprocity, transitivity and same-sex nominations. It therefore makes sense to include all these structural effects in the evaluation function. In any SIENA model outdegree should always be included (as should reciprocity, which we have already included for other reasons) and it is advisable to include other degree-based effects. Two useful effects in this regard are indegree popularity and outdegree popularity; these are basically the sum of the indegrees of the alters chosen and the sum of the outdegrees of the alters chosen. These effects capture the extent to which an actor chooses people who are chosen by many others or who choose many others. Experience has shown that taking the square roots of these sums works best. In the model below we have only included outdegree popularity. In this particular dataset, some of the schoolchildren already knew each other from primary school and this is built into the model. Finally, we include the sender and receiver effects of sex. The results are given in Table 8.6.

Table 8.6 SIENA estimates of friendship evolution.

	Estimate	Standard errors
Evaluation function		
Outdegree	−1.67*	0.38
Reciprocity	1.42*	0.20
Transitive triplets	0.21*	0.03
Transitive ties	0.74*	0.21
3-cycles	−0.26*	0.09
Outdegree popularity	−0.56*	0.23
Sex(M) ego	0.39*	0.13
Sex(M) alter	0.15	0.13
Same sex	0.54*	0.12
Primary school	0.35*	0.14
Rate function		
Rate period 1	9.76	1.91
Rate period 2	10.44	1.83
Rate period 3	8.91	1.39

The first part of the table looks very similar to the output produced for the ERGMs used in the first section. The main difference is that this analysis is about the evolution of ties, and hence reciprocity, for example, measures the extent to which unreciprocated ties become reciprocated over the time period studied. As in previous tables a * indicates a significant result with $p < 0.05$.

The estimates for the rate function are an important part of the SIENA model and are the expected frequencies of the opportunities actors have within the network to make or break ties between successive data waves. It should be noted that p-values are not calculated for these since a value of zero would mean no changes are made and so testing whether they are zero would be meaningless. The values show a fairly consistent rate change, with a slight increase during the second period and a decline towards the end of the study.

We can interpret the significance and parameter estimates in the same way as for ERGMs. Hence we see the strong effects of reciprocity, transitivity,[4] gender homophily, and of prior friendship in primary school. The negative value for 3-cycles means that these tend not to get formed, and this indicates a possible

---

[4] Measured in two different ways: the transitive triplets measure considers the A2P-T paths of Figure 8.10, whereas the transitive ties measure looks for the existence of a 2-path.

hierarchical structure between groups. The significant and negative outdegree popularity shows that children who nominate a lot of friends do not receive many nominations themselves. Also of note is the Sex(M) ego result which indicates that males are more active in the network than females, but the corresponding alter effect is not significant.

8.9 Summary

To statistically test a network hypothesis, we need to use methods which can deal with the interdependencies that are such an important feature of social networks. One approach is to use permutation tests, which are able to generate statistical distributions (against which we can compare observed results) from the network data themselves. Using this approach, we can test for associations between pairs of networks on the same set of actors using correlation, and we can model a dependent network using multiple independent networks (again on the same actors) using regression. Since the relation 'having the same attribute' results in an idealized structural network, we are able to include attribute effects such as homophily or diffusion. In a similar way, we can use differences of attributes (plus other combinations) to include continuous attributes. An alternative approach is to use exponential random graph models, which can test whether certain patterns in the network occur more often than we would expect by chance. These patterns are selected by the researcher and reflect different hypotheses about the network. If we have panel data, we can use Markov methods to capture changes through time by modeling how actors make and break ties. These models are known as stochastic actor-oriented models (SAOMs) and are the basis of the rSIENA software program.

8.10 Problems and Exercises

1. It is sometimes important to hypothesize about the factors that might influence the formation of dyadic ties in social networks. The first problem involves the testing of a dyadic hypothesis. For this problem we will be using the Zachery karate club dataset which has already been unpacked. The two networks are named ZACHE.##h and ZACHC.##h. ZACHE represents the simple presence or absence of ties between members of a Karate Club, and ZACHC contains valued data counting the number of interactions between actors. In UCINET go to Tools|Similarities and Distances and use the cross-product measure to compute similarities among the rows of ZACHE. (The cross product is a very powerful and common matrix operation that, in this case, will count how many friends each pair of actors have in common.) UCINET will name the output "ZACHE-Cro-P". Now go to Tools|Testing Hypotheses|Dyadic (QAP)|QAP Correlation and browse to include both ZACHC and ZACHE-Cro-P to be correlated and click okay. What do the results mean? How

might this reflect the first part of Granovetter's famous 'strength of weak ties' theory, which states that I have stronger ties (ZACHC) with those people with whom I share more friends in common (ZACHE-Cro-P)?

2. For testing a monadic hypothesis, we will be using the KRACK-HIGH-TEC data that contain three dichotomous relations (REPORTS_TO, ADVICE, FRIENDSHIP). HIGH-TEC-ATTRIBUTES contains several attributes about the nodes in KRACK-HIGH-TEC, including Age, Level (CEO, Manager, Staff), Tenure, and Department. We are going to use the ADVICE network dataset. In UCINET go to Network|Centrality and Power|Degree and load the ADVICE network, using the directed version (lower left), telling it NOT to treat the data as symmetric. By default, it will name the output "ADVICE-deg".

    a. We are particularly interested in who is sought after for advice, which is captured by indegree centrality. So, we are going to pull out just that column from the results, by using Data|Filter/Extract|Submatrix. Specify "ADVICE-deg.##h" as your input dataset and that we want to "Keep" "ALL" rows. Then click on the L to the right of the box for "Which Columns" and select the column labeled "InDeg" (for indegree) and call your output dataset ADVISING. This is a measure of how many people said they sought advice from each person.

    b. Now display (D) the HIGH-TEC-ATTRIBUTES dataset to determine which columns the AGE and TENURE attributes are in. To do that go to the "D" in the icon menu and click on the attribute file. Now, it is common wisdom that people look to the 'senior' people for advice, but is unclear in an organizational context whether senior is 'older' or 'longer tenured'. You will test if either of these is supported by the data. In UCINET go to Tools|Testing Hypotheses|Node-Level|Regression specifying ADVISING for your dependent dataset with the appropriate column (Indeg) and HIGH-TEC-ATTRIBUTES and the appropriate columns for your independent dataset (i.e., first adding age and then adding tenure) and set the number of permutations to 10000. Now click OK. Which meaning of 'senior' do the data support? Why did we use the Regression option of Node-Level instead of T-Test or Anova? When would we use those?

3. In this problem, we will test a multivariate dyadic hypothesis using the WIRING dataset. This is a stacked dataset which includes many different files. This is a dichotomous adjacency matrix of 14 employees of the bank wiring room of Western Electric used in the famous Hawthorne Studies. Ties are symmetric and represent participation in games during work breaks. RDGAM records people playing games together, RDCON records conflict between people, RDPOS is positive interactions, RDCON is negative interactions. The dataset has been unpacked. In UCINET go to Tools|Testing Hypotheses|Dyadic (QAP)|QAP Linear Regression|Double Dekker Semi-Partialling MRQAP. Put RDCON (conflict between members about whether the windows should be open or shut) in as the dependent variable. Put in RDPOS (positive relationships), RDNEG (negative relationships), and RDGAM (playing games together) as independent variables. Before running it, what do you think would most significantly predict conflict? After entering the networks click OK. Are your results what you expected? How would you explain the results?

4. For this problem we want to see the extent to which campers' gender is related to the presence of dyadic ties in a social network of methods training course participants using campnet.##h and campattr.##h. Here we want to test a mixed-dyadic

monadic hypothesis. In UCINET go to Tools|Testing Hypotheses |Mixed Dyadic/Nodal|Categorical attributes|Anova Density and run the analysis twice for two different models. For both, specify Campnet as the network matrix, and the "Gender" column of the campattr matrix as the Actor Attribute. For the first run, choose "Constant Homophily" for your model, and for the second, choose "Variable Homophily". Be sure to save the ucinetlog files for comparison. Interpret both sets of results. Is there homophily? Which gender tends to be more homophilous?

5. In this problem, we test a mixed monadic/dyadic hypothesis for the same Campnet network but this time using QAP. In UCINET got to Data|Attribute to matrix, enter the campattr file and create a matrix of exact matches among the actors in Campnet based on Gender. The default name given to the file by UCINET will be "campattr-sameGender". What does the resulting output matrix show? Now go to Tools|Testing Hypotheses|Dyadic (QAP)|MR-QAP Linear Regression|Double-Dekker Semi-Partialling MRQAP to regress the Campnet network (dependent variable) on this new matrix of gender similarity (independent variable), campattr-sameGender. What do the results show?

9

Characterizing Whole Networks

Learning Outcomes

1. Calculate and interpret cohesion measures in a whole network
2. Undertake a triad census
3. Compute and evaluate measures of transitivity, reciprocity and clustering

9.1 Introduction

In the 1950s Alex Bavelas and his student Harold Leavitt conducted a series of experiments at the Massachusetts Institute of Technology. They were interested in which communication structures were best for group problem-solving. For example, they investigated structures like those in Figure 9.1. What they found was, for a variety of outcome measures such as speed and accuracy of solutions, the star-shaped network on the left was generally the best, the circle-shaped network on the right was the worst, and the other two were in between. They concluded that, at least for the simple tasks they were investigating, more centralized networks were better problem-solvers.

Centralization is a property of a network as a whole. When measured, it is a single number that characterizes the whole network. In this chapter we consider how to measure centralization, along with a host of other whole-network properties. Many of these properties can be seen as measures of the cohesiveness of a network. Others are indicators of qualitative differences such as whether the network has a core–periphery shape versus a clumpy shape. Of course, what one regards as the whole network is a matter of choice. Hence, if

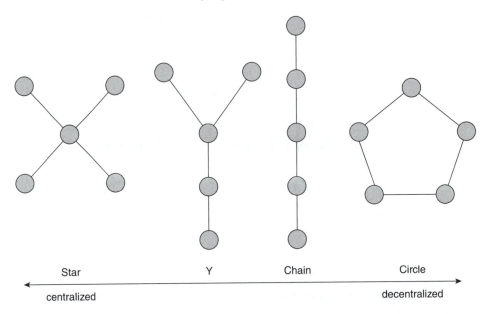

Star   Y   Chain   Circle

centralized   decentralized

Figure 9.1   Network structures studied by Bavelas and Leavitt.

we have collected network data for an entire organization, in the analysis we are free to extract the network of ties within each department, and calculate a measure like centralization for each one. We can then do a comparative analysis of the levels of centralization of each department. If we have enough departments, this can take the form of a regression in which the cases are departments and the variables are attributes of the departments, including such things as performance, size, and, of course, centralization.

9.2 Cohesion

The idea of cohesion is connectedness or 'knittedness'. There is a Spanish word – *enredado* – that expresses it nicely. It means tangled up, like a big clump of electrical wires or fish caught in a trawler's net. It is particularly appropriate because the word is based on the word for network, which is *red*. However, it is important to note that, depending on the nature of ties in the network, the term 'cohesion' may not necessarily correspond to sociological cohesion. For example, if the network consists of 'who hates whom' ties, greater network cohesion would imply less sociological cohesion.

Perhaps the simplest measure of cohesion is density. Density is simply the number of ties in the network, expressed as a proportion of the number possible. In an ordinary undirected non-reflexive graph, the number possible is $n(n-1)/2$, where n is the number of nodes. Density can be interpreted as the

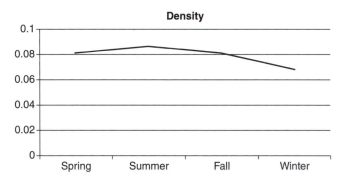

Figure 9.2 Comparison of density by season in Chesapeake Bay ecosystem data.

probability that a tie exists between any pair of randomly chosen nodes; however, the absolute number can be hard to assess. Whether a density of, say, 0.345 should be considered high or low depends on the context. For example, in a small group, such as an academic department, a density of 0.345 for the 'who knows whom' network would be incredibly low – we would expect 1.0. But for the 'who is having sex with whom' network in the department, 0.345 is incredibly high – we would expect something close to 0.0. In general, we see considerably higher density values for positive ties than negative ties.

Density is almost always best used in a comparative way. For example, in the Chesapeake Bay ecological network data (Baird and Ulanowicz, 1989), the density of the 'who eats whom' network varies by season. As shown in Figure 9.2, density is highly correlated with temperature. It is lowest in winter, meaning that dietary variety goes down in winter, perhaps because there are fewer species active and available to be eaten.

In binary data, density is easily computed as the average of all entries in the adjacency matrix (typically omitting the main diagonal, which represents self-ties). In valued data, we again simply compute the average of all values, which is to say we compute average tie strength.

In principle, the advantage of density over the simple number of ties (or total tie strength) is that it adjusts for the number of nodes in the network, making density figures comparable across groups of different sizes. However, care must be taken in comparing densities of small groups with densities of much larger groups. In a network of 10 people, it is quite possible for a node to have ties with all nine other actors. In a network of 50 people, this may still be true. But in a network of 1000 nodes, it seems unlikely that the number of ties an actor will have to others will keep pace with the number available. As a result, densities are almost always lower in large networks than in small networks.

Because of this issue, some researchers prefer to use the average degree of the network. If we compute the degree (number of ties) for each node (i.e., the row sums of the adjacency matrix), and then average these degrees, we obtain the average degree of the network. The average degree is easier to interpret than density because it is literally the average number of ties that each node has. The relationship between average degree $\bar{d}$ and density for undirected non-reflexive graphs is given by

$$\bar{d} = \frac{2T}{n} = \text{density} \times (n-1) \tag{9.1}$$

where T is the number of edges in the network and n is the number of nodes.

So far, we have only considered the density of an entire network. However, density can also be computed within subgroups, and even between subgroups. For example, if we have a network in which nodes can be divided into three types – say, three departments – we can count the number of ties between members of each pair of departments, and divide by the number possible given the number of people in each department. A density table records all densities within and between all groups. As an example, Figure 9.3 shows the Campnet dataset discussed in Chapter 2. In the diagram, node shape is used to distinguish male and female actors.

In this network, each actor has exactly three outgoing ties. As a result, the density of the overall network is of no interest as this has been predetermined by the fixed outdegree. What is interesting and obvious from the diagram is that the women in general select women and the men select men. We can see the extent to which this is true by looking at the density between and within groups as shown in Table 9.1. Note that no entry could be as large as 1.0 because there are more than three actors in each group, and each actor is only allowed three ties.

The Campnet network makes clear that the density of a network need not be uniform throughout the network. A network with a middling density value may have some regions of near perfect density and other regions of near vacuum. In fact, a network could be fragmented into multiple components, as defined in Chapter 2. Another network could have the same density but a very diffuse structure where density is evenly distributed. Density provides a single number that characterizes an aspect of a network, not unlike the mean of a distribution, but tells you nothing about how those ties are distributed throughout the network.

Table 9.1 Density between and within gender groups in the Campnet dataset.

	Women	Men
Women	0.357	0.050
Men	0.063	0.278

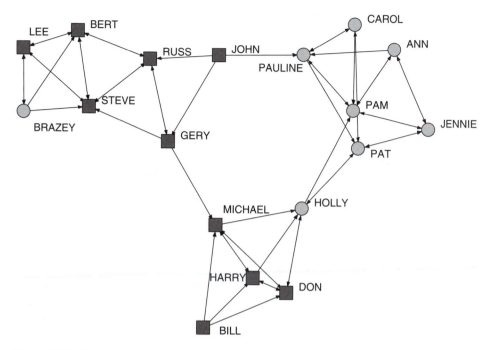

Figure 9.3 Campnet data with gender attribute.

This suggests thinking about cohesion (or non-cohesion) in broadest terms as the number and size of components in the network. The simplest of these is the size of the main component: the bigger the main component (in terms of nodes), the greater the global cohesion of the network. This has been used in looking at networks of HIV transmission (Friedman et al., 1999), and for assessing how well a network survives under attack (Borgatti, 2006b). Of course, this measure assumes there is one large main component, and this is not always the case. We therefore need more sophisticated measures which take into account the different components in a network.

One possibility is to look at the number of components in the graph. If c is the number of components and n is the number of nodes in the graph then we divide $c - 1$ by $n - 1$. This normalized measure – called the 'component ratio' – achieves its maximum value of 1.0 when every node is an isolate, and its minimum value of 0 when there is just one component. Obviously, this is an inverse measure of cohesion as larger values indicate less cohesion. It can be subtracted from 1 to measure cohesion.

One problem with the component ratio is that it is not very sensitive: a large number of networks that vary, at least intuitively, in cohesiveness may have the same score on this measure. A more sensitive measure along these same lines is called 'connectedness' (Krackhardt, 1994) or 'fragmentation' (Borgatti, 2006b). Connectedness is defined as the proportion of pairs of nodes that can reach each other by a path of any length – in other words, the proportion of pairs of nodes that are located in the same component.[1] The formula for connectedness in directed non-reflexive graphs is given by

$$\frac{\sum_{i \neq j} r_{ij}}{n(n-1)} \tag{9.2}$$

where r_{ij} is 1 if nodes i and j are in the same component and 0 otherwise. Fragmentation is 1 minus connectedness, and is interpreted as the number of pairs of nodes that cannot reach each other by any means.

We can see how connectedness captures cohesion by calculating the index for the directed Campnet data shown in Figure 9.3, where the network is defined by each person's top three choices. This has a connectedness index of 0.40. In contrast, if we define the network by each actor's top four choices, the connectedness index jumps up to 0.889.

The typical usage of connectedness or fragmentation is in evaluating changes to a network either in reality or as part of a what-if simulation. For example, if we are trying to prevent a terrorist organization from coordinating attacks, we could figure out which key actors to arrest in order to maximally fragment the network. A computer algorithm could search through the space of combinations of actors to determine a good set whose removal would maximally increase fragmentation (Borgatti, 2006b).

A variation on connectedness, called 'compactness', weights the paths connecting nodes inversely by their length:

$$\frac{\sum_{i \neq j} \left(\dfrac{1}{d_{ij}} \right)}{n(n-1)} \tag{9.3}$$

Compactness just replaces r_{ij} in equation (9.2) with $1/d_{ij}$, where d_{ij} is the geodesic distance from i to j and $1/d_{ij}$ is set to 0 when no path exists from i to j. Compactness is generally better than its simpler cousin, the average geodesic distance in the network. The advantage of average distance is that it can be interpreted as an index of the expected time to arrival of something flowing from one randomly chosen node to another, provided the something always traveled via the shortest paths. Clearly, if things flowing through the network can reach nodes quickly, the network has a certain kind of cohesion. The difficulty with the average geodesic distance and its variants is that it cannot be applied to disconnected graphs (i.e., ones with multiple components), since some distances are not defined. For this

---

[1] Connectedness can also be seen as the density of the reachability matrix R, where R is defined as in Equation 9.2.

reason, we recommend the compactness measure.[2] Note that we can measure fragmentation as 1 minus compactness, a quantity often called breadth.

An approach completely different from cohesion is robustness. Robustness measures how difficult it is to disconnect the network by removing nodes or lines. If you need to remove quite a few nodes or lines to increase the number of components in the graph, then the network is highly robust and in this sense cohesive. Equivalently, if you have to remove many lines or nodes, then there must be many fully independent paths between the nodes, again suggesting cohesion. This suggests that the graph-theoretic concepts of cutpoint and vertex cutset, as well as bridge and edge cutset, might be useful. Indeed, both the vertex connectivity and the edge connectivity of a graph can be seen as measures of cohesion. The greater the value, the more independent paths there are between all pairs of nodes, and the more cohesive the network.

9.3 Reciprocity

If ties are directed, we are often interested in the extent to which a tie from A to B is matched by one from B to A. Hence if we have relations such as 'helps', 'gives advice to' or 'lends money to' and the amount that these are reciprocated varies greatly for similar networks then we may wish to investigate if there is some underlying reason (e.g., hierarchy, wealth inequality or cultural taboo). A simple measure of reciprocity is simply to count the number of reciprocated ties and divide these by the total number of ties. If we do this for the Campnet data in Figure 9.3 we find that just over 54% of the ties have been reciprocated. Note that UCINET also reports the number of symmetric pairs as well as the reciprocated ties. A symmetric pair would include reciprocated ties together with the case where neither actor choses the other, that is, a reciprocated zero in the adjacency matrix.

9.4 Transitivity and the clustering coefficient

For many social relations we might expect that if A is related to B and B is related to C then there would be a relationship from A to C. When this is the case we say the triad is transitive. One way to think of this is that the friends of your friends are your friends. When networks have a lot of transitivity, they tend to have a clumpy structure. That is, they contain knots of nodes that are all interrelated. The tendency toward transitivity is defined by a ratio in which the numerator is the number of triads in which A-->C, and the denominator is the number of triads in which A-->B *and* B-->C. This is expressed in matrix terms as

---

[2] Of course, one could 'fix' average distance by replacing the missing values with a constant, such as 1 + max, where max is the largest distance observed in the network.

$$\frac{\Sigma_{i,j,k} x_{ij} x_{jk} x_{ik}}{\Sigma_{i,j,k} x_{ij} x_{jk}} \tag{9.4}$$

The summations can be restricted to $i \neq j \neq k$ for non-reflexive graphs. Applying this to the Campnet data yields a score of 0.48, which is quite high.

Watts and Strogatz (1998) proposed a measure for undirected networks that they called the 'clustering coefficient' to capture the extent to which a network had areas of high and low density. Their measure starts by measuring the density of ties in each node's ego network (i.e., the density of ties among nodes connected to a given node). This is called the individual clustering coefficient. They then average this quantity across all nodes to get the overall clustering coefficient. It turns out, however, that for measuring clumpiness, it is better to take a weighted average, where the weights are the number of pairs of nodes in each node's ego network. This is $n_i(n_i - 1)/2$, where n_i is the number of nodes that node i is connected to. The weighted average is called the weighted overall clustering coefficient, and this turns out to be identical to the transitivity coefficient defined in equation (9.4). Whether called transitivity or the clustering coefficient, this metric has been used extensively to measure the amount of clustering or clumpiness in a network. However, while it is true that clustered networks tend to have a high clustering coefficient, many other networks can also have high clustering coefficients, so it is not an ideal measure.

Watts and Strogatz used the clustering coefficient as part of an effort to define 'small-world networks'. Essentially, the idea is that human social systems are very clumpy (thanks to factors such as homophily, geographical concentration, and a tendency to develop relations with one's relations' relations), but also, as discovered by Milgram (1967), very compact, in the sense of having surprisingly short paths linking everyone to everyone else. The surprise is both a naïve cultural kind of surprise ('isn't it extraordinary that we millions of people are linked, on average, by no more than six degrees of separation?') but also a more mathematical kind of surprise because the more transitivity there is in a network the longer path distances tend to be. So human systems seemed to present a paradox: they are both clumpy and short-pathed. Watts and Strogatz soon discovered that the paradox was easily resolved: it only takes a few connections between clumps to shorten average path length considerably, so the class of networks that are both clumpy and have shorts paths is quite a bit bigger than initially thought. Still, there remains an interest in the literature in determining whether any given network is a 'small-world network', and this is done by testing that the clustering coefficient of the observed network is large relative to random graphs (in which the clustering coefficient will be very close to graph density) and that the average distance approaches the average distance in random graphs (which is quite small). More information on detecting small-world networks can be found in Chapter 14.

9.5 Triad census

Measuring transitivity involves counting the occurrences of at least two triadic configurations, which are labeled 'transitive' and 'intransitive' in Figure 9.4. One measure of transitivity is the number of transitive triads divided by the number of transitive plus intransitive triads.

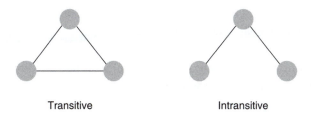

Transitive   Intransitive

Figure 9.4   Transitive and intransitive triads in undirected graphs.

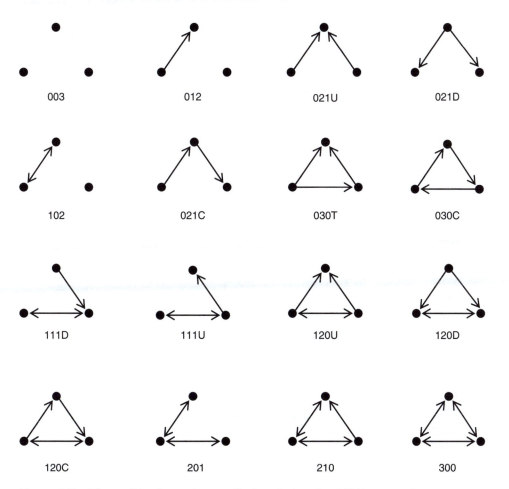

Figure 9.5   All possible directed non-reflexive triads using MAN nomenclature.

However, there are many other triadic configurations we could count which could be used to characterize a network. For directed non-reflexive graphs there are 16 possible configurations, as shown in Figure 9.5. The triads are labeled using the MAN convention (Holland and Leinhardt, 1976) where M stands for 'mutuals' (i.e., dyads with reciprocated ties), A stands for 'asymmetrics' (i.e., dyads with unreciprocated ties), and N stands for 'nulls' (i.e., dyads with no tie). The name of a triad is given by the number of Ms, As and Ns. For example, the first triad is 003, which is a triad that has no mutual dyads, no asymmetric dyads, and in fact consists of three unrelated nodes – three null dyads. The intransitive triad is labeled 021C because it has no mutual dyads, two asymmetric dyads, and one null dyad (the C, for 'cycle', distinguishes it from two other configurations that have the same MAN count).

Given a network, we can count the number of times each of these configurations occurs, creating a profile of measures that characterizes the network. As always, the numbers are not terribly informative in themselves: they are best used comparatively. As an example, we study the triad census in a food web at four points in time (corresponding to the four seasons). The data we use are from the Chesapeake Bay marine ecosystem, collected by Baird and Ulanowicz (1989). The nodes are species, or in some cases compartments, which are aggregations of similar species. For each season, the network consists of who eats whom.

Table 9.2 Triad census of Chesapeake Bay ecosystem data by season.

Triad	Spring	Summer	Fall	Winter
003	4487	4359	4539	4906
012	1937	2001	1884	1663
102	75	71	88	118
021D	115	136	119	88
021U	259	300	273	180
021C	156	153	113	67
111D	25	27	44	37
111U	14	13	11	13
030T	46	54	46	39
030C	7	4	0	0
201	0	0	1	1
120D	8	6	7	8
120U	7	8	7	9
120C	1	5	5	5
210	3	3	3	6
300	0	0	0	0

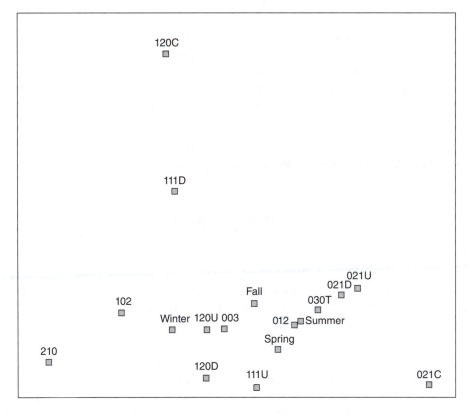

Figure 9.6 Correspondence analysis of triads in Chesapeake Bay ecosystem data.

Table 9.2 shows the raw counts of the number of triads of each type in each season. It is readily noticeable that the proportions of each kind of triad are basically similar across the seasons, but there are differences. For example, winter features quite a few more 003 triads, where no nodes interact, and correspondingly fewer of most other kinds of triads. It is worth pausing to consider what the different triads mean in this context. A transitive triad (030T), represents omnivory – eating at multiple levels in the food chain. That is, species A eats species B, which eats C, but A also eats C, so it is eating at two separate levels of the food chain. A triad containing a mutual dyad, such as 102, reflects a pair of species that eat each other. This is not as rare as it sounds, but is also due to aggregating different species together into a single node.

In order to see the pattern of differences more clearly, we can use correspondence analysis (see Chapter 6). Figure 9.6 shows the results of a correspondence analysis of the triads in Table 9.2, omitting the three rows that have any zeros. It can be seen that seasons trace an arc through the space, starting with spring at the bottom right and moving counterclockwise to winter. This shows that adjacent seasons are particularly similar to each other, as we would expect. Another pattern we see is that on the right-hand side of the plot, corresponding to warmer months, we have triads that begin with 0, meaning they have no mutual dyads. On the left, corresponding to colder months, are triads that have 1s and even 2s as the first number. These are triads in which there are pairs that eat each other. One explanation is that when the weather is warmer, there are more species available and there is no need to resort to reciprocal trophic inter-actions. In winter, there is a kind of contraction of the ecosystem, with less variety available and more reciprocal interactions.[3]

9.6 Centralization and core–periphery indices

We began this chapter by alluding to the concept of centralization. Here, we flesh it out a little more. Centralization refers to the extent a network is domi-nated by a single node. A maximally centralized graph looks like a star: the node at the center of the network has ties to all other nodes, and no other ties exist (see Figure 9.7). A measure of centralization, then, is a measure of the extent to which a network resembles a star.

There are many ways one could think of to construct such a measure, but the one that has become standard is the approach by Freeman (1979). In his approach, we begin by computing a measure of node centrality (see Chapter 10) for each node in the network. For example, we might compute degree centrality, which is simply the number of ties a node has. To calculate centralization, we sum the dif-ference between each node's centrality and the centrality of the most central node. For example, for the network in Figure 9.8, the most central node has 4 ties, and the sum of differences is $(4 - 2) + (4 - 2) + (4 - 2) + (4 - 2) + (4 - 4) = 8$. We then divide this by the maximum possible, which is the score that the star graph would get. Looking at Figure 9.7, it is clear that the sum of differences for the star graph is $(4 - 1) + (4 - 1) + (4 - 1) + (4 - 1) + (4 - 4) = 12$. So for the graph in Figure 9.8, the centralization score, based on degree centrality, is $8/12 = 0.667$.

A network structure similar in spirit to centralization is the core–periphery structure. A network with a core–periphery structure can be seen as having two kinds of nodes: core nodes, which are connected to each other and to others, and periphery nodes, which are connected only to core nodes. A core–periphery network is a clumpy network that only has one clump, which is the core. However, it is not necessary to think of a core–periphery structure in terms of discrete classes of nodes. We can also think of coreness as a continuous property

---

[3] However, there is also an artifactual element here as some of the nodes are collections of species that have been lumped together into what are called 'compartments'.

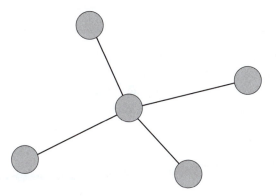

Figure 9.7 A star network with five nodes.

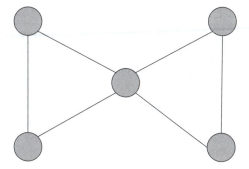

Figure 9.8 A bow-tie network.

of nodes. In this case, a core–periphery structure is one in which the probability (or strength) of a tie between two nodes is a function of the product of each of their corenesses. This neatly generalizes the discrete view we presented first: two nodes that have high coreness will be connected to each other, and two nodes that are peripheral (have low coreness) will probably not be connected to each other. To the extent that we can assign coreness scores to nodes such that the presence or absence of a tie between nodes can be predicted by the product of their coreness scores, we have a core–periphery structure. In this sense, the core-periphery model is analogous to the model of independence in contingency table analysis. This tells us that one way core-periphery structures can arise is when nodes associate at random, differing only in the frequency with which they make connections. Models of core–periphery structures are described in more detail in Chapter 12. For our present purposes, it is enough to note that it is possible to measure the core/peripheriness of a network, and this is essentially done by comparing our observed network to an idealized model.

9.7 Summary

It can be useful to summarize properties of whole networks – such as cohesion – that reflect important aspects of the network. A wide variety of measures are available, including those that simply aggregate lower-level measures such as node or dyad characteristics. Two basic classes of whole-network measures are cohesion measures and shape measures. Cohesion measures include such things as average distance between pairs of nodes and number of nodes that have to be removed from the network in order to disconnect a randomly chosen pair. Shape measures include such properties as centralization, core-peripheriness and clumpiness (e.g., as measured by transitivity).

9.8 Problems and Exercises

1. For the next series of exercises data from a study of the network dynamics of polar research stations will be used. The data represent the social networks of crews at the Amundsen Scott South Pole station at the beginning of the Austral winter and at the end of the winter in terms of reports of social interactions (see Johnson et al., 2003 for a description). A comparison of the characteristics of the social networks of the crew at the beginning and end of the winter at the network level will help inform an understanding of the evolution of network structure over the course of the long winter (March to October). The social networks of the crew in March and October (dichotomized network of strong relations) are shown in Figures 9.9 and 9.10.

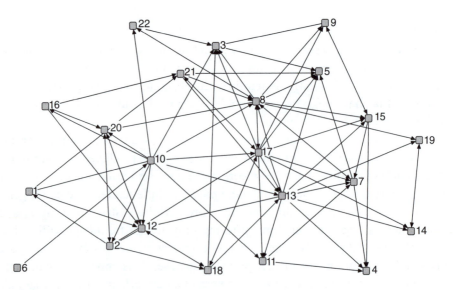

Figure 9.9 Social network at beginning of Austral winter (Beginningwinter.##h)

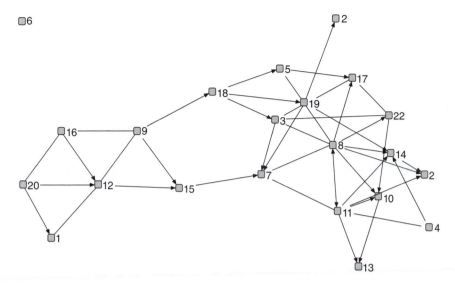

Figure 9.10   Social network at end of Austral winter (Endwinter.##h)

a. One classic measure of network level cohesion is density. Using UCINET deter-
    mine the densities of the social network at both the beginning and end of the
    winter (this will require two separate runs). In UCINET go to Network|Cohesion
    |Density|Density Overall and upload each of the data files and run. What might
    you conclude about the differences in densities over time?
b. Another network level measure of cohesion is transitivity. Similar to the density
    problem above, do an analysis of the changes in transitivity using UCINET for
    each network. Go to Network|Cohesion|Transitivity and upload the matrix and
    click OK. Do a separate run for each. How does transitivity change over the
    course of the winter?
c. Given this is a directed network we can also do a full triad census. For each
    network in UCINET go to Network|Triad Census and load the network file and
    click OK (do a run for each network). Be sure to save each of the ucinetlog files
    for comparison. In comparing the networks how did the number of empty and
    complete subgraphs change in the network over the winter?
d. Another measure of network cohesion is the clustering coefficient. For each
    network in UCINET go to Network|Cohesion|Clustering Coefficient and input
    the networks (be sure to save the ucinetlog files for comparison). How do the
    networks compare?
e. Another important measure of overall cohesion is reciprocity. For each network
    in UCINET go to Network|Cohesion|Reciprocity and input the networks. Using
    the default method of Hybrid click OK (be sure to save the log files). Has reci-
    procity increased or decreased over the winter?

2. In comparing across these different measures of network level cohesion what could
    one conclude about the changes in network level cohesion over the course of the
    austral winter at the station?

10

Centrality

Learning Outcomes

1. Apply centrality measures appropriately
2. Interpret the results of a centrality analysis on undirected, directed and valued data
3. Understand the limitations and constraints of the standard centrality measures

10.1 Introduction

David Krackhardt (1992) tells the story of a unionization drive in a Silicon Valley firm. The union made an enthusiastically pro-union worker named Hal their point man for the campaign. Eventually, there was a vote and the union lost by a good margin. A look at the network of friendships among the workers showed something interesting about Hal, which was that he was quite peripheral in the friendship network. In contrast, Chris, whom the union never approached, was highly central in the friendship network – in fact, the informal leader. Chris was pro-union, but also very friendly with the owner, and concerned that the union might hurt profits. When the election came, Chris abstained. Had he been lobbied by the union and assured that they did not want to harm profits, just make sure the workers shared in them, he would have voted for them – and persuaded many others. Krackhardt uses this story to illustrate the power of centrality in determining events, and also the importance of knowing who is central when you are trying to get something done.

10.2 Basic concept

Centrality is a property of a node's[1] position in a network. It is not one thing but rather a family of concepts. Loosely speaking, one way to think about node centrality is in terms of the contribution the node makes to the structure of the network. In this sense, we might regard centrality as the structural importance of a node. However, there are many different ways in which a node can be important to a structure. For example, a node might be important because removing the node would tend to disconnect the network. Or a node might be important because a large number of ties in the network involve that node.

Another way to think about centrality is in terms of the advantage that accrues to a node by virtue of its position in the network. This is often with respect to things flowing through the network, such as information.[2] A node might be highly central in the sense of being well positioned to catch what is passing from node to node, and to catch it early. Or a node might be central in terms of being able to control the flow of information, whether in the sense of filtering key bits or passing it along but coloring it in ways that benefit the node.

All these different conceptions give rise to different measures of centrality. It should be noted that measures of centrality are normally computed with respect to a single relation – if a dataset contains multiple relations for the same set of nodes, a separate set of centrality scores is computed for each relation, which could then be compared or aggregated. For example, we might construct an overall centrality score for each node by running a factor analysis and taking the first factor as a summary measure.

Sociologically, centrality is interpreted in a wide variety of ways, many of which are quite fanciful. People refer to central nodes as prominent, or influential, or leaders, or gatekeepers, or as having great autonomy, control, visibility, involvement, prestige, power and so on. It is important to realize that these are not definitions or inherent properties of centrality but rather hypotheses about the potential consequences of centrality, either for the node or the group in which they are embedded.

In general, for non-negative relations such as friendship or trust, centrality tends to be viewed as a positive thing for nodes, providing actors with opportunities to influence others and receive flows (including information, support and material aid). As such, centrality is seen as falling under the general rubric of social capital concepts, in which a node's position is a source of opportunities

---

[1] Actually, Everett and Borgatti (1999) have extended centrality to apply to groups of nodes in addition to individual nodes. But this topic is beyond the scope of this book.

[2] See Borgatti (2005) for a discussion of the flow-based view of centrality.

and advantage. Thus, in empirical studies, centrality is often used as an independent variable to predict positive outcomes for nodes, such as the acquisition
of wealth or status, or life satisfaction, health, and so on. Of course, whether the
outcomes are positive or not depends on the nature of what is flowing through
the network. A person central in a face-to-face interaction network may have
many positive consequences, but they are also more likely to be exposed to
contagious diseases.

Network research is also interested in how nodes come to be central. For
example, we might hypothesize that in a given social context one gender would
be more central than the other, or that certain personality types such as extro-
verts and high self-monitors would tend to become central in groups. Another
generic hypothesis is that various kinds of human capital can bring about centrality, as when people with great expertise are sought out for advice.

There are dozens of centrality concepts that have been put forth in the literature, each with associated measures and/or algorithms. In this chapter, we
discuss just a few key constructs that we have found particularly useful in practice or are commonly used (this includes closeness, a measure we do not
recommend using, for reasons discussed later).

10.3 Undirected, non-valued networks

For simplicity of exposition, we initially describe all measures in the context of
undirected (i.e., symmetric) and non-valued networks. Then, in a separate section, we reexamine the measures in the context of non-symmetric and valued
data. The chapter concludes with pointers to additional centrality concepts and
more advanced applications.

10.3.1 Degree centrality

Perhaps the simplest measure of centrality is degree, which is simply the number of ties of a given type that a node has. A node's degree can be calculated
without having information about the full network in which they are embedded.
As such, it could be argued that it is not really a measure of a centrality, which
we defined above as a property of a node's *position* in the network. However, we
include it here out of respect for tradition.

In terms of the adjacency matrix X of an undirected network, degree centrality is simply the row (or column) sums of the adjacency matrix. If d_i is the degree
centrality of actor i and x_{ij} is the (i, j) entry of the adjacency matrix, then

$$d_i = \sum_j x_{ij} \tag{10.1}$$

Depending on the nature of the network ties, we can interpret degree centrality in a variety of ways. For example, if the tie is friendship, degree centrality is the number of friends a node has, and might be hypothesized to relate (though perhaps not linearly) to the amount of emotional support available to the person, the opportunities to attend social events, etc. If the tie is trust, it might be hypothesized to relate to the number of people that the node is in a position to influence directly. Similarly, high-degree nodes are highly visible, and tend to be seen as important. For example, in organizations, nodes with high degree in an organizational network tend to be the same ones that insiders will list as the important people in the group.

If we assume that things – such as information and infections – flow through ties, then degree centrality can be seen as an index of the exposure of a node in the network – that is, the 'risk' of receiving whatever is flowing through the network (whether it is information in a gossip network or an infection in a sexual network). It can be shown mathematically that if something is taking a random walk through the network, the probability that it reaches a particular node is proportional to its degree. It is important to note, however, that many interesting flows probably do not traverse networks as random walks. For example, gossip may flow randomly in many respects, but is usually biased against traveling over the same link multiple times. In other words, a person may receive a given bit of gossip many times, but they tend not to tell the same person the same story over and over again.

Having computed degree (and any other measure of centrality), one would typically add it to a node-level database that contains other variables measured on the same nodes, such as gender, organizational rank, and race. We can then use conventional statistics to relate centrality to these other variables. For example, we might use a t-test to compare the degree centrality of men and women in an organization.

We can run such a test in UCINET using the Tools|Statistics|Vector|T-Test procedure. First we run degree centrality on a symmetrized version of the familiar Campnet data, resulting in Figure 10.1. The individual degree centralities are given in column 1; these are often called the raw scores. The second column gives a normalized score which is the raw score divided by the maximum possible in a network of the same size and expressed as a percentage. Since the network has 18 actors the highest possible centrality would be 17 (as there are 17 others to connect to) and so the second column is derived by dividing the numbers in the first column by 17 and multiplying by 100. The third column is the share; this is the centrality of each actor divided by the sum of all the actor centralities in the network.

We can now run the permutation-based UCINET T-Test procedure to see if there are any differences in the centralities of the women and the men. The inputs

		Degre	nDegr
1	HOLLY	5.000	0.294
2	BRAZEY	3.000	0.176
3	CAROL	3.000	0.176
4	PAM	5.000	0.294
5	PAT	4.000	0.235
6	JENNIE	3.000	0.176
7	PAULINE	5.000	0.294
8	ANN	3.000	0.176
9	MICHAEL	5.000	0.294
10	BILL	3.000	0.176
11	LEE	3.000	0.176
12	DON	4.000	0.235
13	JOHN	3.000	0.176
14	HARRY	4.000	0.235
15	GERY	4.000	0.235
16	STEVE	5.000	0.294
17	BERT	4.000	0.235
18	RUSS	4.000	0.235

Figure 10.1   UCINET degree centrality on symmetrized Campnet data.

		1 Group	2 Group
1	Mean	3.88	3.90
2	Std Dev	0.93	0.70
3	Sum	31.00	39.00
4	Variance	0.86	0.49
5	SSQ	127.00	157.00
6	MCSSQ	6.88	4.90
7	Euc Norm	11.27	12.53
8	Minimum	3.00	3.00
9	Maximum	5.00	5.00
10	N of Obs	8.00	10.00
11	N Missing	10.00	8.00

SIGNIFICANCE TESTS

Difference in Means	...One-Tailed Tests... Group 1 > 2	 Group 2 > 1	Two-Tailed Test
===============	===============	===============	===============
-0.025	0.637	0.591	0.9999

Figure 10.2   Output for t-test on degree centralities.

to this procedure include both the centrality of each node and the gender of each node. It then computes the mean centrality for each gender and calculates the significance of the difference, using a permutation test (see Chapter 8 for a discussion of permutation tests). The result is shown in Figure 10.2. In this output we can see that the means are very similar (3.88 and 3.90), and the two-tailed test has a p-value very close to 1 (0.9999), and hence we conclude that there is no difference in centralities between the two groups.

An advantage of degree centrality is that it is basically interpretable in all kinds of networks, including disconnected networks. A disadvantage of degree centrality is that it is a relatively coarse measure of centrality. For example, if a node is connected to five others that have no other ties, the centrality of this node is no different from the centrality of a node that is connected to five others that are well connected themselves and in the center of a network.

10.3.2 Eigenvector centrality

Eigenvector centrality can be described from a number of different perspectives (Bonacich, 1972). We present it here as a variation of degree centrality in which we count the number of nodes adjacent to a given node (just like degree centrality), but weight each adjacent node by its centrality:

$$e_i = \lambda \sum_j x_{ij} e_j \tag{10.2}$$

where e is the eigenvector centrality score and λ (lambda) is a proportionality constant called the eigenvalue. The equation basically says that each node's centrality is proportional to the sum of centralities of the nodes it is adjacent to – in effect, when it comes to eigenvector centrality, a node is only as central as its network. It should be noted that an adjacency matrix could have many vectors (and associated eigenvalues) that satisfy the equation, and each of these vectors is an eigenvector of the adjacency matrix. By convention (and for good mathematical reasons), we regard eigenvector centrality as the eigenvector with the biggest eigenvalue. One further issue with eigenvectors is that a multiple of an eigenvector is also an eigenvector (this can easily be seen by multiplying both sides of equation (10.2) by a constant). A simple way to make them unique is to make all the entries positive and force the sum of squares to be equal to 1, but other approaches can be taken. This is not an issue when comparing centrality scores with each other within a network, but it can be an issue when comparing scores across different networks.

We can interpret eigenvector centrality as a measure of popularity in the sense that a node with high eigenvector centrality is connected to nodes that are

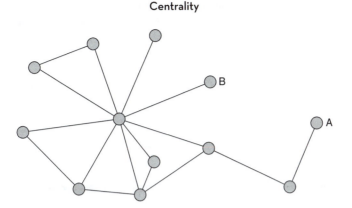

Figure 10.3 A sexual contact network.

themselves well connected. This means that a node with small degree could have a higher score than a node with high degree if the first node's friends are very popular while the second node's friends are not.

In a flow context, we could also view eigenvector centrality as a more sophisticated measure of risk.[3] For example, consider the hypothetical network of sexual ties in Figure 10.3. Nodes A and B both have degree 1. But they do not have the same level of risk because the node that B is having sex with, is having sex with many others. Eigenvector centrality captures this difference and assigns B a higher score. However, we need to be careful here in making this risk-based interpretation, because eigenvector centrality does not take into account the fact that your friends' connections might be to the same people you are already connected to, yielding an inflated estimate of risk.

An important issue with eigenvector centrality is that in disconnected networks it will assign zeros to all members of the smaller components. Furthermore, if a network has a bow-tie structure such as shown in Figure 10.4, the scores for all the nodes in the smaller subgroup will have uniformly lower scores than the nodes in the larger subgroup. This is not precisely a flaw since in fact the nodes in the smaller group are connected to nodes that really are less well connected, but it is something one might want to take account of, particularly in the case where the groups correspond to, say, organizational subunits and the size of the subunits is determined by a variable extraneous to the processes being researched.

One final point relates to the fact that we are interested in the eigenvector associated with the largest eigenvalue. If this is similar in size to the second largest

---

[3] Since we are dealing only with undirected networks at this point, we should note that the risk of receiving something is the same as the capacity to transmit.

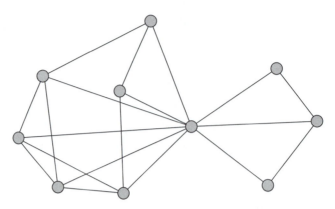

Figure 10.4 A bow-tie network structure.

eigenvalue then our centrality scores can be seen as somewhat arbitrary. Ideally, the largest eigenvalue should be two or three times as large as the second largest. Otherwise, it could be argued that you really need more than one eigenvector to represent the position of the node in the network, which may be inconvenient when testing hypotheses. For example, if you expect centrality to moderate the relationship between an employee's tenure in the organization and their performance, the interaction terms involving two variables that jointly represent centrality can get complicated and the results difficult to interpret.

10.3.3 Beta centrality

An interesting measure that in a sense generalizes both degree and eigenvector centrality is beta centrality (Bonacich, 1987). Beta centrality is defined as the row sums of the matrix represented by the equation

$$c = (I - \beta A)^{-1} A1 \tag{10.3}$$

although this is not very illuminating.[4] What is more illuminating is that, under certain conditions, the matrix in equation (10.3) is equal to the convergent infinite sum as shown in the equation

$$c = \sum_{k=1}^{\infty} \beta^{k-1} A^k 1 = A1 + \beta A^2 1 + \beta^2 A^3 1 + \dots \tag{10.4}$$

---

[4] We omit Bonacich's alpha parameter which serves to normalize the resulting centrality score.

which is much easier to interpret. The terms in equation (10.4) consist of powers of the adjacency matrix, and it is well known that the (i, j) cell of the kth power of an adjacency matrix gives the number of walks of length k from i to j. The β parameter (which is chosen by the user) serves as a length-based weight. Hence the sum of the series gives the total number of walks between each pair of nodes of all possible lengths, weighted by β^{k-1}.

When β is zero, the beta centrality reduces to simple degree centrality, because zero to any non-zero power is zero, thus all but the first matrix in the infinite series will be weighted zero and so knocked out. As we increase β, though, longer walks will begin to count as well. For example, if β is 0.2, then walks of length 2 will be weighted 0.2, walks of length 3 will be weighted $0.2^2 = 0.04$, and so on. Really long walks – say, of length 10 – will still be largely ignored, since 0.2^9 is only 0.000000512. If we think of a walk from a node to another node as a channel of potential indirect influence, what β does is determine how much we are going to count long walks in measuring the amount of influence a node might have on others. Therefore, we can think of beta centrality as a measure of the total amount of potential influence a node can have on all others via direct and indirect channels, where indirect channels are weighted (inversely) by their length, and β controls how much the longer walks are counted.

Now let us consider what happens if we continue to increase β. When the absolute value of β equals $1/\lambda$ (the reciprocal of the largest eigenvalue of the adjacency matrix), the infinite sum no longer converges and equation (10.4) cannot be calculated. However, if we let the absolute value of β get as close as we like to $1/\lambda$ without actually reaching that value, the corresponding measure will become as indistinguishable as we like from eigenvector centrality. Thus, from the lens of beta centrality we can view degree centrality and eigenvector centrality as two poles in a continuum of measures that vary in the extent to which longer walks are counted.

Thus, the advantage of beta centrality is that we can choose in-between values of β that reflect our conception of how much longer channels of influence matter. The problem is that we must somehow figure out what value that should be. Ideally, we would have some kind of theory that would say that, in the particular context of our study, β should be a certain value. Unfortunately, we are unlikely to have such a theory.

Alternatively, we can choose β empirically to maximize predictive ability. For example, suppose we are investigating how social position in an organization relates to knowledge of recent gossip. We use surveys to measure the network at time T, and the amount of knowledge each person has at $T + 1$. We then calculate beta centrality for a wide range of βs from 0 to just under the reciprocal of the largest eigenvalue, and correlate each with knowledge. The β that yields the largest correlation is the one we choose. We then interpret the value of the optimal β by looking at where it is in the range. If it is closer to zero, we know that, in our research setting, it is only short paths that are important. If it is closer to $1/\lambda$, we know that we are looking at a phenomenon where even long paths really matter. In UCINET's command line interface (CLI), we can compute centralities for multiple betas like this:

```
->mb = betacent(campnet 0 0.3)
->dsp mb
```

The result will be 10 columns of scores, corresponding to beta = 0, beta = 0.03, beta = 0.06 and so on up to beta = 0.3 (we chose 0.3 as the upper end because the reciprocal of the largest eigenvalue of the Campnet adjacency matrix is 0.33).

One thing we have not explicitly mentioned is that β can be negative. When it is, we can see that what equation (10.4) does is subtract the weighted counts of walks of even length (corresponding to k being 2, 4, 6, ...) from the count of walks of odd length. As a result, a node like X in Figure 10.5 gets a higher score than the Ys when β is positive but a lower score than the Ys when β is negative. This is because there are so many nodes (the Zs) that are even lengths from X.

The thought here is that beta centrality with a negative β captures power dynamics in settings where power is a function of (a) the number of alters a node Y has to exchange with, and (b) the paucity of alternatives to Y that Y's

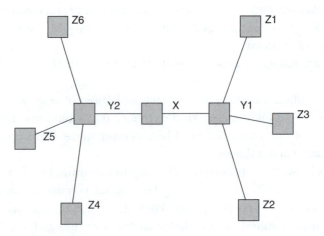

Figure 10.5 An exchange network.

alters have. For example, in a trading context, if you have many potential partners to trade with, but they only have you, you are in the driver's seat. Since the
number of nodes you can reach in two links corresponds to the number of alternatives your partners have to you, subtracting these from your power score
makes sense. In practice, using a negative β can make surprisingly little difference. In part, this is a function of the structure of the network, and in part it
occurs because beta centrality counts walks rather than the number of distinct
nodes at various distances. One other issue when selecting negative β is that the
centrality scores themselves can be negative, implying that an actor would be
better off not having any connections. It is possible to think of situations in
which this could occur but these are rare, and in those cases it is probably better
to increase the value of β to eliminate negative scores.

10.3.4 Closeness centrality

Freeman (1979) defined closeness centrality as the sum of geodesic distances
from a node to all others. (Recall that the geodesic distance from a node to
another node is the length of the shortest path connecting them.) Closeness is
an inverse measure of centrality in the sense that large numbers indicate that
a node is highly peripheral, while small numbers indicate that a node is more
central. In actual usage, people often use a normalized version in which each
node's centrality is divided into $n - 1$, which is the minimum possible score
(and occurs when a node has a direct tie to all $n - 1$ other nodes in the network). This has the effect of not only reversing the values so that large
numbers correspond to greater centrality, but also normalizing the values to
have a maximum of 100%.

In a flow context, we typically interpret closeness centrality in terms of
the minimum time until the arrival of something flowing through the network. A node that has a high normalized closeness score is a short distance
from most others, so information originating at a random node can potentially reach the central node very quickly. Also, since the diffusion process
tends to introduce distortion, we expect the information received by central
nodes to have higher fidelity on average. Thus, a high normalized closeness
would seem a significant advantage for a node (in the case of something useful
being transmitted).

Closeness centrality is problematic in disconnected networks. The distance
from a node to a node in another component is undefined since there is no path
between them. Some people view this distance as infinite, and then represent
this infinite distance with a large constant, such as one more than the maximum
distance observed anywhere in the network. Other approaches include taking

the reciprocal of each dyadic distance and assigning zero as the proximity of two disconnected nodes, or subtracting each dyadic distance from a constant. Unfortunately, none of these is well-justified and tends to result in closeness scores with little variance, a problem that closeness suffers from anyway, leading it to have poor correlations with any variable. For this reason, it is of limited use as a centrality measure.

10.3.5 *k*-step reach centrality

We now turn to k-step reach centrality, which is defined as the number of distinct nodes within k links of a given node (Borgatti, 2006). In other words, it tells you how many nodes a given node can reach in k or fewer steps. A typical number for k would be 2. From the point of view of assessing the risk of catching something, we might view this as an (admittedly simplistic) improvement over eigenvector centrality. A node that is within two links of many others can be seen as (a) having a high probability of catching what they have, and (b) catching it early. By the same token, such a node can also transmit something to many others very quickly. Note that by counting distinct others, the measure avoids the problem with eigenvector centrality that a node may appear to be well connected simply because its alters are well connected to each other.

One issue with interpreting k-step reach in terms of the ability to receive/ send from/to other nodes is that it assumes that paths of length k are just as certain and as high quality as paths shorter than k. For example, if k is 5, a node gets a high score if it can reach many nodes within k steps. But if the process of transmission is at all uncertain, it may be a too optimistic to weight nodes five steps away the same as nodes just one step away. At the same time, if we make k very small, as in 2, we are probably being too pessimistic about the chances of eventually influencing a node many links away.

A better approach might be to weight the nodes being counted inversely by how far away they are. Hence if a node is directly tied to 3 nodes, and two links away from 5 nodes and three links from 12 nodes, then we would construct a score of 3/1 + 5/2 + 12/3 rather than 3 + 5 + 12 as in the unweighted version. This measure (or one proportional to it) is referred to as average reciprocal distance (ARD) in UCINET. Alternatively, we could weight by a fractional constant taken to the power of the distance minus 1. For example, suppose we think that the probability of a node passing something on to another in a given time period is a constant 0.5. Then, in our example, the node's score would be $3 \times 0.5^0 + 5 \times 0.5^1 + 12 \times 0.5^3$. Since the constant 0.5 is smaller than 1, the increasing distances yield a smaller and smaller weight. This approach is very similar to the use of β in beta centrality. In UCINET, this measure is called beta reach centrality.

10.3.6 Betweenness centrality

Betweenness centrality (Freeman, 1979) is a measure of how often a given node falls along the shortest path between two other nodes. More specifically, it is calculated for a given focal node by computing, for each pair of nodes other than the focal node, what proportion of all the shortest paths from one to the other pass through the focal node. These proportions are summed across all pairs and the result is a single value for each node in the network. The formula for the betweenness centrality of node j is given by

$$b_j = \sum_{i<k} \frac{g_{ijk}}{g_{ik}} \tag{10.5}$$

where g_{ijk} is the number of geodesic paths connecting i and k through j, and g_{ik} is the total number of geodesic paths connecting i and k. A node's betweenness is zero when it is never along the shortest path between any two others. This can occur when the node is an isolate, or when every alter of a node is connected to every other alter. Betweenness reaches its maximum value when the node lies along every shortest path between every pair of other nodes.

Betweenness is typically interpreted in terms of the potential for controlling flows through the network – that is, playing a gatekeeping or toll-taking role (Brass, 1984). In a sense, nodes with high betweenness are in a position to threaten the network with disruption of operations. More generally, high-betweenness nodes are in a position to filter information and to color or distort it as they pass it along. However, the ability to exploit a high-betweenness position varies inversely with the ease with which nodes can create ties. For example, suppose that a given node has high betweenness, meaning that many nodes need that node to reach other nodes via efficient paths. In principle, this node has power because it can threaten to stop transmitting, making nodes use less efficient paths to reach one another. But this threat only works if the other nodes cannot easily create new ties to simply go around the recalcitrant node.

An appealing example is provided by the medieval Russian trade networks studied by Forrest Pitts (1979). He notes that, in the twelfth century, Moscow was just another principality indistinguishable in all respects from hundreds of others. Soon, however, it began to grow, outstripping the other principalities in the region. The question is why. Was it perhaps due to good leadership? Better than average natural resources? Or something more structural? Pitts notes that every principality was located on a river, which was used for trade. The rivers connect the principalities to form a network of highly durable and difficult-to-create ties in a network of principalities. In this network, Moscow and another town turned out to have the highest betweenness centrality. It was therefore in an excellent position to make demands (e.g., exact tolls) on the traders. Since the traders could not easily create new ties (e.g., redirect rivers), Moscow could effectively enforce its demands.

It is useful to note that, in practice, the variance of betweenness tends to be quite high, providing effective discrimination between nodes and potentially correlating well with other variables.

10.4 Directed, non-valued networks

At least one of the centrality concepts discussed above – namely, betweenness – can be applied to directed data without any important change. For the rest we can usually define an 'out' version and 'in' version, reflecting outgoing versus incoming ties or paths.

10.4.1 Degree

In the previous section, degree was defined as the row sums of an adjacency matrix. Since we were working with undirected networks, the adjacency matrix was symmetric, and we could just as easily have defined degree in terms of the column sums. For directed data, however, the adjacency matrix is not necessarily symmetric, and the row and column sums may be different. For convenience, we refer to the row sums as outdegree, and the column sums as indegree. Outdegree counts the number of outgoing ties (arcs) whereas indegree counts the number of incoming ties. Depending on the social relation in question, we might interpret outdegree as the 'gregarious-ness' or 'expansiveness' of the node and the indegree as the 'prestige' or 'popularity' of the node. For example, this interpretation would make sense for friendship ties. In the case of trust ties, we interpret outdegree as a meas-ure of how trusting a node is, while indegree is a measure of how trustworthy they are. In the case of dislike ties, outdegree is a kind of 'curmudgeonliness' measure, while indegree is a 'dislikeability' measure.

One situation that is worth describing in detail occurs when we collect data of the form 'who do you get X from', as in 'who do you seek advice from'. If a respondent A lists person B, this is an outgoing tie from A, but the flow of advice is incoming to A. So high outdegree in the 'gets advice' relation means that a node is receiving advice from many others, while high indegree indicates the node is sending advice to many others. In cases like this, it often makes sense to transpose the data so that 'gets advice' becomes 'gives advice', and that way ties point in the direction of the motion of whatever is flowing.

In survey data, it is not unusual to regard node outdegree with some suspi-cion as it may reflect differences in interpretation by different respondents, or different levels of social desirability bias. For example, in asking about friend-ship ties within an organization, a node's high outdegree may indicate a very liberal interpretation of the word 'friend', or a feeling that they 'should' list everyone in their work unit as a friend.

10.4.2 Eigenvector and beta centrality

Similar to degree centrality, eigenvector centrality can be 'split' into two con-cepts, right eigenvectors (corresponding to outdegree), and left eigenvectors (corresponding to indegree). If ties indicate who gives advice to whom, the right eigenvector can be seen as a measure of potential to influence others via both direct and indirect ties (i.e., they give advice to many people who in turn give advice to many people, etc.), whereas the left eigenvector indicates the amount of direct and indirect potential influence on the node.

However, there are issues with eigenvectors in directed data. Consider the left eigenvector for the network in Figure 10.6. We see that nodes 1, 2 and 3 have no incoming ties so they get a value of zero. The centrality of node 4 is in turn the sum of its incoming ties, which is also zero. Following on, we would expect node 5 to also have a score of zero but it has a value of 1. The reason is that in this network the constant λ has a value of zero and so the sum model we used breaks down, although the eigenvector is still defined. Of course, we intuitively are happy with a result that gives node 5 higher centrality than the others, but we would also have liked node 4 to have greater centrality than nodes 1, 2 and 3. The right eigenvector is even more problematic. In this

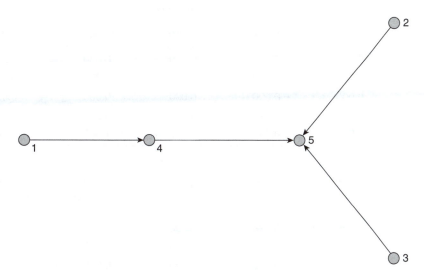

Figure 10.6   A directed network.

instance nodes 4 and 5 get a value of zero but nodes 1, 2 and 3 can take any value, including zero.

As a result, for directed data a much better approach is to use beta centrality. Applying beta centrality to the network in Figure 10.6 for different values of β gives the results shown in Table 10.1. The scores have been normalized so that the sum of squares of all values equals one. The top half of the table gives the 'in' scores. When $\beta = 0$, which gives zero weight to walks longer than one link, we get (normalized) indegree, which is zero for all nodes except 4 and 5. As beta increases, the normalized value of node 4 moves toward zero, and the beta centrality vector converges on the left eigenvector. For the 'out' scores, a $\beta = 0$ gives us normalized outdegree, which means nodes 1, 2, 3 and 4, all have the same score, while node 5 has zero. As β increases, node 1 becomes increasingly more important while the scores for all other nodes tends to zero. Clearly for networks where eigenvector centrality gives sensible results, beta centrality gives the same results (by setting β as close to $1/\lambda$ as possible). And for networks like Figure 10.6, where eigenvectors yield undesirable results, beta centrality manages to give useful results, particularly for lower values of β.

An application of 'in' beta centrality is summarized in the scatterplot shown in Figure 10.7. The data are from a management consulting project. The x-axis is an index of formal power in the client organization, constructed by computing the first principal component of a weighted average of power indicators including rank, tenure (years in the organization), and number of direct subordinates.

Table 10.1 Beta centrality scores for Figure 10.6.

	In scores				
Node	$\beta = 0$	$\beta = 1$	$\beta = 10$	$\beta = 100$	$\beta = 1000$
1	0.000	0.000	0.000	0.000	0.000
2	0.000	0.000	0.000	0.000	0.000
3	0.000	0.000	0.000	0.000	0.000
4	0.316	0.243	0.077	0.010	0.001
5	0.949	0.970	0.997	1.000	1.000
	Out scores				
Node	$\beta = 0$	$\beta = 1$	$\beta = 10$	$\beta = 100$	$\beta = 1000$
1	0.500	0.756	0.988	1.000	1.000
2	0.500	0.378	0.090	0.010	0.001
3	0.500	0.378	0.090	0.010	0.001
4	0.500	0.378	0.090	0.010	0.001
5	0.000	0.000	0.000	0.000	0.000

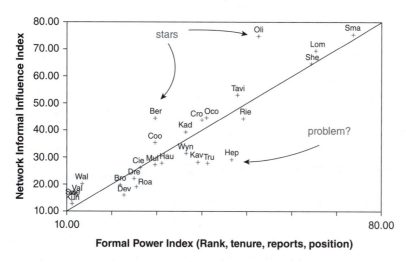

Figure 10.7   Scatterplot of informal power (beta centrality) by formal power.

The weights were determined by factor analysis. The y-axis is an index of informal power, measured as the 'in' beta centrality of the who seeks advice from whom network. A high score indicates that the person is sought after for advice by people who are themselves sought after for advice. The scatterplot shows a strong correlation between formal position and informal position. What is interesting, however, is the outliers. For example, the node 'Oli' is way above the regression line, indicating that in the informal network he is as important as anybody in the organization, including the president. This is someone who is ready to be promoted, and indeed is at risk of leaving if formal recognition isn't forthcoming. In contrast, 'hep' is below the line, indicating that they are much lower in the informal network than would be expected given their formal position. This person might be a candidate for executive coaching.

10.4.3 Closeness and k-reach centrality

Closeness centrality is not well suited to directed data. While we can easily define in-closeness as the column sums of the geodesic distance matrix and out-closeness as the row sums, the problem we run into is that directed graphs are particularly likely to be fragmented, so there are pairs of actors X and Y in which either X cannot reach Y or Y cannot reach X. Graphs in which every pair of actors is mutually reachable are called 'strongly connected' and closeness can be defined for these networks, but these are unusual in real data. We can, of course, apply the same techniques for our weakly or disconnected graphs as we did in the undirected case, but with an increased number of undefined distances, the closeness scores become even less meaningful, and variance across actors gets very low.

10.5 Valued networks

Degree centrality is easily extended to valued networks by taking the tie values into account – we define the valued degree centrality simply as the average value of each row (or column) of the adjacency matrix (for outdegree), or even more simply we can use the sum. Both eigenvector and beta centrality work without modification on valued data (provided the values are not negative). For eigenvector centrality, a node's centrality is proportional to the sum of centralities of its alters, but weighted by the strength of tie to that alter. This means that a high-valued connection to a low-centrality actor would produce a similar result as having a low-valued connection to a highly central actor.

Both betweenness and closeness rely on identifying optimal paths, which in the case of binary data can be unproblematically identified as shortest paths. But if the ties are valued, there are a variety of possibilities in assessing the optimality of a path. We now need to consider whether a long path of strong ties is better than a short path of weak ties. For example, if our tie strengths are probabilities of passing along a bit of information, we might consider the value of a path to be the product of the weights of each link in the path. Or if our tie strengths represent the capacities of pipes, we might consider the value of a path to be the strength of the weakest link in the path. Finally, if the tie values represent costs, we might consider the value of a path to be the sum of the costs. Having decided how to assess optimality, we then need to decide (at least for closeness) whether to sum the number of links in these optimal paths, or the values of the paths. All of this means that there is no one generalization for valued data, but there are a number of alternatives. Choosing among these alternatives requires careful consideration of what the tie values mean, and what kinds of network processes we are studying. In addition, identifying optimal paths is computationally intensive. As a result, most studies take the approach of binarizing their valued data and running the traditional measures of centrality. By taking different cut-off values for dichotomizing the data and comparing results, we often obtain better, more robust and interpretable centrality results than the more sophisticated valued extensions.

10.6 Negative tie networks

As we have noted, many centrality measures can be interpreted in terms of network flows (Borgatti, 2005). For example, given a network of roads, a measure of centrality such as betweenness centrality gives you an indication of how much traffic can be expected to flow over each node, given a preference for taking the shortest paths. A measure such as closeness gives an indication of how long things take, on average, to reach a given node.

This interpretation works well for many of the kinds of social relations we study, but falls apart when we consider negative ties such as dislike. First, the kinds of things that might flow over a negative tie are somewhat restricted. If John dislikes Sally, he might tell her something nasty, but there are many things John would not tell Sally. Second, whatever John chooses to transmit to Sally, it is hard to imagine Sally then relaying it to someone she dislikes. In other words, if John lets Sally know she is incompetent, do we really expect Sally to then tell Bill, whom she dislikes, that she is incompetent? The point is that even though dyads in negative tie networks may transmit things from one node to the other, it is not clear that paths of a length greater than one serve this function. As a result, it is hard to know what to make of measures like closeness centrality and betweenness when applied to negative tie networks. In contrast, degree centrality works well with negative ties, requiring only a simple reversal of the usual hypotheses. For example, we interpret indegree as a measure of unpopularity instead of popularity, and we expect an increase in indegree to be associated with a reduction of power and influence rather than an increase. Although eigenvector centrality can be thought of as a kind of iterated degree centrality, it is unclear how useful eigenvector centrality is in a negative tie context. For instance, in the case of a left eigenvector, an actor would have a high score if they were disliked by many people who themselves were disliked. This works if being disliked by the disliked is even more damning than being disliked by popular actors, but in reality it is probably more problematic to be disliked by the ones everybody likes. Indeed, being disliked by the despised may be considered a positive sign.

10.6.1 PN centrality

Some datasets contain both positive and negative relations among the same actors. In fact, it is quite possible and not uncommon for actors to say they have both positive and negative ties to the same others. Consider first just the negative tie network. The recipient of a negative tie would be less affected by receiving a negative tie from an actor who gave out a lot of negative ties than if they were the sole recipient of a negative tie from an actor that only gave one negative tie. Now imagine a situation in which lots of actors giving just a single negative tie did so to the same individual. In this case we would expect that individual to be on the margins of the network and so not be very central. This can be further compounded when we take account of the positive ties as well. Receiving single negative ties from actors that each attract a lot of positive ties would make the recipient very low in centrality. Everett and Borgatti (2014) capture these ideas and incorporate them into a measure they call PN centrality that is closely related to the β-centrality measure discussed above. The undirected version of the measure is given by equation 10.6.

$$PN = \left(1 - \frac{1}{2n-2}A\right)^{-1}1 \qquad (10.6)$$

In the equation, $A = P - 2N$, P denotes a positive tie matrix and N denotes a negative tie matrix. Note that the negative ties are recorded so that the entries of N are all non-negative. If there are no negative ties so that A is simply P then the measure ranges from 1 to a maximum of 2. If there are no positive ties so that A is just N then it ranges from 0 to 1. If both positive and negative ties are possible then it ranges from -1 to 2. The value of -1 occurs when all the actors bar one have positive ties between them and they all have a negative tie to the remaining actor. There is a directed version of equation 10.6 and the method can also be used on valued data under certain conditions.

10.7 Summary

Centrality is one of the most widely used concepts in social network analysis. A centrality measure scores each node in the network in terms of its structural importance. Simple measures such as degree, which looks at how many connections a node has, are local, but most measures use the whole network to determine the centrality score. Being connected to actors who are themselves well connected gives rise to a family of measures including eigenvector and beta centrality. The beta centrality score in some sense captures the extent to which distant nodes contribute to the centrality score: as we approach the maximum allowable score for β, we get eigenvector centrality, and a value of zero gives degree centrality. Betweenness centrality serves a very different purpose: it reflects the amount of brokerage each node has between all other nodes in the network. Often, betweenness scores provide strong discrimination, with very few nodes having high scores and many nodes having low or zero scores. The ability of a node to exploit betweenness is highly dependent on the ease with which the nodes it is between can create ties.

10.8 Problems and Exercises

1. For each of the following centrality measures discuss the appropriateness for analyzing both directed and undirected binary networks.

    a. Degree Centrality
    b. Betweenness Centrality
    c. Eigenvector Centrality
    d. Closeness Centrality
    e. Beta Centrality

2. In the problems that follow we will primarily be using the bank wiring game network (wiringRDGAM.##h) for analyzing a select set of centrality measures. The social network is an undirected graph of who plays games with whom in the bank wiring room. For each of the following centrality measures conduct an analysis one measure at a time and save the results as an attribute file. Be sure to note the name of the output files since you will be using them later.

    a. Degree Centrality (in UCINET go to Network|Centrality and Power|Degree and input the game network and click OK).
    b. Closeness Centrality.
    c. Eigenvector Centrality.
    d. Betweenness Centrality.

3. Create four visualizations of the bank wiring room game network. In each of the visualizations make the size of the nodes proportional to the value of each of the four centrality measures. Compare and contrast the differences and similarities of the measures across the four visualizations. From a social and behavioral perspective how might you interpret these comparisons?

4. Using the advice relations among actors in Krackhardt's advice network (KRACKAD.##h) provide an analysis of node centrality for each of the measures below. The network is a directed dichotomous network.

    a. Degree Centrality in a directed network (in UCINET go to Network|Centrality and Power|Degree. Given this is a directed network "Directed" must be highlighted at the far left. Upload the network and click OK. Make sure to note the names of the output files).
    b. As in Problem 3 above, create two visualizations of the advice network with one having a node size proportional to indegree centrality and one with a node size proportional to outdegree centrality.

5. The science collaboration network used in Chapter 6 is a symmetric valued network reflecting the number of grants researchers have in common. Provide an analysis of node centrality in this valued symmetric network for each of the following centrality measures.

    a. Degree Centrality (in UCINET go to Tools|Univariate statistics and input the collaboration network. Note the name of the output file).
    b. Eigenvector Centrality (in UCINET go to Network|Centrality and Power|Eigenvector Centrality. Upload the network and click OK. Make sure to note the names of the output files).
    c. Create three visualizations of the scientific collaboration network with one having a node size proportional to the average row sum, one with a node size proportional to the row sum and one with a node size proportional to eigenvector centrality.
    d. What can you say about the relationship between the various centrality measures?

Don't forget to visit the website at
https://study.sagepub.com/borgatti2e

11

Subgroups

Learning Outcomes

1. Understand the similarities and differences of the main approaches in detecting cohesive subgroups or communities
2. Select appropriate methods given the size and nature of the network
3. Perform a cohesive subgroup analysis or community detection on a variety of types of network

11.1 Introduction

Embedded within a network there are often groups of actors who interact with each other to such an extent that they could be considered to be a separate entity. In a friendship network this could be a group of close friends who all socialize together, in a work environment a collection of colleagues who all support the same football team, or in a network of interacting organizations a collection of organizations which behave as a single unit (so-called 'virtual organizations'). We call any such group a 'cohesive subgroup', although a number of other terms are also used, such as 'cluster' and 'community'. In the examples above we have identified the underlying cohesive theme which unites the group, but this would not necessarily be apparent from the network under study. In examining network data, we would first try to detect the cohesive subgroups and then, by looking at common attributes, see if there was some underlying principle that could explain why they identify with each other. For example, we may be interested to see if the cohesive groups consist of people who smoke, drink or take drugs. This information would be useful in the design of any public health initiative that had the aim of reducing these activities.

Actors within cohesive subgroups tend to share norms and often have common goals and ideals. They can also exert considerable peer pressure on their members to conform to these norms. This means that group members frequently have similar outcomes with respect to adoption of innovation, behaviors and attitudes. In-group members can easily develop negative attitudes toward out-group members, and networks divided into multiple subgroups can suffer from warring factions. Clearly, structural information alone does not tell us about these issues, but it does tell us where we should be focusing our attention.

Alternatively, the cohesive groups within the network may explain, or partially explain, certain outcomes. For example, in the Kapferer tailor shop study (Kapferer, 1972), which looked at ties within a work setting at two different time periods, there were significant changes in the network structure between the two time periods. In the first time period there was a more disjointed cohesive subgroup structure than in the second. As it happens, there was an unsuccessful call for a strike in the first time period but a successful strike in the second, and this is probably related to the structural changes.

Certain roles are played out within and between cohesive subgroups. Internally, there may well be group leaders providing a role model for others in the group to follow or dictating the group norms and attitudes. Alternatively, some actors may be spanners between groups, providing important conduits for information flow or acting as brokers between the groups.

Finally, if there are shared norms and similar actions for group members, we may be able to replace cohesive group members by a single 'super-node'. This would reduce the complexity and size of the network and consequently aid visualization and analysis.

At first sight, it may appear easy to identify cohesive subgroups in a network by simply visualizing it. Unfortunately, it is very easy to miss group members or even whole groups when trying to find cohesive subgroups by looking at a network. The position of actors on the page and the preponderance of edges make this task almost impossible to do by hand, so we often need to resort to algorithms and computers to perform the task for us. This is particularly true if the data were collected either from digital archives or by questionnaire, but even with observational data it is recommended that a computer analysis be undertaken.

It should be remembered that some cohesive subgroups are open and want to be identified, but for others there is a strong disbenefit in identification (e.g., a cartel or a drug ring). It is therefore necessary to have some formal definitions that capture exactly what a cohesive subgroup is. Within the social sciences, the notion of a social group is often used casually. It is assumed that the reader has an intuitive grasp of the concept involved and that it is not necessary to present an exact definition. Clearly, such an approach cannot be used to analyze real data, and we are thus forced to define precisely what is meant by a cohesive subgroup. There are a large number of possible realizations of the social group concept, but we shall only concern ourselves with the more commonly used practical techniques.

We start by discussing several methods of identifying cohesive subgroups in undirected and non-valued networks, and then, in separate sections, we consider how to apply subgroup concepts to directed data and to valued data. Finally, we end the chapter with a tutorial on finding cohesive subgroups in a directed, valued dataset.

11.2 Cliques

A clique is a subset of actors in which every actor is adjacent to every other actor in the subset and it is impossible to add any more actors to the clique without violating this condition. Formally, a clique is defined as a maximal complete subgraph (Luce and Perry, 1949). 'Complete' means that every node in the clique is adjacent to every other. 'Maximal' means that we cannot increase its size and still have it be complete. This definition is the same for both directed and undirected networks, hence we need not consider these as different cases. In applications we usually insist that any clique have at least three actors, since normally we do not think of a singleton or a couple as a group.

We can illustrate the idea of a clique by examining the undirected network in Figure 11.1. We see that nodes 1, 2, 3 and 4 are all connected to each other. In addition, we cannot increase this group and still retain this property. Node 5 is connected to 3 and 4 but not to 1 and 2. It follows that {1, 2, 3, 4} is a clique. Other cliques are {3, 4, 5}, {7, 9, 10} and {7, 8, 10}. Note that {1, 2, 3}

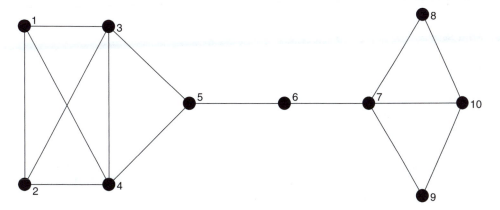

Figure 11.1 A network with four cliques.

		1 I1	2 I3	3 W1	4 W2	5 W3	6 W4	7 W5	8 W6	9 W7	10 W8	11 W9	12 S1	13 S2	14 S4
1	I1	0	0	1	1	1	1	0	0	0	0	0	0	0	0
2	I3	0	0	0	0	0	0	0	0	0	0	0	0	0	0
3	W1	1	0	0	1	1	1	1	0	0	0	0	1	0	0
4	W2	1	0	1	0	1	1	0	0	0	0	0	1	0	0
5	W3	1	0	1	1	0	1	1	0	0	0	0	1	0	0
6	W4	1	0	1	1	1	0	1	0	0	0	0	1	0	0
7	W5	0	0	1	0	1	1	0	0	1	0	0	1	0	0
8	W6	0	0	0	0	0	0	0	0	1	1	1	0	0	0
9	W7	0	0	0	0	0	0	1	1	0	1	1	0	0	1
10	W8	0	0	0	0	0	0	0	1	1	0	1	0	0	1
11	W9	0	0	0	0	0	0	0	1	1	1	0	0	0	1
12	S1	0	0	1	1	1	1	1	0	0	0	0	0	0	0
13	S2	0	0	0	0	0	0	0	0	0	0	0	0	0	0
14	S4	0	0	0	0	0	0	0	0	1	1	1	0	0	0

Matrix 11.1   Games matrix from the bank wiring room data.

is not a clique because it is not maximal (we can add 4 to it). Clearly, cliques can overlap so that individual actors can be in more than one clique. In our example, we see that nodes 3, 4, 7 and 10 are all in two cliques. Finally, there can be actors who are not in any cliques. In our example, we can see that node 6 is not in any cliques.

As a practical example, we return to the 14 Western Electric employees working in a bank wiring room introduced in Chapter 2. The employees worked in a single room and included two inspectors (I1 and I3), three solderers (S1, S2 and S4) and nine wiremen (W1 to W9). One of the observed relations was participation in horseplay, and the adjacency matrix referred to as the games matrix is given in Matrix 11.1.

The cliques routine in UCINET was used to identify the following five cliques:

1   I1 W1 W2 W3 W4
2   W1 W2 W3 W4 S1
3   W1 W3 W4 W5 S1
4   W6 W7 W8 W9
5   W7 W8 W9 S4

We note that, although these cliques overlap, there are two distinct groups, namely {I1, W1, W2, W3, W4, W5, S1} and {W6, W7, W8, W9, S4}, together with two outsiders, I3 and S2. These two groupings are in exact agreement with the findings of Roethlisberger and Dickson (1939), who identified the groups as those at the front of the room and those at the back. In this instance a simple clique analysis has been successful in identifying important structural properties of the network. Unfortunately, most analyses are not as straightforward as this one. Often there are a large number of overlapping cliques, and it is difficult to deduce anything directly from the clique list.

11.2.1 Analyzing clique overlaps

When there are a large number of cohesive subgroups, the overlap itself can hide features of the clique structure. A network with just 21 nodes can have up to 2187 different cliques! While it is true that this is unlikely to occur in any real data, it does give an indication of the possible scale of the problem.

One possible way forward when we have too many cliques is to try to reduce the number of cliques by increasing the minimum size to more than three. While this approach has some merit, it has the disadvantage of ignoring some possibly important smaller cliques. An alternative strategy would be to try to remove or reduce the overlap by performing some additional analyses on the cliques themselves. We shall now explore this approach in some detail.

We can use the cliques to obtain a measure of association between each pair of actors. If actor X is in a large number of cliques with actor Y, it is reasonable to assume that X and Y are reasonably close. In fact, we can build a proximity matrix which tells us how many times each pair of actors in our network are in the same clique together. We call this matrix the 'clique co-membership matrix' A, where $A(i, j)$ is the number of times i is in a clique with j. The ith diagonal entry gives the number of cliques containing actor i. Matrix 11.2 gives the clique co-membership for the games matrix in the bank wiring room study we just examined.

If we look at row 5, column 6 of Matrix 11.2, we can see that W3 was in a clique with W4 on three occasions, and the diagonal entry for row 4 indicates that W2 was in two cliques. These results can be checked by referring back to the list of cliques displayed earlier.

We note that the clique co-membership matrix is a proximity matrix in which larger values indicate a stronger link – that is, it is a similarity matrix. This matrix can then be submitted to a hierarchical clustering procedure such as the average-link method. The result will be sets of non-overlapping nested clusters of actors. Applying this technique to the clique co-membership matrix for the games data results in the cluster diagram given in Figure 11.2, in this diagram we can clearly see the two outsiders, S2 and I3, and at the 0.381 level the two major groupings {I1, W1, W2, W3, W4, W5, S1} and {W6, W7, W8, W9, S4} identified previously. In addition, we can see that W1, W3 and W4 are the most active in the first group and W7, W8 and W9 are the most

Analyzing Social Networks

		1	2	3	4	5	6	7	8	9	10	11	12	13	14
		I1	I3	W1	W2	W3	W4	W5	W6	W7	W8	W9	S1	S2	S4
1	I1	1	0	1	1	1	1	0	0	0	0	0	0	0	0
2	I3	0	0	0	0	0	0	0	0	0	0	0	0	0	0
3	W1	1	0	3	2	3	3	1	0	0	0	0	2	0	0
4	W2	1	0	2	2	2	2	0	0	0	0	0	1	0	0
5	W3	1	0	3	2	3	3	1	0	0	0	0	2	0	0
6	W4	1	0	3	2	3	3	1	0	0	0	0	2	0	0
7	W5	0	0	1	0	1	1	1	0	0	0	0	1	0	0
8	W6	0	0	0	0	0	0	0	1	1	1	1	0	0	0
9	W7	0	0	0	0	0	0	0	1	2	2	2	0	0	1
10	W8	0	0	0	0	0	0	0	1	2	2	2	0	0	1
11	W9	0	0	0	0	0	0	0	1	2	2	2	0	0	1
12	S1	0	0	2	1	2	2	1	0	0	0	0	2	0	0
13	S2	0	0	0	0	0	0	0	0	0	0	0	0	0	0
14	S4	0	0	0	0	0	0	0	0	1	1	1	0	0	1

Matrix 11.2 Clique co-membership matrix for the games data.

active in the second. The cliques routine in UCINET produces these analyses automatically as part of the routine.

In this simple example the method has clearly worked well. But care is needed in interpreting the results when using a technique like this. The clustering is based upon the amount of activity of pairs of actors and not on the strength or overlap of the groups. A consequence of this is that in a network with, say, one large homogeneous group and another group consisting of a large

```
             I  I  W  W  W  W  W  S  S  W  W  W  W  S
             3  1  5  2  1  3  4  1  2  6  7  8  9  4

                                 1  1        1  1  1
   Level      2  1  7  4  3  5  6  2  3  8  9  0  1  4
   -----      -  -  -  -  -  -  -  -  -  -  -  -  -  -
   3.000      .  .  .  .  X  X  X  X  X  .  .  .  .  .  .
   2.000      .  .  .  X  X  X  X  X  X  X  .  .  .  X  X  X  X  X  .
   1.800      .  .  .  X  X  X  X  X  X  X  X  X  .  .  X  X  X  X  X  .
   1.000      .  .  .  X  X  X  X  X  X  X  X  X  .  X  X  X  X  X  X  X  .
   0.911      .  .  X  X  X  X  X  X  X  X  X  X  X  .  X  X  X  X  X  X  X  .
   0.800      .  .  X  X  X  X  X  X  X  X  X  X  X  .  X  X  X  X  X  X  X  X  X
   0.381      .  X  X  X  X  X  X  X  X  X  X  X  X  X  .  X  X  X  X  X  X  X  X  X
   0.000      X  X  X  X  X  X  X  X  X  X  X  X  X  X  X  X  X  X  X  X  X  X  X  X  X  X  X  X
```

Figure 11.2 Hierarchical clustering of the clique overlap matrix.

number of overlapping cliques, the analysis will be biased towards the complex overlapping structure. Another possible objection to the method is that it completely eliminates one of the desirable features of cohesive subgroups, namely overlap. Our own experiences tell us that it is quite common for actors to be in more than one group. One possible solution would be to cluster the cliques as opposed to the actors; this is a useful approach, and details of how to do it are given at the end of the chapter. We shall now turn our attention to a completely different approach.

11.2.2 Bimodal method

The bimodal method (Everett and Borgatti, 1998) examines both the cliques and the actors simultaneously by constructing a two-mode data matrix of actors by cliques called a 'clique participation matrix'. This matrix has the actors as the rows and the cliques as the columns. The entries measure the extent to which an actor is in a clique. Actors with no direct connections to a clique member score 0, clique members score 1, and values in between give the number of ties which connect the actor to the clique divided by the number of ties required for the actor to be a clique member. Hence, if a clique has four members then adding a new node requires five more reciprocated edges. It follows that if an actor is already connected to three clique members by reciprocated ties then they have three of the five required ties. In this case the entry in the clique participation matrix would be $3/5 = 0.6$. This matrix can then be visualized as a two-mode data matrix in NetDraw or analyzed using a two-mode technique such as correspondence analysis (see Chapter 13 for more details on two-mode networks).

We first demonstrate this technique on the games data from the wiring room before showing both methods in a more complex example. The clique participation matrix derived from the five cliques found in the wiring data above is given in Matrix 11.3; this is automatically produced in the UCINET clique routine. Figure 11.3 shows the data visualized as a two-mode dataset in NetDraw. The actors are represented by gray circles and the cliques by squares. The thickness of the lines represents the values in the clique participation matrix, with higher values having thicker lines. We note the two isolates I3 and S2, and we can see that cliques 1, 2 and 3 are placed close together, as are cliques 4 and 5. We clearly see the two groups of actors – one at the top, the other at the bottom of the diagram – with W5 and W7 occupying bridging positions between the groups. The thicknesses of the lines show that W5 identifies with the bottom group, whereas W7 is associated with the top group. The groups would be more clearly identified if we only visualized the stronger links, but we would then

	1	2	3	4	5
I1	1.000	0.800	0.600	0.000	0.000
I3	0.000	0.000	0.000	0.000	0.000
W1	1.000	1.000	1.000	0.000	0.000
W2	1.000	1.000	0.800	0.000	0.000
W3	1.000	1.000	1.000	0.000	0.000
W4	1.000	1.000	1.000	0.000	0.000
W5	0.600	0.800	1.000	0.250	0.250
W6	0.000	0.000	0.000	1.000	0.750
W7	0.000	0.000	0.200	1.000	1.000
W8	0.000	0.000	0.000	1.000	1.000
W9	0.000	0.000	0.000	1.000	1.000
S1	0.800	1.000	1.000	0.000	0.000
S2	0.000	0.000	0.000	0.000	0.000
S4	0.000	0.000	0.000	0.750	1.000

Matrix 11.3   Clique participation matrix for the games data.

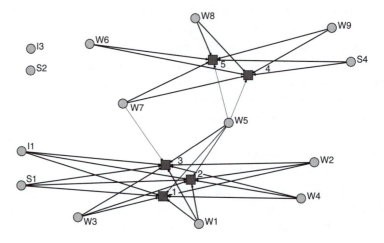

Figure 11.3   Visualization of the clique participation matrix.

hide the important roles played by W5 and W7. We now demonstrate both methods on a more complex example.

We first introduced the karate club data in Chapter 7 and used it in our ERGM example in Chapter 8, but we need to give a bit more detail to help with our analysis. Zachary (1977) collected data on the members of a university karate club. One of the data matrices he collected is a record of interactions between members of the club outside of club activities. During the study there was a dispute, and this resulted in the club splitting in two. The data only consider those members of the club who joined one of the two new clubs created by the split. There were 34 actors involved in the study. A clique analysis reveals 25 overlapping cliques. The results of the clique co-membership clusterings are presented in Figure 11.4.

We can see two distinct groupings which are identified at level 0.001: one containing the set {1, 2, 3, 4, 5, 6, 7, 8, 11, 13, 14, 17, 18, 20, 22} and the other containing the set {9, 15, 16, 19, 21, 23, 24, 25, 26, 27, 28, 29, 30, 31, 32, 33, 34}, with 10 and 12 being outside the clique structure. In addition, we have some information on the activities of individuals. Actors 33 and 34 are in eight different cliques together, indicating that this pair are important within the group and are possibly taking on some kind of leadership role (we could use centrality to measure this). Actors 1 and 2 are similarly highly active, and we could draw the same conclusions. Now consider the bimodal method. The NetDraw visualization is given in Figure 11.5.

```
      1
      1 1   1     1 1              1 1 2 2 2 2 2 3 2 2 2 2 1 1 1   3 3 2 3 3
Level 0 2 5 1 6 7 7 3 1 2 3 4 8 4 8 0 2 9 5 6 2 8 7 3 1 9 6 5 9 1 0 4 3 4
----- - - - - - - - - - - - - - - - - - - - - - - - - - - - - - - - - - -
8.000 . . . . . . . . . . . . . . . . . . . . . . . . . . . . . . . . XXX
5.000 . . . . . . . . XXX . . . . . . . . . . . . . . . . . . . . . . XXX
2.333 . . . . . . . . XXXXX . . . . . . . . . . . . . . . . . . . . . XXX
2.133 . . . . . . . . XXXXXXX . . . . . . . . . . . . . . . . . . . . XXX
2.000 . . . . . XXX . . XXXXXXX . . . . . . . . . . . . . . . . . . . XXX
1.667 . . . . . XXX . . XXXXXXX . . . . . . . . . . . . . . . . . XXXXX
1.500 . . . . . XXX . . XXXXXXX . . . . . . . . . . . . . . . . XXXXXXX
1.000 . . XXX XXXXX . XXXXXXXXX . . . . . XXXXX . . . . . . . XXX XXXXXXX
0.667 . . XXX XXXXX . XXXXXXXXX . . . . . XXXXX . . . . . . . XXXXXXXXXXX
0.600 . . XXX XXXXX . XXXXXXXXX . . . . XXXXXXX . . . . . . . XXXXXXXXXXX
0.450 . . XXX XXXXX . XXXXXXXXX . . . . XXXXXXX . . . . . . XXXXXXXXXXXXX
0.444 . . XXX XXXXX . XXXXXXXXXX . . . XXXXXXX . . . . . . XXXXXXXXXXXXX
0.394 . . XXX XXXXX . XXXXXXXXXX . . . XXXXXXX . . . . . XXXXXXXXXXXXXXX
0.350 . . XXX XXXXX . XXXXXXXXXX . . . XXXXXXX . . . . XXXXXXXXXXXXXXXXX
0.315 . . XXX XXXXX . XXXXXXXXXXX . . . XXXXXXX . . . XXXXXXXXXXXXXXXXXX
0.286 . . XXX XXXXX . XXXXXXXXXXX . . . XXXXXXX . . XXXXXXXXXXXXXXXXXXXX
0.263 . . XXX XXXXX . XXXXXXXXXXX . . . XXXXXXX . XXXXXXXXXXXXXXXXXXXXX
0.242 . . XXX XXXXX . XXXXXXXXXXX . . . XXXXXXX XXXXXXXXXXXXXXXXXXXXXX
0.210 . . XXX XXXXX . XXXXXXXXXXX . . . XXXXXXXXXXXXXXXXXXXXXXXXXXXXX
0.178 . . XXXXXXXXX . XXXXXXXXXXX . . . XXXXXXXXXXXXXXXXXXXXXXXXXXXXX
0.127 . . XXXXXXXXX XXXXXXXXXXXX . . . XXXXXXXXXXXXXXXXXXXXXXXXXXXXX
0.030 . . XXXXXXXXX XXXXXXXXXXXXXXXX . . XXXXXXXXXXXXXXXXXXXXXXXXXXXXX
0.014 . . XXXXXXXXX XXXXXXXXXXXXXXXXXXXX . XXXXXXXXXXXXXXXXXXXXXXXXXXXXX
0.007 . . XXXXXXXXX XXXXXXXXXXXXXXXXXXXXXX XXXXXXXXXXXXXXXXXXXXXXXXXXXXX
0.001 . . XXXXXXXXXXXXXXXXXXXXXXXXXXXXXXXX XXXXXXXXXXXXXXXXXXXXXXXXXXXXX
0.000 . . XXXXXXXXXXXXXXXXXXXXXXXXXXXXXXXXXXXXXXXXXXXXXXXXXXXXXXXXXXXXX
0.000 XXXXXXXXXXXXXXXXXXXXXXXXXXXXXXXXXXXXXXXXXXXXXXXXXXXXXXXXXXXXXXXXX
```

Figure 11.4 Hierarchical clustering of the karate club clique overlap matrix.

The cliques are represented by the gray squares and the actors by the circles. In addition, we have colored the circles black for the actors who ended up in one club and white for the actors who went to the other club. It should be noted that one club was led by actor 1, the other by actor 34. The diagram clearly identifies two sets of cliques: one on the right of the picture and one on the left. At the extreme left and right are clearly identified two separate groups associated with each cluster of cliques. Towards the center, there are actors associated with the left group (10, 28, 29, 31, 33 and 34) and some associated with the right group (1, 2, 4 and 8). These two groups clearly have links with both major groupings but have stronger links to the groups they are closest to. In the diagram actors 3, 9, 14, 20 and 32 are placed in the center between the two major groupings. By examining the stronger links (not shown here) as we did for the wiring data, it is possible to associate these actors uniquely with each group. Actors 9 and 32 are closer to the group on the left, whereas 3, 14 and 20 are linked more strongly to the right group. This is consistent with the co-membership method, but in this case we were able to assign the actors 10 and 12. If we had used this method to predict which clubs the actors would have joined after the split, we would have only wrongly assigned actor 9. Zachary gives an ethnographic reason for actor 9 joining the club with which he was less associated. The new club the clique analysis associated him with were going to do a different type of karate. He was only three weeks away from gaining a black belt, and if he joined that club he would be required to give up his brown belt and start again.

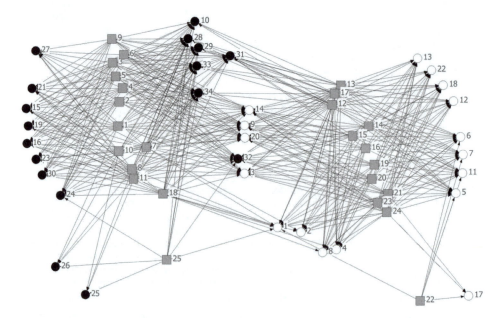

Figure 11.5 Bimodal analysis of the karate club clique participation matrix.

In doing an analysis, we should not view co-membership and bimodal techniques as alternatives but as providing different views of the same data. They
are both, after all, a secondary analysis of the clique structure and are adding to
the information we have already gleaned. The co-membership method did not
successfully place actors 10 and 12, but it gave us leadership information not
provided by the bimodal method. Thus, it would always make sense to use both
methods to obtain the maximum benefit from any clique analysis.

A clique has a formal definition and we use computer algorithms to search
for cliques in the data (often followed by a secondary analysis of the clique
overlap). In large or complex data, a clique analysis can be difficult to interpret
or simply not possible as it would not be computationally feasible. An alternative approach is to define cohesive subgroups in terms of the output of a
particular algorithm rather than starting from a definition. We now look at two
methods which take this approach.

11.3 Girvan–Newman algorithm

One approach to finding cohesive subgroups is to try to find the structurally
important edges whose removal fragments the network rather than finding
cohesive groups directly. These edges cannot be within the cohesive groups and
so must be between them. The removal of these edges will leave just the cohesive groups. This is the approach taken by the Girvan–Newman algorithm
(Girvan and Newman, 2002).

Edge betweenness is defined in a similar way to vertex betweenness. Edge
betweenness is a count of the number of times an edge lies on a geodesic path
between a pair of vertices. Hence, as in the vertex case, we take all pairs of
vertices and simply count in the same way the number of times each edge is
part of a geodesic path. If we delete the edge with the highest score, we will
either increase the number of components or increase the fragmentation. If we
iteratively repeat this process, the number of components will continue to
increase until we are only left with isolates. We usually stop the process before
this happens. The algorithm proceeds as follows:

1. Set the maximum number k of cohesive subsets required.
2. Calculate the edge betweenness of the network and find the edge (or edges) with
    the highest score.
3. Delete this edge (or edges) and count the number of components that now exist.
4. If the number of components exceeds k then stop, otherwise go to Step 2.

As the algorithm iterates, we obtain different partitions. These do not increase
necessarily by 1 each time, as there may be more than one edge with the highest score.

In addition, the algorithm makes an assessment of how good each partition is in terms of a numerical score called 'modularity', denoted by Q. Modularity compares the number of internal links in the groups to how many you would expect to see if they were distributed at random. Higher values mean that the algorithm has found more significant groupings. Negative values are possible, indicating that the groups are less cohesive than a purely random assignment. We now present the formal definition of modularity Q. Suppose a network with n vertices and m edges has adjacency matrix A. Let P be a matrix of probabilities in which the (i, j)th entry is the probability that actor i has an edge to actor j given that the edges are distributed at random (but with the expected degrees made to match those in A). Given a partition of the vertices into c groups, let S be the n × c indicator matrix in which the (i, j)th entry is a 1 if actor i is a member of group j and 0 otherwise. Let B = A − P then the modularity Q is given by equation 11.1

$$Q = \frac{1}{2m} Tr(S^T BS)$$
(11.1)

where $Tr(X)$ is the trace of matrix X, which is to say, the product of the diagonal elements.

If we used the Girvan–Newman algorithm on the karate club data, we would obtain very similar results to the clique analysis. As an alternative, we return to the tailor shop data briefly mentioned in the first section of this chapter. We first look at time period 1 when the strike was not successful. We run the algorithm for up to 10 groups and obtain the following measures:

- Partition with 4 clusters: $Q = 0.000$
- Partition with 5 clusters: $Q = 0.000$
- Partition with 6 clusters: $Q = -0.001$
- Partition with 7 clusters: $Q = -0.001$
- Partition with 8 clusters: $Q = 0.004$
- Partition with 9 clusters: $Q = 0.225$
- Partition with 10 clusters: $Q = 0.226$

The partition measure for 4, 5, 6, 7 and 8 clusters is very small. In fact, each of these consists of one large group with just a single actor in each of the other groups. These represent an unsuccessful attempt to partition the data, and the first (and only) success is into 9 clusters. Of course, 7 of these clusters will consist of singleton actors, but the higher score shows that the main group has been split. The fact that the 10-cluster partition has nearly the same score as the 9 shows that this has simply added another singleton group. Figure 11.6 shows the 9-cluster solution.

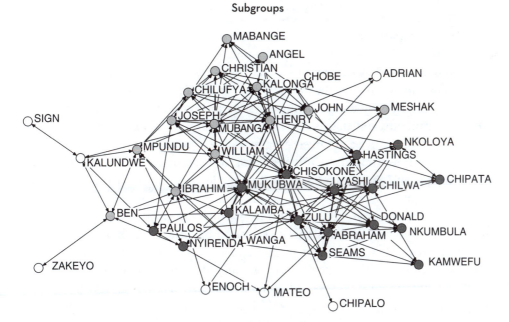

Figure 11.6 Girvan–Newman split of the tailor shop data.

Each of the white actors is in their own cluster and the main split of the large group is into black and gray. The partition in Figure 11.6 divides the large central group into two, indicating that they are not as united as they should have been in order to organize a strike. If this analysis is repeated at time period 2, there is no split of the main group, which might explain why the strike was successful.

11.4 Factions and modularity optimization

In this section we shall look at a general method that partitions the whole population into a predetermined number of cohesive groups. Since we have a partition, every actor must be placed into a unique group. When we determined cliques, we allowed actors to be placed in more than one group and also accepted that some actors did not belong to any group. We now insist that every single actor in the network be assigned to one and only one group. Furthermore, when applying this method, we shall have to determine the number of groups a priori. This is because the algorithm we shall be using tries to fit the actors into the groups and then measures how well this has been achieved.

We shall illustrate the ideas by a simple example. We first need some measure of how well a partition has divided the actors into cohesive subgroups. One way would be to calculate the density of each of the groups and then sum them up.

If we wish to partition our data into three groups, the best value we could achieve using this measure is 3. This would occur when each group had the maximum density. Any measure used in this fashion is more commonly referred to as a 'cost function', and the value of the function for a particular partition is called the fit. Unfortunately it is not possible in general to evaluate all possible group assignments and then select the best. There are simply too many for a computer to examine, so we need an alternative approach.

The algorithm proceeds as follows. First, arbitrarily assign everyone to one of the groups and then calculate the fit to see how good the partition is. Next, move some actors from one group to another, calculate the fit again and see if there is any improvement. Continue in this way until no more improvement is possible and the result is the required partition. The hard part is how to decide on what is a good move. There is a class of methods called 'combinatorial optimization' which are specifically designed to try to do this. It should be noted that this is a deliberately vague description of how the methods work; the interested reader would be advised to look at the specialist literature on combinatorial optimization techniques. When applying any of these algorithms to a real problem, the user needs to be aware of the possible pitfalls in interpreting the results. The most important factor to be remembered is that there will always be a solution. That is, if the data contain no real groups, the data will still be partitioned into the prescribed number of classes and the method finds the best of the possible solutions it has looked at. The fact that none of the solutions is any good is ignored. As an extreme example, consider a network in which everyone is connected to everyone else. If we selected three groups, any partition into three would have the same fit as any other. The algorithm would therefore retain the original arbitrary split and this would be reported as the partition. Clearly, there is only one group within the data and yet the algorithm would report three factions

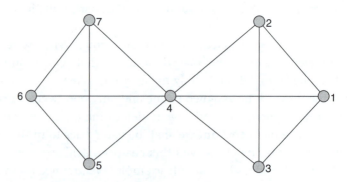

Figure 11.7 A network with two cliques.

as requested. Note, further, that the density cost function proposed above would be at the maximum fit of 3. This could be fixed by having a more sophisticated cost function, but the underlying problem of always finding a solution remains. Linked to this is the problem of the uniqueness of the solution. That is, there may be more than one partition into factions with the same maximum fit.

Consider two complete networks of the same size together with one actor linked to all the actors in the network. Figure 11.7 is such a network: each of the complete networks consists of three actors {1, 2, 3} and {5, 6, 7}, with actor 4 connected to everyone. Suppose now we wish to search for two factions. The two complete graphs will each be in a separate faction, but to which group does actor 4, who is connected to everyone, belong? The density fit will be perfect whichever group is selected. That is, the partition {1, 2, 3, 4} {5, 6, 7} is as good as {1, 2, 3}{4, 5, 6, 7}. There are therefore two possible partitions, both of which are valid. In more complex data there may be a number of very different partitions all of which have the same or very similar fit values. One way to check the robustness of a partition is to repeat the analysis a number of times to see whether the final factions are the same or similar.

The simple density cost function used to illustrate the principles in factions is often not effective. The reason is that it only captures part of the intuitive notion discussed in the first section of this chapter. Since we are trying to partition the whole network, we are able to include both the idea of internal cohesion between group members and a separation or distancing from members outside

0	1	1	0	0	0	0	0	0	0	0	0
1	0	1	0	0	0	0	0	0	0	0	0
1	1	0	0	0	0	0	0	0	0	0	0
0	0	0	0	1	1	1	1	0	0	0	0
0	0	0	1	0	1	1	1	0	0	0	0
0	0	0	1	1	0	1	1	0	0	0	0
0	0	0	1	1	1	0	1	0	0	0	0
0	0	0	1	1	1	1	0	0	0	0	0
0	0	0	0	0	0	0	0	0	1	1	1
0	0	0	0	0	0	0	0	1	0	1	1
0	0	0	0	0	0	0	0	1	1	0	1
0	0	0	0	0	0	0	0	1	1	1	0

Matrix 11.4 An ideal cohesive subgroup structure.

the group. One way to achieve this is to measure the similarity of the partitioned data matrix to an 'ideal' structure matrix. We now explore this approach.

By way of an example, let us consider a partition of a network into three groups. If we apply the intuitive notions discussed in the first section of this chapter, the idealized structure consists of three groups, each of which is a complete component. We can use this information to construct the adjacency matrix of the idealized structure. Suppose that our three groups consist of 3, 5 and 4 actors, respectively, and for clarity we will assume that actors 1, 2 and 3 are in the first group, actors 4, 5, 6, 7 and 8 are in the second group, and actors

```
Group Assignments:

  1:  1 2 3 4 5 6 7 8 10 11 12 13 14 17 18 20 22
  2:  9 15 16 19 21 23 24 25 26 27 28 29 30 31 32 33 34

Grouped Adjacency Matrix

                       1 1 1 1 1 1 2 1 2   1   1 2 1 2 2 2 2 2 2 3 3 3 3
         1 2 3 4 5 6 7 8 7 0 1 2 3 4 0 8 2   5 9 9 1 6 3 4 5 6 7 8 9 0 1 2 3 4
       -----------------------------------------------------------------------
    1 | 1 1 1 1 1 1 1 1   1 1 1 1 1 1 1 |  1                       1         |
    2 | 1 1 1 1         1           1 1 1 1 |             1                   |
    3 | 1 1 1 1       1   1     1       |  1             1 1         1       |
    4 | 1 1 1 1         1         1 1   |                                   |
    5 | 1         1   1         1       |                                   |
    6 | 1         1 1   1     1         |                                   |
    7 | 1             1 1 1   1         |                                   |
    8 | 1 1 1 1         1               |                                   |
   17 |             1 1     1           |                                   |
   10 |     1               1           |                               1 |
   11 | 1           1 1       1         |                                   |
   12 | 1                     1         |                                   |
   13 | 1     1               1         |                                   |
   14 | 1 1 1 1               1         |                               1 |
   20 | 1 1                         1   |                               1 |
   18 | 1 1                           1 |                                   |
   22 | 1 1                             1 |                                 |
       -----------------------------------------------------------------------
   15 |                                 | 1                           1 1 |
    9 | 1   1                           | 1                       1   1 1 |
   19 |                                 |   1                         1 1 |
   21 |                                 |     1                       1 1 |
   16 |                                 |       1                     1 1 |
   23 |                                 |         1                   1 1 |
   24 |                                 |           1   1   1   1     1 1 |
   25 |                                 |             1 1   1       1     |
   26 |                                 |             1 1 1         1     |
   27 |                                 |                 1     1     1 |
   28 |       1                         |                 1 1   1       1 |
   29 |       1                         |                       1   1 1 |
   30 |                                 |                 1   1   1   1 1 |
   31 |   1                             | 1                   1   1 1 |
   32 | 1                               |                 1 1   1   1 1 1 |
   33 |       1                         | 1 1 1 1 1 1 1                 1 1 1 1 1 |
   34 |                     1       1 1 | 1 1 1 1 1 1 1     1 1 1 1 1 1 1 1 |
       -----------------------------------------------------------------------
```

Figure 11.8 A factions analysis of the karate club data.

9, 10, 11 and 12 are in the last group. The resultant matrix has the structure shown in Matrix 11.4.

We can now compare this matrix with our data matrix to provide a measure of how good our partition is. There are a number of possible measures which compare matrices, but we mention just two here. Each will give rise to a cost function. The first is to simply count the number of cells that are different between the data matrix and the idealized structure matrix. The second method is to calculate the correlation coefficient between the matrices (to do this we simply treat the entries of each matrix as if it is one long vector split over a number of rows, as discussed in Chapter 8). It must be remembered that, since we do not have statistical independence, the correlation coefficient can have no statistical significance associated with it. This means we are unable to interpret any particular value of the coefficient in absolute terms. We are, however, able to establish that one particular partition is closer to the ideal than another. Obviously, every time there is a new distribution of actors between the groups, we need to construct a different idealized matrix and use this as the basis of our cost function.

We shall now take as an example the karate club data that were analyzed in the previous section. We already know from the study that every actor joined one of the two clubs, so the data should split into two factions. The Factions routine in UCINET was run using the correlation cost function. The process was repeated a number of times using different starting configurations, but the same groups always emerged. The results are shown in Figure 11.8. The group assignments are in agreement with those reported by Zachary, both in terms of the factions identified by observation and subsequent club membership, with the exception of actor 9. They are also the same as the analysis we obtained using the bimodal method.

11.4.1 Modularity optimization

The factions method we have just described as already discussed can be implemented with any suitable cost function. One obvious candidate is the modularity function Q introduced by Girvan and Newman described in Section 11.3. This method has gained a considerable following among the network science community and a number of extensions and modifications have been proposed, for example to deal with valued and two-mode data. Subgroups found by this method are often referred to as communities and the approach is known as community detection. If we apply modularity optimization to the karate club data then the two-community partition produced is exactly the same as in Figure 11.8, where we used the correlation method.

While it is a much-used method, there are some well-known shortcomings and in some circumstances it fails to find the communities when they are small compared with the size of the network. More details can be found in the article by Fortunato and Barthelemy (2007). The second issue with modularity optimization is shared with all methods that use this method and that is the computational cost. In essence if we want robust methods then the computation cost is high but if we are more relaxed about the quality of our optimization then we are able to implement much faster algorithms. One approach is to use an agglomerative method such as hierarchical clustering as discussed in Chapter 6. An even faster approach is to use a greedy algorithm with a data reduction step which allows us to examine large networks. This is known as the Louvain method and is discussed in more detail in Chapter 14.

11.5 Directed and valued data

With directed data, the maximum cohesion can only be achieved when every tie is reciprocated. The approach to directed data is therefore to simply symmetrize the data first to produce an undirected network of reciprocated ties. There may be circumstances when it makes more sense to examine the underlying graph, which means that we consider an edge to be present if there is a link in either direction. For example, perhaps there are very few (or even no) reciprocated links, but in this case we are really finding cohesive groups based on a different relation to the one that is being analyzed. Again, care should be taken in interpreting the groups.

In principle, concepts like cliques can be reformulated for valued data, but at the current time there is no generally accepted valued definition of cliques. So the standard approach to using cliques with valued data would be to dichotomize the data in the ways outlined in Chapter 5. Often, one would want to dichotomize at different levels and compare the results.

In contrast, the factions technique is easily adapted to valued data including Newman community detection. In the case of the UCINET program, the decision was made to simplify things by having the factions procedure handle only dichotomous data, and include a separate routine, called Clustering|Combinatorial Optimization, to handle the more general case of valued data, although not Newman community detection. The procedures are identical except that the measures of correspondence between ideal and real datasets available in each are different, since some procedures for valued data would be less than appropriate for dichotomous data, and vice versa.

As an example, we consider the now familiar valued and non-symmetric dataset called Camp92 available in UCINET. The values are ranks indicating how highly the row person has ranked the column person in terms of how much interaction they have had over the last week. A smaller value indicates more interaction. If we block the matrix according to the factions produced by the Optimization algorithm (see Figure 11.9), the smallest values occur with the blocks along the main diagonal, meaning that social 'distances' are mostly small within factions, as they should be. The density table at the bottom of the output gives the average rank within and between factions.

```
r-square = 0.334
```

		1	10	12	14	9	17	2	15	16	18	11	4	13	3	6	7	8	5
		HO	BI	DO	HA	MI	BE	BR	GE	ST	RU	LE	PA	JO	CA	JE	PA	AN	PA
1	HOLLY		12	2	5	4	9	7	16	11	10	15	1	14	17	13	8	6	3
10	BILL	8		2	3	1	6	9	7	5	4	10	15	12	14	17	13	16	11
12	DON	2	17		3	1	9	13	4	11	16	10	5	14	15	7	8	12	6
14	HARRY	2	5	3		1	12	16	9	7	13	6	10	4	15	17	14	8	11
9	MICHAEL	3	14	1	2		8	15	4	9	16	17	6	12	5	13	11	10	7
17	BERT	5	13	12	16	14		4	6	1	3	2	7	17	10	11	8	9	15
2	BRAZEY	4	17	11	16	15	3		14	2	12	1	5	13	8	9	7	6	10
15	GERY	13	17	7	10	3	4	6		2	1	8	14	5	9	15	12	16	11
16	STEVE	14	17	7	16	12	1	5	4		3	2	15	10	6	11	8	13	9
18	RUSS	4	11	10	14	12	2	8	1	3		5	15	6	9	7	17	16	13
11	LEE	10	16	9	7	11	2	3	12	1	5		13	8	6	14	15	17	4
4	PAM	4	16	10	11	9	12	7	15	14	17	13		8	5	3	1	2	6
13	JOHN	16	13	11	7	10	15	5	2	6	3	17	8		4	14	1	9	12
3	CAROL	16	17	14	15	7	8	10	12	6	9	13	1	5		4	3	11	2
6	JENNIE	9	17	11	15	14	7	8	13	6	10	12	3	16	5		4	2	1
7	PAULINE	10	15	16	17	13	7	6	14	9	12	11	1	8	3	5		4	2
8	ANN	5	15	12	10	9	13	8	16	11	17	14	2	6	4	1	3		7
5	PAT	2	17	15	16	14	7	6	10	8	11	9	13	12	3	1	5	4	

Density Table

	1	2	3
3	4.550	10.133	10.571
2	11.433	4.200	10.690
3	12.229	10.214	5.095

Figure 11.9 Clustering of valued data into three groups.

Most computer implementations of the Girvan–Newman algorithm do not allow valued data, although in principle the procedure can be applied to valued data, particularly where the values represent costs or distances as in the Camp92 dataset, as explained by Brandes (2008).

Finally, we should mention that symmetric valued data are proximity data, so the standard methods of hierarchical clustering and multidimensional scaling can be directly applied to the data.

11.6 Computational considerations

All the techniques in this chapter require a computer to carry out any analysis. The algorithms employ direct search methods for the cliques, combinatorial optimization for the factions, and a simple polynomial-time algorithm for the Girvan–Newman procedure. The time required for the searches can increase exponentially with the size of the problem, making this a practical issue. For the clique analysis, the important factors are the number of edges and the number of cliques. Since larger networks tend to be less dense in general, the number of edges is not a major issue. Thus, a clique analysis on networks containing hundreds and even thousands of actors is feasible, provided there are not too many groups. If there is a problem in terms of computation, the analyst should consider increasing the minimum size of a group (this significantly decreases the number of groups, and sophisticated software can use this information to reduce the number of edges). For very large networks, we advise breaking them down into smaller portions before undertaking an analysis – see Chapter 14.

The combinatorial search routines have computation times that depend upon the number of actors and the number of factions. They are best suited to fewer than 100 actors and partitions into five or fewer groups. It would be computationally impossible to take, say, 10,000 actors and partition them into 150 groups. Again, the basic approach in dealing with large networks or many groups is to break the network down into smaller portions. There are however some fast optimization methods and some computational tricks which can make community detection efficient for very large networks. A well established and tested method that does this is known as the Louvain method which we outline in Chapter 14. This has the added advantage of being able to deal with valued data and also determines the number of communities in the data.

Girvan–Newman is a polynomial-time algorithm and so does not suffer from the same computational constraints. However, when the networks become large, the algorithm does have a tendency to create many clusters containing singleton actors.

11.7 Performing a cohesive subgraph analysis

In this section we give a step-by-step procedure for examining the cohesive subgraph structure within a network. These steps are intended as a guide only and should not be seen as the definitive approach to analyzing data. The guide is naive, since we make no assumptions about the nature of the data and have no knowledge of the research questions being investigated. A sophisticated analyst can take the steps in a different order and/or bypass some of them.

Step 1

If the data are binary, go to Step 2. If the data are valued, either use a technique designed for valued data (e.g., multidimensional scaling, hierarchical clustering, or UCINET's Clustering|Combinatorial Optimization routine) or dichotomize the data. When dichotomizing, it is important to make the 1s in the resulting matrix correspond to stronger social ties, which could mean taking values greater than a given threshold for similarity data, or values smaller than a given value for distance data. Once the data are in binary form, go to Step 2. Always repeat the analysis with different cut-off values to test for robustness and to get a more complete picture of the data. For data with multiple relations, analyze each relation separately.

Step 2

Establish the components. For directed data, find both the weak and strong components (see Chapter 2). Components represent the simplest form of cohesive subgroup analysis and can sometimes provide sufficient information to answer research questions (particularly with large datasets). If this is the case, the analysis is complete. If not, proceed to Step 3.

Step 3

If a partition is required and the approximate number of groups has been decided, go to Step 6. If the data (or largest component) are very large then use the Louvain method discussed in Chapter 14. Otherwise, find all the cliques. If there are no or very few cliques, try the following:

If the minimum clique size is 4 or more, reduce it (but do not go below 3).

If the data were directed, look at the underlying graph – that is, symmetrize the data by taking the minimum; in this case care needs to be taken in interpreting the cliques as the relation has been changed.

If the data were dichotomized, reduce the cut-off value for similarity data or increase it for distance data.

If all these steps fail, proceed to Step 5. If too many cliques are found (this may only be apparent after Step 4), try the reverse of the options above for too few cliques. If a simple listing of the cliques is sufficient, stop; however, unless the structure is very simple, it is worth going on to Step 4.

Step 4

Analyze the pattern of overlap. Both methods of analyzing the overlaps described earlier in the chapter should be used to try to identify major groupings of cliques and actors – outsiders and possible leaders and spanners of the groups. It should also be possible to deduce the approximate number of groupings; this informa-tion can be used to perform a factions analysis. If a partition of the data is required, go to Step 6; otherwise, the analysis is complete.

Step 5

Apply the Girvan–Newman algorithm. If this gives a satisfactory result, stop; otherwise, continue to Step 6.

Step 6

Partition the network into factions or Newman community detection (ncd) or implement the Louvain method. Factions and ncd should be implemented on each weak component of the network, since separate components will always fall into different factions or communities. Therefore, only components which need to be broken into smaller groups need to be analyzed. Decide how many groups should be used. This number can sometimes be determined from the clique analysis or is known/decided from external sources. If there is no source of information, try different numbers of groups starting from 2 moving up to 3, 4 and 5. If the outcome of the analysis is one large group with all other groups consisting of single or few actors, then the data cannot be split into this many groups. If repeated runs produce the same actors in the smaller groups, the rou-tine is identifying outsiders. Remove the outsiders and repeat the analysis. Outsiders can also be identified using the clique methods. If this and all the other methods fail, it is reasonable to assume that the data do not possess any cohesive subgroups.

An example

We shall now use the steps outlined in the previous section to analyze the Newcomb fraternity data discussed in Chapter 8. Recall that the data are from a study in which 17 previously unacquainted undergraduate transfer students were allowed to live for free in a fraternity house on the campus of the University of Michigan in the fall of 1956. In return for board and lodgings, each student supplied data over a 16-week period, including a complete rank ordering of the other 16 members by 'favorableness of feeling'. We shall examine the data for week 15: rankings are from 1, most favorable, to 16, least favorable, and no ties were allowed. The data are given in Matrix 11.5.

STEP 1

As we have valued non-symmetric data, we first try the Clustering|Combinatorial Optimization method. We tried two and three groups: the three-group split was not very successful; the two-group split produced clusters {1, 2, 4, 5, 6, 7, 8, 9, 11, 12, 13, 14, 17} and {3, 10, 15, 16}, with a blocked data matrix as shown in Figure 11.10.

Rather than accept this, we will continue with subsequent steps to see if the other methods agree with these groupings. We first need to dichotomize the data. We shall start by assuming that the actors' top five choices are important and we will therefore replace rankings from 1 to 5 with the value 1 and change all other values to zero. We shall change these values later to check that we have robust groupings. The results are given in Matrix 11.6.

	1	2	3	4	5	6	7	8	9	10	11	12	13	14	15	16	17
1	0	12	15	5	10	11	6	4	7	16	8	9	2	3	13	14	1
2	8	0	13	2	3	6	9	10	5	15	7	4	11	12	14	16	1
3	8	11	0	10	12	3	5	13	4	14	6	2	9	15	7	16	1
4	6	4	15	0	3	2	10	11	5	16	9	8	7	14	12	13	1
5	5	4	13	2	0	8	10	6	1	14	12	11	3	9	15	16	7
6	6	9	14	3	8	0	7	1	2	15	13	11	4	10	12	16	5
7	12	4	8	6	14	10	0	5	9	16	2	1	7	11	13	15	3
8	1	9	15	3	6	4	13	0	11	14	10	8	2	7	12	16	5
9	10	5	13	3	7	1	12	9	0	16	11	6	8	4	14	15	2
10	2	12	14	11	10	6	3	4	7	0	9	1	15	13	5	16	8
11	9	3	6	4	7	13	5	14	8	16	0	2	10	11	12	15	1
12	8	2	12	7	11	14	1	10	3	16	5	0	6	9	15	13	4
13	1	10	14	9	8	5	3	2	7	15	12	11	0	6	13	16	4
14	4	9	16	10	15	2	8	11	1	14	3	7	6	0	12	13	5
15	12	8	11	3	16	7	9	13	4	14	15	5	6	10	0	2	1
16	12	5	16	3	11	8	7	15	2	14	9	1	13	10	6	0	4
17	4	3	14	2	6	10	9	11	1	16	8	7	5	13	12	15	0

Matrix 11.5 Newcomb fraternity data.

Analyzing Social Networks

	1	2	11	4	5	6	7	8	9	14	13	12	17	10	3	16	15
1		12	8	5	10	11	6	4	7	3	2	9	1	16	15	14	13
2	8		7	2	3	6	9	10	5	12	11	4	1	15	13	16	14
11	9	3		4	7	13	5	14	8	11	10	2	1	16	6	15	12
4	6	4	9		3	2	10	11	5	14	7	8	1	16	15	13	12
5	5	4	12	2		8	10	6	1	9	3	11	7	14	13	16	15
6	6	9	13	3	8		7	1	2	10	4	11	5	15	14	16	12
7	12	4	2	6	14	10		5	9	11	7	1	3	16	8	15	13
8	1	9	10	3	6	4	13		11	7	2	8	5	14	15	16	12
9	10	5	11	3	7	1	12	9		4	8	6	2	16	13	15	14
14	4	9	3	10	15	2	8	11	1		6	7	5	14	16	13	12
13	1	10	12	9	8	5	3	2	7	6		11	4	15	14	16	13
12	8	2	5	7	11	14	1	10	3	9	6		4	16	12	13	15
17	4	3	8	2	6	10	9	11	1	13	5	7		16	14	15	12
10	2	12	9	11	10	6	3	4	7	13	15	1	8		14	16	5
3	8	11	6	10	12	3	5	13	4	15	9	2	1	14		16	7
16	12	5	9	3	11	8	7	15	2	10	13	1	4	14	16		6
15	12	8	15	3	16	7	9	13	4	10	6	5	1	14	11	2	

Figure 11.10 Clustering of raw Newcomb fraternity data.

STEP 2

Perform a component analysis. The data have only one weak component, consisting of all the actors. There is one large strong component and four trivial strong components consisting of the singleton actors 3, 10, 15 and 16. This analysis has not provided us with any insight into the internal structure of the group. We therefore proceed to Step 3.

STEP 3

A standard clique analysis reveals seven cliques, shown in Figure 11.11. We see that actors 3, 10, 14, 15 and 16 are not in any cliques. We note that 3, 10, 15 and 16 were one of the groups found by the clustering method in Step 1. This analysis shows they were removed, since they are outsiders from the main group and are not a group within themselves. The number of cliques clearly provides us with some information, and we therefore proceed to Step 4.

STEP 4

The clique co-membership method yields a large group consisting of actors {1, 2, 4, 5, 6, 8, 9, 13, 17} with a smaller group of {7, 11, 12} and the outsiders. The bimodal method agrees with this, but provides some additional insight into the structure of the larger group; the latter can be split into {2, 4, 5, 9}

```
                          1 1 1 1 1 1 1 1
          1 2 3 4 5 6 7 8 9 0 1 2 3 4 5 6 7
          - - - - - - - - - - - - - - - - -
    1     0 0 0 1 0 0 0 1 0 0 0 0 1 1 0 0 1
    2     0 0 0 1 1 0 0 0 1 0 0 1 0 0 0 0 1
    3     0 0 0 0 0 1 1 0 1 0 0 1 0 0 0 0 1
    4     0 1 0 0 1 1 0 0 1 0 0 0 0 0 0 0 1
    5     1 1 0 1 0 0 0 0 1 0 0 1 0 0 0 0
    6     0 0 0 1 0 0 0 1 1 0 0 0 1 0 0 0 1
    7     0 1 0 0 0 0 0 1 0 0 1 1 0 0 0 0 1
    8     1 0 0 1 0 1 0 0 0 0 0 0 1 0 0 0 1
    9     0 1 0 1 0 1 0 0 0 0 0 0 0 1 0 0 1
   10     1 0 0 0 0 0 1 1 0 0 0 1 0 0 1 0 0
   11     0 1 0 1 0 0 1 0 0 0 0 1 0 0 0 0 1
   12     0 1 0 0 0 0 1 0 1 0 1 0 0 0 0 0 1
   13     1 0 0 0 0 1 1 1 0 0 0 0 0 0 0 0 1
   14     1 0 0 0 0 1 0 0 1 0 1 0 1 0 0 0 1
   15     0 0 0 1 0 0 0 0 1 0 0 1 0 0 0 1 1
   16     0 1 0 1 0 0 0 0 1 0 0 1 0 0 0 0 1
   17     1 1 0 1 0 0 0 0 1 0 0 0 1 0 0 0 0
```

Matrix 11.6 Dichotomized fraternity data.

```
        1:    2  4  9  17
        2:    2  4  5
        3:    1  8  13
        4:    1  13  17
        5:    4  6  9
        6:    6  8  13
        7:    7  11  12
```

Figure 11.11 Clique analysis results.

and {1, 8, 13}, with actors 6 and 17 as part of both and acting as brokers between these two groups.

A repeat analysis taking just the top three choices gives similar results. In this instance, the groups reported come from the component analysis and a clique analysis is not required. Taking the top seven choices produces similar results, but the outsiders tend to cloud the standard clique analysis. The faction method with three groups, however, gives the groupings {1, 2, 4, 5, 6, 8, 9, 13, 14, 17}, {10, 15, 16} and {3, 7, 11, 12}, in close agreement with our previous analysis. In this instance, the {10, 15, 16} group had no ties with the other two groups. We therefore conclude that our analysis is robust and represents the structure inherent in the data, and we terminate our analysis.

11.8 Supplementary material

In the group co-membership method outlined above, the approach was to cluster the actors based upon the frequency of pairwise group membership. A dual approach would be to cluster the groups based upon a measure of pairwise overlap. The result would be a hierarchical clustering of groups, where each group at a particular level would be uniquely placed in a cluster. But, since the actors can belong to more than one group, the clusters of groups could consist of actors belonging to more than one cluster. We assume that group X and group Y are similar if they share a lot of actors. We therefore define a similarity matrix called the 'co-group matrix' B, where $B(i, j)$ is the number of actors group i has in common with group j. The diagonal entries will give the size of the groups. Matrix 11.7 is the co-group matrix for the clique analysis of the games data. Notice that the matrix is 5×5 since we identified five cliques.

We see that, since the (2, 3) entry is 4, cliques 2 and 3 have four actors in common: W1, W3, W4 and S1. If this is now submitted to an average link hierarchical clustering procedure, we obtain the clustering given in Figure 11.12.

Here we see that cliques 1, 2 and 3 form a cluster, and cliques 4 and 5 form a separate cluster. The actors in cliques 1, 2 and 3 are {I1, W1, W2, W,3 W4, W5, S1} and in cliques 4 and 5 are {W6, W7, W8, W9, S4}, repeating the results obtained from the actor-based clustering. The reason these two methods agree is that there is no overlap between the two basic groups. However, in general this would not be the case. Again, this analysis is done automatically within UCINET.

```
          1   2   3   4   5
          --  --  --  --  --
     1     5   4   3   0   0
     2     4   5   4   0   0
     3     3   4   5   0   0
     4     0   0   0   4   3
     5     0   0   0   3   4
```

Matrix 11.7   Co-group matrix for the games data.

```
     Level      1 2 3 4 5
     -----      - - - - -
     4.000      XXX . . .
     3.500      XXXXX . .
     3.000      XXXXX XXX
     0.000      XXXXXXXXX
```

Figure 11.12   Hierarchical clustering of the co-group matrix.

11.9 Summary

Cohesive subgroups (sometimes referred to as communities) are portions of the network in which actors interact more with each other than they do with actors who are not in the group. Such groups often share common ideals, goals and/or attributes and are therefore of particular interest. There are two distinct approaches to looking for such groups. The first is to start with an explicit definition such as a clique and then look for cliques in the data. The second is to devise an algorithm which captures subgroup properties and then use this to identify the groups; factions, Newman community detection and Girvan–Newman take this approach. Clique analysis usually requires a secondary analysis to untangle the complex overlapping structures which result. The two approaches to this are to use hierarchical clustering on the clique overlap matrix or to use two-mode techniques on the clique participation matrix. The first approach prevents an actor from being in more than one clique, although other techniques could be used (such as multidimensional scaling) which do not suffer from this problem. The second approach allows for a visualization, which can be explored interactively. More complex methods, discussed in Chapter 13, could also be used, but these are not usually necessary. The methods of factions and Newman community detection use optimization techniques to try to partition the data into meaningful groups. The Girvan–Newman algorithm searches for central edges which hold the network together and deletes these to recursively uncover the cohesive subgroups. Neither of these methods allows for overlap. Computationally, factions can be limiting and Girvan–Newman does not always yield groups. In analyzing any real data, a combination of approaches is usually recommended.

11.10 Problems and Exercises

1. The network data in the file "campnet.##h" will be used for the problems and exercises in this chapter. First, we want to symmetrize the network. In UCINET go to Transform|Symmetrize… and input Campnet.##h. In this case symmetrize by using the "Maximum". Once maximum has been selected click OK. The symmetrized network we will be using is called "campnet-maxsym.##h". Now visualize the network using NetDraw (this is something you should be able to do by now). With just a visual inspection of the network how might you characterize the subgroupings among actors in the network? Now we want to analyze the network using the various approaches discussed in the chapter for detecting cohesive subgroups.

2. Initially we want to identify the cliques in the network. In UCINET go to Network| Subgroup|Cliques… and input the file "campnet-maxsym.##h". Be sure to name all the output files accordingly. For example, you might want to add the name of the network to the output file default name as in "CliqueOverlapcampnet-maxsym". Once the file has been loaded and the output files properly named click OK. Be sure to save the "ucinetlog" for later use. How many cliques are there? Are actors members of more than one clique?

3. Using the same output from Problem 2 above, what does the "Actor-by-Actor Clique Co-Membership Matrix" tell you? Using the "HIERARCHICAL CLUSTERING OF OVERLAP MATRIX" in the same output, how many subgroups would you say are in this network?

4. We can also examine the actors and the cliques simultaneously. Referred to as the bimodal method, we want to use one of the output files created during the run of the clique analysis in Problem 2 above. This involves the clique participation matrix, which if using the naming method outlined above would be named "Clique Participationcampnet-maxsym.##h". Go to NetDraw and click on File|Open|2_Mode network. Enter the clique participation network and click OK. What does this bimodal representation inform us about the subgroupings in the network?

5. Another way to determine cohesive subgroups is factions. Using "campnet-maxsym.##h" in UCINET go to Network|Subgroup|Factions and load the network. You have to determine the prescribed number of partitions or subgroups in advance. For the purposes of this problem we will run a series of analyses with different numbers of prescribed blocks or subgroups. With number of blocks designated as 2 click on OK. Save the ucinetlog file for later comparison (be sure to save the file to your working folder). Now run the factions again only this time designating the number of blocks as 3 (remembering to save the ucinetlog output). Finally, run the factions again only this time designating the number of blocks as 4 (remembering to save the ucinetlog output). Does a 2, 3 or 4 block solution best reflect the cohesive subgroup structure of the network?

6. Another method for detecting cohesive subgroups, also referred to as community detection, is the Girvan-Newman algorithm. Using the Campnet symmetrized network go to UCINET and click on Network|Subgroup|Girvan-Newman and load "campnet-maxsym.##h" and click OK. The output shows partitioning of the network into subgroups at different levels. However, we can visualize the various levels of partitioning using NetDraw. An output file was produced called "campnet-maxsym-gn.##h". Go to NetDraw and click on File|Open|Ucinet dataset|Network and enter the Campnet symmetrized network and click OK. We now want to use the Girvan-Newman attribute file containing the partitions. Go to File|Open|Ucinet dataset|Attribute data and load the file "campnet-maxsym-gn.##h" and click OK. The attribute file is now loaded. Now go to Properties|Nodes|Symbols|Color|Attribute-based. Click on the Select Attribute pull down menu. There will be a list of attributes for various levels of partitioning and an attribute for ID. We are interested in the partitions designated with a "C". So C2 is for two subgroups, C3 for three subgroups and so on. In the pull-down menu click on C2. Two boxes with colors should be displayed representing each of the two partitions. Click on the green check mark. Now go back to the pull-down menu and click on C3 and click the green arrow. Repeat for C4. How do the various levels of partitioning compare?

7. In comparing the various methods for detecting cohesive subgroups what might you conclude?

8. Cohesive subgroup can also be determined in valued networks. We will use a valued network for the South Pole crew at the end of the winter. The valued network is named "End_Winter_Valued.##h". Similar to Chapter 6, Problem 4 we can determine cohesive subgroups in this valued network using Hierarchical Clustering. In UCINET go to Tools|Cluster Analysis|Hierarchical and input the name of the network data file. Since this is valued data on a 11 point Likert Scale, with 0 being no social interaction and 10 being a lot, we want to make sure "Similarities" is entered. We will use the default method of WTD_AVERAGE. Also, make sure the "Output Partition Matrix" is properly named for later visualization of the partitions in the network. Once the file is loaded click OK. How many cohesive subgroups would you say are in this valued network?

12

Equivalence

Learning Outcomes

1. Understand the underlying model of structural and regular equivalence
2. Construct and interpret blockmodels for both regular and structural equivalence
3. Undertake a core–periphery analysis of a network

12.1 Introduction

Ideas of social role have been important to social theorists since the middle of the last century. Some social theorists have emphasized the set of rights and obligations associated with social roles. Others, however, such as Nadel (1957), view roles from a relational perspective. A teacher is a teacher because she has certain characteristic relations with her students, who in turn are defined in terms of their relations with their teachers. Social networks provide an ideal environment in which to formalize relational perspectives on role and position.

We recall that a social network in its largest sense may consist of a number of different relations collected on the same set of actors. One of the fundamental aspects of social role is that it is determined over a number of different relations. It follows that any relational definition of role or position should be capable of simultaneously taking account of multiple different kinds of ties among nodes.

Nodes that occupy the same structural roles or positions are said to be relationally equivalent.[1] The positional approach to network analysis is based upon identifying

[1] We would like to say 'structurally equivalent', since we mean equivalence with respect to structural position. Unfortunately, the term was used early on by Lorrain and White (1971) to refer to one specific type of structure-based equivalence, so we avoid using the term except when referring to the more specific concept.

similar positions and should be contrasted with the relational or cohesive subgroup approach of Chapter 11. Whereas positional approaches seek classes of
nodes that have similar structural properties, cohesive subgroup approaches
seek clusters of nodes that are connected to each other. Formal definitions have
been developed for directed and undirected networks. These definitions have
then been relaxed so as to allow for the analysis of noisy and valued data.

Over the years, network researchers have developed a number of different concepts of structure-based equivalence that each have their utility. In this chapter,
however, we shall only address two concepts: Lorrain and White's (1971) structural
equivalence and White and Reitz's (1983) regular equivalence (which includes
structural equivalence as a special case). We begin with structural equivalence.

12.2 Structural equivalence

In its simplest form, structural equivalence examines the direct connections of
an actor to other actors in the network. Two actors are structurally equivalent if
they send ties to the same third parties, and receive ties from the same third
parties. They do not need to have a direct tie to each other to be equivalent.
Thus, an actor's position is defined by whom he is connected to – his 'location'
in social space.

A useful question to ask is why we should care about structural equivalence.
One reason is that there is a lot of empirical evidence that shows that structurally
equivalent actors share other similarities as well, such as similarities in attitudes
(Erickson, 1988) and behaviors (Burt, 1980). In other words, actors in the same
equivalence class tend to show a certain amount of homogeneity, very much like
actors in the same cohesive subgroup. The mechanism, however, can be different.
For example, in the case of cohesive groups, actors are interacting with each other
and being exposed to each other's ideas, language, infections, and the like. It is a
contagion process. In the case of structurally equivalent actors (who may not even
know each other), it is that their similar social environments provoke similar
responses. For example, if two people are connected to the same set of very gossipy
people, they might both learn to keep their mouths shut for their own protection.
Notice how different this is from a contagion process, where they would be closed-
mouthed because their friends were close-mouthed. In contagion, having gossipy
friends would mean becoming gossipy as well. Thus, one mechanism underlying
the relationship between structural equivalence and homogeneity is the idea that
persons adapt to their social environments, and therefore actors with similar social
environments will tend to have certain similarities. Since the concept of sharing a
niche in both ecology and marketing involves sharing the same environment
(whether physical/biological or client-based), structural equivalence provides a
network definition of the concept of niche.

Another way to think about structural equivalence is in terms of substitutability. Nodes that are structurally equivalent are structurally indistinguishable and therefore substitutable. For example, a computer programmer working on a project may fall sick, and her role might then be taken over by a contract programmer. In terms of whom he reports to and whose code his code has to connect with, the new programmer relates to all other members of the project team in the same way as the previous programmer. It follows that the new and the old programmer have exactly the same connections in the work network and, as such, are structurally equivalent and substitutable.

A final reason for paying attention to structural equivalence is that we can use it as a kind of data reduction device because it enables us to build a simplified model of the network without sacrificing essential features. Hence, it provides a high-level description of the relations within the network.

We shall now give a formal definition of structural equivalence. Although it is possible to give a sophisticated mathematical definition (see Lorrain and White, 1971), we shall give a slightly longer but less technical one. This definition is valid for undirected data that allow self-loops. Two actors i and j are structurally equivalent if the following two statements are true for every relation in our dataset:

- For every actor k different from i and j, whenever i is connected to k, then j is also connected to k, and if i is not connected to k then neither is j.
- If i is connected to itself then so is j, and if i is not connected to itself then neither is j – so that both actors share the same relationship with themselves.

Hence, for undirected graphs without self-loops, the definition reduces to the following: Actors i and j are structurally equivalent if, excepting each other, they are connected to exactly the same other actors.

The extension to directed data simply deals with both the incoming ties and outgoing ties separately. This also adds another level of complication in dealing with the relationship between i and j, but fundamentally the concept is the same.

Let us now consider some examples on single-relationship networks. If we examine R_1 in Figure 12.1, we can easily see that actors 3, 4 and 5 are all connected to 1 and 2 and are all therefore structurally equivalent. Notice further that actor 1 is connected to 2, 3, 4, 5 and actor 2 is connected to 1, 3, 4, 5; therefore, outside of each other they are both connected to 3, 4, 5 and both have self-loops and hence are structurally equivalent. In relation R_2, actors 3 and 4 both only receive ties from actors 1 and 2 and are therefore structurally equivalent. Actors 1 and 2 are both connected to 3 and 4 and both receive ties from 5; in addition, the connection from actor 1 to 2 is matched by the connection from 2 to 1 so that they too are structurally equivalent. Note that 5 is not structurally equivalent to any of the other actors.

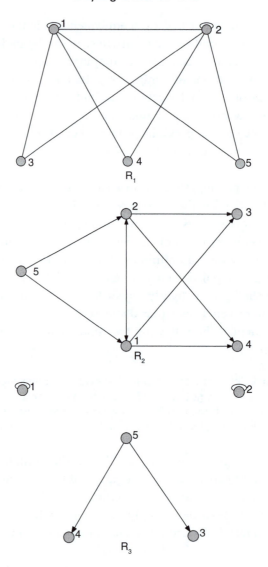

Figure 12.1 A multirelational network.

We now look at Figure 12.1 as a multirelational example consisting of five actors on three relations. In relation R_1 actors 1 and 2 are structurally equivalent and so are actors 3, 4 and 5. However, in relations R_2 and R_3 actors 1 and 2 are structurally equivalent and so are 3 and 4, but 5 is not structurally equivalent to any other actor in either relation. It follows that the structurally equivalent actors are 1 and 2 as one pair and 3 and 4 as another pair.

Another way of thinking about structural equivalence is that if we remove the labels that identify two structurally equivalent actors, *i* and *j*, say, on a diagram, it will no longer be possible to tell which is which. This is because they have exactly the same pattern of relationships over all relations. If we look back at R_1 in Figure 12.1 and remove the labels 3 and 5, we have no way of knowing which label belongs to which vertex. This would not be the case if labels 2 and 3 were removed: we know that the actor of degree 4 is 2 and the one of degree 2 is 3. A consequence of this is that structurally equivalent actors are identical with respect to any structural property. They have the same degree, the same centrality, participate in the same number of cycles, etc. They are perfectly substitutable for each other.

To extend the definition to valued data, we simply insist that the identical connections to other actors have identical values. If in relation R_2 in Figure 12.1 actors 1 and 2 are structurally equivalent and the edge (1, 3) has a value of 5.0, the edge (2, 3) must have a value 5.0. Furthermore, if the edge (1, 2) has a value of 7.0, so must the edge (2, 1).

12.3 Profile similarity

Our definition of structural equivalence is an ideal mathematical model and would rarely occur in real data. It does, however, provide a theoretical framework on which we can base measures that try to capture the degree to which actors are structurally equivalent to each other. This will allow us to analyze data that contain measurement error, respondent variability and all the other inevitable inaccuracies associated with collecting real data.

We first observe that structural equivalence is a local property in the sense that to determine whether a pair of actors are structurally equivalent we only need to know to whom they are directly connected. As a result, ego network data are sufficient for calculating structural equivalence. The rows and columns of the adjacency matrix of the relation contain all the relevant information and can be used to determine the sets of alters; they are known as profiles (Burt, 1976). The profile of actor i in an undirected single relation is simply the ith row (or column, as this is the same) of the adjacency matrix. For directed data, the profile is the ith row concatenated with the ith column.

We illustrate this with some examples. In Figure 12.1 the profile of actor 3 is (1, 1, 0, 0, 0), which shows that actor 3 is adjacent to actors 1 and 2 and not adjacent to itself nor to actors 4 and 5. Consider actor 2 in the network given by the adjacency matrix in Matrix 12.1. The second row of the adjacency matrix is (1, 0, 1, 1, 0), and the second column is (1, 0, 0, 0, 1). The fact that 2 is not connected to itself is recorded in the second entry of both the row and column vectors – that is, this value has been noted twice. The profile is therefore (1, 0, 1, 1, 0, 1, 0, 0, 0, 1). Once we have the profiles, we can compare them and

```
              1 2 3 4 5
              - - - - -
          1   0 1 0 1 1
          2   1 0 1 1 0
          3   1 0 0 1 1
          4   1 0 1 0 0
          5   0 1 0 0 1
```

Matrix 12.1   A directed adjacency matrix.

check whether they satisfy the structural equivalence definition. To do so, they need to be identical except for the entries that correspond to the actors that are compared. Hence, if we are comparing the profile of actor i with that of actor j, we need to pay particular attention to the ith and jth entry of the two profiles. If the two profiles compared in this way are not identical, the actors are not structurally equivalent. It would be useful to know how similar the two vectors are to each other. To do this, we could use any of the standard measures for comparing vectors. These include, but are not limited to, matches, correlation and Euclidean distance. One advantage of using the existing comparison methods for vectors is that they can be applied to valued data.

When we compare two profile vectors, we have to make sure that we meet all the conditions of structural equivalence. Suppose that we wish to use matching to compare the profile of row i with the profile of row j. For each element except the ith and jth entry in each row or column that makes up the profile, we match the corresponding element in each vector. We then match the ith entry in row i with the jth entry in row j and the jth entry in row i with the ith entry in row j, repeating the process for the corresponding column entries. This process is known as 'reciprocal swapping' and is applied regardless of the method of comparing vectors.

We then proceed to compare every pair of actors and from this information construct a structural equivalence matrix. The (i, j) entry in this matrix is the profile similarity measure of actor i with actor j. Regardless of how many relations are being considered, and whether they were directed or not, the structural equivalence matrix is a square symmetric matrix with the same number of rows (and columns) as the number of actors in the dataset. Note that if a standard statistical measure such as correlation is used, we could not apply classical statistical inference on the results since the independence assumption has been violated. We can, however, treat the matrix as a proximity measure and apply classification and clustering techniques. This is necessary since one of the goals of positions is to place actors into mutually exclusive equivalence classes.

If we used Euclidean distance, a pair of structurally equivalent actors would yield a distance of zero. Values close to zero would indicate that the actors involved are nearly structurally equivalent. Clearly, if we used correlation,

(a) Esteem

		1R	2B	3A	4B	5P	6L	7V	8W	9J	10G	11H	12B	13M	14A	15A	16B	17E	18S
1	ROMUALD	0	0	0	0	0	0	0	0	0	0	0	0	0	0	0	0	0	0
2	BONAVENTURE	0	0	1	0	3	2	0	0	0	0	0	0	0	0	0	0	0	0
3	AMBROSE	0	0	0	0	3	0	2	0	1	0	0	0	0	0	0	0	0	0
4	BERTHOLD	0	0	0	0	3	2	0	0	0	0	0	0	0	0	0	0	0	0
5	PETER	2	0	0	1	0	3	0	0	0	0	0	0	0	0	0	0	0	0
6	LOUIS	0	2	3	0	0	0	0	0	0	0	0	0	0	0	0	0	0	0
7	VICTOR	0	1	0	2	3	0	0	0	0	0	0	0	0	0	0	0	0	0
8	WINFRID	0	0	0	0	0	0	0	0	3	2	1	0	0	0	0	0	0	0
9	JOHN	0	1	0	0	0	0	3	2	0	0	0	0	0	0	0	0	0	0
10	GREGORY	0	1	0	0	0	0	2	0	3	0	0	0	0	0	0	0	0	0
11	HUGH	0	0	0	0	0	0	0	1	3	2	0	2	0	0	0	0	0	0
12	BONIFACE	0	0	0	0	0	0	0	0	1	3	2	0	0	0	0	0	0	0
13	MARK	0	0	0	0	0	0	0	1	0	3	0	1	0	2	0	0	0	0
14	ALBERT	0	0	0	0	0	0	0	1	0	3	0	2	2	0	0	0	0	0
15	AMAND	0	3	0	0	0	1	0	0	0	0	0	0	2	0	0	0	0	0
16	BASIL	0	0	0	0	0	0	0	0	3	0	0	0	0	0	2	0	1	1
17	ELIAS	0	0	0	0	0	0	0	0	0	1	0	0	0	0	1	2	0	3
18	SIMPLICIUS	0	0	0	0	0	0	0	0	0	2	0	0	0	0	0	3	1	0

(b) Disesteem

		1R	2B	3A	4B	5P	6L	7V	8W	9J	10G	11H	12B	13M	14A	15A	16B	17E	18S
1	ROMUALD	0	0	0	0	0	0	0	0	0	0	0	0	0	0	0	0	0	0
2	BONAVENTURE	0	0	0	0	0	0	0	0	0	0	0	0	0	0	0	1	3	2
3	AMBROSE	0	0	0	0	0	0	0	0	0	0	0	0	0	0	1	0	3	2
4	BERTHOLD	0	0	0	0	0	0	1	0	0	0	0	0	3	0	0	2	2	0
5	PETER	0	0	0	0	0	0	0	0	2	3	1	0	0	0	0	0	0	0
6	LOUIS	0	0	0	0	0	0	0	0	1	3	0	0	0	1	0	2	0	0
7	VICTOR	0	0	0	0	0	0	0	0	0	0	1	0	0	0	0	0	2	3
8	WINFRID	0	0	0	0	0	0	0	0	0	0	0	0	0	0	0	0	0	0
9	JOHN	0	0	0	0	0	0	0	0	2	0	0	3	0	0	1	0	0	0
10	GREGORY	0	0	0	0	3	0	0	0	0	0	0	0	0	0	1	2	0	0
11	HUGH	0	0	0	0	2	2	0	0	0	0	0	0	0	0	3	0	1	1
12	BONIFACE	0	0	0	0	3	1	0	0	0	0	0	0	0	0	0	2	1	1
13	MARK	0	0	0	3	2	0	2	0	0	0	0	0	0	0	0	2	1	0
14	ALBERT	0	0	0	0	3	0	0	0	0	0	0	0	0	0	0	2	2	1
15	AMAND	0	0	0	3	0	0	0	0	2	0	0	0	0	0	0	1	0	0
16	BASIL	0	0	0	2	3	0	0	0	0	1	0	0	0	0	0	0	0	0
17	ELIAS	0	0	0	3	2	0	1	0	0	0	0	0	0	0	0	0	0	0
18	SIMPLICIUS	1	0	0	2	2	0	3	0	0	0	0	0	0	0	0	0	0	0

Matrix 12.2 Sampson monastery: (a) esteem matrix; (b) disesteem matrix.

structurally equivalent actors would have a correlation coefficient of 1. However, in contrast to the Euclidean distance measure, it would also be possible for actors that were not structurally equivalent to have a perfect correlation score. This would occur if one profile were a straight multiple of another, which in some circumstances would be desirable. We shall return to this topic later.

In 1968 Sampson collected data on social relations in a contemporary isolated American monastery. Towards the end of his study, there was a major crisis, resulting in a number of members being expelled or resigning. Sampson (1969) defined four sorts of relation: affect, esteem, influence and sanction. Breiger et al. (1975) report these matrices for the period just before the dispute. We shall consider just the esteem relation, which we split into two relations of esteem and disesteem. Each novitiate ranked the other monks, giving his top three choices for that relation. In all rankings, 3 is the highest or first choice and 1 the lowest; ties and no choices were permissible. The esteem matrix is shown in Matrix 12.2a and the disesteem matrix in Matrix 12.2b.

Shortly after these data were collected, Gregory, Basil, Elias and Simplicius were expelled. Almost immediately, John departed voluntarily. A few days later Hugh, Boniface, Mark and Albert left, and within a week Victor and Amand departed. One month later Romuald also left. Sampson grouped the monks and then named the groups as follows:

- {Winfrid, John, Gregory, Hugh, Boniface, Mark, Albert}, the Young Turks;
- {Bonaventure, Ambrose, Berthold, Peter, Louis}, the Loyal Opposition;
- {Basil, Elias, Simplicius}, the Outcasts;
- {Romuald, Victor, Amand}, indeterminate.

The esteem and disesteem matrices were submitted to the profile similarity routine in UCINET. The program constructs a profile for each actor by appending its row in the disesteem matrix to its row in the esteem matrix. Because the data are not symmetric, it also appends to these profiles the columns of each data matrix, yielding profiles on the order of $4N$ cells in length. This is often referred to as 'including the transposes'. Euclidean distance was selected as the choice for measuring the amount of structural equivalence between the profiles. The results are shown in Matrix 12.3, where the distances have been rounded up to the nearest whole number.

Since we used Euclidean distance, a value of zero would indicate perfect structural equivalence. The only zero values are on the diagonal (actors are structurally equivalent to themselves), so no two actors are perfectly structurally equivalent. The smallest values are 5, so the most similar actors are pairs such as Bonaventure and Ambrose or Albert and Boniface. The least similar actors have a score of 13 – for example, Peter and John. To obtain some form of structurally equivalent groups, we can submit this matrix to either a multidimensional scaling routine or

	1	2	3	4	5	6	7	8	9	10	11	12	13	14	15	16	17	18
	RO	BO	AM	BE	PE	LO	VI	WI	JO	GR	HU	BO	MA	AL	AM	BA	EL	SI
	--	--	--	--	--	--	--	--	--	--	--	--	--	--	--	--	--	--
ROMUALD	0	7	7	8	11	7	8	5	9	10	7	7	8	7	7	9	8	8
BONAVENTURE	7	0	5	8	12	8	7	8	10	12	9	8	9	8	9	11	10	10
AMBROSE	7	5	0	9	12	9	7	7	10	11	8	8	10	8	9	10	10	10
BERTHOLD	8	8	9	0	10	10	9	10	11	12	11	10	9	10	10	10	10	11
PETER	11	12	12	10	0	10	12	12	13	13	12	12	13	13	11	12	12	13
LOUIS	7	8	9	10	10	0	10	8	10	12	10	9	10	9	7	10	10	10
VICTOR	8	7	7	9	12	10	0	8	11	12	10	9	11	9	10	11	10	9
WINFRID	5	8	7	10	12	8	8	0	8	9	6	5	8	7	8	8	9	9
JOHN	9	10	10	11	13	10	11	8	0	10	10	10	11	10	9	11	11	11
GREGORY	10	12	11	12	13	12	12	9	10	0	9	9	11	10	11	9	12	12
HUGH	7	9	8	11	12	10	10	6	10	9	0	5	9	7	9	9	10	9
BONIFACE	7	8	8	10	12	9	9	5	10	9	5	0	7	5	9	9	9	9
MARK	8	9	10	9	13	10	11	8	11	11	9	7	0	6	9	9	9	9
ALBERT	7	8	8	10	13	9	9	7	10	10	7	5	6	0	9	9	9	9
AMAND	7	9	9	10	11	7	10	8	9	11	9	9	9	9	0	9	9	9
BASIL	9	11	10	10	12	10	11	8	11	9	9	9	9	9	9	0	7	9
ELIAS	8	10	10	10	12	10	10	9	11	12	10	9	9	9	9	7	0	5
SIMPLICIUS	8	10	10	11	13	10	9	9	11	12	9	9	9	9	9	9	5	0

Matrix 12.3 Structural equivalence matrix of Sampson data.

HIERARCHICAL CLUSTERING OF EQUIVALENCE MATRIX

```
                 1         1     1 1 1   1 1 1 1
Level      5 9 0 4 2 3 7 3 1 8 1 4 2 6 5 6 7 8
------     - - - - - - - - - - - - - - - - - -
 5.099     . . . . XXX . . XXX . XXX . . . XXX
 6.267     . . . . XXX . . XXX XXXXX . . . XXX
 6.395     . . . . XXX . . XXXXXXXXX . . . XXX
 7.393     . . . . XXXXX . XXXXXXXXX . . . XXX
 7.416     . . . . XXXXX . XXXXXXXXX XXX . XXX
 7.514     . . . . XXXXX XXXXXXXXXXX XXX . XXX
 8.168     . . . . XXXXX XXXXXXXXXXX XXX XXXXX
 8.674     . . . XXXXXXX XXXXXXXXXXX XXX XXXXX
 8.762     . . . XXXXXXX XXXXXXXXXXXXXXX XXXXX
 9.188     . . . XXXXXXX XXXXXXXXXXXXXXXXXXXXX
 9.856     . . . XXXXXXXXXXXXXXXXXXXXXXXXXXXXX
10.000     . XXX XXXXXXXXXXXXXXXXXXXXXXXXXXXXX
10.912     . XXXXXXXXXXXXXXXXXXXXXXXXXXXXXXXXX
12.012     XXXXXXXXXXXXXXXXXXXXXXXXXXXXXXXXXXX
```

Figure 12.2 Clustering of structural equivalence matrix.

a clustering method. Figure 12.2 is the clustering diagram associated with a single-link hierarchical clustering of the structural equivalence matrix given in Matrix 12.3. The following groupings are obtained from this clustering at the level 8.674:

- {Bonaventure, Ambrose, Berthold, Victor}
- {Romuald, Winfrid, Hugh, Boniface, Mark, Albert}
- {Louis, Amand}
- {Basil, Elias, Simplicius}

Peter, John and Gregory are singletons and have not been taken into any clusters at this level. Each group is consistent with Sampson's assignment, as none of the members of the three major groupings are placed together. It also has to be remembered that this is an analysis of just one pair of the relations and thus is not as rich in data as taking all the relations.

12.4 Blockmodels

Once we have identified a partition of the nodes based upon structural equivalence, we can produce a simplified or reduced matrix. We first arrange the rows and columns of the adjacency matrix so that structurally equivalent actors are grouped together. This grouping induces blocks within the matrix. Matrix 12.4 shows this process for relation R_1 in Figure 12.1. We note that the blocks consist of either all zeros or all ones. We could therefore replace each block by a zero or a one without losing any information. This results in a new and smaller adjacency matrix which represents a reduced graph. We call these the 'image matrix' and 'image graph', respectively. The reduced adjacency matrix and image graph for Matrix 12.4 are given in Figure 12.3.

This process is called blockmodeling. For pure structural equivalence, the blocks are either all ones or all zeros and are called '1-blocks' and '0-blocks', respectively (White, Boorman and Breiger, 1976). For real data, the blocks will not be perfect, but the 0-blocks will be predominantly filled with zeros and the

```
        1 2   3 4 5
      -------------
  1 | 1 1 | 1 1 1 |
  2 | 1 1 | 1 1 1 |
      -------------
  3 | 1 1 | 0 0 0 |
  4 | 1 1 | 0 0 0 |
  5 | 1 1 | 0 0 0 |
      -------------
```

Matrix 12.4 Blocks for R_1 in Figure 12.1.

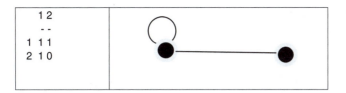

Figure 12.3 Reduced adjacency matrix and image graph from Matrix 12.4.

1-blocks should contain nearly all ones. The extent to which this is true is a measure of how well the method has managed to partition the data into structurally equivalent blocks. To illustrate blockmodeling, we have repeated the profile analysis on the Sampson esteem data but dichotomized the data first and used correlation as the measure of similarity, which is usually considered the better option. We have selected a four-block solution, and Figure 12.4 gives the blockmodel.

The results show four groups, resulting in 16 matrix blocks in each of the two relations (esteem and disesteem). The density of each of the blocks is given below each relation. Of the 32 blocks, only eight are perfect, of which seven are 0-blocks and one is a 1-block. This is fairly common when analyzing data of this type. The blockmodel allows us to uncover structural properties of the data. We can see, for example, that none of the groups has any esteem for the Outcasts

```
                              1      1 1 1 1      1      1 1 1
                   1 2 3 4 5 7  0 8 9 4 1 2 3    6 5    6 7 8
                   R B A B P V  G W J A H B M    L A    B E S
                  -------------------------------------------------
 1    ROMUALD    |             |             |       |       |
 2 BONAVENTURE   |     1   1   |             |   1   |       |
 3    AMBROSE    |       1 1   |     1       |       |       |
 4    BERTHOLD   |       1     |             |   1   |       |
 5    PETER      | 1     1     |             |   1   |       |
 7    VICTOR     |   1   1 1   |             |       |       |
                  -------------------------------------------------
10    GREGORY    |   1     1   |     1       |       |       |
 8    WINFRID    |             | 1   1   1   |       |       |
 9    JOHN       |   1     1   |   1         |       |       |
14    ALBERT     |             | 1 1     1 1 |       |       |
11    HUGH       |             | 1 1 1   1   |       |       |
12    BONIFACE   |             | 1   1 1     |       |       |
13    MARK       |             | 1 1   1 1   |       |       |
                  -------------------------------------------------
 6    LOUIS      |   1 1       |             |       |       |
15    AMAND      |   1         |         1   | 1     |       |
                  -------------------------------------------------
16    BASIL      |             |   1         |   1   | 1 1   |
17    ELIAS      |             | 1           |   1   | 1   1 |
18  SIMPLICIUS   |             | 1           |       | 1 1   |
                  -------------------------------------------------
```

(Continued)

Figure 12.4 (Continued)

Reduced BlockMatrix

	1	2	3	4
1	0.333	0.024	0.250	0.000
2	0.095	0.476	0.000	0.000
3	0.250	0.071	0.500	0.000
4	0.000	0.143	0.333	1.000

		1	2	3	4	5	7	10	8	9	14	11	12	13	6	15	16	17	18
		R	B	A	B	P	V	G	W	J	A	H	B	M	L	A	B	E	S
1	ROMUALD																		
2	BONAVENTURE																1	1	1
3	AMBROSE														1			1	1
4	BERTHOLD			1									1				1	1	
5	PETER							1		1		1							
7	VICTOR												1					1	1
10	GREGORY				1										1		1		
8	WINFRID																		
9	JOHN							1				1					1		
14	ALBERT			1													1	1	1
11	HUGH			1											1	1		1	1
12	BONIFACE			1											1		1	1	1
13	MARK		1	1	1												1	1	
6	LOUIS							1		1	1							1	
15	AMAND			1				1										1	
16	BASIL		1	1				1											
17	ELIAS		1	1	1														
18	SIMPLICIUS	1	1	1	1														

Reduced BlockMatrix

	1	2	3	4
1	0.033	0.119	0.083	0.500
2	0.167	0.048	0.286	0.571
3	0.083	0.286	0.000	0.333
4	0.500	0.048	0.000	0.000

Figure 12.4 Blockmodel of the Sampson data.

(except themselves!) and also that there is a high level of disesteem from each of the groups to the Outcasts. This confirms that Sampson was correct in his observation and that calling this group the Outcasts was justified.

In general, one looks for certain patterns in the blockmodel that equate to known structures. Core–periphery is one such pattern, and we discuss this later in the chapter. Another common pattern is to have the 1-blocks on the diagonal in the image matrix; these equate to cohesive subgroups, and the blockmodel gives additional insight into the interactions between these groups. This is precisely what was done using the factions method in Chapter 11.

For valued data, we would expect the blocks to contain similar values. For example, instead of 1-blocks and 0-blocks, we may have, say, a 5-block (i.e., a block in which each value is a 5). The image matrix will now consist of entries that are the average of all the values in the blocks. We can again judge how good the blockmodel is by looking at the variation in the values in each block. The standard deviation is one obvious way to do this, and this is reported in UCINET.

Finally, when using the profile structural equivalence method on non-valued data, it is common practice to first convert the data to geodesic distances. Two actors that are structurally equivalent in the original data will still be structurally equivalent in the geodesic distance matrix. One reason for doing the conversion is that the geodesic distance matrix contains information about how well an actor is connected into the whole network and not just their local neighborhood. This is particularly useful for sparse networks, but at a penalty of making the interpretation of the results more difficult.

12.5 The direct method

We have constructed our blockmodels by first performing a profile analysis and then using this to partition our adjacency matrix. An alternative is to use a direct method to partition the data (Panning, 1982; Batagelj et al., 1992b). As already mentioned, we are able to assess how close a partition is to an ideal blockmodel by examining the entries of each block. To compare two different partitions on the same data, we just need to count the number of changes that are required to make the blockmodel fit the ideal structure of zeros and ones. We call this the 'fit', and we can now try to optimize the fit over all the possible assignments of actors to different groups. One disadvantage of this approach is that we have to specify the number of groups. For valued data, it is not possible to simply count the number of errors. In this situation, more sophisticated fit functions are used, but the principle remains the same. We demonstrate the direct method on the dichotomized esteem data. Currently, the UCINET optimization routine only accepts a single relation, so we did not include the disesteem relation. Matrix 12.5 is a three-block optimization of the data. We see that it has identified the

Outcasts, but that two of the Young Turks are now in the Loyal Opposition. In this example, since the monks were asked only to rank their top three choices, it is not possible for the larger blocks to have all ones. This means that the larger blocks cannot be made to fit well, with the consequence that the technique struggles to find good solutions. The researcher needs to be aware that, regardless of the inherent structure, the method will produce an answer. This answer may not be particularly good – it may simply be the best of a bad set. It is always good practice to examine the results carefully to see if they fit the model well.

One of the expectations we had of the structural equivalence model was that actors who are structurally equivalent would exhibit similar behaviors and outcomes. This did seem to happen to a significant extent with the Sampson data. All members of the Outcasts were expelled, and both the direct and the profile similarity methods identified these as structurally equivalent. The Young Turks all left, and, again, they were identified using the structurally equivalent models. The four core members of the Loyal Opposition remained, and each method placed three of these together and one method included all four.

```
                             1 1 1       1 1 1                   1     1 1
                             0 1 2 8 9   8 6 7   4 6 2 3 5 1 5 7 3 4
                             G H B W J   S B E   B L B A P R A V M A
                            -------------------------------------------
  10     GREGORY   |            1 |         |       1           1       |
  11        HUGH   | 1    1 1 1   |         |                           |
  12    BONIFACE   | 1 1        1 |         |                           |
   8     WINFRID   | 1 1        1 |         |                           |
   9        JOHN   |       1      |         |       1           1       |
                   --------------------------------------------------
  18  SIMPLICIUS   | 1          |     | 1 1 |                           |
  16       BASIL   |        1 1 | 1 | 1   1 1 |               1          |
  17       ELIAS   | 1          |   | 1 1   |                1          |
                   --------------------------------------------------
   4    BERTHOLD   |            |         | 1      1                    |
   6       LOUIS   |            |         |    1 1                      |
   2 BONAVENTURE   |            |         | 1      1 1                  |
   3     AMBROSE   |        1   |         |            1        1       |
   5       PETER   |            |         | 1 1           1             |
   1     ROMUALD   |            |         |                             |
  15       AMAND   |            |         |    1 1              1       |
   7      VICTOR   |            |         | 1      1   1                |
  13        MARK   | 1     1 1  |         |                        1    |
  14      ALBERT   | 1     1 1  |         |                        1    |
                   --------------------------------------------------
```

Matrix 12.5 Three-block optimization of the Sampson esteem data.

Table 12.1 MR-QAP regression of structural equivalence on gender and role similarity, with controls. R-square was 0.417.

	Un-Stdized	Stdized Coef	P-value
week_2	0.168916196	0.206286713	0.00049975
week_2-Reciprocity	0.203460485	0.24847348	0.00049975
week_2-Transitivity (Closure)	0.155448377	0.23357299	0.00049975
Gender similarity	0.132871106	0.212603197	0.010494753
Role similarity	0.028867932	0.044548016	0.2103948
Intercept	–0.209991813	0	0

More generally, a standard way to use the results of a structural equivalence analysis would be to use QAP regression to relate structural equivalence to an outcome of interest, such as being expelled together, or adopting an innovation at similar times. In addition, there is no reason why we cannot treat structural equivalence as a dependent variable and investigate how nodes come to be structurally equivalent. Table 12.1 shows the results of predicting structural equivalence at time 3 in the Camp92 dataset as a function of being the same gender and playing the same occupational role, while controlling for direct ties, reciprocity and transitivity at time 2. The results show that gender does seem to affect a node's position, but occupational role does not.

12.6 Regular equivalence

One of the restrictions of structural equivalence is that, to be equivalent, actors need to be connected to the same actors. However, actors can be structurally similar in ways that do not involve being connected to the same actors. Krackhardt and Porter (1986), for example, looked at turnover of staff in a number of fast-food outlets. They examined whether people with similar patterns of advice-seeking exhibited similar turnover patterns. Clearly, they could not use structural equivalence, since the actors were in different restaurants and so could not be connected to each other. In the study they used a generalization of structural equivalence called regular equivalence (White and Reitz, 1983). Regular equivalence relaxes the strict condition on the 1-blocks in blockmodeling. Rather than having blocks that have a 1 in every row and column, we simply require at least one 1 in each row and column (Batagelj et al., 1992a). An example of a regular blockmodeling is given in Matrix 12.6. The blockmodel has three 0-blocks as in structural equivalence, and we note that one of the blocks is a 1-block but the other blocks each have at least one 1 in every row and every column. In structural equivalence, if two actors are equivalent they have to be connected to exactly the same others. Hence, two teachers are structurally equivalent if they teach the same students. In regular equivalence, the teachers have to teach at least one student each (and not all students) and, equally, the students all need at least one teacher.

To find a regular equivalence, we can use methods similar to structural equivalence. The direct method simply needs a small change to the fit measure, but in all other respects is the same as for structural equivalence. As an example, we consider the taro data collected by Schwimmer (1973), representing the relation of gift-giving (taro exchange) among 22 households in a Papuan village. Schwimmer points out how these ties function to define the appropriate persons to mediate the act of asking for or receiving assistance among group members. We submitted the data to the UCINET direct regular equivalence optimization routine, selecting three groups. The routine returned a perfect solution – that is, one in which each block satisfies the condition for regular equivalence. The solution is given in Matrix 12.7.

This three-group solution consists of a group that exchanges within itself and with the other two groups. The two other groups only exchange outside of their groups. This suggests a status system where the top group exchanges with everyone else, but the lower group exchanges with the top and the other group but not with themselves. There are, however, many other exact solutions which have similar structures but where actors are assigned to different groups. This indicates that the solution is not stable and it would not be wise to read too much into this blocking. One approach to stabilize the solution is to be more prescriptive on the nature of the blocks. We see in the solution

```
                                          1
                    1 2 3 4   5 6 7   8 9 0
                    ---------------------------
        1  |            1 |        | 1    1 |
        2  | 1           |        |    1    |
        3  |    1    1 |        | 1    1 |
        4  |       1    |        |    1 1 |
                    ---------------------------
        5  | 1 1 1 1 |   1 1 | 1        |
        6  | 1 1 1 1 |     1 |    1     |
        7  | 1 1 1 1 | 1        | 1 1 1 |
                    ---------------------------
        8  |            | 1 1 1 |          |
        9  |            |    1 |          |
       10  |            |    1 1 |          |
                    ---------------------------
```

Matrix 12.6   Regular blockmodel.

```
                  1 2 1 1   1 1           1 1 2   1   1       1 2
                6 2 4 0 0 1 7 3 7     4 1 5 9 1 9 8     2 3 8 5 6 2
                -----------------------------------------------------
     6 |                    1       | 1                 |       1       |
     2 |                        1   | 1                 |   1           |
    14 |                  1         | 1                 | 1             |
    20 |              1             |           1       | 1             |
    10 |              1             |             1     |     1         |
    11 |         1 1                |           1   1 | 1             |
     7 | 1                          | 1         1       |       1   1   |
    13 |   1                        |             1     | 1             |
    17 |   1                        |   1           1 | 1         1 1 |
                -----------------------------------------------------
     4 | 1                 1        |                   |     1   1     |
     1 |   1                     1  |                   |       1       |
    15 |     1                      |                   | 1         1   |
    19 |             1              |                   | 1           1 |
    21 |         1 1                |                   |         1     |
     9 |           1       1        |                   |       1       |
    18 |                 1     1    |                   |             1 |
                -----------------------------------------------------
    12 |     1         1   1        |     1 1           |               |
     3 |   1                   1    | 1                 |               |
     8 |           1   1            |             1     |               |
     5 | 1         1                | 1 1         1     |               |
    16 |                 1     1    |   1               |               |
    22 |                       1    |         1       1 |               |
                -----------------------------------------------------
```

Matrix 12.7 Regular blockmodel of the taro data.

in Matrix 12.6 there is a structurally equivalent block, i.e. a block of all 1s. We could therefore mix the block structures, insisting some blocks are null, some are regular, and some are structural. This is the approach taken in generalized block modeling, which uses a variety of specified block types to fit the data. UCINET has not implemented this type of block modeling, and the interested reader would need to use Pajek; further details can be found in Doreian et al. (2005).

12.7 The REGE algorithm

The extension of profile similarity to regular equivalence is not as simple. Unlike structural equivalence, where the measure is local and depends on the direct connections to other actors, we now have to compare profiles of actor equivalences. This is a far more complicated process, since the equivalences will not be known until the process is completed. This problem is solved by itera-tively moving toward an equivalence matrix and using the interim scores as equivalence measures between iterations. The REGE algorithm accomplishes this. We do not present the details here, but we note some important facts which anyone using REGE needs to know. First, the algorithm only works on directed data (valued data must therefore not be symmetric) which contains at least one actor with either zero outdegree (a sink) or zero indegree (a source). Second, the similarity values produced can be difficult to interpret in absolute terms (except scores of 100, which signify perfect equivalence). Scores are usually used to partition the data via a clustering routine, as we did when we applied profile structural equivalence. As with structural equivalence, if you have binary data, some analysts suggest converting the adjacency matrix to a geodesic distance matrix and submitting this to REGE.

The REGE algorithm is designed to converge to the maximum equiva-lence, and, as this is a unique solution, we do not have the difficulty of the multiple solutions that can occur with the direct method. Also, like profile structural equivalence, the REGE algorithm can be applied to datasets containing multiple relations.

To see how REGE can be used, we return to the Sampson esteem/disesteem data, running the UCINET routine with the default values. The results are shown in Figure 12.5. If we examine the groups at the 74.855 level, we obtain the clusters:

- {Bonaventure, Ambrose}
- {Louis, Mark, Hugh, Albert, Boniface}
- {Berthold, Victor}
- {Peter, Gregory}
- {Basil, Elias, Simplicius}

The other monks form singleton clusters. These groupings do not fit Sampson's description as well. The Outcasts have been clearly identified, and two of the singleton clusters were labeled as indeterminate by Sampson. The pairing of Bonaventure and Ambrose is consistent with Sampson's description, as they are both members of the Loyal Opposition; we also note that the pairing of Berthold and Victor is not inconsistent, since Victor was seen as indeterminate by Sampson. The inclusion of Louis, a member of the Loyal Opposition, in the oth-erwise Young Turks group, and the pairing of Peter and Gregory are interesting. It turns out that Gregory was seen as the leader of the Young Turks and Peter as the leader of the Loyal Opposition. Hence, this pairing can be seen as a leaders group. The largest cluster contains core members of the Young Turks together with the solid supporter of the Loyal Opposition, Louis, and these could be viewed as core group members. It should be noted that, since structurally equiv-alent actors (with the exception of isolates) are connected to the same others, they

	1 ROM	2 BON	3 AMB	4 BER	5 PET	6 LOU	7 VIC	8 WIN	9 JOH	10 GRE	11 HUG	12 BON	13 MAR	14 ALB	15 AMA	16 BAS	17 ELI	18 SIM
ROMUALD	100	30	19	30	31	37	37	35	33	35	20	20	22	21	31	35	28	29
BONAVENTURE	30	100	85	57	47	70	69	59	65	60	72	80	73	79	60	52	51	58
AMBROSE	19	85	100	55	47	63	72	51	66	65	69	78	66	73	61	50	48	56
BERTHOLD	30	57	55	100	74	57	80	33	59	70	57	55	77	61	66	67	77	76
PETER	31	47	47	74	100	69	76	30	63	79	53	46	70	54	67	75	68	77
LOUIS	37	70	63	57	69	100	66	48	71	67	71	74	73	78	74	69	62	68
VICTOR	37	69	72	80	76	66	100	43	65	75	65	64	76	67	65	72	69	72
WINFRID	35	59	51	33	30	48	43	100	45	44	53	58	43	51	42	36	34	37
JOHN	33	65	66	59	63	71	65	45	100	68	64	61	63	63	66	61	54	62
GREGORY	35	60	65	70	79	67	75	44	68	100	67	64	73	63	65	76	62	72
HUGH	20	72	69	57	53	71	65	53	64	67	100	80	75	80	67	62	61	63
BONIFACE	20	80	78	55	46	74	64	58	61	64	80	100	77	88	62	54	51	58
MARK	22	73	66	77	70	73	76	43	63	73	75	77	100	80	71	71	78	77
ALBERT	21	79	73	61	54	78	67	51	63	63	80	88	80	100	69	64	63	68
AMAND	31	60	61	66	67	74	65	42	66	65	67	62	71	69	100	68	72	68
BASIL	35	52	50	67	75	69	72	36	61	76	62	54	71	64	68	100	75	78
ELIAS	28	51	48	77	68	62	69	34	54	62	61	51	78	63	72	75	100	85
SIMPLICIUS	29	58	56	76	77	68	72	37	62	72	63	58	77	68	68	78	85	100

HIERARCHICAL CLUSTERING OF EQUIVALENCE MATRIX

```
               B
               O                           S
               N                           I
               A           B   B           M
         R W   V A         O   E     G     P
         O I   E M       A N   R V   R     L
         M N   N B L     L I A T I P E B E I
         U F J T R O M H B F M H C E G A L C
         A R O U O U A U E A A O T T O S I I
         L I H R S I R G R C N L O E R I A U
         D D N E E S K H T E D D R R Y L S S

                     1 1 1 1       1 1 1 1
Level    1 8 9 2 3 6 3 1 4 2 5 4 7 5 0 6 7 8
------   - - - - - - - - - - - - - - - - - -
88.377   . . . . . . . XXX . . . . . . . . .
85.295   . . . XXX . . . XXX . . . . . . . .
85.003   . . . XXX . . . XXX . . . . . . XXX
80.413   . . . XXX . . . XXX . XXX . . . XXX
79.855   . . . XXX . . XXXXX . XXX . . . XXX
78.725   . . . XXX . . XXXXX . XXX XXX . XXX
78.004   . . . XXX . XXXXXXX . XXX XXX . XXX
77.247   . . . XXX . XXXXXXX . XXX XXX XXXXX
74.855   . . . XXX XXXXXXXXX . XXX XXX XXXXX
74.075   . . . XXX XXXXXXXXX . XXXXXXX XXXXX
72.096   . . . XXXXXXXXXXXXX . XXXXXXX XXXXX
72.066   . . . XXXXXXXXXXXXX . XXXXXXXXXXXXX
67.788   . . . XXXXXXXXXXXXX XXXXXXXXXXXXXXX
64.734   . . XXXXXXXXXXXXXXX XXXXXXXXXXXXXXX
63.138   . . XXXXXXXXXXXXXXXXXXXXXXXXXXXXXXX
41.968   . XXXXXXXXXXXXXXXXXXXXXXXXXXXXXXXXX
29.298   XXXXXXXXXXXXXXXXXXXXXXXXXXXXXXXXXXX
```

Figure 12.5 REGE coefficients and clustering.

are more likely to be members of the same cohesive subgroups. This restriction does not apply to regular equivalence, so this concept may well capture the concept of role independent of group membership.

12.8 Core–periphery models

A common equivalence pattern in social networks and other fields is that of a core–periphery structure. Networks with core–periphery structures have been observed to function better than networks with multiple clique structures (Johnson et al., 2003). Core–periphery is a partition of the nodes into two groups, namely the core and the periphery; this was first examined in detail by Borgatti and Everett (2000). The partition produces four blocks, as depicted in Table 12.2. The core block contains the core-to-core interactions, and the peripheral block contains the periphery-to-periphery interactions, with the two off-diagonal blocks containing the core-to-periphery and the periphery-to-core interactions. Clearly, in an undirected network the two off-diagonal blocks are simply the transpose of each other.

In a core–periphery structure, we expect core nodes to be well connected to other core nodes. We also expect peripheral nodes not to be connected to other peripheral nodes. Hence, in an ideal structure the core block would be a 1-block and the peripheral block would be a 0-block. Let us now assume that our network is undirected. If we used structural equivalence as our underlying model, the core-to-periphery blocks could either be 0-blocks or 1-blocks. If they were 0-blocks, the ideal structure would consist of a clique serving as the core, and only isolates as the periphery. This would not really capture the notion of a core–periphery structure as we expect the periphery to be related in some way to the core. If the core-to-periphery blocks were 1-blocks, this would fit our intuitive notion, but with the rather strict condition that every peripheral member is connected to every core member. The network shown in Figure 12.6 has this structure, with nodes 1, 2, 3 and 4 in the core and the remainder in the periphery.

Clearly, such idealized patterns are not likely in real data, so we relax the conditions. One approach is to consider only the core and periphery blocks and in essence ignore the off-diagonal blocks. In so doing, it would make sense to at

Table 12.2 Core–periphery blockmodel structure.

	Core nodes	Peripheral nodes
Core nodes	Core	Core–Periphery
Peripheral nodes	Periphery–Core	Peripheral

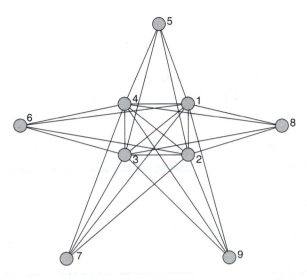

Figure 12.6 A simple core–periphery structure.

least insist on some core–periphery interaction. This can be achieved by making sure that the network is connected, or weakly connected if it is directed. We can in this instance apply the direct method discussed above and measure the extent to which assignments of nodes to core and periphery fit the ideal core model in Table 12.2. This is known as the 'discrete core–periphery method'. If we use the criterion that minimizes the number of changes required, for non-valued data this can be done very efficiently. It turns out that this criterion is closely related to the degree of the nodes, and if we ordered the nodes in decreasing degree, we just need to check at what point we need to draw the line between core and periphery. In our ideal example the core nodes have degree 8 and the peripheral nodes have degree 4, so this boundary is set between 4 and 8. It follows that with this fit function, degree centrality is a node-level core–periphery measure and all we need to do to identify the core and periphery is decide at what value of degree we will divide core from periphery.

This approach is straightforward but does have a few problems. First, it cannot be directly applied to valued data. Second, and more important, it does not give information about the core–periphery structure of the network. It is quite possible for the best assignment of nodes to a core and periphery structure to result in a core block that is a 0-block or has very few entries. This happens when the core contains a lot of errors but the periphery has very few, for example in a very sparse network. One way to overcome this problem is to use a measure of fit that is based on the correlation between the data matrix and the idealized block model. In this instance, we treat the off-diagonal blocks as if they contain missing data. As an example, we take the co-citation data among the top social work journals in a one-year period (1985) reported by Baker (1992). The results of the core–periphery analysis using the correlation method are given in Matrix 12.8.

We note that the journals do cite their own papers, producing the 1s down the diagonal, which the algorithm ignores. The correlation between the data matrix in Matrix 12.8 and the idealized block structure is 0.81, indicating a strong core–periphery structure. The core block has a density of 0.86, and the peripheral block has a density of 0.05. These results indicate even more strongly the core–periphery structure of these data in which core journals cite other core journals and peripheral journals do not cite other peripheral journals. This is further reinforced by examining the two off-diagonal blocks. The top right core–periphery block has a density of 0.15, whereas the bottom left periphery-to-core block has a density of 0.32. This shows that peripheral journals cite twice as many core journals as core journals cite peripheral journals, providing further evidence of the hierarchical structure of the journals.

```
                                        1 1 1 1 1 1 1 1 1 2
                         1 2 3 4 5 6 7  8 9 0 1 2 3 4 5 6 7 8 9 0
                         C S J S S S A  C F C A J B P C J C S S I
                        -------------------------------------------
      1    CW | 1 1 1 1 1     | 1              1       1           |
      2    SW | 1 1 1 1 1 1 1 |              1           1 1       |
      3  JSWE |   1 1 1 1 1 1 |                              1     |
      4   SSR | 1 1 1 1 1 1 1 |                                    |
      5   SCW | 1 1 1 1 1 1 1 | 1 1 1              1       1 1     |
      6  SWRA | 1 1 1 1 1 1   |                                    |
      7   ASW |   1 1 1   1 1 |                  1                 |

      8   CAN | 1 1     1     | 1                                  |
      9    FR |   1     1     |   1                                |
     10  CSWJ |   1   1 1     |     1                              |
     11   AMH |   1           |         1                          |
     12   JSP |       1       |           1                        |
     13  BJSW |   1 1         |             1                      |
     14    PW | 1             | 1           1                      |
     15   CCQ | 1       1     |                 1                  |
     16  JGSW |   1     1     |                   1                |
     17  CYSR | 1 1   1 1 1   | 1 1             1 1   1            |
     18   SWG |   1 1 1 1     |             1             1 1      |
     19  SWHC |   1     1     |                             1      |
     20  IJSW |   1           |                                 1  |
                        -------------------------------------------
```

Matrix 12.8   A core–periphery model of co-citation data.

As already mentioned, we are able to use the correlation method on valued data, but it can still be computationally challenging for large datasets. One other issue is that this method places nodes either in the core or in the periphery, which may be too simplistic. Some authors have suggested the idea of a semi-periphery, which is equivalent to introducing more blocks into the block structure. But this increases the complexity of the problem, and it becomes even more difficult to decide on the nature and structure of the additional blocks. An alternative formulation is to try to find a node-level measure of the amount of core–periphery. We have already mentioned that degree centrality does precisely this if we use the model of fit corresponding to the number of changes required. High-degree actors must be in the core, low-degree actors must be in the periphery, and actors who are close to the boundary value would be in the semi-periphery or on the edge of the core. But as mentioned earlier, degree is not always a good measure and does not extend to valued data. To overcome this, we use an ideal structure, matrix Δ, constructed as the outer product of a vector $\mathbf{c}$ of coreness values,

$$\Delta = \mathbf{c}\mathbf{c}^{\mathsf{T}} \tag{12.1}$$

Hence the (i, j) entry of the matrix Δ is simply the product of $\mathbf{c}_i$ with $\mathbf{c}_j$. If two nodes have a high coreness score, their product and hence the corresponding value in Δ will be high. If both entries are low, the product will be low and so the corresponding value in Δ will be low. If one is high and one is low, the corresponding Δ value will be intermediate. In the extreme case in which we constrain the entries of $\mathbf{c}$ to be either 0 or 1, Δ would correspond exactly to a blockmodel structure of core–periphery as described in Table 12.2; $\mathbf{c}$ would be an indicator vector where a value 1 would indicate a core node and 0 a peripheral node. It follows that our discrete method can be formulated as finding a binary vector $\mathbf{c}$ in which the correlation between our data matrix A and our product matrix Δ is as large as possible. If we now relax the condition that $\mathbf{c}$ is binary and allow $\mathbf{c}$ to take on any positive values, we obtain the continuous core–periphery model. The values of $\mathbf{c}$ now give the coreness of each node within the network. This generalization from the discrete to the continuous is remarkably similar to the extension of degree centrality to eigenvector centrality. As mentioned earlier, degree centrality can be thought of as a coreness measure when we use the 'number of changes' measure of fit for core–periphery, and eigenvector serves a similar purpose for the continuous approach. (In fact, if we use Euclidean distance between matrices instead of correlation, this similarity becomes explicit.)

Applying the continuous method to the citation data used for the discrete method in Matrix 12.8 yields the results given in Table 12.3. The two columns

Table 12.3 Continuous core–periphery scores for citation data.

Node	Name	Score
5	SCW	0.473
2	SW	0.358
17	CYSR	0.349
1	CW	0.308
4	SSR	0.284
6	SWRA	0.256
3	JSWE	0.255
18	SWG	0.239
7	ASW	0.180
8	CAN	0.167
10	CSWJ	0.164
9	FR	0.120
16	JGSW	0.120
19	SWHC	0.120
15	CCQ	0.113
13	BJSW	0.088
14	PW	0.068
11	AMH	0.051
20	IJSW	0.051
12	JSP	0.041

are the split between core and periphery recommended by the software. This recommendation is based on correlating the scores above with an ideal set of scores. The ideal scores are when core members score a value of 1 and peripheral members score a value of 0. Correlations are examined for all possible core sizes from 1 to $n - 1$, and the recommended split is the highest correlation from these $n - 1$ values – in this case a vector of eight 1s and twelve 0s. This measure is called 'concentration'. If we compare this output to the one in Matrix 12.8, we see that the two results have six core journals in common. We note that ASW is the highest-scoring peripheral journal and that the discrete method has this journal in the core. Two journals that were peripheral for the discrete method – SWG and CYSR – are placed in the core of the continuous method. The discrete output shows that these are the only journals with multiple peripheral block entries. There is one further important characteristic of the continuous method: the matrix Δ must be symmetric by definition. It follows that the continuous method, which must take account of the off-diagonal blocks, cannot differentiate between core–periphery and periphery–core interaction. This means that it

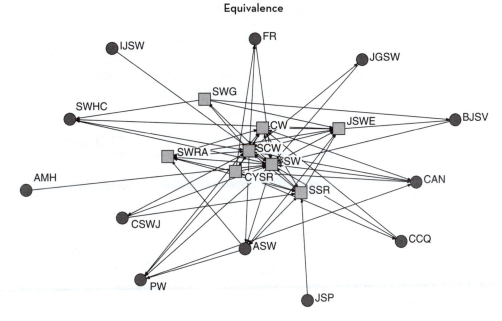

Figure 12.7 Core–periphery layout of citation data.

is better suited to symmetric data (or at least data that are very nearly symmetric). In fact, if the two methods are compared on symmetrized versions of the citation data, they are in complete agreement.

The continuous model has one other advantage in that we can use the Δ matrix to help us get a good visualization of the data. If we submit Δ to metric multidimensional scaling, then use this output to position the nodes, we will obtain a network in which the nodes in the core will be placed at the center and the nodes in the periphery will be around the outside. We can then immediately see which nodes are on the edge of the core or part of the semi-periphery, particularly if we shape or color the nodes that are in the recommended core. We have done this for the citation data, and the results are shown in Figure 12.7, with core nodes as gray squares and peripheral nodes as black circles. The position of the core journals in the center and the strong connections between them are apparent. In addition, we see that ASW is placed near to the core and so must be close to being considered a member of the core; SWG, JSWE, SSR and SWRA are clearly on the edge of the core and are close to being in the periphery.

A natural question in examining for core–periphery patterns is what method to use – discrete or continuous? The data may give an indication. Both methods can handle valued data, so this is not an issue. If the data are not symmetric, the discrete method has some obvious advantages, provided the dataset is not too large. The continuous model can be used for data that are mildly non-symmetric, but if using UCINET, one should be careful to choose the "For large datasets".

The continuous method has computational advantages, and the visualization as shown in Figure 12.7 is a real advantage. The recommended approach is to use both methods whenever possible and to take account of the advantages and disadvantages of each to gain an overall view of the data.

12.9 Summary

Actors in similar structural positions across multirelational networks share certain behavioral patterns. We try to capture these positions by using equivalences. Structural equivalence captures the extent to which equivalent actors are connected to the same others, whereas regular equivalence looks at the extent to which equivalent actors are connected to equivalent others. These concepts need to be relaxed when applied to real data. Profile methods measure the similarity among the rows and columns of the adjacency matrix to produce a proximity matrix that measures the extent to which any pair of actors is equivalent. The REGE algorithm has the same goal for regular equivalence but uses an iterative technique based on fuzzy sets. The proximity matrices can then be clustered to find the equivalent groups. Alternatively, we can measure the amount of equivalence in a particular partition by examining the blocks it induces. Structural equivalence requires blocks of all 0s or all 1s, whereas regular equivalence relaxes the 1-blocks so that there is at least one 1 in every row and every column. Once we have a measure, we can apply optimization techniques to try to find the best fit. Partitioned matrices are known as blockmodels, which can be used to give summary reductions of the data. One particularly useful blockmodel is the core–periphery model in which core actors interact with other core actors but not the peripheral actors, and peripheral actors also interact with the core actors and not the peripheral actors. Core–periphery structures are commonly found in social network data and have important implications for their functioning.

12.10 Problems and Exercises

1. Another way to find clusters of nodes in a network, besides cohesion, is by looking at the structural similarity or structural equivalence among nodes. Using the "campnet-maxsym.##h" in UCINET go to Network|Roles & Positions|Structural|Profile... and load the symmetrized Campnet network. Since this is a symmetric matrix we do not need to include the transpose. For the similarity measure use the default Euclidean Distance. Be sure to properly name the output files for future use. For example, they could be named SEcampnet and SEPartcampnet respectively. Once the file is loaded click OK. A ucinetlog file will have the equivalence matrix and an HCL of the matrix. In looking at the clusters in the HCL how does this compare to the identification of cohesive subgroups for the Campnet data in Chapter 11?

2. Now let's examine some different ways of looking at measuring the structural equiv-
    alence among actors. We will be using the wiring bank room game network called
    RDGAM.##h. Before running the analysis visualize the network in NetDraw. How
    many isolates are there? Using this network run a profile similarity analysis as in
    Problem 1. In UCINET go to Network|Roles & Positions|Structural|Profile... and load
    the game network. For the similarity measure use the default Euclidean Distance. Be
    sure to properly name the output files for future use as in Problem 1 above. Click OK.
    What do you notice about the Euclidean distance between I3 and S2? The two nodes
    are structurally equivalent in that each is similar in that they are not connected to any
    nodes in the network. We should remove the isolates and run the analysis again. To
    remove the isolates, go to Data|Remove|Remove isolates. Enter the games network
    and click OK. Note that the output file is automatically named RDGAM-NoIsolates.
    In UCINET go to Network|Roles & Positions|Structural|Profile... and load the game
    network with isolates removed. For the similarity measure use the default Euclidean
    Distance. Be sure to properly name the output files for future use as in Problem 1
    above. Click OK. Reviewing the ucinetlog, which actors are structurally equivalent?
    What is it about actor W5 that makes him/her structurally unique (look at the network
    visualization of the games network)?
3. Now let's use the same WIRING games network to fit a blockmodel. In UCINET go
    to Network|Roles & Positions|Structural|Optimization|Binary and load the RDGAM-
    NoIsolates network. For this run make the number of blocks 2. Click OK. What can
    you conclude about the structure of the network?
4. In this problem we want to test for core–periphery structures at the beginning and
    end of the winter for the South Pole networks. Johnson et al. (2003) found that net-
    works that had core–periphery structures tended to have higher group morale. The
    data involve strong ties among crew in terms of who interacts socially with whom. In
    UCINET go to Network|Core/Periphery|Continuous and load "Beginning_Winter_
    Valued_GT_6" and hit OK. Be sure to save the ucinetlog output for later comparison
    (you can also minimize it for later use). Do the same for the "End_Winter_Valued_
    GT_6." Run the analysis again only this time use the categorical model for both time
    periods. How did the core–periphery nature of the network structure change over the
    course of the winter?

Don't forget to visit the website at
https://study.sagepub.com/borgatti2e

13

Analyzing Two-mode Data

Learning Outcomes

1. Represent two-mode data as an affiliation matrix and a bipartite network
2. Project two-mode data to a single mode effectively
3. Extend one-mode methods to bipartite networks

13.1 Introduction

In most of this book, we have focused on data in which we have ties among a single set of actors, and the ties are measured directly, either by asking the actors involved or collecting archival data on, say, transactions between actors. However, as touched on elsewhere, we often have the situation where we cannot collect ties among the actors directly, but can infer or predict ties based on belonging to the same groups or attending the same events. Our basic data, therefore, consist of two types of actors in which there are only connections between the two types and not within. As we discussed in Chapter 2, this is known as two-mode data or affiliation data.

A simple example would be a group of students and a set of classes. We could construct a network which ties students to classes. The relationship is 'attends class'. There would be no ties directly between students, nor would there be ties between classes, only ties connecting students to classes. Recall that we can represent these data by a matrix, typically referred to as a two-mode incidence matrix or an affiliation matrix. This is like an adjacency matrix, except the rows would represent one group, the students, say, and the columns represent a different group, the classes.

		1	2	3	4	5	6	7	8	9	1 0	1 1	1 2	1 3	1 4
1	EVELYN	1	1	1	1	1	1	0	1	1	0	0	0	0	0
2	LAURA	1	1	1	0	1	1	1	1	0	0	0	0	0	0
3	THERESA	0	1	1	1	1	1	1	1	1	0	0	0	0	0
4	BRENDA	1	0	1	1	1	1	1	1	0	0	0	0	0	0
5	CHARLOTTE	0	0	1	1	1	0	1	0	0	0	0	0	0	0
6	FRANCES	0	0	1	0	1	1	0	1	0	0	0	0	0	0
7	ELEANOR	0	0	0	0	1	1	1	1	0	0	0	0	0	0
8	PEARL	0	0	0	0	0	1	0	1	1	0	0	0	0	0
9	RUTH	0	0	0	0	1	0	1	1	1	0	0	0	0	0
10	VERNE	0	0	0	0	0	0	1	1	1	0	0	1	0	0
11	MYRNA	0	0	0	0	0	0	0	1	1	1	0	1	1	1
12	KATHERINE	0	0	0	0	0	0	0	1	1	1	0	1	1	1
13	SYLVIA	0	0	0	0	0	0	1	1	1	1	0	1	1	1
14	NORA	0	0	0	0	0	1	1	0	1	1	1	1	1	1
15	HELEN	0	0	0	0	0	0	1	1	0	1	1	1	0	0
16	DOROTHY	0	0	0	0	0	0	0	1	1	0	0	0	0	0
17	OLIVIA	0	0	0	0	0	0	0	0	1	0	1	0	0	0
18	FLORA	0	0	0	0	0	0	0	0	1	0	1	0	0	0

Matrix 13.1   Southern women dataset.

In Chapter 2 we discussed the Davis et al. (1941) data on the attendance at 14 society events by 18 Southern women. For ease of reference, the data are given again in Matrix 13.1, where the rows of the affiliation matrix are the women and the columns are the 14 events.

Data in this form are very common in certain areas of application. For example, there has been a long tradition of studying data on interlocking directorates. In this case, the actors are company directors and the second mode (the events, in our language) consists of the companies on whose board they sit. Data from social movements often consist of actors and meetings or events they have attended or organizations to which they are affiliated. Methods for finding connections between more difficult-to-reach populations have also used two-mode data techniques. For example, in looking at sexual health issues, the two-mode networks of gay men attending saunas or of swingers attending parties are often easier to collect than detailed sexual practices between named individuals. Large two-mode datasets can be constructed from the Internet Movie Database (e.g., actors by movies), as discussed in Chapter 4.

In analyzing two-mode data, we typically assume that attending the same event is either an indicator of an underlying social relationship between the actors or a potential opportunity for one to develop. When events are very large, however, such as sporting events, co-attendance may be a very poor indicator or predictor of a social relationship. It is also worth noting that two-mode data not involving interactions (e.g., subscribing to the same magazines or watching the same TV shows) are even more tenuously related to social relationships.

As an aside, two-mode data are normally treated as undirected, even when it is clear that there is agency in only one direction. For example, if the data consist of a person's attendance at public events, it is the person who chooses the event, and not the other way around. However, if all the ties point from person to event, there is little benefit to keeping the ties directed and, in fact, doing so would make many of the analyses we discuss impossible. Occasionally, however, we find two-mode data that really do have direction. A rule of thumb is that if both the persons and groups are sending ties, and ties need not be reciprocated, then the data can profitably be analyzed as directed. An example occurs in the US college football recruiting process, where schools publicly announce which recruits they are interested in, and recruits similarly announce which schools they are interested in. Similar data occur in a number of matching situations, such as heterosexual dating sites where males and females choose each other and do not choose within-sex partners.

Two-mode data can be analyzed in a number of different ways. The most commonly used methods are converting to one-mode data or analyzing the two-mode data directly as a bipartite graph. Although the first method is the most common, conventional wisdom until recently has considered the second method to be better. This is based on the assumption that conversion to one-mode necessarily entails loss of data. Recent work, however, suggests that this concern has been exaggerated (Everett and Borgatti, 2013). We consider both methods in this chapter.

As a terminological convenience, we shall assume one mode consists of a set of actors and the other mode a set of events. We should emphasize that this is only to simplify the exposition and we do not require the modes to actually consist of actors and events.

13.2 Converting to one-mode data

One approach to dealing with data of this type is to convert them to one-mode data – a new dataset in which a pair of actors is said to be tied to the extent

Analyzing Social Networks

	EV	LA	TH	BR	CH	FR	EL	PE	RU	VE	MY	KA	SY	NO	HE	DO	OL	FL
EVELYN	8	6	7	6	3	4	3	3	3	2	2	2	2	2	1	2	1	1
LAURA	6	7	6	6	3	4	4	2	3	2	1	1	2	2	2	1	0	0
THERESA	7	6	8	6	4	4	4	3	4	3	2	2	3	3	2	2	1	1
BRENDA	6	6	6	7	4	4	4	2	3	2	1	1	2	2	2	1	0	0
CHARLOTTE	3	3	4	4	4	2	2	0	2	1	0	0	1	1	1	0	0	0
FRANCES	4	4	4	4	2	4	3	2	2	1	1	1	1	1	1	1	0	0
ELEANOR	3	4	4	4	2	3	4	2	3	2	1	1	2	2	2	1	0	0
PEARL	3	2	3	2	0	2	2	3	2	2	2	2	2	2	1	2	1	1
RUTH	3	3	4	3	2	2	3	2	4	3	2	2	3	2	2	2	1	1
VERNE	2	2	3	2	1	1	2	2	3	4	3	3	4	3	3	2	1	1
MYRNA	2	1	2	1	0	1	1	2	2	3	4	4	4	3	3	2	1	1
KATHERINE	2	1	2	1	0	1	1	2	2	3	4	6	6	5	3	2	1	1
SYLVIA	2	2	3	2	1	1	2	2	3	4	4	6	7	6	4	2	1	1
NORA	2	2	3	2	1	1	2	2	2	3	3	5	6	8	4	1	2	2
HELEN	1	2	2	2	1	1	2	1	2	3	3	3	4	4	5	1	1	1
DOROTHY	2	1	2	1	0	1	1	2	2	2	2	2	2	1	1	2	1	1
OLIVIA	1	0	1	0	0	0	0	1	1	1	1	1	1	2	1	1	2	2
FLORA	1	0	1	0	0	0	0	1	1	1	1	1	1	2	1	1	2	2

Matrix 13.2 Single-mode projection of the women.

that they share affiliations. This can be a relatively simple process. As an example, consider the Davis data above. We can construct a new one-mode matrix in which both the rows and columns represent women, and the matrix cell values indicate the number of events the women with the relationship attended an event together. The co-membership matrix for the Davis data in Matrix 13.1 is given in Matrix 13.2. A visualization of the network is shown in Figure 13.1 where the thickness of the lines corresponds to the values in the matrix.

It is important to remember that ties inferred from two-mode data are not the same as ties obtained directly from, say, a survey. For example, if the events are large (e.g., political demonstrations), two actors may attend several of the same events and never even meet each other, let alone pass information. In such cases, we need to interpret the co-membership tie as, at best, a potential for interaction – the more events a pair of women attend in common, the greater the chance of meeting, establishing a relationship, etc. Or we may see

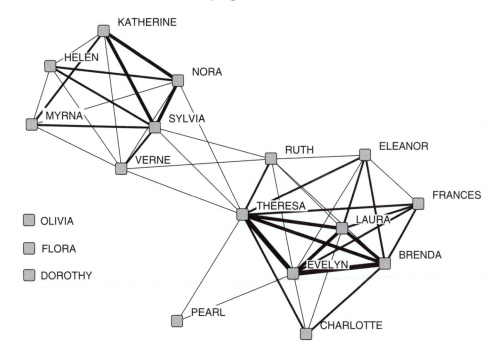

Figure 13.1 Woman-by-woman co-attendance network.

co-attendance or co-membership as a potential for activation. For example, suppose you and I are strangers, but I would like to enlist you to join me in donating some money to a charitable cause. I may have an easier time if I can point out that we attended the same university, belong to the same country club, and so on. (Of course, as discussed in Chapter 1, we can also see co-attendance as the observed result of an otherwise hidden relationship between the two actors.)

Mathematically, we can construct the one-mode matrix of co-occurrences by post-multiplying the two-mode matrix by its transpose:

$$c_{ij} = \sum_k x_{ik} x_{jk} \qquad (13.1)$$

Or, more simply, for each pair of rows, we look at each column and count the number of times that both are 1. Hence, Evelyn and Laura have a link in this new dataset since they both attended event 1, for example. On the other hand, Flora did not attend any events with Laura, so they are not connected. In fact, we can do more than simply construct a binary matrix; we can form a proximity

	E1	E2	E3	E4	E5	E6	E7	E8	E9	E10	E11	E12	E13	E14
E1	3	2	3	2	3	3	2	3	1	0	0	0	0	0
E2	2	3	3	2	3	3	2	3	2	0	0	0	0	0
E3	3	3	6	4	6	5	4	5	2	0	0	0	0	0
E4	2	2	4	4	4	3	3	3	2	0	0	0	0	0
E5	3	3	6	4	8	6	6	7	3	0	0	0	0	0
E6	3	3	5	3	6	8	5	7	4	1	1	1	1	1
E7	2	2	4	3	6	5	10	8	5	3	2	4	2	2
E8	3	3	5	3	7	7	8	14	9	4	1	5	2	2
E9	1	2	2	2	3	4	5	9	12	4	3	5	3	3
E10	0	0	0	0	0	1	3	4	4	5	2	5	3	3
E11	0	0	0	0	0	1	2	1	3	2	4	2	1	1
E12	0	0	0	0	0	1	4	5	5	5	2	6	3	3
E13	0	0	0	0	0	1	2	2	3	3	1	3	3	3
E14	0	0	0	0	0	1	2	2	3	3	1	3	3	3

Matrix 13.3 Event-by-event matrix.

matrix in which the entries give the number of events each pair attended. We can see from the matrix that Brenda attended six events with Evelyn. These are sometimes called 'co-membership matrices'. Note that the diagonal elements give the number of events each woman attended.

We could also form a one-mode matrix of the events instead of the women by pre-multiplying the two-mode matrix by its transpose. This would result in an event-by-event matrix in which the entries would show how many women attended both events in common (see Matrix 13.3). These should not be viewed as two independent data matrices, since they are clearly linked. In a classic paper, Breiger (1974) explored the duality between the actors and the events and suggested that consideration should be given to both projections – an issue we shall return to later in the chapter.

One thing to think about in this kind of conversion is the effects of varying row and/or column sums. For example, in Matrix 13.3, events 7, 8 and 9 have many 'ties' with each other (and with all other events), in part because they are simply well attended. Even if people attended events at random, these events would be highly co-attended by chance alone. In some ways, this is the right answer. If we were studying the spread of disease, we would be very interested in those big events that are capable of spreading disease to many other events (assuming they occur after the big event). In other cases, however, we think of the effects of variation in size as a nuisance that we would like to normalize

	E1	E2	E3	E4	E5	E6	E7	E8	E9	E10	E11	E12	E13	E14
E1	100	84	100	78	100	100	57	100	30	0	0	0	0	0
E2	84	100	100	78	100	100	57	100	50	0	0	0	0	0
E3	100	100	100	100	100	79	59	56	24	0	0	0	0	0
E4	78	78	100	100	100	70	63	47	39	0	0	0	0	0
E5	100	100	100	100	100	78	68	63	21	0	0	0	0	0
E6	100	100	79	70	78	100	56	63	33	32	37	27	43	43
E7	57	57	59	63	68	56	100	54	27	53	46	59	57	57
E8	100	100	56	47	63	63	54	100	44	52	14	56	41	41
E9	30	50	24	39	21	33	27	44	100	61	56	65	100	100
E10	0	0	0	0	0	32	53	52	61	100	66	100	100	100
E11	0	0	0	0	0	37	46	14	56	66	100	61	59	59
E12	0	0	0	0	0	27	59	56	65	100	61	100	100	100
E13	0	0	0	0	0	43	57	41	100	100	59	100	100	100
E14	0	0	0	0	0	43	57	41	100	100	59	100	100	100

Matrix 13.4   Event-by-event associations using Bonacich's (1972) normalization.

away. In this case, a solution is to create a metric that measures the extent to which events are co-attended relative to the amount we would expect by chance given the size of the events. UCINET's affiliations procedure provides Bonacich's (1972) metric as an option. Using it on the Davis dataset yields Matrix 13.4 which is represented graphically in Figure 13.2. Now, the strengths of tie between events 7, 8 and 9 are much smaller than the strengths among 1 through 5, and among 12 through 14.

The choice between using the raw and the normalized numbers can be put in the following terms. Let us focus not on the event-by-event matrix above but the women-by-women matrix of co-attendances at events. If we use the raw counts, those women who go to a lot of parties will be highly central, and two women with this characteristic will tend to have a strong tie with each other. If we use the normalized values, the effects of these differences will be removed and what will remain is the underlying tendency for two women to co-attend events. One method gets the actual pattern of co-attendance, while the other tries to get the underlying preferences for co-attendance, correcting for the confounding influences of differential tendencies to attend in general. It is similar to the situation in the measurement of homophily. Suppose there is a population that is 90% white and 10% black. Unnormalized measures of homophily will tend to show that whites are heavily homophilous while blacks are heterophilous. This is

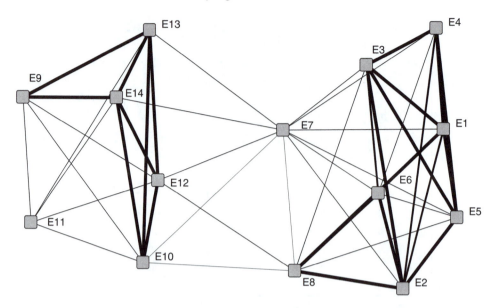

Figure 13.2 Normalized associations among events. Line thickness corresponds to tie strength.

because almost all available interaction partners are white. Normalized measures of homophily seek to unpack the underlying preferences that may be masked by the unequal distributions of group sizes. They would typically show both groups being fairly homophilous.

To summarize, then, when converting two-mode data to one-mode, we can make use of two kinds of normalizations – one associated with the mode serving as variables and the other associated with the mode serving as cases. To make this less abstract, let us take the case of converting the women-by-events data to women-by-women. First, we realize that some events are larger than others, so co-attendance at those events could be counted less than co-attendance at small events. One way to implement this that would allow us to retain equation 13.1 unchanged is simply to divide each value in the original two-mode matrix by the square root of the column sums. Second, we realize that some women attend more events than others, and therefore have higher probabilities of having a co-attendance tie with others. Again, to implement this without changing equation 13.1, we could further divide the cell entries by the square roots of the row sums of the original matrix. This division by the roots of the row and column sums is precisely the first step in a correspondence analysis (see Chapter 6). Alternatively, we can accomplish this row-wise normalization implicitly by using a measure of row–row association that automatically takes care of that. Bonacich's (1972) measure is one example that was specifically designed for working with two-mode data, but there are dozens of other measures of association that have similar properties, including Cohen's Kappa (1960) and Freeman's S (1978).

13.3 Converting valued two-mode matrices to one-mode

So far, we have only considered binary affiliation matrices. If the original two-mode data were valued, we would need to take account of this when constructing our one-mode datasets. As noted earlier, Matrix 13.2 can be constructed from Matrix 13.1 by simply multiplying the former by its transpose. Effectively, for each pair of rows, we simply multiply the entries in each column and sum them up. Since zero times anything is zero, the sum is only greater than zero when there are columns in which both values are 1s. We can use the same method for valued data. However, this would mean the elements would be multiplied and then summed to give a value in the one-mode data. This is a figure that is rather difficult to interpret, although clearly high values would indicate strong ties to the same events.

A more interpretable approach would be to sum the minimums of the two cell values rather than the products. Hence, if row i was (5, 6, 0, 1) and row j was (4, 2, 4, 0) then $AA^T(i, j)$ would be $5 \times 4 + 6 \times 2 + 0 \times 4 + 1 \times 0 = 32$ for the normal matrix product and $\min(5, 4) + \min(6, 2) + \min(0, 4) + \min(1, 0) = 6$ for the minimum method. These would produce the same answers for binary data. To see why the minimum is more interpretable, suppose the two-mode dataset recorded how many hours each member of a consulting company spent on each client project. That is, the rows are persons and the columns are projects. Then, constructing the person-by-person one-mode matrix using the minimum method would yield the maximum possible time each pair of persons could have spent together.

As in the case of binary data, what we are really doing here is computing measures of similarity on the rows or columns of the two-mode matrix. Dozens of measures have been devised in different contexts that could be applied here, and the researcher should make an effort to consider whether one of these other measures would suit their research better.

13.4 Bipartite networks

One of the problems with converting the affiliation matrix to one-mode is that there can be a loss of information.[1] For example, two women could have the same degree of overlap as another pair of women but through entirely different events.

---

[1] However, Everett and Borgatti (2013) have recently shown that this need not be the case if we consider both projections together.

An alternative approach is to treat the affiliation matrix as if it were a piece of a much larger adjacency matrix in which the rows consist of both women and events, and the columns also consist of both women and events, as shown in Matrix 13.5. Note that ties exist only between women and events – there are no ties among women or among events. A network with this structure is known as bipartite.

A graphical representation of the bipartite version of the Davis data is shown in Figure 13.3. In order to easily differentiate the modes of the nodes, we have represented the events as squares and the women as circles. There are no edges connecting pairs of circles or pairs of squares. An alternative visualization is to

```
0 0 0 0 0 0 0 0 0 0 0 0 0 0 0 0 0 0 | 1 1 1 1 1 0 1 1 0 0 0 0 0 0
0 0 0 0 0 0 0 0 0 0 0 0 0 0 0 0 0 0 | 1 1 1 0 1 1 1 1 0 0 0 0 0 0
0 0 0 0 0 0 0 0 0 0 0 0 0 0 0 0 0 0 | 0 1 1 1 1 1 1 1 1 0 0 0 0 0
0 0 0 0 0 0 0 0 0 0 0 0 0 0 0 0 0 0 | 1 0 1 1 1 1 1 1 0 0 0 0 0 0
0 0 0 0 0 0 0 0 0 0 0 0 0 0 0 0 0 0 | 0 0 1 1 1 0 1 0 0 0 0 0 0 0
0 0 0 0 0 0 0 0 0 0 0 0 0 0 0 0 0 0 | 0 0 1 0 1 1 0 1 0 0 0 0 0 0
0 0 0 0 0 0 0 0 0 0 0 0 0 0 0 0 0 0 | 0 0 0 0 1 1 1 1 0 0 0 0 0 0
0 0 0 0 0 0 0 0 0 0 0 0 0 0 0 0 0 0 | 0 0 0 0 0 1 0 1 1 0 0 0 0 0
0 0 0 0 0 0 0 0 0 0 0 0 0 0 0 0 0 0 | 0 0 0 0 0 0 1 1 1 0 0 1 0 0
0 0 0 0 0 0 0 0 0 0 0 0 0 0 0 0 0 0 | 0 0 0 0 0 0 1 1 1 0 1 1 1 1
0 0 0 0 0 0 0 0 0 0 0 0 0 0 0 0 0 0 | 0 0 0 0 0 0 1 1 1 1 0 1 1 1
0 0 0 0 0 0 0 0 0 0 0 0 0 0 0 0 0 0 | 0 0 0 0 0 1 1 0 1 1 1 1 1 1
0 0 0 0 0 0 0 0 0 0 0 0 0 0 0 0 0 0 | 0 0 0 0 0 0 1 1 0 1 1 1 0 0
0 0 0 0 0 0 0 0 0 0 0 0 0 0 0 0 0 0 | 0 0 0 0 0 0 1 1 0 1 1 1 0 0
0 0 0 0 0 0 0 0 0 0 0 0 0 0 0 0 0 0 | 0 0 0 0 0 0 0 1 1 0 0 0 0 0
0 0 0 0 0 0 0 0 0 0 0 0 0 0 0 0 0 0 | 0 0 0 0 0 0 0 1 1 0 0 0 0 0
0 0 0 0 0 0 0 0 0 0 0 0 0 0 0 0 0 0 | 0 0 0 0 0 0 0 1 0 1 0 0 0 0
0 0 0 0 0 0 0 0 0 0 0 0 0 0 0 0 0 0 | 0 0 0 0 0 0 0 1 0 1 0 0 0 0
─────────────────────────────────────────────────────────────────────
1 1 0 1 0 0 0 0 0 0 0 0 0 0 0 0 0 0 | 0 0 0 0 0 0 0 0 0 0 0 0 0 0
1 1 1 0 0 0 0 0 0 0 0 0 0 0 0 0 0 0 | 0 0 0 0 0 0 0 0 0 0 0 0 0 0
1 1 1 1 1 1 0 0 0 0 0 0 0 0 0 0 0 0 | 0 0 0 0 0 0 0 0 0 0 0 0 0 0
1 0 1 1 1 0 0 0 0 0 0 0 0 0 0 0 0 0 | 0 0 0 0 0 0 0 0 0 0 0 0 0 0
1 1 1 1 1 1 1 0 1 0 0 0 0 0 0 0 0 0 | 0 0 0 0 0 0 0 0 0 0 0 0 0 0
1 1 1 1 0 1 1 1 0 0 0 0 1 0 0 0 0 0 | 0 0 0 0 0 0 0 0 0 0 0 0 0 0
0 1 1 1 1 0 1 0 1 1 0 0 1 1 1 0 0 0 | 0 0 0 0 0 0 0 0 0 0 0 0 0 0
1 1 1 1 0 1 1 1 1 1 1 1 1 0 1 1 0 0 | 0 0 0 0 0 0 0 0 0 0 0 0 0 0
1 0 1 0 0 0 0 1 1 1 1 1 1 1 0 1 1 1 | 0 0 0 0 0 0 0 0 0 0 0 0 0 0
0 0 0 0 0 0 0 0 0 0 1 1 1 1 1 0 0 0 | 0 0 0 0 0 0 0 0 0 0 0 0 0 0
0 0 0 0 0 0 0 0 0 0 0 0 1 1 0 1 1 | 0 0 0 0 0 0 0 0 0 0 0 0 0 0
0 0 0 0 0 0 0 0 1 1 1 1 1 1 0 0 0 | 0 0 0 0 0 0 0 0 0 0 0 0 0 0
0 0 0 0 0 0 0 0 0 0 0 1 1 1 0 0 0 0 | 0 0 0 0 0 0 0 0 0 0 0 0 0 0
0 0 0 0 0 0 0 0 0 0 1 1 1 0 0 0 0 | 0 0 0 0 0 0 0 0 0 0 0 0 0 0
```

Matrix 13.5 Bipartite matrix of Southern women data.

put the women on one side of the picture and the events on the other so that the edges only go across the page.

Since the bipartite network is simply a network, we can apply all the normal network methods. However, we need to be aware that our results will be affected by the fact that edges cannot occur within the two groups. For example, we cannot find any cliques since the shortest possible cycle is of length 4. Also, standard normalizations of measures such as centrality usually assume that all actors could in principle be connected to each other. Take as an example degree centrality. Ruth has degree 4, so the normalized degree centrality would take the 4 and divide it by $n - 1$, which is 31 in this case, to yield a normalized centrality of 13%. But Ruth could only attend a maximum of 14 events and so her normalized degree centrality should be 29%. We can run all the standard centrality and centralization routines, but we need to adjust the normalization scores to reflect the nature of the data. (Details can be found in Borgatti and Everett, 1997.) UCINET has special routines which perform the correct normalization for both degree and betweenness centrality (and also closeness, but, as already noted, this is not a very useful centrality measure).

Density can similarly be adjusted. We just count the number of edges, as we normally do (see Chapter 9) and then divide by the maximum possible, $m \times n$,

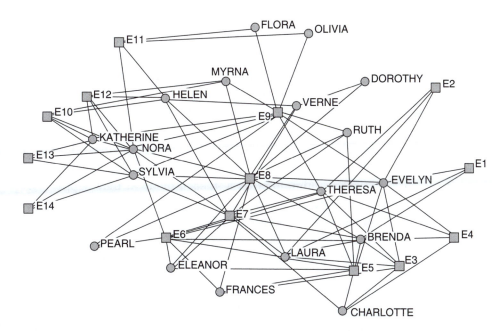

Figure 13.3 Bipartite graph of Southern women data. Circular nodes indicate women, square nodes indicate events.

where m is the number of actors and n is the number of events. For valued bipartite networks we simply sum the edge weights instead of counting.

Other cohesion methods such as average geodesic distance need not be renormalized, but in comparing networks we need to be aware that the bipartite networks have different properties and we should not, for example, compare these scores with ones derived from single-mode networks.

The general approach of adapting methods for bipartite networks works for a number of other techniques, but it does not work for all. For example, as noted earlier, most two-mode networks are not directed in the usual sense, so reciprocity is either 100% or zero. For another example, bipartite networks have no transitive triples, since that would require a within-mode tie. For properties such as transitivity, we have to construct a new concept that in some sense retains the spirit of the original concept. For example, one way to think about transitivity in ordinary networks is in terms of closure: if A is connected to B and B is connected to C, then the open structural hole between A and C would be closed if A and C became connected. In a bipartite network, closure can be defined in terms of 4-cycles. In other words, if A and B attend event X and A attends event Y, we have closure if B also attends Y. Other generalizations of transitivity also exist (Opsahl, 2012).

13.5 Cohesive subgroups and community detection

Clearly, a bipartite network cannot contain any cliques as described in the cohesive subgroup chapter since we cannot have connections within the modes. However, recall that a clique is defined as a maximally connected subgraph. This definition can still hold for a bipartite network; we just need to refine it to be a maximally complete bipartite subgraph, which we call a 'bi-clique'. Cliques usually contain at least three actors; for bi-cliques, we normally look for at least three actors from each mode, but this can be lowered. Also, there is no reason for us to require the same minimum criteria in each mode. It may happen that one mode contains a lot more vertices than the other. We can then analyze the bi-cliques in the same way as we did for the cliques.

The Davis data have 22 bi-cliques with at least three actors in each mode. We then constructed an actor-by-actor bi-clique co-membership matrix and submitted this to the average method hierarchical clustering to obtain the diagram given in Figure 13.4. In this figure, we can clearly identify two groups of women and the events associated with each group.

It is also possible to analyze the bi-clique overlap using the bimodal method discussed in Chapter 4. In this case, any visualization would have three different

```
                        C                                   K
                        H                                   A
            D           A           E F             T       T
            O O         R           L R E           B H     H   S
            R L F   P   L       V   E A V   L       R E   H   M   E   Y
            O I L   E   O   R E A N E   A   A   E R E N Y   R   L
            T V O E A   T   U R N C L   U   N E   L O R E I   V E E
            H I R 1 R E E T E T N E O E Y E R E D S E E E R N 1 N E I 1 1 1
            Y A A 1 L 2 1 E 4 H E 7 R S N 3 A 6 A A 5 8 N A A 0 E 9 A 2 3 4

            1 1 1 2   2 1   2   1 2       2   2       2 2 1 1 1 2 1 2 1 3 3 3
   Level    6 7 8 9 8 0 9 5 2 9 0 5 7 6 1 1 2 4 4 3 3 6 5 4 1 8 2 7 3 0 1 2
   -------  - - - - - - - - - - - - - - - - - - - - - - - - - - - - - - - -
  11.0000   . . . . . . . . . . . . . . . . . . . . . XXX . . . . . . . . . .
   9.5000   . . . . . . . . . . . . . . . . . . . . XXXXX . . . . . . . . . .
   8.2500   . . . . . . . . . . . . . . . . . . . XXXXXXX . . . . . . . . . .
   8.0000   . . . . . . . . . . . . . . . . . . . XXXXXXX . . . . . . XXX . .
   7.2500   . . . . . . . . . . . . . . . . . . XXXXXXXXX . . . . . . XXX . .
   6.5625   . . . . . . . . . . . . . . . . . XXXXXXXXXXX . . . . . . XXX . .
   5.5000   . . . . . . . . . . . . . . . . . XXXXXXXXXXX . . . . XXXXX . .
   5.2813   . . . . . . . . . . . . . . . . XXXXXXXXXXXXX . . . . XXXXX . .
   5.0625   . . . . . . . . . . . . . . . XXXXXXXXXXXXXXX . . . . XXXXX . .
   4.5000   . . . . . . . . . . . . . . . XXXXXXXXXXXXXXX . . . XXXXXXX . .
   4.0000   . . . . . . . . . . . . . . . XXXXXXXXXXXXXXX . . . XXXXXXXXX . .
   3.3750   . . . . . . . . . . . . . . . XXXXXXXXXXXXXXX . . XXXXXXXXXXX . .
   3.0000   . . . . . . . . . XXX . . XXXXXXXXXXXXXXX . . XXXXXXXXXXX . .
   2.0000   . . . . . . XXX . XXX . . XXXXXXXXXXXXXXX . . XXXXXXXXXXX . .
   1.9375   . . . . . . XXX . XXX . . XXXXXXXXXXXXXXX . XXXXXXXXXXXXX . .
   1.7500   . . . . . . XXX . XXX . XXXXXXXXXXXXXXXXX . XXXXXXXXXXXXX . .
   1.5000   . . . . . . XXX XXXXX . XXXXXXXXXXXXXXXXX . XXXXXXXXXXXXX . .
   1.1563   . . . . . . XXX XXXXX . XXXXXXXXXXXXXXXXX XXXXXXXXXXXXXXX . .
   1.0938   . . . . . . XXX XXXXX XXXXXXXXXXXXXXXXXXX XXXXXXXXXXXXXXX . .
   1.0000   . . . . . . XXX XXXXX XXXXXXXXXXXXXXXXXXX XXXXXXXXXXXXXXX XXX
   0.7090   . . . . . . XXX XXXXXXXXXXXXXXXXXXXXXXXXX XXXXXXXXXXXXXXX XXX
   0.4004   . . . . . . XXXXXXXXXXXXXXXXXXXXXXXXXXXXX XXXXXXXXXXXXXXX XXX
   0.3750   . . . . . . XXXXXXXXXXXXXXXXXXXXXXXXXXXXXXXXXXXXXXXXXXXXXXXX
   0.0877   . . . . . . XXXXXXXXXXXXXXXXXXXXXXXXXXXXXXXXXXXXXXXXXXXXXXXX
   0.0310   . . . . . XXXXXXXXXXXXXXXXXXXXXXXXXXXXXXXXXXXXXXXXXXXXXXXXXX
   0.0154   . . . . XXXXXXXXXXXXXXXXXXXXXXXXXXXXXXXXXXXXXXXXXXXXXXXXXXXX
   0.0057   . . . . XXXXXXXXXXXXXXXXXXXXXXXXXXXXXXXXXXXXXXXXXXXXXXXXXXXX
   0.0000   XXXXXXXXXXXXXXXXXXXXXXXXXXXXXXXXXXXXXXXXXXXXXXXXXXXXXXXXXXXX
```

Figure 13.4 Clustering of bi-cliques in the Southern women data.

node types: actors, events and bi-cliques. However, the actors and events would be treated as if they belonged to the same mode, and the bi-cliques would be the second mode. This would require sophisticated use of any of the current software tools, and thus is not discussed here in any detail.

13.5.1 Modularity optimization

Modularity optimization or Newman community detection can be extended to two-mode networks. The communities would consist of both actors and events and so we are looking to partition both the rows and the columns of the affiliation matrix so that the diagonal (not necessarily square) blocks are dense and the off-diagonal blocks are sparse. One method to do this is to find communities of one of the projected matrix and then to associate the other mode with the communities they are most closely associated. Guimerà et al. (2007) take this approach and use a simple extension to modularity to deal with the valued data. When they apply this technique to the Davis data they report a straight split of the women into two groups namely {Evelyn, Laura, Theresa, Brenda, Charlotte, Frances, Eleanor, Ruth} and attach events 1 through 8 to this group. All the other women and events belong to the second group.

An alternative approach is to extend the modularity measure Q given by equation 11.1 to two-mode data as discussed by Barber (2007). In the two-mode version the adjacency matrix is replaced by an affiliation matrix and the P matrix is adapted to take account of the bipartite structure, so that B is replaced by $\check{B}$. In addition, instead of a single S indicator matrix we need to have one matrix for each mode which we call R and T. The resultant formula has the form shown in equation 13.2.

$$Q = \frac{1}{m} Tr(R^T BT) \tag{13.2}$$

If we have c communities and our bipartite network has p actors and q events then R is p × c, $\check{B}$ is p × q and T is q × c. Barber also proposes an algorithm BRIM (Bipartite, Recursive Induced Modules), which uses the singular vectors of B to recursively partition both actors and events into groups. The algorithm does not however provide a method to find the maximum value for c the number of groups. To overcome this he suggests starting with c = 1, calculating Q and then keep doubling c until Q decreases. At this stage use bisection to find the value of c which maximizes Q. Full details and an example using the Davis data can be found in the paper.

13.6 Core–periphery models

Core–periphery structures generalize naturally to two-mode data. The events and the actors are both divided into core and periphery groups. Core actors attend core events and peripheral actors attend peripheral events. As with the single-mode case, the core–periphery interactions are often defined by the data and are not always specified. In general, we might expect core actors to attend some peripheral events and peripheral actors to only attend a few core events; these can be built into the models.

As with the single-mode case, we can use either a categorical approach and use optimization methods to fit our data to an ideal model, or use a continuous approach. Note that the number of actors in the actor core will in general be different from the number of events in the event core, so the optimization algorithm will be a lot slower for two-mode data. This is true to such an extent that only relatively small networks can be analyzed using this approach.

We can adapt the continuous method to the bipartite network by analyzing the affiliation matrix directly, using methods designed for non-square matrices (singular-valued decomposition). However, it turns out that this technique is basically equivalent to finding the core–periphery structures of the actor-by-actor and event-by-event one-mode networks and using these results to define the relevant cores and peripheries. Hence, an analysis of a two-mode dataset would proceed by first constructing the two one-mode datasets of actors and events as described in the second section of this chapter and then applying the continuous core–periphery model to each of these separately. These results are then combined and represented on the original affiliation matrix. Applying this to the Davis data and taking the recommended core and periphery sizes provided by UCINET results in the partition shown in Figure 13.5.

We note that, as shown in Figure 13.5, there are eight core women and five core events. It is easy to see that the core events are simply the most popular, since they were all attended by eight or more women, and the peripheral events had six or fewer. The core women, on the other hand, have a more subtle structure: to be in the core, a woman had to either attend either four or more core events or three core events and at least four peripheral events. We see that Ruth, for example, only attended four events but they were all core, whereas Katherine attended six events but only two of these were core, so she

```
                                                1 1 1 1 1
                            8 9 6 7 5     3 4 1 2 0 1 2 3 4
                            E E E E E     E E E E E E E E E
                          -------------------------------------
         1     EVELYN |  1 1 1     1 |  1 1 1 1                  |
         2      LAURA |  1     1 1 1 |  1     1 1                |
         3    THERESA |  1 1 1 1 1 |  1 1     1                  |
         4     BRENDA |  1     1 1 1 |  1 1 1                    |
        14       NORA |     1 1 1   |               1 1 1 1 1   |
         7    ELEANOR |  1     1 1 1 |                           |
         9       RUTH |  1 1   1 1 |                             |
        13     SYLVIA |  1 1   1   |             1   1 1 1 1     |
                          -------------------------------------
         6    FRANCES |  1   1   1 |  1                          |
         8      PEARL |  1 1 1     |                           1 |
        10      VERNE |  1 1   1   |                           1 |
        12  KATHERINE |  1 1       |             1   1 1 1 1     |
        11      MYRNA |  1 1       |             1     1         |
         5  CHARLOTTE |         1 1 |  1 1                       |
        15      HELEN |  1       1 |               1 1 1         |
        16    DOROTHY |  1 1       |                             |
        17     OLIVIA |     1       |               1             |
        18      FLORA |     1       |               1             |
                          -------------------------------------
```

Figure 13.5 Core–periphery analysis of the Southern women data.

is placed in the periphery. We also note that the peripheral women Frances, Pearl and Verne all attended three core events but very few peripheral events (at most only one), and this was not enough to compensate for their lower attendance at the core events.

The approach taken here can be seen as a more general technique for analyzing two-mode networks. We have taken both projections (women-by-women and event-by-event), analyzed these separately, and then combined the results. This is what Everett and Borgatti (2013) call the 'dual projection approach'. They show that provided you use both projections and do not dichotomize, there will almost never be any structural data loss.

13.7 Equivalence

The approach taken in Chapter 12 on equivalence requires very few modifications to apply directly to affiliation matrices. Core–periphery models can be seen as nearly structural equivalence blockmodels with a 1-block for core–core interaction and a 0-block for periphery–periphery interaction. They are not quite a structural equivalence, since we do not specify any patterns in the off-diagonal blocks. The block specifications are the same for one-mode and two-mode data; the only difference is in the fact that we allow non-square blocks in the two-mode data as we partition the rows independently of the columns.

13.7.1 Structural equivalence

As normally conceived, two-mode data cannot contain self-loops and do not have directed ties. As a consequence, we can use a very simple definition for structural equivalence: actors i and j are structurally equivalent if they are connected to exactly the same events. Events A and B are structurally equivalent if they were attended by exactly the same actors.

We can apply profile similarity in exactly the same way as for the single-mode case. We take the rows as the profiles of the actors and the columns as the profiles of the events. We can then form a structural equivalence matrix of the actors by comparing the rows using correlation Euclidean distance or matching, and a structural equivalence matrix of the events by comparing the columns in the same way. Each matrix can then be clustered in the same way as for the one-mode case. This is another example of using the dual projection approach to guard against data loss when converting from two-mode to one-mode. Figure 13.6 gives the structural equivalence matrix for the women and the events of the Davis data. The measure of equivalence is matches, and the values give the fraction of matches between the profiles to a single (truncated) decimal place.

We can see from Figure 13.6 that Olivia and Flora are structurally equivalent, as are events 13 and 14. The least structurally equivalent women are Evelyn and Nora, and the least structurally equivalent events are 8 and 11. We could proceed with a clustering of these matrices, but we shall postpone this so we can make a direct comparison with the optimization approach.

A blockmodel for structural equivalence has exactly the same form as for the single-mode case. That is, the matrix blocks are either all 0s or all 1s. We can therefore apply the direct method to the Davis data. The computational complexity of this approach means that it is often quite difficult to find good partitions of the data, and there are often very many competing solutions, making this very challenging for the researcher. The structural equivalence partition

		1 EVE	2 LAU	3 THE	4 BRE	5 CHA	6 FRA	7 ELE	8 PEA	9 RUT	10 VER	11 MYR	12 KAT	13 SYL	14 NOR	15 HEL	16 DOR	17 OLI	18 FLO
1	EVELYN	1.0	0.8	0.9	0.8	0.6	0.7	0.6	0.6	0.6	0.4	0.4	0.3	0.2	0.1	0.2	0.6	0.4	0.4
2	LAURA	0.8	1.0	0.8	0.9	0.6	0.8	0.8	0.6	0.6	0.5	0.4	0.2	0.3	0.2	0.4	0.5	0.4	0.4
3	THERESA	0.9	0.8	1.0	0.8	0.7	0.7	0.7	0.6	0.7	0.6	0.4	0.3	0.4	0.3	0.4	0.6	0.4	0.4
4	BRENDA	0.8	0.9	0.8	1.0	0.8	0.8	0.8	0.6	0.6	0.5	0.4	0.2	0.3	0.2	0.4	0.5	0.4	0.4
5	CHARLOTTE	0.6	0.6	0.7	0.8	1.0	0.7	0.7	0.5	0.7	0.6	0.4	0.3	0.4	0.3	0.5	0.6	0.6	0.6
6	FRANCES	0.7	0.8	0.7	0.8	0.7	1.0	0.9	0.8	0.7	0.6	0.6	0.4	0.4	0.3	0.6	0.7	0.6	0.6
7	ELEANOR	0.6	0.8	0.7	0.8	0.7	0.9	1.0	0.8	0.9	0.7	0.6	0.4	0.5	0.4	0.6	0.7	0.6	0.6
8	PEARL	0.6	0.6	0.6	0.6	0.5	0.8	0.8	1.0	0.8	0.8	0.8	0.6	0.6	0.5	0.6	0.9	0.8	0.8
9	RUTH	0.6	0.6	0.7	0.6	0.7	0.7	0.9	0.8	1.0	0.9	0.7	0.6	0.6	0.4	0.6	0.9	0.7	0.7
10	VERNE	0.4	0.5	0.6	0.5	0.6	0.6	0.7	0.8	0.9	1.0	0.9	0.7	0.8	0.6	0.8	0.9	0.7	0.7
11	MYRNA	0.4	0.4	0.4	0.4	0.4	0.6	0.6	0.8	0.7	0.9	1.0	0.9	0.8	0.6	0.8	0.9	0.7	0.7
12	KATHERINE	0.3	0.2	0.3	0.2	0.3	0.4	0.4	0.6	0.6	0.7	0.9	1.0	0.9	0.7	0.6	0.7	0.6	0.6
13	SYLVIA	0.2	0.3	0.4	0.3	0.4	0.4	0.5	0.6	0.6	0.8	0.8	0.9	1.0	0.8	0.7	0.6	0.5	0.5
14	NORA	0.1	0.2	0.3	0.2	0.3	0.3	0.4	0.5	0.4	0.6	0.6	0.7	0.8	1.0	0.6	0.4	0.6	0.6
15	HELEN	0.2	0.4	0.4	0.4	0.5	0.6	0.6	0.6	0.6	0.8	0.8	0.6	0.7	0.6	1.0	0.6	0.6	0.6
16	DOROTHY	0.6	0.5	0.6	0.5	0.6	0.7	0.7	0.9	0.9	0.9	0.9	0.7	0.6	0.4	0.6	1.0	0.9	0.9
17	OLIVIA	0.4	0.4	0.4	0.4	0.6	0.6	0.6	0.8	0.7	0.7	0.7	0.6	0.5	0.6	0.6	0.9	1.0	1.0
18	FLORA	0.4	0.4	0.4	0.4	0.6	0.6	0.6	0.8	0.7	0.7	0.7	0.6	0.5	0.6	0.6	0.9	1.0	1.0

		1 E1	2 E2	3 E3	4 E4	5 E5	6 E6	7 E7	8 E8	9 E9	10 E10	11 E11	12 E12	13 E13	14 E14
1	E1	1.0	0.9	0.8	0.8	0.7	0.7	0.5	0.4	0.3	0.6	0.6	0.5	0.7	0.7
2	E2	0.9	1.0	0.8	0.8	0.7	0.7	0.5	0.4	0.4	0.6	0.6	0.5	0.7	0.7
3	E3	0.8	0.8	1.0	0.9	0.9	0.8	0.6	0.4	0.2	0.4	0.4	0.3	0.5	0.5
4	E4	0.8	0.8	0.9	1.0	0.8	0.7	0.6	0.3	0.3	0.5	0.6	0.4	0.6	0.6
5	E5	0.7	0.7	0.9	0.8	1.0	0.8	0.7	0.6	0.2	0.3	0.3	0.2	0.4	0.4
6	E6	0.7	0.7	0.8	0.7	0.8	1.0	0.6	0.6	0.3	0.4	0.4	0.3	0.5	0.5
7	E7	0.5	0.5	0.6	0.6	0.7	0.6	1.0	0.6	0.3	0.5	0.4	0.6	0.5	0.5
8	E8	0.4	0.4	0.4	0.3	0.6	0.6	0.6	1.0	0.6	0.4	0.1	0.4	0.3	0.3
9	E9	0.3	0.4	0.2	0.3	0.2	0.3	0.3	0.6	1.0	0.5	0.4	0.6	0.5	0.5
10	E10	0.6	0.6	0.4	0.5	0.3	0.4	0.5	0.4	0.5	1.0	0.7	0.9	0.9	0.9
11	E11	0.6	0.6	0.4	0.6	0.3	0.4	0.4	0.1	0.4	0.7	1.0	0.7	0.7	0.7
12	E12	0.5	0.5	0.3	0.4	0.2	0.3	0.6	0.4	0.6	0.9	0.7	1.0	0.8	0.8
13	E13	0.7	0.7	0.5	0.6	0.4	0.5	0.5	0.3	0.5	0.9	0.7	0.8	1.0	1.0
14	E14	0.7	0.7	0.5	0.6	0.4	0.5	0.5	0.3	0.5	0.9	0.7	0.8	1.0	1.0

Figure 13.6 Structural equivalence of women and events from the Davis data.

Analyzing Social Networks

```
                                        1 1 1 1 1
                      1 2 3 4 5   6 7 8 9   0 1 2 3 4
                      E E E E     E E E E   E E E E
                      -----------------------------------
 1     EVELYN  | 1 1 1 1 1 | 1     1 1 |             |
 2      LAURA  | 1 1 1   1 | 1 1 1     |             |
 3    THERESA  |   1 1 1 1 | 1 1 1 1   |             |
 4     BRENDA  | 1   1 1 1 | 1 1 1     |             |
 5  CHARLOTTE  |     1 1 1 | 1         |             |
 6    FRANCES  |   1   1 1 | 1   1     |             |
 7    ELEANOR  |       1 1 | 1 1 1     |             |
 9       RUTH  |       1 1 |   1 1 1   |             |
                      -----------------------------------
17     OLIVIA  |           |           | 1     1     |
10      VERNE  |           | 1 1 1     |     1       |
11      MYRNA  |           |   1 1 1   | 1     1     |
12  KATHERINE  |           |   1 1 1   | 1   1 1 1   |
13     SYLVIA  |           | 1 1 1     | 1   1 1 1   |
14       NORA  |         1 1|     1     | 1 1 1 1 1   |
15      HELEN  |           | 1 1       | 1 1 1       |
18      FLORA  |           |     1     |     1       |
                      -----------------------------------
 8      PEARL  |           | 1   1 1   |             |
16    DOROTHY  |           |     1 1   |             |
                      -----------------------------------
```

Figure 13.7 Direct blockmodel of the Davis data.

of the Davis data given in Figure 13.7 has been proposed as a good solution (found using the Pajek software) and published by Doreian et al. (2004). This required relatively sophisticated use of the software, specifying the model precisely together with certain (non-default) penalties for violating the structural equivalence criteria.

We can see that the proposed solution has four pure non-zero blocks and contains 63 errors in the 1-blocks. It divides the women into three groups. One group attends two sets of events; the second group also attends two sets of events but with one set in common with the first group; and the final pair of women only attend the events the first two sets of women had in common. This solution is consistent with many other analyses of these data.

To compare this solution with the profile method directly, we will first cluster each of the matrices of Figure 13.6 into three groups. We use the UCINET Cluster Optimization routine with the Density option to generate the clusters from the equivalence data. The resultant two-mode blockmodel constructed using the woman and event partitions is given in Figure 13.8.

The event blocking is similar in both models, with just event 6 differently allocated. The first block of women is also similar, with just one woman, Ruth, placed in another block. However, the remaining blocks are quite different. The overall structure is very similar, inasmuch as all women attend one group of events (the middle group in both cases), there is a group of women who attends these and one other set of events, and another group who attends these and a different set of events. As previously noted, Figure 13.7 has 63 errors, whereas the model in Figure 13.8 has just 43 errors and as such is a better solution.

```
                            1 1 1 1 1
         1 2 3 4 5 6    7 8 9    0 1 2 3 4
         E E E E E E    E E E    E E E E
        ----------------------------------
 1     EVELYN | 1 1 1 1 1 1 |   1 1 |             |
 2      LAURA | 1 1 1   1 1 | 1 1   |             |
 3    THERESA |   1 1 1 1 1 | 1 1 1 |             |
 4     BRENDA | 1   1 1 1 1 | 1 1   |             |
 5  CHARLOTTE |   1 1 1     | 1     |             |
 6    FRANCES |   1   1 1   |   1   |             |
 7    ELEANOR |       1 1   | 1 1   |             |
        ----------------------------------
 8      PEARL |         1   |   1 1 |             |
 9       RUTH |       1     | 1 1 1 |             |
10      VERNE |             | 1 1 1 |     1       |
11      MYRNA |             |   1 1 | 1     1     |
16    DOROTHY |             |   1 1 |             |
17     OLIVIA |             |     1 |   1         |
18      FLORA |             |     1 |   1         |
        ----------------------------------
15      HELEN |             | 1 1   | 1 1 1       |
12  KATHERINE |             |   1 1 | 1     1 1 1 |
13     SYLVIA |             | 1 1 1 | 1     1 1 1 |
14       NORA |         1   | 1   1 | 1 1 1 1 1   |
        ----------------------------------
```

Figure 13.8 Structural blockmodel derived from profile similarity.

13.7.2 Regular equivalence

Unfortunately, the fact that there is no simple profile similarity method for regular equivalence means that we are more constrained when implementing two-mode techniques for regular equivalence. As our two-mode data are not directed, the maximal regular equivalence found will always be trivial, and even if we extended the REGE algorithm to two-mode, it would simply cluster together all actors in each mode. It is possible to have profile methods that find approximations to other regular equivalences (such as automorphic), but they have not been extensively used. This means that the direct method is really the only technique available besides converting the data to one-mode.

The blocks for a regular partition of a two-mode dataset are exactly the same as in the one-mode case. That is, any block must either be a 0-block or contain a 1 in every row and every column. We can therefore use this fact exactly as in the single-mode case to construct a direct optimization method. Highly sophisticated methods to do this have been implemented in Pajek. In fact, the structural equivalence solution given in Figure 13.7 has only one regular error (in the center block of the bottom row) and, if viewed as a regular equivalence, is an excellent solution. This same solution can be found by using the regular equivalence model rather than the structural equivalence model. The blockmodel in Figure 13.8 has seven errors and as such is a far worse regular model than the one in Figure 13.7. The interested reader should look at Borgatti and Everett (1992) and Doreian et al. (2004) for more details.

13.8 Summary

Network data consisting of ties between and not within two distinct groups are known as two-mode data. Such data naturally arise when examining structures of people attending events or with memberships in organizations. They can be converted to standard proximity data by constructing relations such as 'number of events attended in common' or 'number of actors attending a pair of events'. These are examples of projections, which can be analyzed directly (as proximity matrices) or dichotomized and analyzed as networks. If only one projection is examined, or if the data are dichotomized, there is a loss of structural information. However, there is no real loss of information if both projections are used. An alternative is to examine the network as a bipartite graph and then take account of the bipartite structure. This can be done either by normalizing the results to reflect the fact that ties do not occur within the modes, or by modifying the concepts so that they are consistent with the two-mode structure. The first approach is recommended for centrality, whereas the second approach can be used to define bi-cliques – for example, to find cohesive subgraphs. Both approaches can be used to define equivalences. One important thing to keep in mind is that, for bi-cliques and centrality, attending the same event or having events with actors in common is a proxy for the related one-mode relation. This is not necessarily true for equivalence, but care in this case needs to be taken in interpreting the results so as not to conclude that some kind of relationship exists when in reality it does not.

13.9 Problems and Exercises

1. For the problems in this chapter we will use the United States Supreme Court decisions in the Rehnquist court (1986–2005) for the year 1997 (SupremeCourt97.##h). The data consist of the nine justices' decisions on n cases (for matters of simplicity a 1 reflects agreement with the majority decision while a 0 reflects agreement with the minority decision). First visualize the two-mode network using NetDraw. Go to NetDraw, click on the File|Open|Ucinet dataset|2-Mode network and enter the two-mode matrix and click OK. Do there appear to be any patterns with respect to the clustering of the justices? If so, describe the patterns.
2. It is important to visualize the relationship among justices vis-à-vis court decisions on cases and the relationship among court cases vis-à-vis the justices. For this we convert the two-mode matrix into a one-mode matrix of relationships either among cases or justices. The converted one-mode is called an affiliation network.

    a. Create an affiliation network of relations among justices. In UCINET go to Data|Affiliations(2-mode to 1-mode) and input the Supreme Court two-mode matrix. Since the justices are the rows of the matrix the "Mode:" to the far left should be highlighted as "Rows". In this example use the default "Method" sums of cross-product (overlaps). Click OK.

b. How would you interpret the values in each of the off-diagonal cells of the resulting one-mode affiliation network? What about the values in the diagonal cells of the matrix?

c. Create an affiliation network of relations among cases. In UCINET go to Data|Affiliations(2-mode to 1-mode) and input the Supreme Court two-mode matrix. Since the cases are the columns of the matrix the "Mode:" to the far left should be highlighted as "Columns". In this example use the default "Method" sums of cross-product (overlaps). Click OK.

d. How would you interpret the values in each of the off-diagonal cells of the resulting one-mode affiliation network? What about the values in the diagonal cells of the matrix?

3. Another way to treat two-mode matrices as one-mode data is to convert the matrix to a bipartite network. Using the original two-mode Supreme Court matrix (SupremeCourt97.##h), in UCINET go to Transform|Graph Theoretic|Bipartite... and input the two-mode matrix and then click OK. How would you now characterize the rows and columns of the resulting bipartite matrix?

4. The Rehnquist Court was known by the division between liberal and conservative justices. There are a number of ways of looking for cohesive subgroups in the Supreme Court data. We will explore three of them.

a. The first is 2-mode factions. Go to Network|2-Mode networks| 2-Mode Factions and enter the "SupremeCourt97.##h" for input (be sure to properly name the output files) and hit OK. How might you interpret the resulting blocked adjacency matrix in terms of a possible division in the court between liberal and conservative justices?

b. As with one-mode networks we can also look for structural equivalence by calculating profile similarities for the rows and columns of the matrix. Since we are mostly interested in the justices we will only examine row profile similarity. In UCINET go to Tools|Similarities & Distances and input the "SupremeCourt97.##h" data file. Make sure that "Rows" are checked. For the purposes of this exercise we will use the "Matches" similarity measure. We will want to use the output file in order to run a cluster analysis (if you input SupremeCourt97 the output dataset will automatically be named SupremeCourt97-Mat-R). This yields a similarity matrix of matches among the justices reflecting similarities in their decision-making behaviors. Which justices have the highest similarity in their decisions across the cases?

c. The similarity matrix of matches on court decisions among the justices lends itself to hierarchical cluster analysis (HCL) to better understand the presence of subgroupings among the justices. In UCINET go to Tools|Cluster Analysis| Hierarchical... and input the file "SupremeCourt97-Mat-R.##h" and hit OK. What does the cluster diagram tell you about the divisions among the justices?

Don't forget to visit the website at
https://study.sagepub.com/borgatti2e

14

Large Networks

Learning Outcomes

1. Understand the challenges of dealing with large networks
2. Implement techniques to reduce the size of the problem
3. Correctly use and interpret sampling methods
4. Identify small-world and scale-free networks

14.1 Introduction

Social network researchers are increasingly interested in analyzing large networks. Typically, large datasets are obtained from secondary data sources rather than direct survey methods. For example, researchers interested in how the network structure of project teams affects project success might analyze the Internet Movie Database, which contains data on collaborations among more than 2 million persons. Sociologists interested in elites and inequality might study the pattern of who sits on the boards of what companies. These data are available from a number of sources and potentially involve millions of persons and organizations. Within organizations, a convenient (even if problematic) method of assessing communication patterns is to analyze the pattern of emails among all employees.

A useful first question to ask is what are the consequences of network size. There are three basic issues associated with large networks: space (e.g., computer memory), time (i.e., execution time), and usability (e.g., usefulness of results). Today, space is rarely a problem except insofar as accessing all the data affects time. In general, time is the biggest problem. There are many analyses we would like to do which are feasible for very small networks that are simply impossible for networks of even 50 nodes. For example, when we discussed factions in Chapter 11 we stated that it was difficult to look at all possible assignments to groups for larger networks. If we had a network of 20 nodes and wanted to look for all assignments into three groups and our computer could do 1000 million calculations a second, it would complete the calculation in just over 2 seconds making this a fairly easy task. If we increased this to 50 nodes it would take over 3 million years.

Usability is a more subtle problem. An example is the network visualization problem. Programs like NetDraw can easily draw a network with thousands of edges. However, whether the result is useful depends on the structure of the network. Diffuse structures of even a few hundred nodes can look like a bowl of spaghetti. But a large network with clear subgroups can be usefully visualized even if it has many thousands of nodes and edges. Another example is a measure like closeness centrality (Chapter 10). In large networks, we typically find that most nodes are pretty far from a lot of nodes, so the closeness measure tends to have very low variance, making it difficult to distinguish between nodes.

Another good question to ask is what is meant by network size. Most people intuitively think in terms of the number of nodes, and indeed in many cases the running time and space requirements of an algorithm are in fact a direct function of the number of nodes. This is almost always true for methods derived from multivariate statistics, such as correspondence analysis or extracting eigenvectors, and is true for many methods derived from graph theory as well. More commonly, however, for graph-theoretic algorithms the number of edges in the graph provides a better guide to an algorithm's running time and space requirements, and so is a better way to think about network size.

Some programs such as Pajek (Batagelj and Mrvar, 1998) have been designed specifically for large networks and are capable of handling networks far larger than UCINET.[1] However all programs will at some point be unable to cope well with networks of a certain size and so all have limitations and all need to take account of usability.

Based on these considerations, in this chapter we present some strategies for working with large networks.

14.2 Reducing the size of the problem

One obvious approach is to reduce the problem from a large network to one of a reasonable size. This must involve losing some data and so needs to be done carefully and in the full knowledge that something will be lost.

---

[1] Recently, Pajek has introduced an XL version that can literally handle billions of nodes. See the Pajek website for details: http://mrvar.fdv.uni-lj.si/pajek/

14.2.1 Eliminating edges

For most graph-theoretic algorithms, including visualizing networks with graph layout algorithms, the single best thing you can do is reduce the number of edges in the graph. If the data are valued, this means dichotomizing at increasingly high levels. For example, if the data consist of the number of days that pairs of people worked together on a project in the previous year, you can increase the cut-off for what counts as a tie from anything greater than 0, to greater than 1, greater than 2, and so on until the number of edges is just small enough to be tractable, or until some other criterion is reached, such as splitting a previously connected graph into components.

An example of this strategy is provided by the PV960 network that is distributed with UCINET. It represents the number of days that pairs of scientists in a research organization have worked together on funded projects. The initial visualization of the network is shown in Figure 14.1. Simply restricting the links to those representing at least 3 days of work together gives the result in Figure 14.2, which shows significant structure. We can see two large dense groups one to the left and one to the right and a slightly smaller dense area below the left-hand group. An analysis of the attributes of the nodes (not shown) shows that these three clusters correspond to a number of correlated differences (gender, salary, discipline and so on) between the groups.

If the data are not valued, one strategy is to delete ties that do not have a certain property. For example, if the data are logically undirected but in practice not symmetric, you could choose to analyze only reciprocated ties, perhaps on

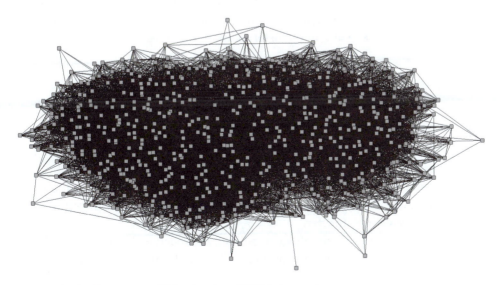

Figure 14.1   Ties among 960 scientists (PV960 dataset).

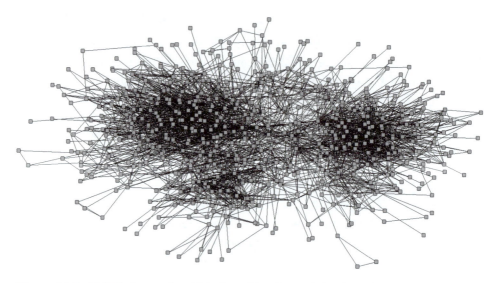

Figure 14.2 PV960 dataset in which ties with edge weights less than 3 are removed.

the theory that these are 'real' or 'corroborated' ties. For example, if you were analyzing friendship ties, you would construct a new undirected network in which there is a tie between two people only if both mentioned the other as being a friend. Similarly, Krackhardt (1999) argues that Simmelian ties are especially important ties that can usefully be analyzed alone. He defines Simmelian ties as existing between nodes A and B if both A and B have a tie to each other, and both have a reciprocated tie to at least one third party in common. Reducing your network to just Simmelian ties will significantly reduce the number of edges and often make subgroup clustering more obvious.

14.2.2 Pruning nodes

An obvious tactic is to try to reduce the number of nodes in the network, whether in addition to (recommended) or instead of removing ties. For example, we might start by removing nodes that have no ties (i.e., isolates). Since these might be few, we might go a step further and remove nodes that have just one tie (i.e., pendants and isolated dyads). If degree varies widely, we might take this process many steps further until we are only left with nodes that are pretty well connected.

One problem with this simple degree-based approach is that when you delete all nodes with, say, just one tie, you may still be left with a network that has a bunch of nodes with just one tie – these will be the nodes that used to have two ties but one of those ties was to a node that was just deleted. We can fix this by taking an approach based on k-cores (Seidman, 1983). A k-core is a subgraph in which every actor has degree k or more with the other actors in the subgraph. Hence in a 2-core every actor is connected to at least two other actors. A k-core analysis can be run relatively quickly even on large graphs. Once we have run a k-core analysis, we can successively eliminate nodes starting from the most peripheral (those who only participate in a 1-core) to the next most peripheral (those who participate only in a 2-core) and so on until left with only those that are members of the inner core of the network. Figure 14.3 shows the results of retaining only nodes who are members of a 10-core or higher. This is the inner core of the network in Figure 14.1, but it can now be seen that the inner core consists of several subgroups.

K-cores are related to cohesive subgroups but are far more relaxed. Cohesive subgroups live in k-cores, but a k-core itself need not be very cohesive. For example, a k-core may contain two unconnected cliques. Hence if the goal of the network analysis were to find cohesive subgroups, it would be economical to look for them within k-cores rather than in the graph as a whole.

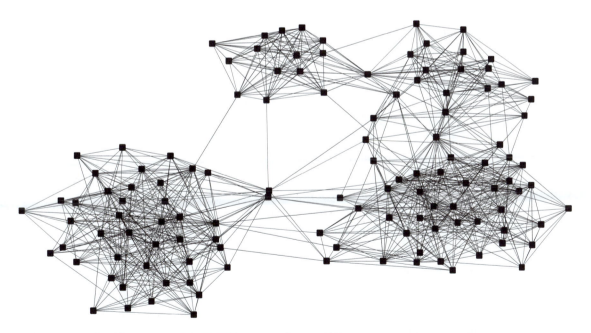

Figure 14.3 Nodes belonging to a 10-core or higher in PV960 dataset, after removing ties with edge weights less than 3.

14.2.3 Divide and conquer

One approach to reducing the size of the problem is to analyze sections of the network separately. These could be a priori sections, such as different departments within an organization, or something based on the structure of the graph itself. The most obvious approach is to search for the components of the graph. Most network methods yield the same answer (normalization aside) for a given node whether they are applied to the whole network or just to the component that node is in. Hence the logical strategy is to break up the large network and analyze each component separately. Finding components is, fortunately, an efficient process and can be readily applied to large networks. For directed networks we can look at breaking into weak components or strong components, although in this case it is no longer true that we will generally get the same answer for a node-level measure when comparing the whole-network result to the strong-component result.

Unfortunately, many networks have just one large component. A common pattern is a giant component together with a number of little fragments too small to analyze. In these cases, the component approach does not help much. To overcome this we can generalize the component approach to a less perfect partitioning of the network. Essentially, we apply a clustering technique to find sections of the network that have more connections within than to outsiders, even if they are not perfectly separate. The problem now becomes how to cluster a large network.

For networks under, say, 10,000 nodes, standard clustering approaches such as Johnson's hierarchical clustering and k-means clustering can be used. (If the edges are not valued, then we must first convert to geodesic distances or the like in order to provide the clustering algorithms with some variance to work with.) For larger datasets, there are graph partitioning algorithms (e.g., Kernighan and Lin, 1970) that are extremely fast but unfortunately not very accurate. They are usually used to do things like distribute tasks for parallel computing where the only consequences of generating a poor partition are reduced efficiency rather than getting wrong or misleading answers. For social network analysis, however, a partition that does not correspond well to actual clusters could possibly do much more harm than good.

14.2.4 Aggregation

Finding the components or k-cores often helps in reducing the network but it is rarely a complete answer. Sometimes, the network has just one large component and our k-cores do not help, and so we must find other ways to cut the problem down to size. One approach is to reduce the network by aggregating nodes. One technique is to aggregate nodes based on categorical attributes. For example, suppose we have the entire communication network among employees of a large organization. Instead of working with the individual-level data, we could look at the communications between departments. That is, we could merge together all the actors in the same department to form a department 'super-node'. This is repeated for all the departments so that we have a network of ties between departments. This is a smaller network in which the nodes are departments and the ties are the number of communications among employees of the departments. We now analyze this reduced network so that we get an overall view of the communication structure. We then separately analyze each department to uncover the internal communication structure.

This process is relatively easily accomplished using standard software such as UCINET. We illustrate this with a network of 504 actors available in UCINET (as PV504); the actors are in 10 departments ranging in size from 4 to 108. We can run UCINET's density by groups routine to obtain the average tie strengths within and between the departments as shown in Matrix 14.1.

	1	2	3	4	5	6	7	10	20	30
1	0.573	0.291	0.152	0.021	0.126	0.037	0.026	0.881	0.530	0.538
2	0.291	0.422	0.145	0.064	0.124	0.090	0.063	0.435	0.672	0.284
3	0.152	0.145	0.687	0.082	0.095	0.092	0.215	0.263	0.733	0.139
4	0.021	0.064	0.082	1.000	0.089	0.201	0.473	0.040	0.467	0.054
5	0.126	0.124	0.095	0.089	0.310	0.167	0.163	0.335	0.424	0.122
6	0.037	0.090	0.092	0.201	0.167	0.657	0.210	0.083	0.443	0.030
7	0.026	0.063	0.215	0.473	0.163	0.210	0.589	0.073	0.488	0.012
10	0.881	0.435	0.263	0.040	0.335	0.083	0.073	1.487	0.856	1.346
20	0.530	0.672	0.733	0.467	0.424	0.443	0.488	0.856	2.071	0.656
30	0.538	0.284	0.139	0.054	0.122	0.030	0.012	1.346	0.656	1.500

Matrix 14.1 Average values within and between departments.

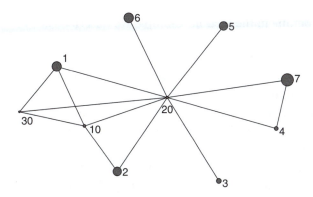

Figure 14.4 Inter-department communication for the PV504 data.

Looking down the diagonal we see that the department coded 5 has the low-est average within-department communication. This may of course reflect their function as we also see their values to other departments are quite low. While we could examine this matrix in some detail, we could look at a graphical display of the network of average values to try to get a better feel for our data. The network in Figure 14.4 uses these data but we have only shown links between departments if the average value is greater than 0.4, and we have sized the nodes according to the department size (an alternative would have been to size the nodes according to the average value of the internal communication). We can now see the central role played by the small department labelled 20. We note the clique involving departments 1, 10, 20 and 30 and can see the relative isolation of 3, 5 and 6.

14.3 Choosing appropriate methods

In dealing with large networks there are two main considerations when selecting particular methods. The first relates to the speed of the algorithm. When the network becomes large, this imposes restrictions on which algorithms are able to complete the analysis in a reasonable time. It is useful to understand a little about how efficiency of algorithms is measured. It is normal to give a worst-case value related to the size of the problem, which, as discussed earlier, is usually indexed by the number of nodes n. We use the O notation to give an approximate idea of the efficiency. A time $O(n^3)$ means that for sufficiently large n the time to execute will increase at the rate of n^3, although it is possible for a 2-fold increase in n to result in a 20-fold increase in execution time, instead of the expected 8-fold increase. This would be because n was not sufficiently large and factors other than size are at play.

Timings which are exponential mean that the user should be aware that small increases in n may cause very large increases in execution time; this is precisely what was happening in the factions example we described above. These routines cannot be used on even moderately sized networks. On the other hand, as discussed earlier, the number of nodes is not always the best indicator of the size of the problem. A number of algorithms have an efficiency rating that is related to the number of edges as opposed to the number of actors. This is important since many large networks are sparse and as they increase in size the number of edges may not increase in proportion to the number of actors. However, the help routines in UCINET give the timings in terms of n and so do not highlight when it is the number of edges that determine the efficiency.

The following methods (among others) are very efficient and can be used on large networks: components, bicomponents, degree centrality, brokerage, structural holes, ego density, ego betweenness, density, EI index (see Chapter 15), reciprocity, transitivity (clustering coefficient) and k-cores.

There are some slightly less efficient methods which are usually not a problem but may require a long time even with a fairly powerful machine. These are: geodesic distances, betweenness, closeness and profile similarity for structural equivalence. In addition, methods for finding eigenvectors have received a lot of attention from the computing and mathematics communities due to the large number of applications that require them. As a consequence, there are a number of approximate and highly efficient algorithms which achieve this and this means that any of the techniques that use such concepts (often known as spectral methods) can often be applied to large networks.

Theoretically, finding cliques should take too long to be practical, but in many cases it can work fine – this rather depends on the structure of the network. The optimization methods and permutation tests are not possible on large networks.

To show the running times we run a number of these methods on three different size networks in UCINET. It should be noted that when running larger networks and the results are a matrix larger than 200 × 200 the output is suppressed and has to be viewed by running Display. The networks are PV960, an undirected network which has 960 nodes and 38,540 edges; a directed network, Terro_4275, which has 4275 nodes but only 7874 edges; and a random network with 1000 nodes but with 499,422 edges (density of 0.5). The times in seconds for the three networks are shown in Table 14.1.

The first thing to note is that all these methods had no real problems for any of these networks. The highly efficient algorithms for density, clustering coefficient and components mean there is little variation in the timings over the three networks. Comparing columns 1 and 3, we can see that the number of edges is the important factor for the last three methods.

It should be noted that certain methods are not suitable for large networks simply because they are based upon small-network assumptions. As already

Table 14.1 Running times (seconds) for large networks.

	PV960 (960 nodes)	Terro_4275 (4275 nodes)	Random (1000 nodes)
Density	1	3	1
Clustering coefficient	1	1	2
Components	1	1	1
k-cores	1	8	18
Geodesic distances	1	21	16
Betweenness	1	3	18

mentioned, closeness centrality would be one such example as there is little variance in the resulting closeness centrality measure. Betweenness tends to produce much more variance and can often detect structurally distinctive nodes in large networks. However, the interpretation of betweenness in large networks can get complicated; very long paths count just as much as short paths in the betweenness calculations, but may be sociologically much less meaningful. Restricting the path lengths used can help address this (and is an option in UCINET); it has been suggested that path lengths of 2 are often sufficient (Everett and Borgatti, 2005), and this is the same as ego betweenness.

14.3.1 Using specialized algorithms: The Louvain method for community detection

For some problems, special algorithms have been developed specifically to deal with problems involving large networks. One of the most successful is the so-called Louvain method for finding communities by optimizing modularity, proposed by Blondel et al. (2008). In this section we provide a simple description of the algorithm to give a feel for how it works. The algorithm proceeds in two stages, a greedy stage followed by an aggregating stage. The algorithm starts with each node in its own community and the modularity Q is then calculated. Then for each node we calculate the value of Q when it is merged into a community it is adjacent to. If this is a positive increase then we merge the node into the community with the largest gain. If none of the Qs result in a positive increase then the node stays in its current community. This process is applied repeatedly until it is impossible to increase Q. A new graph is then formed in the second aggregating stage in which the communities of the first stage are the nodes and the edges have values which are the sums of the weights of all the edges connecting each pair of communities. Once this is done the algorithm again applies the first greedy stage. This is done until no increase in Q is found. Note to do this we need to extend the definition of Q given in Chapter 11 to deal with edge weights. This is a simple extension given in equation 14.1

$$Q = \frac{1}{2m} \sum_{i,j} \left[A_{i,j} - \frac{k_i k_j}{2m} \right] \delta\left(c_i, c_j\right) \tag{14.1}$$

where $A_{i,j}$ is the weighted adjacency matrix, $k_i = \sum_j A_{i,j}$, $m = \sum_{i,j} A_{i,j}$, c_i is the community that i belongs to and $\delta(u,v) = 1$ if $u = v$ and 0 otherwise. A result of using this extension is that the algorithm can be applied to valued data and does not require a binary network. Figure 14.5 gives a simple visualization of the algorithm.

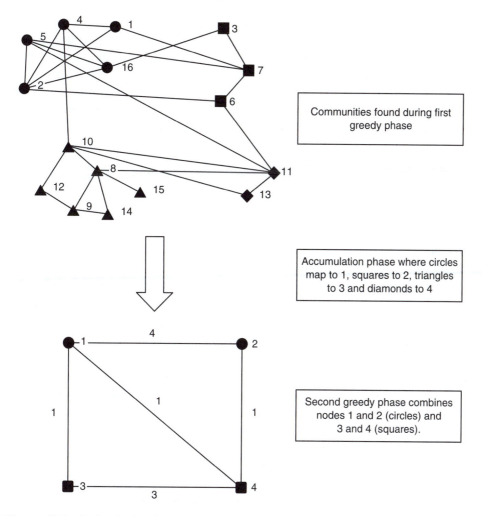

Figure 14.5 A simple visual representation of the Louvain algorithm.

During the first greedy phase the 16 vertices are placed into four communities given by the shapes of the nodes. In the second phase these communities are shrunk to a smaller valued network containing 4 nodes. The first phase is then applied for a second time to obtain the two communities given by merging the circular groups 1 and 2 with each other and merging the square groups 3 and 4 with each other.

The algorithm has shown to be very efficient and has been used on networks containing millions of nodes. In addition, the quality of the partition has been shown to be high considering the speed of the algorithm. It should be noted that the order in which the nodes are examined during the first phase can affect the final partition, although the differences are often minor. For this reason, it is advisable to run the algorithm a number of times to test the robustness of any partition.

As an example, we run the Louvain method on the network Terro_4275 introduced in Section 14.3. These data are directed and for the purpose of this
example we ignored the direction of the ties. In the first greedy pass the algorithm identified 503 clusters and Q had a value of 0.68. These are then
aggregated into a new graph of 503 nodes and this is then submitted to the
greedy phase. The second greedy application finds 105 clusters and Q has a
value of 0.85. In the third and final pass the algorithm identifies 66 clusters and
finishes with a modularity score of 0.87. The data actually consisted of 32 components, the largest of which contains 4085 nodes with the second largest
containing 35. None of the smaller components are split and the final partition
splits the large component into 34 different clusters.

14.4 Sampling

The vast majority of the efficient methods are based on ego networks. That is,
to calculate the measure we only use local information captured by ego and its
alters. Such methods are always efficient as they depend on the size of each ego
network, and this is nearly always limited by constraints (we can only maintain
so many friends). In this case we have the added advantage that we may not
need to calculate the value for every ego. Suppose, for a large network, that we
wanted to calculate the average degree. We could simply randomly sample a
number of egos drawn from the whole network and use the mean of these as
an unbiased estimate of the average degree. We could use this value to predict
the density of the whole network (although this is rarely of much use in large
networks). As examples we apply this method to the three networks used in
Table 14.1. Two of the networks are directed and in this case we use both the
indegree and the outdegree; overall the average indegree will be the same as
the average outdegree. The PV960 and Terro_4275 networks are valued, so the
average degree is simply the average tie strength for the network as a whole.
We sample just 1% of the nodes uniformly at random, repeating the process
10 times. The aggregated results are shown in Table 14.2.

We can see, with just 10 repeated sweeps of 1% of the nodes sampled, that
the results are reasonable without being excellent. The random example is very

Table 14.2 Sampled degree.

	PV960	Terro_4275	Random
Actual average degree	80.29	1.84	499
Sampled average degree	64.69	2.14	501

close; this is because it was generated from a uniform distribution and so all the degrees are very similar and it has a very low standard deviation. The other two are actual networks and have very high standard deviations, and so the sampled values are far less accurate. In applying this method to real data, thought needs to be given to the possible distribution of degrees. If we were looking at data taken from the World Wide Web, this is well known to have a power law distribution (see the next section for a detailed description), that is, it has a large number of low-degree nodes and a small number of nodes of very high degree. In such cases sampling at random means you are unlikely to get a distribution that reflects the population, since it is very likely you would not get a high-degree node and so you would underestimate the average degree. However, if by chance you did have a high-degree node then you would overestimate the average degree. If the degree distribution is more evenly spread (as we would expect in a social network in which it takes resources to maintain links) then this approach would provide a reasonable estimate. We have used degree as an example of ego-based estimation, but any ego measures discussed in the final chapter of the book could be used.

In the example above we tried to capture summary global properties that require us to deduce information from every node in the network. In general, we do not know the structure and so this makes it a difficult task to do accurately. However, we can use more sophisticated methods to help us find information about certain properties of the network. Suppose, instead of wanting to know the average degree, we wanted to know what the maximum degree was. If we just randomly sampled the network, the chances of finding the node with highest degree would be remote. A better strategy would be to select a smaller number of seed nodes and then trace random walks within the network. To create a random walk, we just randomly select a node adjacent to the current node. Since high-degree nodes are connected to lots of other nodes we are more likely to find them using this technique. To illustrate this, we used this method to try to locate the high-degree nodes in the Terro_4275 network. We first dichotomized and then symmetrized it to form the underlying graph. We used five seeds and created random walks of length 3; this gives us a maximum of 20 nodes. This was repeated just three times. The first run produced a maximum degree of 71, the second run 72, and the final run 65. The real maximum for these data are 114, but 72 is the second highest, 71 the third and 65 the sixth. As a comparison, we randomly selected 20 nodes uniformly three times. The first run gave a maximum degree of 10, the second 45 and the final 17. In this instance, it is clear that the random walk technique is a significant improvement on uniform sampling. This is just a simple illustration of a more general approach, and the interested reader should look at the paper by Backstrom and Kleinberg (2011).

14.5 Small-world and scale-free networks

Certain network properties can only be observed in large networks, and we now turn our attention to two of these. As already mentioned briefly in the previous section, some networks have a degree distribution that follows a power law. That is, the number of nodes of degree k is proportional to $k^{-\gamma}$, where the power γ is usually in the range from 2 to 3. We call networks with this distribution 'scale-free' networks. If the degree distribution followed this law and γ was at the lower range of 2 and we had 1,000,000 nodes of degree 1, then we would expect around 10,000 nodes of degree 10, 100 nodes of degree 100 and just 1 node of degree 1000. For the higher value of 3 it would be 1000 nodes of degree 10 and just 1 node of degree 100. In this case the networks are dominated by low-degree nodes with just a very small number of high-degree nodes – we do, however, expect some high-degree nodes to exist. This last statement has important consequences for social networks. In almost any social network, it requires resources to make or maintain links. There is only a limited amount of resource, and so there are often natural boundaries on the degree of a node. An actor can only have so many friends, and this cannot be unbounded. There are, however, a few situations in directed networks where the resources are only required from one of the actors in any dyad. Two examples are citation networks and the 'follow' relation on Twitter. The citing article is the one that needs to provide some resource to do the citing, whereas the cited article is a passive recipient. Similarly, the follower on Twitter needs to implement the relation and the one being followed provides no resource to make or maintain the relation. In these cases, it is the indegree that follows the power law if a directed relation is considered, but often the scale-free concept is applied to the underlying (undirected) graph.

One mechanism that gives rise to scale-free networks is the Matthew effect (a term coined by Robert Merton and taken from the Gospel according to Matthew: 'For everyone who has will be given more'), also known as preferential attachment. A new node creates links to existing nodes in proportion to the existing nodes' degree, so that nodes of high degree attract edges and so their degree increases even more (often expressed as 'the rich get richer'). There is evidence that this is the case for citation networks and for the structure of the World Wide Web; it is also a plausible explanation for the distribution of followers on Twitter. The usefulness of identifying scale-free networks is still debated and, given the nature of the distribution, it is only when networks are of the sizes mentioned here (i.e. hundreds of thousands or millions of nodes) that it makes any sense to try to fit the distribution.

Most people are familiar with the idea of six degrees of separation – that is, that between any two people there is a path of length 6 or less. The value of 6 was a result of an experiment by Stanley Milgram in which he distributed letters randomly to people in two US cities and asked them to pass them to a target, and, if they did not know the target, to pass them to someone who might. He found the average number of steps from originator to target was 6.4. A second example was the analysis of Microsoft Messenger in 2007 which at the time had 180 million nodes and 1.3 billion edges; it was calculated that the average geodesic path length was 5.5. A good overview of work done in this area can be found in the article by Schnettler (2009).

Recall that in Chapter 9 we looked at the average geodesic distance L. We are interested in the size of L for specific networks and classes of networks. There is no agreement on what constitutes a small value for L, but it has been suggested that we require L to be proportional to $\log N$ (where N is the size of the network). This definition relates to a class of networks and not to an individual network. It can be shown that scale-free networks fall into this category. In fact, even if we uniformly randomly generate edges on a set of nodes, then this too will create a network in which L is small; and even if we start with a network with a large L and randomly rewire a few edges L is quickly reduced. It would seem that nearly all networks have a small average path length. As discussed in Chapter 9, Watts and Strogatz (1998) noted that these random graphs differed from observed social networks inasmuch as the observed networks had higher than expected clustering coefficients (recall that the clustering coefficient is the average density of all the open neighborhoods). As a consequence, they defined a small-world network to be one with low average path length and a high clustering coefficient (also known as Watts and Strogatz networks). Such networks consist of highly connected cliques or clumps which are linked together by relatively short paths and are the sort of structures commonly found in observed social networks.

Investigations into small-world and scale-free networks are usually confined to describing these properties, that is, deciding whether a network is scale-free or small-world. The consequences of such structures are not well understood, and it would be difficult to draw conclusions about individual actors or even small groups of actors in such networks. The main goal is to gain some understanding of the overall network structure.

14.6 Summary

Large networks present a number of challenges in terms of both computation and interpretation. We can try to reduce the size of the problem either by cutting the network into smaller pieces, pruning away less important parts of the network, or merging together nodes and edges. If we are unable to reduce the size of the problem, we need to think carefully about what methods we are able to use. This decision is based on our ability to make meaningful interpretations for large datasets, as well as on computational considerations of what is feasible. We can uniformly sample from large networks to obtain average ego-based measures; this is a useful approach, provided the network does not have a highly skewed structure. If the network is skewed, techniques based on random walks allow us to glean some global information. Finally, large networks give us an opportunity to look for structures such as small-world and scale-free networks which would not be apparent in more modest-sized networks.

14.7 Problems and Exercises

1. One way of reducing complexity of the problem in large networks is to use K-Cores. The network file "Antarctica.##h" involves relationships among Wikipedia pages that contain the word "Antarctica". The network contains 1337 nodes. First, visualize the network. In NetDraw go to File|Open|Ucinet dataset|Network and load Antarctica.##h and click OK (it may take a while to load). It is hard to see anything because of the sheer size of the network and the overlapping labels. To toggle off the labels go up to the "L" in the icon menu across the top and click. Click the green check mark to toggle off the labels. It is still very difficult to understand the network. To do an analysis of K-cores in NetDraw go to Analysis|K-cores and click on K-cores. The nodes will change various colors reflecting K-core membership. To view the core nodes, click on the "Nodes" tab in the right corner. In the pull-down menu select K-cores. Uncheck boxes 1 through 11. This now leaves the most central nodes in the network. We can now add the labels for interpretation. Click on the "L" to toggle on the labels. Can you now interpret relationships among the nodes?
2. Besides using K-cores, what are two other methods for reducing the size of larger networks? Explain your answers.
3. Run the Louvain method for community detection on the Antarctica data. Compare your results with the K-cores found in Question 1.
4. Sampling is often used to estimate the characteristics of larger social networks, such as average degree. What are some of the issues that will affect the accuracy of these estimates in large networks?

15

Ego Networks

Learning Outcomes

1. Collect ego network data using standard personal-network research design tools
2. Analyze ego networks consisting of just ego–alter ties and both ego–alter and alter–alter ties
3. Format and analyze ego network data using appropriate software

15.1 Introduction

As discussed in Chapter 2, an ego network (or ego net) is the part of a network that involves a particular node we are focusing on, which we call ego. The ego network consists of ego, the nodes ego is connected to (referred to as ego's alters), and the ties between ego's alters. An example is shown in Figure 15.1. As discussed in Chapter 3, there are two fundamental ways of obtaining ego network data. One way is via a whole-network research design, in which the ties among all pairs of actors are collected. Once the whole network is obtained, we can simply extract the subgraph corresponding to any particular node's first-order neighborhood, which we call an ego network. The other way is via a personal-network research design, in which we sample a population to obtain a set of respondents (egos) and then collect from each ego the list of people (alters) they are connected to, along with the nature of the ties connecting them to ego, characteristics of the alters, and the respondent's perceptions of the ties among the alters. In this chapter we focus on personal-network research designs, although most of our comments on the analysis of the data will also apply to ego network data extracted from whole networks.

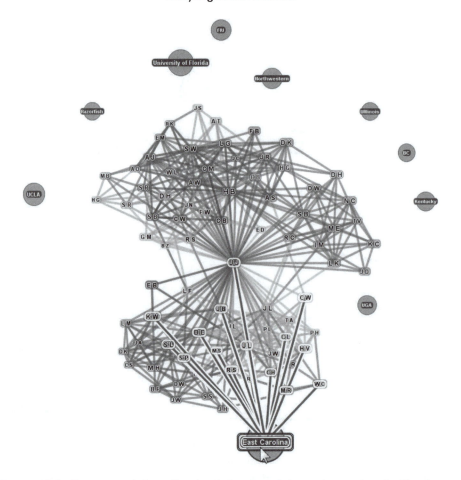

Figure 15.1 Ego network from Facebook for one of the authors using the Touch-Graph app showing 80 'friends' and 10 'networks', in this case universities.[1]

The personal-network research design has become particularly popular in the social sciences in part because it fits well within a standard survey approach (McCallister and Fischer, 1978).[2] Personal-network questions can be readily added to a standard survey instrument, and (unlike whole-network designs) do not require respondents to identify themselves. Hence, the survey can remain anonymous. In addition, the personal-network approach lets you sample randomly from a large population, and then generalize results to that population.

---

[1] Unfortunately, Facebook no longer provides public access to their data.

[2] The personal-network research design also maps well onto ethological designs where biologists pick an individual animal at random and then follow it around all day to see who it interacts with. The next day a new focal animal is chosen, and so on. For an example, see Rushmore et al. (2013).

A limitation of whole-network designs is that it is not clear what they generalize to. In this chapter we review data collection in a personal-network research design, and also discuss the analysis of ego network data (including ego network data drawn from a whole-network study).

15.2 Personal-network data collection

In a personal-network research design, ego network data are ideally collected in three steps or questionnaire sections, although these can also be intertwined. The first step is generally referred to as a 'name generator' and consists of a series of open-ended questions designed to generate a list of unique people (alters) in a person's life.[3] The second step is the 'name interpreter', in which we ask the respondent about each unique alter that came up in the name generator. Two kinds of data are requested: attributes of the alter, such as gender and age, and qualities of ego's relationship with the alter, such as whether they are friends, co-workers, kin, etc. Sometimes these questions are asked immediately after a name is generated, so the generators and interpreters do not actually form different sections of the survey. The third (optional) step is what we call the 'name inter-relator', where we ask the respondent about ties among the alters. For instance, we might ask 'does Mary know Jane?' or 'do Mary and Jane talk?'

15.2.1 Name generators

Classically, the primary purpose of the name generator is to develop a list of distinct names that we can then systematically ask the respondent about. The idea is that respondents are known to forget names, so we want to give them several opportunities to name relevant alters, ensuring that all relevant names eventually come up. Then, in the name interpreter portion of the questionnaire, we go back and clarify the respondent's relationship with each person named. This ideally includes asking the name generator questions again because a respondent might neglect to mention a friend when asked 'who are your friends?' but mention them later in response to a different question (Brewer, 2000). If the respondent is then shown every name that came up in any question and asked to check off whether they are a friend, the neglected name will be properly identified as a friend.

What questions should be asked to generate names? The answer, of course, is determined by the research context. In general, the questions asked can be drawn from any of the social-tie categories listed in the typology of Chapter 1 (see Table 15.1). There are usually just a handful of name-generating questions, and

---

[3] An important advantage of personal-network research designs is that actual names of a person's contacts need not be collected. Nicknames, initials or any code the respondent can remember will do. In addition, the respondents themselves can remain anonymous.

Table 15.1   Types of relations used in name generators.

Tie type	Sample elicitation	Comments
Role-based relations (e.g., friends, kin, teachers)	Please name all the people in Hartford that you consider a friend.	Respondents may have different definitions of 'friend'
Interactions (e.g., communicating with, going to movies with)	Who are the people you have talked to about health-related matters at the gym over the last two weeks?	Respondents are more accurate at answering who they usually talk to than who they talked to during a given period
Affective ties (e.g., like, dislike)	Who are the people in the office that you feel particularly close to?	Respondent is sole authority on their feelings
Exchanges and flows (e.g., help around the house, borrow from)	Who are the people that helped you by giving financial aid after the storm?	Respondents typically feel these are easy questions to answer
Cognitive ties (e.g., is an acquaintance of, know what they eat for breakfast)	You've been here for a month now. Who have you met? (By 'met' we mean you have interacted, can attach a face to the name, and they are likely to say they have met you as well)?	Responses can be voluminous if not well circumscribed

they can be mixed and matched, although there is a tendency in actual studies to ask questions within a given type, such as only affective questions, or only exchange-based questions (Marin and Hampton, 2007). For example, in studies of corporate employees, the name-generating questions tend to be highly circumscribed, focusing on co-workers and ignoring ties to family and non-work friends. Here we might use a mixture of questions based on the relationship (friends, mentors, subordinates), individual characteristics (people in the marketing department, people on the 2nd floor), or activities (people you have a drink with after work, people you have lunch with). In contrast, in anthropology, it is not unusual to be interested in the totality of everyone in a person's life – ideally, everyone they know. In this case, the name-generating questions are like mnemonic devices designed to stimulate the respondent's memory. For example, one might use 'grand tour' questions, such as 'take me through your neighborhood. Who lives next to you on the right?'. One can also go through a list of common names and ask, 'do you know any Andersons?', 'what about Borgattis?', etc. This sort of methodology typically comes up with about 1500 names (Freeman and Thompson, 1989; Killworth et al., 1990).

15.2.2 Position and resource generators

An alternative type of name generator – the position and/or resource generator – elicits *types* of persons rather than individuals. For example, the respondent is asked if they know any doctors (a role or position), or anybody who owns a car (control of a resource). This approach is often used in studies of social capital (Lin and Dumin, 1986; Van der Gaag and Snijders, 2005) where the objective is to provide estimates of ego's access to various kinds of resources through their ties. In this type of study, position and resource generators can be more efficient than name generators.

However, position generators limit the kinds of analysis that can be done. For example, it usually does not make sense to ask the respondents how the positions are related to each other, as in 'do any of your priests know any of your nurses?'. In addition, these kinds of questions can be difficult for respondents, since they may not index alters in their minds by categories. For example, they may have trouble recalling whether they know anyone who enjoys gardening. In contrast, eliciting names of friends and then asking, 'do they like gardening?' may be more successful.

An example of the position-based approach is the study by Avenarius and Johnson (2012) on beliefs about the rule of law and social capital in China. Table 15.2 shows the structure of the matrix used in the survey instrument to collect the position-based data. The instrument was administered in Mandarin. Egos were shown a list of jobs and asked, for each job in turn, 'would you please tell me if you happen to know someone doing this job?'. This was followed by the series of questions about an alter corresponding to each job type, such as the gender of the person doing the job, the duration of ego's relationship with them, and so on. The data were used to construct measures of individual-level social capital that could be used as either an independent or dependent variable.

The resource-based approach elicits ego's access to whichever resources are important to the study. Collection of this type of data requires preliminary research in order to produce a list of resources that are both relevant to the respondents and of theoretical interest. Resource-based approaches may also limit comparability across studies performed in research sites, since resources seen as essential in one location may not be important in another.

An example of this approach can be found in Van der Gaag and Snijders (2005). The authors obtained data from a representative sample ($N = 1004$) of the Dutch population between 1999 and 2000. They were interested in how a multidimensional approach to the study of social capital might aid in better understanding the relationship between social capital and what they term 'productivity' or the attainment of an actor's goals as well as the accumulation of resources. The resource-generator portion of the instrument included a series of questions eliciting ego's access to a predetermined list of social resources. The resource questions first ask ego 'do you know anyone who ...', followed by a list of resources such as 'can repair a car, bike, etc.', 'owns a car', 'is handy repairing household equipment', 'reads a professional journal', etc. Egos respond either yes or no and then are queried about the nature of their relationship(s) to the alters in question. For example, if they say yes to knowing a person handy with household repairs, they are then asked if the person is an acquaintance, friend, or family member. (In this case, the name-interpreter questions are mixed in with the name-generator questions.) Ego is also asked whether they can serve as their own resource for repairing cars or bicycles, reading professional journals, owning a car, etc. For a review of instruments and measures employing these approaches, see Van der Gaag and Webber (2008).

Table 15.2 Position-based data survey matrix.

Type of job	1. Do you know anyone in this job? (How many people?)	2. Gender of the person(s)	3. How long have you known this person(s) (in number of years)?	4. What is your relationship with this person? How do you know this person? (from list)	5. If you don't know such a person yourself, does a friend or relative know such a person? Who? (from list)
A manager					
A director of a company					
A university professor					
A police officer					
A doctor					
A lawyer					
A judge					
A low level civil servant					
A county or city official					
A prefecture level official					
A province level official					
A current army member					
An insurance agent					
An accountant or banker					

15.2.3 Name interpreters

Once a set of names has been generated by the name generator, the researcher compiles them into a roster of unique names and asks a series of questions about each name. Two kinds of questions are asked: (a) what kinds of ties ego has with the alter, and (b) characteristics of the alter. The former questions are typically the same as one would ask in a whole-network design (e.g., 'is this person a friend?', 'is this person a neighbor?'), and the same considerations of format and wording apply (see Chapter 4). One special point is worth mentioning however – because the name interpreter offers the respondent an aided list of all contacts that emerged in the name-generator section, it is freer of the recall issues that plague open-ended questions. As a result, it is usually good practice to re-ask the name-generator questions here, though possibly in a slightly different form. For example, the name-generator phase might have asked 'who do you talk with about health-related matters?', but the name-interpreter step might ask for a rating such as 'how often did you talk with this person about health-related matters in the last month?'.

The alter-attribute questions are interesting in a personal-network design because they are not collected from the alters themselves, but rather reported by ego. This means the alter characteristics are perceptions, and could be quite wrong. Whether this is a problem depends on the mechanisms that link network properties to outcomes. For example, if we are interested in the wealth of information about diseases available to a person through their social contacts (in order to predict ego's health outcomes), it is important to know who their contacts really are and what they really know. Ego may think their friend is an expert, but they may be wrong, and this would mean that in reality ego does not have good information on health. Both ego and our measurements of ego's available resources would be wrong. On the other hand, if we are interested in social influence and how that changes ego's attitudes and behavior, it is far more important to know what ego thinks is true of their friends than what is really true. If I think you are a wine maven, I will be more inclined to take your advice on wines, even if in reality you know little about wines. Similarly, if I believe my friends are getting regular mammograms, perhaps I am more likely to do the same. It is the belief, not the reality, that motivates.

15.2.4 Name inter-relators

The name inter-relator is the section of the survey that asks egos about ties among his or her alters. The name inter-relator section is probably the most challenging ego network data to collect for two reasons: (a) ego may have limited knowledge of the ties among their alters; and (b) the task can be tedious and time-consuming. With respect to the first issue, there are real questions about the accuracy of respondents' knowledge about the ties among their alters. In fact, in cognitive social structure designs, where every respondent is asked about the ties among the same set of alters, it is evident that individuals vary widely in their knowledge of the network around them (Krackhardt, 1987). In an ego network setting, there is no way to assess accuracy or even consensus because ego is the only person responding about that particular set of alters. Once again, though, whether this constitutes a problem depends on what social processes we are studying. If it is peer influence on behavior, perceptual data may in fact be preferred. For example, if I think my friends talk to each other about me, it can have a constraining effect on my behavior (e.g., I avoid lying), even if in reality they do not talk to each other about me at all.

With respect to the tediousness of the task, there is a real danger of respondent fatigue. As McCarty et al. (2007) point out, for an ego network of 50 alters, ego would have to report on 1225 undirected ties, which is quite a daunting task that might have to be spread out over multiple data collection sessions. Van der Gaag and Snijders (2005) report that an interview in their study typically took an hour and a half to administer. There have been a number of suggestions for reducing respondent burden in ego network studies. An obvious solution is to simply limit the number of alters that ego lists (Marsden, 1990). The disadvantage of such a fixed-choice methodology is that it severely limits one's ability to measure a variety of constructs, starting with simple density. In addition, respondents typically do not list alters in random order (Brewer, 2000), so that limiting alters to the first k could introduce significant bias.

Another solution keeps the name generator unlimited, but then for the name interpreter we sample from the list of alters. Marin and Hampton (2007) advocate using what they call the 'multiple generator random interpreter'. This involves using multiple name-generator questions to create an exhaustive list of alters, but then randomly selecting alters from that list for use in the name interpreters and inter-relators. McCarty et al. (2007) also suggest using a sampling approach and find that a random sample of 20 alters for use in the name interrelator is sufficient to capture many of the structural measures of interest.

There are a number of different formats for collecting these types of data. One approach is the matrix form shown in Figure 15.2 in which respondents simply check a box to show an alter–alter tie. Another approach, particularly useful for directed data, is to have a page or screen for each alter. Each page prominently displays the alter's name (let us call them the focal alter) and then presents a roster of all alters. The respondent is instructed to fill out the survey as the focal alter would do it. For example, if the social relation is 'talks to', the respondent is asked to check off the names of all the people that the focal actor talks to. Figure 15.3 gives a variation on this approach drawn from Krackhardt (1984).

	John	Sue	Pete	George	Pat	Steve
Please place a check in the box if the two people would talk to each other even if you were not present.						
John						
Sue	☐					
Pete	☐	☐				
George	☐	☐	☐			
Pat	☐	☐	☐	☐		
Steve	☐	☐	☐	☐	☐	

Figure 15.2 Example of format for name inter-relator.

Who would Ana consider to be a personal friend?

__Bob __Cara __Cherie ___Dawn __Eric ___Gina ___Hani ___Joe ___Kim W.
___Laura P. ___Leslie W. ___Lisa A. ___Lisa K. ___Lucy ___Mark ___Max
___Mike R. ___Molly ___Monique ___Nina ___Rondi ___Rotasha ___Steve ___Terry
__Tim

Who would Bob consider to be a personal friend?

__Ana __Cara __Cherie ___Dawn __Eric ___Gina ___Hani ___Joe ___Kim W.
___Laura P. ___Leslie W. ___Lisa A. ___Lisa K. ___Lucy ___Mark ___Max
___Mike R. ___Molly ___Monique ___Nina ___Rondi ___Rotasha ___Steve ___Terry
__Tim

Who would Cara consider to be a personal friend?

___Ana __Bob __Cherie ___Dawn __Eric ___Gina ___Hani ___Joe ___Kim W.
___Laura P. ___Leslie W. ___Lisa A. ___Lisa K. ___Lucy ___Mark ___Max
___Mike R. ___Molly ___Monique ___Nina ___Rondi ___Rotasha ___Steve
___Terry __Tim

Who would Cherie consider to be a personal friend?

___Ana __Bob __Cara ___Dawn __Eric ___Gina ___Hani ___Joe ___Kim W.
___Laura P. ___Leslie W. ___Lisa A. ___Lisa K. ___Lucy ___Mark ___Max
___Mike R. ___Molly ___Monique ___Nina ___Rondi ___Rotasha ___Steve
___Terry __Tim

Who would Dawn consider to be a personal friend?

___Ana __Bob __Cara ___Cherie __Eric ___Gina ___Hani ___Joe ___Kim W.
___Laura P. ___Leslie W. ___Lisa A. ___Lisa K. ___Lucy ___Mark ___Max
___Mike R. ___Molly ___Monique ___Nina ___Rondi ___Rotasha ___Steve
___Terry __Tim

Figure 15.3 An alternative approach to collecting alter–alter ties.

15.2.5 Specialized data collection software

EgoNet (McCarty et al., 2007) is a program specifically designed for the collection of ego network data, using both name-generator and name-interpreter types of questions. EgoNet also allows for visualization of ego networks and provides a number of standard network measures. The measures can then be output directly into an SPSS data file. A more recent data collection and analysis tool similar to EgoNet is EgoWeb (EgoWeb 2.0, computer software, http://egoweb. info) which can be run from a webserver or installed on Windows and Mac systems.

Some programs employ a visual approach to the collection of ego network data. VennMaker (Gamper et al., 2012), for example, uses a visual interface that allows the respondents to move alters around the screen to indicate their relationships with them. The screen looks like a bullseye with concentric circles that are used to indicate closeness to ego. The screen can also be divided into pie slices representing different categories of alters, such as work friends, high school buddies, family, etc. Once the respondent is satisfied with the visualization of their network, the data are written to a file for analysis. Similarly, the OpenEddi (http://www.openeddi.com/) package has the respondent create a network diagram using a browser (no internet connection required). At the start, all the alters are isolates. The respondent then drags a tie from one node to another. As the respondent fills in the ties, the program can be set to continuously run a graph layout algorithm to maximize readability (and simultaneously entertain the respondent). The resulting diagram is often quite illuminating to the respondent.

15.3 Analyzing ego network data

Research on ego networks (like all node-level network analysis) generally falls into one of two basic camps that we refer to as social capital and social homogeneity (see Table 15.3). In the social capital camp, the canonical research agenda is to investigate how a person's achievement and success are a function of their social ties, particularly how those ties enable access to resources and support. Given this view of ties as social capital, there is of course also an interest in investigating how individuals acquire the network ties that they do.

In the social homogeneity camp, there is a strong interest in how ego's ties determine ego's attitudes and behavior, with a particular focus on the contagion mechanism – how the attitudes and behavior of ego's alters infect or influence ego's own attitudes and behavior. There is an equally strong interest in understanding how the characteristics of actors determine which actors become involved with each other. For example, when the nodes are firms, we are interested in how firms

Table 15.3 Social capital and social homogeneity.

Role of network variable	Performance (social capital paradigm)	Similarity (social homogeneity paradigm)
Ego network characteristics as explanatory variables	Social capital as explanation for success, performance, power, rewards, etc.	Influence and adoption of innovation. How one's behavior and attitudes are affected by the behavior and attitudes of one's alters
Ego network characteristics as outcomes	The acquisition of social capital. How actors come to have the ego networks that they do	Actor characteristics determine who has ties with whom e.g., homophily, where individuals tend to have ties to those who are similar to themselves on socially significant attributes

choose alliance partners. When the nodes are persons, we are interested in how they choose their friends. Here, a frequent finding is homophily – the tendency to form positive ties with actors who are similar to ego in socially significant ways.

In general, much of ego network analysis consists of constructing measures describing each actor's ego network. These measures become new actor-level variables, which are then related statistically to other actor-level variables, such as demographics, attitudes, performance and behavior.[4] Table 15.4 categorizes some of the main ego network measures that are used. We discuss each row of the table in turn.

Table 15.4 Classification of measures used in the analysis of ego networks.

Tie analysis: central tendency Data needed: • ego–alter ties	For binary tie data, counting the number or proportion of ties of a given type, such as number of friends, percentage of weak ties
	For valued ties, the total or average or maximum, etc. tie strength of a given tie type, as in average duration of relationship
Tie analysis: dispersion Data needed: • ego–alter ties	For binary tie data, dispersion refers to how evenly ego's ties are distributed across tie categories (e.g., instrumental and expressive ties). Measures include Blau's H or Agresti's IQV
	For valued ties, dispersion is assessed via standard deviation or coefficient of variation in tie strengths, frequencies, etc.
Alter analysis: central tendency Data needed: • ego–alter ties • alter attributes	For categorical alter attributes, characterization refers to counts or proportions of number of alters in each category, as in percentage of alters that are gay
	For continuous alter attributes, characterization refers to statistics like the mean, total, minimum, or maximum of the alters on some attribute, as in average education
	For valued ties, alters can be weighted by the strength of tie

(Continued)

---

[4] However, see Section 15.3.6 for a different approach.

Table 15.4 (Continued)

Alter analysis: dispersion or heterogeneity Data needed: • ego–alter ties • alter attributes	For categorical alter attributes, dispersion refers to how evenly alters are distributed across categories (e.g., equal numbers of friends who are freshmen, sophomores, juniors and seniors). Measures include Blau's H or Agresti's IQV
	For continuous alter attributes, dispersion is assessed via standard deviation and the coefficient of variation
	For valued ties, alters can be weighted by the strength of tie
Ego–alter similarity Data needed: • ego–alter ties • alter attributes	Ego–alter similarity can reflect homophily (choosing similar others) or influence (becoming similar because of interacting)
	For categorical attributes, such as gender, there are a number of measures available including the percent same, the EI index. When non-ties are available, measures like PBSC and Yule's Q are used
	For continuous attributes, such as age, measures like average absolute difference and the identity coefficient are used
Ego network structural shape measures Data needed: • ego–alter ties • alter–alter ties	Measures of the extent to which ego's contacts are connected to each other, such as ego-net density, structural holes measures, ego betweenness
	Dropping ego, treat the remaining network of ties among alters as a whole network and apply all the usual measures and analyses for whole networks, such as counting the number of components, calculating a triad census, measuring average distance, etc.

15.3.1 Tie analysis: central tendency

At the top of the table is 'tie analysis: central tendency', which refers to statistically summarizing the kinds and magnitudes of ties that egos have. For binary data (recording only the presence or absence of a tie), this means basically measuring network size with respect to different kinds of ties – for example, how many friends a person claims to have, or how many different people they discuss confidential matters with. In terms of using variables of this type in research, we might predict that the more friends a person has, the better their mental health (with causality running in both directions).

For valued data (recording, say, strengths of social relations or frequencies of interactions) this analysis of central tendencies of tie characteristics means measuring things like the average tie strength for each ego, or the average duration of ego's friendships. A social capital perspective might argue that stronger ties can be counted on for providing help when needed, so we would predict that the stronger their average tie to others, the better off the person will be. A social embeddedness perspective might argue that the effect would have an inverted 'U' shape, because the strong ties also imply a heavy load of obligations to others. In a social homogeneity study, we typically expect stronger ties to be more influential, so that a person's attitude toward something would be more similar to the attitudes of their alters when ties are strong, and more a function of ego's own characteristics when ties are weaker.

15.3.2 Tie analysis: dispersion

The next category is 'tie analysis: dispersion'. For binary data, this category refers to measuring the extent to which a person's ties are equally distributed across types. For example, does a person have mostly instrumental relationships, or do they have equal numbers of expressive relationships? For valued data, this refers to having a wide range or high standard deviation in tie characteristics such as strengths, durations, frequencies, and so on. For example, older people can potentially have a mix of friends they have known for decades along with friends they have just met. We might predict that variety along this dimension would be an indicator of a healthy, happy lifestyle in which one retains old friends but is open to new ones.

15.3.3 Alter analysis: central tendency and dispersion

The next two categories are 'alter analysis: central tendency' and 'alter analysis: dispersion'. These are analogous to the tie characterizations described above, but refer to attributes of the alters, such as their gender and wealth. These categories are probably the most commonly used types of variables. For instance, in social capital research, we expect that, say, entrepreneurs with ties to a diverse set of others (computer experts, finance experts, human resource experts) will be in a better position to cope with threats to their fledgling enterprises. In social homogeneity research, we might expect that people surrounded by unhappy people will tend to become less happy themselves.

15.3.4 Ego–alter similarity

The penultimate category is ego–alter similarity. These are measures of the extent to which ego is similar to their alters on attributes such as demographics, personality, attitudes and behavior. These are often used to test hypotheses of homophily (the tendency to have positive ties with socially similar others) and hypotheses of diffusion (the tendency to adopt the attitudes and practices of one's relevant alters). This is one area where ego networks drawn from whole-network data are superior to ego networks obtained via a personal-network research design. In the ego networks drawn from whole networks, in addition to whom the respondent has chosen, we know whom the respondent did *not* choose. With the personal-network design, we do not have this information. This matters because the non-choices can help us distinguish between homophily due to availability and homophily due to preference (which we might regard as true homophily). For example, if a white person's friends at work are 85% white and 15% black, this looks highly homophilous. But if we find that the people our respondent is *not* friends with are also 85% white and 15% black, we realize that they are not actually showing a differential interest in whites.

		Alter-Ego Similarity	
		Same	Different
Ego	Tie	9	1
	No Tie	27	3

Matrix 15.1   Crosstab of tie status and alter–ego similarity for one respondent.

This can be expressed as a contingency table or crosstab, as shown in Matrix 15.1. A chi-square test on this table would show perfect independence.

Moreover, we can use standard measures of association such as Yule's Q to assess the degree to which ties (and non-ties) tend to correspond with being similar or different, controlling for the relative sizes of the different categories. Given a generic contingency table as shown in Matrix 15.2, Yule's Q is defined as

$$Q = \frac{ad - bc}{ad + bc} \tag{15.1}$$

For the case of Matrix 15.1, Yule's Q is a perfect 0.0, indicating no relationship between tie status and similarity.

An important advantage of Yule's Q as a measure of alter–ego similarity is that it is invariant under changes of category sizes. For example, doubling the values in the first column of the table would not change the value of the measure. In contrast, the well-known EI index (Krackhardt and Stern, 1988), an inverse measure of homophily, is defined entirely in terms of the first row of the contingency table:

$$EI = \frac{b - a}{b + a} \tag{15.2}$$

As a result, the EI index is sensitive to differences in group sizes. For example, if a population consists mostly of whites, the first column of the contingency

	Same	Different
Tie	a	b
No Tie	c	d

Matrix 15.2   Generic contingency table.

table will be large (because most people are the same race) and the EI index will indicate strong homophily (−0.8 in the case of Matrix 15.1). However, because it only pays attention to ties present (the first row), the EI index is actually computable in data collected via a personal-network design, whereas Yule's Q is not.

15.3.5 Ego network structural shape measures

The final category in Table 15.4 is structural shape measures. This category refers to measures that characterize the pattern of ties among an ego's alters. In personal-network designs these ties are as perceived by ego; in whole-network designs these ties are reported by the alters themselves.

Because an ego network is a network unto itself, all the measures discussed in Chapter 9, which characterize whole networks, are applicable to ego networks. In the case of ego networks, however, we must decide whether to include ego and her ties in the calculations. In general, we do not, but there are some notable exceptions that we will discuss later.

One of the most commonly used measures in this category is density. This is normally computed without ego, so it is, loosely, the proportion of ego's friends who are connected to each other. More exactly, it is the number of ties between ego's friends divided by the total number of ties possible. This is usually seen as an indicator of constraint on ego's behavior since communication between my friends makes it more difficult for me to present inconsistent images of myself.

Another useful analysis is to identify components (see Chapter 2) and cohesive subgroups (Chapter 11) within the ego network (leaving out ego). The presence of separate components indicates that ego has friends from different social worlds, which could suggest a greater level of cosmopolitanism in ego, either as cause or effect.

Perhaps the most common measures to calculate in ego networks are the set of measures corresponding to potential for brokerage, such as Burt's (1995) structural holes measures. A structural hole is the lack of a tie between two alters within an ego network. Burt argues that unconnected alters are more likely to offer ego different points of view (non-redundant information) and can also be played off against each other to ego's benefit. One measure of structural holes is effective size. In the case of binary data, effective size can be defined as ego's degree (i.e., the number of alters ego has) minus the average degree of her alters within the ego network (which can be seen as a measure of their redundancy). For example, for the ego network shown in Figure 15.4, ego has degree 6, and the average degree of her alters (not including ties to ego) is 1.33. So the effective size of ego's

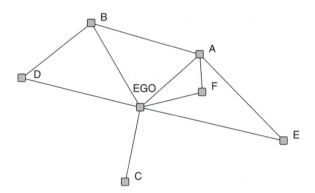

Figure 15.4   An ego network with few structural holes.

network is 4.67. If none of the alters had ties with each other, the effective size would be 6, and if all the alters had ties with all the others, the effective size would be 1.

Another measure of structural holes is constraint. Constraint is another way of measuring the extent to which ego's alters have ties to each other by measuring the extent to which ego invests time and energy in alters who invest in each other. Investment in another actor is measured by the proportion of contacts they have; in a binary network. it assumes time is evenly divided. As an example, in Figure 15.4 the actor B spends a third of their time with each of D, EGO and A. The constraint matrix has as its entries the square of the sum of the direct and indirect proportions (the indirect proportions are the products along paths of length 2). The row sum of this matrix gives the constraint of an actor; it is an inverse measure of structural holes in that a smaller number indicates more structural holes. It should be noted that for small ego networks, the measure can be larger than 1.

Alter-level analysis

At the alter level of analysis, we don't aggregate the ego network data up to the ego level, although we can include ego-level variables in the analysis. For example, suppose we are interested in which alters egos listen to the most in making decisions about their health. Is it family members (who are highly motivated to help) or more distant acquaintances (who may be more knowledgeable)? Is it men or women that ego is more comfortable talking to about health? For data, we have asked egos to rate each of their alters in terms of how much they discuss health-related issues. We have also asked ego to indicate, for each alter, whether they are family, friends, etc. We have asked about each alter's gender, and a host of other variables. The data structure looks like this:

Ego	Alter	sex	age	race	educ	relig	talkto	known	spouse	parent	child	sibling	othfam	friend	cowork
1	0001_001	1	32	1	7	3	2	3	2	2	2	2	2	1	2
1	0001_002	2	29	1	6	1	1	2	1	2	2	2	2	2	2
1	0001_003	1	32	1	7	3	3	3	2	2	2	2	2	1	2
1	0001_004	1	35	1	6	3	3	3	2	2	2	1	2	2	2
1	0001_005	2	29	1	4	2	2	2	2	2	2	2	2	1	2
2	0002_001	2	42	1	3	2	1	3	1	2	2	2	2	1	2
2	0002_002	1	44	1	7	3	2	3	2	2	2	2	2	1	2
2	0002_003	1	45	1	6	3	1	3	2	2	2	2	2	1	1
2	0002_004	2	40	1	3	2	1	2	2	2	2	2	2	1	1
2	0002_005	1	50	1	7	3	1	3	2	2	2	2	2	1	1
3	0003_001	2	25	1	6	3	2	2	2	2	2	2	2	1	2
3	0003_002	2	24	1	3	3	2	3	2	2	2	2	2	1	2
3	0003_003	2	46	1	7	3	2	3	2	1	2	2	2	1	2
3	0003_004	2	21	1	6	3	1	3	2	2	2	1	2	1	2
3	0003_005	2	35	1	7	3	2	1	2	2	2	2	2	2	2
4	0004_001	2	26	1	7	4	1	3	2	2	2	2	2	1	2
4	0004_002	1	27	1	7	1	1	1	2	2	2	2	2	1	1
4	0004_003	1	28	1	7	4	3	3	2	2	2	2	2	1	2
4	0004_004	1	27	1	7	4	2	1	2	2	2	2	2	1	2
4	0004_005	2	25	1	6	3	1	2	2	2	2	2	2	1	2

The first five data rows all pertain to the five alters belonging to ego 1. The next five are the alters for ego 2, and so on. Unfortunately, the data collection design required each ego to name no more than 5 alters. Let us assume that our dependent variable is Talkto and our independent variables are Sex and Friends. One approach is to run a single regression on the entire dataset, in order to be able to draw a general conclusion about explaining which alters egos talk to most as a function of the gender and friendship status of the alters. The difficulty with this is that each ego network is something of a world unto itself and alters are nested within these networks. From a statistical point of view, it seems very likely that the observations within each ego will be auto-correlated, suggesting that at the very least we should control for ego (e.g., add a dummy variable for each ego).

Both constraint and effective size are a function of not only ego network density but also of ego's degree, the logic being that a person's social capital increases with the number of alters they have and decreases with the extent to which the alters are connected to each other. As a result, researchers using structural holes as an independent variable in a regression should not control for degree, as degree is one of the two factors that make up the concept. If one is interested in the relative importance of density and degree, it would make more sense to use both as independent variables and omit the structural holes measures. If Burt is right, we should normally find density to be negatively related to performance and/or reward and find degree to be positively related.

15.3.6 Correlating tie characteristics with alter attributes

The previous sections were concerned with constructing ego-level measures that would then be correlated with other ego-level variables. For example, we might have correlated a person's degree of homophily with their attitudes toward for-eigners. However, we can also do analyses directly on the most disaggregate ego network data, without constructing ego-level variables first. For example, suppose we are interested in what kind of person tends to provide the most emotional support. Emotional support is a type of tie. We might hypothesize that women are more likely to provide this type of tie. So what we are looking at is regressing emotional support on gender across all ego networks in our study. Now, we could ignore the fact that each datum (an emotional support value and a gender code) is nested within an ego. But common sense dictates that the relationship between emotional support and gender could be very different within different egos. So it makes sense to run a multilevel or mixed effects model that allows for different intercepts and slopes for each ego. For more information about this approach, see the book by Perry et al. (2017).

15.4 Example 1 of an ego network study

Here we give an example of an ego network study (Johnson and Griffith, 2010a) using a personal-network research design. The study was concerned with the relationship between access to social and institutional resources and psycho-logical well-being. Data were collected from a small sample of individuals who experienced catastrophic property loss from flooding in the aftermath of Hurricane Floyd in North Carolina in 1999.

The study used exchange-type name generators to measure the social and institutional resources available to respondents. The name generator was a sin-gle question asking respondents to list the names of alters that provided 'informal' help during the flood. The term 'informal' was used here to distin-guish between aid received from ordinary individuals and actors serving as agents of more formal organizations such as the Federal Emergency Management Agency (FEMA) or even local churches.

Respondents were encouraged to list as many alters as possible. The number of alters could have been fixed or a cut-off could have been used, limiting the number by some level of tie strength. However, for the purposes of this study, it was important to know the full inventory of alters that may have provided help.

The name generator was followed by a name-interpreter phase asking ego to identify their relationship to each alter (e.g., immediate family, extended family, co-workers) and the type of aid received (e.g., emotional support, food, money). Table 15.5 provides examples of the types of assistance and role relations used in the study. In addition, respondents were asked to provide data on more formal sources of aid during and following the flood via this question: 'please list the names of all institutions/organizations that assisted you during the flood. List as many names as possible.' Formal institutions included such things as the FEMA, Salvation Army and Red Cross. This was followed by an elicitation of the types of assistance provided by each organization.

Because the data were collected using a personal-network design, the analysis was conducted using E-Net (Borgatti, 2006a; Halgin and Borgatti, 2012), a software package specifically designed for data collected using a personal-network design. Figures 15.5–15.7 show a simplified dataset in a format known as the row-wise format. For simplicity, just three egos are shown. In the row-wise

Table 15.5 List of assistance and relational variables used in the Hurricane Floyd study.

Types of assistance	Types of relations
Financial/money support	Immediate family
Emotional support	Extended family
Clothing	Friends
Food	Acquaintances
Shelter/place to stay	Co-workers
Use of phone	Neighbors
Help in gathering/moving belongings prior to flood	Other
Help in gathering/moving belongings during flood	
Help in gathering/moving belongings after flood	
Furniture	
TV/electronics	
Rides/transportation	
Help in cleaning damaged residence	
Help with filling out forms	
Babysitting	
Transportation to help in moving belongings	

format, there are three sections of data. The first consists of ego attributes (e.g., gender, age, education). The second consists of data on alters, including alter attributes (as perceived by ego) and information on the types of tie ego has with each alter. This is followed by a list of alter–alter ties, characterized by strength and/or type of tie. As we will see in the next example, there is also a column-wise format in which each row is an ego and the columns are variables for ego and alter characteristics and ego–alter characteristics (e.g., tie strength, length of time known).

Once the data were entered into E-Net, a set of simple compositional analyses were conducted (corresponding to the first four rows of Table 15.4). A screenshot of E-Net is shown in Figure 15.8, and additional measures are listed in Table 15.6.

These were then related statistically with measures of depression and psychological well-being. Ego network variables can be analyzed in a number of different ways. For the purposes of this example we present the results of a series of regressions relating ego network composition variables with depression, controlling for

```
*ego data
ID            Age      Gender      Depression
Ego45         52       Male            32
Ego26         48       Female          25
Ego31         38       Male            40
```

Figure 15.5 Row-wise format in E-Net: ego attributes section.

```
*alter data
From    To    Im-Family Ex-Family    Friends Coworkers Relation
Ego45   45-1   0 0 0 0 1   other
Ego45   45-2   0 0 0 0 1   other
Ego45   45-3   0 0 1 0 0   Friend
Ego45   45-4   0 0 1 0 0   Friend
Ego45   45-5   1 0 0 0 0   Ifam
Ego26   26-1   0 0 1 0 0   Friend
Ego26   26-2   1 0 0 0 0   Ifam
Ego26   26-3   0 0 0 1 0   Cowork
Ego26   26-4   0 0 0 1 0   Cowork
Ego26   26-5   0 0 0 1 0   Cowork
Ego26   26-6   0 0 0 1 0   Cowork
Ego31   31-1   1 0 0 0 0   IFam
Ego31   31-2   1 0 0 0 0   IFam
Ego31   31-3   1 0 0 0 0   IFam
Ego31   31-4   1 0 0 0 0   IFam
Ego31   31-5   0 1 0 0v0   Xfam
Ego31   31-6   1 0 0 0 0   IFam
Ego31   31-7   0 0 1 0 0   Friend
Ego31   31-8   0 0 1 0 0   Friend
```

Figure 15.6 Row-wise format in E-Net: alter attributes section.

```
*alter-alter data
from      to       knows
45-1      45-2       1
45-1      45-3       1
45-1      45-4       0
45-1      45-5       0
45-2      45-3       1
45-2      45-4       0
45-2      45-5       0
45-3      45-4       0
45-3      45-5       0
45-4      45-5       1
26-1      26-2       1
26-1      26-3       0
26-1      26-4       0
26-1      26-5       0
26-1      26-6       0
26-2      26-3       0
26-2      26-4       0
26-2      26-5       0
26-2      26-6       0
26-3      26-4       1
26-3      26-5       1
26-3      26-6       1
26-4      26-5       1
26-4      26-6       1
26-5      26-6       1
```

Figure 15.7   Row-wise format in E-Net: alter–alter ties.

Table 15.6   Compositional variables constructed by E-Net.

Individual sources of aid

- % of immediate family
- % of extended family
- % of acquaintances/friends
- % of co-workers
- % of new (met during crisis)
- % of neighbors
- % of males that helped
- % neighbors
- % Greenville area
- % outside area
- % outside state
- average age of those who helped
- % of same ethnicity that helped
- top type of assistance
- second highest type of assistance
- median (in days) period of help received

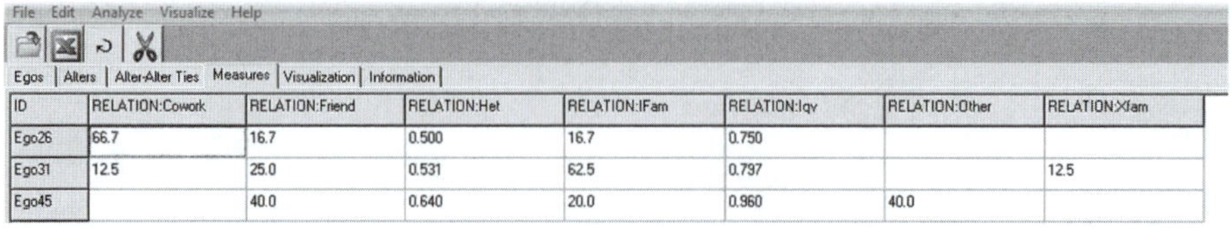

ID	RELATION:Cowork	RELATION:Friend	RELATION:Het	RELATION:IFam	RELATION:Iqv	RELATION:Other	RELATION:Xfam
Ego26	66.7	16.7	0.500	16.7	0.750		
Ego31	12.5	25.0	0.531	62.5	0.797		12.5
Ego45		40.0	0.640	20.0	0.960	40.0	

Figure 15.8 E-Net output measures for Hurricane Floyd study.

Table 15.7 Regression models comparing the effects of the various composition network variables on the dependent variable depression while controlling for demographic variables (included are standardized coefficients with t–values in parentheses).

Effect	Model 1	Model 2	Model 3	Model 4
Education	–0.284* (–1.86)	–0.299* (–1.64)	–0.235 (–1.25)	–0.224 (–1.41)
Organizations	–0.037 (–0.24)	–0.120 (–0.71)	–0.089 (–0.52)	–0.094 (–0.60)
Age	0.042 (0.24)	–0.030 (–0.18)	–0.014 (–0.09)	0.056 (0.35)
Immediate	0.412** (2.66)	–	–	–
Extended	–	–0.131 (–0.71)	–	–
Friends	–	–	–0.019 (–0.10)	–
Neighbors	–	–	–	–0.320* (–2.00)
Constant	0.000 (2.58)	0.000 (2.74)	0.000 (2.67)	0.000 (2.75)
Squared Multiple R	0.226	0.079	0.066	0.163

P<0.1*, p<0.001**

some basic demographic variables (see Table 15.7). The analysis shows a clear relationship between dependency on immediate family for help and levels of depression. It is also the case that the extent of help from neighbors had a mediating effect on depression. This analysis focused on compositional variables, but of course a number of more structural variables, such as ego network density, could have been used.

15.5 Example 2 of an ego network study

In this example we demonstrate the use of E-Net's column-based data format. The data are taken from the 1985 General Social Survey – see Burt (1985) for a discussion. A name generator was used to elicit alters where the relation of interest was people with whom the respondent, ego, discussed important matters over the last six months. The actual question was as follows (Burt, 1985: 19): 'From time to time, most people discuss important matters with other people. Looking back over the last six months, who are the people with whom you discussed matters important to you? Just tell me their first names or initials.' This was followed by a name interpreter that asked about the sex, race/ethnicity, education, age, and religious preference of the alters, as well as respondents' strength of tie to each alter (closeness), frequency of contact, and duration of acquaintance. Finally, there was a name inter-relator that asked respondents to judge the level of closeness between each pair of alters.

Figures 15.9 and 15.10 provide an example of the GSS data in a column-wise format in Excel. This follows the standard survey format of one row per respondent with columns containing the variables for each respondent, including dyadic information. For example, in Figure 15.9 the variables on the left are attributes of ego, the respondent. The variable 'rclose1' refers to how close the ego is to their first-named alter. 'Age1', 'sex1', 'educ1' and so on are ego's perceptions of attributes of Alter 1. Farther to the right (not seen in the figure) are the same variables for Alter 2, Alter 3, and so on. If one of several naming conventions is used, the E-Net program can automatically detect which variables are ego characteristics and which are dyadic. Figure 15.10 shows the far right-hand side of the data file, which gives ego's estimation of the level of closeness between each pair of her alters.

As an illustration, we use these data to examine how a person's social capital, as measured by structural holes, might vary with their race/ethnicity. Figure 15.11 shows output from E-Net giving a number of structural hole measures. The race variable in this study consisted of a categorical variable with three classes. A simple

id	sex	race	degree	rincome	rclose1	age1	sex1	educ1	race1	relig1
1	male	white	bachelor	$20000 - 24999		32	male	grad or pr	white	jewish
2	male	white	graduate	$25000 or	especially close	42	female	h.s. grad	white	catholic
3	female	white	bachelor	lt $1000		25	female	bach. deg	white	jewish
4	female	white	graduate	$10000 - 14999		26	female	grad or pr	white	none
5	female	white	high schoc	$10000 - 14999		44	female	h.s. grad	white	catholic

Figure 15.9 Example of column-wise E-Net format for the GSS data.

close1-3	close1-4	close1-5	close2-3	close2-4	close2-5	close3-4	close3-5	close4-5
know each othe	know each other	know each other	especially close	especially close	especially close	know each other	know each other	know each other
know each othe	especially close	especially close	total strangers	especially close	total strangers	especially close	know each other	especially close
know each othe	know each other		know each other	know each other		especially close		total strangers
total strangers	total strangers	know each other	total strangers	know each other	know each other	know each other	total strangers	know each other

Figure 15.10 Continuation of the column-wise format in E-Net showing alter–alter ties.

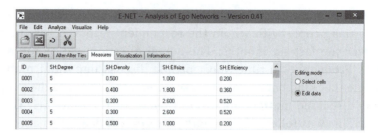

Figure 15.11   E-Net structural holes output.

Analysis of Variance					
Source	Type III SS	df	Mean Squares	F-Ratio	p-Value
RACE	0.089	2	0.045	0.921	0.398
Error	56.458	1,164	0.049		

Figure 15.12   ANOVA output for the test of the hypothesis concerning constraint and race/ethnicity.

first cut at the analysis is to use analysis of variance to see whether there is a significant difference in social capital among the three race/ethnicity groups. Figure 15.12 shows that there is not a significant difference in Burt's effective size measure among the three ethnic categories.

15.6 Summary

Ego networks consist of a focal node together with the nodes connected to the focal node. We refer to the focal node as 'ego' and the nodes connected to ego as 'alters'. In addition, we often collect one or more of the following: ego attributes, alter attributes and alter–alter connections. In personal-network research designs, the data (including alter characteristics and alter–alter ties) are collected entirely from ego, and the survey can be completely anonymous. In addition, egos can be sampled at random from a larger population. In a whole-network research design, information about alters is collected from the alters themselves, and the surveys cannot be anonymous. The ego networks are then extracted from the whole network as needed. Personal-network designs make use of name generator, name interpreter and name inter-relator questions. The analysis of ego network data generally consists of characterizing the ego network in some way (e.g., the average income of the alters, the density of ties among alters) and then relating these variables statistically to characteristics of ego.

15.7 Problems and Exercises

1. Provide three examples of network studies where a personal network approach is more appropriate than a sociocentric study design.

2. A researcher decides to limit the number of alters' ego names to six (alter1, alter2, alter3, and so on). Construct an alter name inter-relator matrix that could be used in a survey to collect alter–alter tie data.

3. A researcher is interested in doing a study of social capital and its relationship to wealth in cattle in a number of small villages in Northern Kenya using both position and resource generators. Provide some examples of the types of positions and resources that the researcher may want to use in the study. Which of the two approaches might be more appropriate for this ethnographic context? Explain your answer.

4. Using the E-NET row-wise example file from the chapter "enet_example.txt" open E-NET and click on File|Import and click on Row-Wise selection and click OK. Load the ENET example file and click OK. This is just a simple dataset containing three egos (the attributes for egos should be displayed). Before we can visualize the ego networks we must make certain to filter the Alter-Alter Ties to include only alters that 'know' of each other. Go to Alter-Alter Ties and in the box to the upper right (Alter-Alter ties filter criteria) type into the box "knows>0". This will filter out alter–alter ties in which alters do not know one another. Click on Filter and create the working dataset. To visualize each of the ego networks click on Visualization and the network for one of the egos should be displayed. To move through the visualizations of the ego networks go over to the left or right arrows (upper right) and click to display the next ego network. Go through all three ego networks. How would you describe the differences (or similarities) in network structure across the three networks? We can also compare the structural and compositional characteristics of the ego networks using structural holes and cohesion measures. Go to Analyze|Structural holes and leave the default "None" for each of the tie strength variables and click OK. Which of the three egos has the most social capital according to structural holes theory?

5. For this problem we will use the GSS dataset used in the column-wise example in the chapter (GSS 1985 network data.xlsx). To load the data into ENET go to File|Import and click on Column-Wise and click OK. Load in the GSS dataset and click on Load. To load the variables for ego, ego–alter and alter–alter go to the Auto button on the bottom left and click (this will automatically load the variables). Once the variables are loaded click OK. Now the data are ready for analysis. One interesting question to examine is do the ego networks show more homophily on the basis of sex or race? To exam this go to Analyze|Homophily. In the middle box highlight SEX=SEX and click on the right arrow to the right and move it to the box to the right. Do the same for the RACE=RACE variable. Once loaded click OK. A text output file will open showing the E-I index for sex and race for the entire sample. Also a set of measures were calculated for each ego including the E-I index and the proportion of alters in the ego network of the same sex and race. Does homophily by sex and race in ego networks differ? Also, what is the relationship between the "same proportion" variable and the E-I index for sex and race?

6. Provide examples of the types of analyses and hypothesis testing you can conduct with the data generated in Problem 5 above.

Glossary

A

Actor A node in a network. Also known as a vertex or point. Actors may be individuals (e.g., individual person or chimpanzee) or collectivities (e.g., firms or countries).

Actor-oriented Model A model used in statistical network analysis of panel data with the underlying assumption that actors in the network control their outgoing ties. In such models, the pattern of ties and the attributes of the nodes co-evolve in response to each other.

Adjacency Matrix A matrix in which the rows and columns represent nodes and an entry in row i and column j represents a tie from i to j.

Adjacent (Adjacency) When two vertices share an edge (i.e., a tie)

Affective Tie A tie relating to mood, feelings, and attitudes.

Affiliation Matrix A 2-mode incidence matrix. For example, in a person-by-event matrix, the matrix entry in row i and column j would indicate that person i attended event j.

Alter A node with a tie to a focal node (called ego in this context).

"Alter Analysis: Central Tendency" For a continuous alter variable, this would be a measure like the mean or median. For a categorical alter variable, this would be the mode.

"Alter Analysis: Dispersion and Heterogeneity" A measure of the diversity of ego's alters with respect to some alter variable. In the case of a categorical variable, this would typically be Blau's heterogeneity. In the case of continuous variable, this would typically be standard deviation.

AND (intersection) Rule In the context of symmetrizing an adjacency matrix, a rule that considers a tie to exist between two actors only if both name the other, as when both name each other as a friend; stricter than the OR (union) Rule.

Arbitrage In theory, a mechanism through which brokers derive advantage from their position connecting otherwise disconnected others. The broker is able to bring something useful to a group that comes from a different group that already has it.

Arc An alternative name for an edge in a directed graph.

Attribute A node-level attribute, such as their gender or age. Sometimes used for structural variables as well, such as their centrality.

Auctioning When a node that is located between two other nodes uses its position in the network to demand more from the other two nodes, as in a buyer deciding between two competing sellers.

Average Reciprocal Distance (ARD) A nodal measure in the closeness family. It is average reciprocal distance (geodesic) to all other nodes in the graph.

B

Backcloth and Traffic Model The view of ties as conduits through which things flow (material goods, ideas, instructions, diseases, and so on). Backcloth refers to the path through which the traffic, or flow, travels.

Balance Theory A theory which states the networks with positive and negative ties tends to result in two groups with positive ties within groups and negative ties between groups.

Beta Centrality A centrality measure that counts the total number of direct and indirect walks that emanate from a node, weighted inversely by length. When beta is chosen appropriately, the measure gives the same result as eigenvector centrality.

Betweenness Centrality Loosely speaking, a measure of the number of times a given node falls along the shortest paths between two other nodes.

Bi-clique A maximally complete bipartite graph. In a bi-clique, every pair of nodes from different modes is adjacent.

Bimodal Method Examines cliques and actors simultaneously as a two-mode matrix of actors-by cliques.

Bipartite A graph that can be divided into two groups such that the only edges that are exist are those that connect one group to the other.

Block In the context of blockmodeling, a submatrix of an adjacency matrix. Blocks consisting of all 0s are called 0-blocks; blocks that contain 1s are called 1-blocks.

Blockmodeling The process of partitioning a network into classes of equivalent actors. The adjacency matrix is then re-arranged so that nodes in the same class are placed next to each other, and lines separating the classes are superimposed on the matrices. This results in visually dividing the matrix into blocks, much like the panes in a window.

Boundary Specification In the context of research design, this is the problem of selecting which actors will be part of the study. In personal networks, two sets of actors need to be selected: the egos or index persons, and the alters they are allowed to mention. In whole networks, just one set of actors needs to be chosen.

Bridge An edge that, if removed, would increase the number of components. A network with many bridges is brittle – susceptible to being disconnected through the loss of a few ties.

Brokerage The function associated with having structural holes. A broker can bring value to an alter A by passing along something learned from alter B. This is enabled by the lack of a direct tie between A and B.

C

Categorical Attribute Qualitative traits comprised of a limited number of categories, such as male and female.

Census A set of research subjects that encompasses all persons matching the research – a population rather than a sample.

Centrality A class of theoretical constructs that characterize a node's position within the network structure.

Centrality Analysis The process of scoring each node in the network according to its structural importance.

Centralization The extent to which a network is dominated by a single node. Specifically, the extent to which one node is much more central than all others.

Chain Another term for a path or walk.

Clique A maximal subset of actors in which every actor is adjacent to every other actor in the subset. Maximal means that a subset of a clique is not a clique: it has to include every node that matches the criteria that everyone can reach everyone else.

Clique Analysis A technique designed to identify the cliques within a network.

Clique Co-Membership Matrix An actor-by-actor proximity matrix which tells us how many times each pair of actors in our network are members of the same clique.

Clique Participation Matrix A two-mode data matrix where rows are actors and columns are cliques. The entries measure the extent to which an actor has ties to members of each clique.

Closed-Ended (aided) In the context of a network survey, a question in which a roster of names is presented and the respondent must select those he/she has ties with.

Closeness Centrality The sum of geodesic distances from a node to all other nodes. Commonly normalized by dividing into N – 1. Closeness is often interpreted as the minimum time until the arrival of something flowing through the network.

Closure Configuration In ERGM, the shape of a k-triangle where the main triad is closed, or has a tie between each node.

Cluster A group of items that are closer to each other than to other items.

Cluster Analysis A set of techniques for assigning items into groups or classes based on the similarities or distances between them.

Clustering Coefficient For an individual node it is simply the density of its open neighborhood. For an overall network, it is the mean of the individual clustering coefficients for each node.

Cognitive Social Structures Each network member's report on the network connections of all other actors in the network.

Co-group Matrix A similarity matrix where the rows and columns indicate the number of actors two groups have in common.

Cohesion Refers to the connectedness of a network.

Cohesive Subgroup Groups of actors embedded in a network who interact with each other to such an extent that they potentially form a separate entity or subgroup.

Co-membership Matrix A proximity matrix in which the entries give the number of events each pair of nodes attended.

Combinatorial Optimization A class of algorithms that attempt to find good partitions or permutations by maximing a fitness function.

Commission Error The erroneous inclusion of nodes and edges that can affect the ultimate determination of node-level measures and the identification of key nodes.

Compactness The average reciprocal distance between all pairs of nodes.

Complete-link Clustering Where the distance between one cluster and another cluster is equal to the longest distance from any member of one cluster to any member of the other cluster; also referred to as the diameter or maximum method.

Component A maximal set of nodes in which every node can reach every other by some path.

Component Analysis A process to determine the number of weak and strong components in a network.

Compositional Variable Variables related to the attribute properties of nodes and networks.

Concentration A measurement that examines correlations between all possible core sizes from 1 to $n - 1$.

Conditional Dependence When two edges share a common vertex. These are considered dependent and are conditional on the rest of the graph.

Configuration Objects, such as stars and triangles, that are selected by the researcher on the basis of a particular hypothesis.

Conformable Matrices The number of columns in matrix A equals the number of rows in matrix B.

Connectedness The proportion of nodes that are located in the same component.

Connectivity Configuration Diagram that clearly depicts the connectivity of k-2-paths of a network.

Constraint An actor's position in the network that determines the potential for brokerage opportunities. High constraint offers few opportunities.

Continuous Attribute A variable that has an infinite amount of possible values.

Convex Hull In a Euclidean space, the smallest area that encompasses every point of a given set. Like the outline of a country or region on a map.

Co-occurrence Data Relational data where there is overlap in the answers of the actors (e.g., co-membership in groups, co-participation in events, etc.).

Coreness A measure referring to core–periphery structure as a continuous property of the nodes as opposed to a discrete property.

Core–Periphery Structure A network that consists of a single group (a core) together with hangers-on (a periphery). It can involve a model of a network partitioned into two blocks, a central and highly connected core and a sparsely connected and external periphery (or as a continuous property as in coreness).

Correspondence Analysis Refers to a collection of closely related techniques used for a variety of purposes, primarily as a visualization technique. It allows for the visualization of both row and column items of a matrix or contingency table in the same low dimensional space.

Cost Function A measurement of how well a partition has divided the actors into cohesive subgroups.

Cross-sectional Research design pertaining to data collected at one point in time.

Cutpoints Nodes which, if removed, would increase the number of components.

D

Data Fusion/Aggregation Clustering of data into categories often on different temporal, relational, and spatial scales.

Datum A single bit of data.

Degenerate In Markov random graph models difficulties with estimation where only a small number of graphs have any meaningful probability under the model.

Degree The number of edges incident on a node or the number of nodes adjacent to another node.

Density The number of ties in the network, expressed as a proportion of the total number possible.

Dependencies In the context of ties of models of tie formation, this refers to non-independence of ties, as when a tie from A to B increases probability of a tie from B to A.

Dependent Variable An outcome variable that is explained or influenced by other variables (independent/explanatory variables).

Dichotomize The process of turning valued data into binary data.

Diffusion The spread of something through the network (i.e. virus, information, item).

Directed Refers to edges that have direction (e.g., advice relations). A tie going from one node to another, but not necessarily returned.

Discrete Core-Periphery Method A more relaxed method of blockmodeling that only analyzes the fit to either the core or the periphery blocks.

Distance Matrix (Geodesic Matrix) A matrix with the geodesic distances, or shortest paths, between all nodes in a network.

Dual-projection Approach A method for analyzing two-mode networks, where each mode is analyzed separately and the results are recombined.

Dyad A pairwise relation between actors.

Dyadic Cohesion The extent to which actors are close to one another in a network.

E

Edge Connection between two nodes. Another term for a tie or link.

Edge Betweenness Loosely, a count of the number of times an edge lies on a geodesic path between a pair of nodes.

Edgelist A format that consists of a set of rows in which each row represents a dyadic tie in the network.

Edge/Node Attribution Errors Errors that result from assigning a behavior or attributing something to either an edge or node incorrectly.

Ego The focal node of ego-network or personal-network study. Also referred to as 'index node.'

Ego–Alter Similarity The degree to which a node is similar to its alters with respect to some node-level attribute. Similarity can be the result of either homophily or influence.

Ego Bias The tendency for actors in the network to report more or less ties then they really have.

Ego-centric/Ego-centered A network research design in which egos are sampled from a population, and data are collected about the set of alters in their lives. Contrasts with a sociocentric research design.

Ego Density The density of ties among nodes connected to a focal node (ego).

Ego Network Structural Shape Measure Measures that characterize the pattern of ties among an ego's alters, such as measures of structural holes.

EI Index An inverse measure of ego-alter similarity, typically used to measure heterophily.

Eigenvector Centrality A variation of degree centrality in which we sum the number of nodes adjacent to a given node, but weight each adjacent node proportionally by its centrality.

Emic From the native's point of view or from within the social group.

Equivalence Matrix A matrix where the (i, j) entry is the profile similarity measure of actor i with actor j.

Ethnographic Sandwich Conducting ethnographic work before and after a quantitative study.

Etic Refers to research viewpoints from outside the social group.

Euclidean Norm The square root of the sum of squared values. We often normalize measures so that the Euclidean norm is 1.

Experimental Research Research that involves the random assignment of units to treatment and control groups and manipulation of the independent variable while controlling for all other factors, both known and unknown.

Exponential Random Graph Models A family of statistical network models that can test whether certain patterns in the network occur more often than we would expect by chance.

F

Factions A set of mutually exclusive groups of actors such that the cohesion of ties within groups is greater than the cohesion of ties between groups.

Factor Analysis A statistical method for understanding and describing the variability among a set of observed variables (e.g., correlations) as a lower number of unobserved variables called factors.

Flow The outcomes of interactions that may be intangibles such as beliefs, attitudes and norms that are passed on from one person to another.

Formatting Error Errors that can be due to differences in document or website formatting.

Fragmentation The number of pairs of nodes that cannot reach each other by any means (1 minus connectedness).

Free-list A structured interviewing technique designed to elicit elements of a cognitive or cultural domain.

G

Geodesic A shortest path between two vertices.

Geodesic Distance The length of a geodesic path between two vertices.

Girvan-Newman Algorithm An approach where the removal of edges based on edge betweenness is used as a means of fragmenting the network and revealing cohesive subgroups.

Graph Layout Algorithm An algorithm used to visualize networks. The GLA determines the locations of the points, often by optimizing some fitness function.

Graph Theory Refers to a specific branch of mathematics that studies graphs.

H

Heterophily The opposite of homophily, where individuals tend to collect in diverse groups.

Hierarchical Clustering (HCL) A part of clustering analysis that produces a series of successive partitions that are nested within each other in the sense that you can get from the partition with fewer (but larger) classes to the partition with more (smaller) classes by subdividing one or more of the larger classes.

Homophily The opposite of heterophily, where individuals tend to bond and congregate with other similar individuals.

I

Image Graph/Matrix The new adjacency matrix and reduced graph resulting from blockmodeling or other equivalence methods. In the image graph, each block in the original adjacency matrix is a node, and there is a tie between two block nodes if the matrix blocks they correspond to are 1-blocks.

Incident Two ties are said to be incident if they share a node. Incidence is also used to refer to a tie in a 2-mode network.

Inclusion of False Nodes/Ties Refers to data errors in the measurement of a network.

Indegree The number of incoming ties received by a node. The column sums of a non-symmetric adjacency matrix.

Independent Variable A variable that helps to explain the dependent or outcome variable.

Inflow Where something comes into a network or to a specific node.

Interaction Behaviors with respect to others that are often observable by third parties.

Intransitivity The phenomenon that leads to potential transitive triads remaining 'open', thus not fulfilling the act of transitivity.

Isolate A vertex or node that has no connections.

K

K-core A subgraph in which every actor has degree k or more with the other actors in the subgraph.

K-plex A set of nodes in which every node has a tie to at least $n - k$ others in the set.

K-step Reach Centrality The number of distinct nodes within k links of a given node.

K-triangles Similar to k-2-paths except the two vertices are adjacent.

K-2-paths A configuration which has k independent paths of length 2 connecting two non-adjacent vertices.

L

Layout Refers to the location of all nodes in a network diagram.

Level of Analysis There are three levels of analysis in the study of networks: node level, dyad level, and network level.

Likert Scale An n-point psychometric scale, often anchored with words, used to scale actor's responses (e.g., states, beliefs, amount of social interaction, etc.).

Link/Line Synonyms for edge and tie.

Longitudinal Occurring across multiple points in time. In network datasets, this often refers to collecting network data at multiple points in time in order to study network change.

M

Main Diagonal In an adjacency matrix where the ties are self-loops, or sending a tie from one actor to themselves.

MAN A method for labeling triads, where M stands for 'mutual' (i.e., dyads with reciprocated ties), A stands for 'asymmetrics' (i.e., dyads with unreciprocated ties), and N stands for 'nulls' (i.e., dyads with no ties).

Markov Process A process in which the next state of the system is determined solely by the current state. For example, in the case of network flow, when something reaches a given node, it then jumps to the next adjacent node without regard for where it has been before.

Markov Random Graph Model A special class of exponential random graph models that describes how a network is built up from smaller constituent parts called configurations.

Matrix Multiplication If A and B are conformable matrices (which means that the number of columns in A equal the number of columns in B), then the product of A and B is written C = AB.

Matthew Effect/Preferential Attachment Where a new node creates links to existing nodes in proportion to the existing nodes' degree, so that nodes of high degree attract edges and so their degree increases even more.

Membership Data Data related to belonging to the same group or entity.

Micro-configurations Referring to network structures such as transitive triplets, 4-cycles, etc.

Mode The kinds of entities being represented in a network (e.g., people, events, organizations).

Modularity Compares the number of internal links in the groups to how many you would expect to see if they were distributed at random.

Monadic Of or pertaining to the node level, as in a monadic hypothesis.

Monte Carlo Simulation Also known as a probability simulation that is used to understand the impact of uncertainty.

Multidimensional Scaling Plot Provides a visual representation of the pattern of proximities among a set of objects.

Multigrid A data collection format that places lists in a series of columns with each column associated with a relational question.

Multiple Generator Random Interpreter A name-generating process that uses multiple name-generating questions to create an exhaustive list of alters, but then randomly selects alters from that list for use in the name interpreters and inter-relators.

Multirelational Dataset (or Networks) Involving more than one type of relation.

Multivariate Dealing with more than two variables.

N

N-clique A maximal set of nodes in which every pair is within distance *n* of one another.

Name Generator A technique for data collection that consists of a series of open-ended questions designed to generate the names or nicknames of people in an ego's life (or with whom they have a specific relation).

Name Interpreter A section of an egocentric survey in which ego reports on the characteristics of the names that came up in the name generator (e.g., age, gender, etc.).

Name Inter-relator An additional step in personal-network data collection where the respondent is asked to report on the ties between alters.

Neighborhood The set of all nodes to which a node is adjacent or connected (first-order neighborhood).

Network A way of thinking about social systems that focuses our attention on the connections or relations among the entities that make up the system.

Node An actor or entity that makes up the system or network. Also known as a vertex, point or agent.

Nodelist The simplest and most economical data format, where the first name in a row sends a tie to the subsequent names in the same row.

Normalize Refers to any of a number of normalization measures, typically applied to node-level measures, often with the goal constraining the values to a given range such as 0 to 1. Normalization is also performed on each row of an adjacency matrix in order to reduce bias or increase comparability.

O

Observational Research Also known as field research, it is a form of correlational research.

Omission Errors Errors due to missing edges and nodes in the network.

One-Mode Network A network that consists of only one set of actors or nodes and the rows and columns of the matrix are the same entities.

Open-Ended In the context of a network survey, a question format where no preset list of responses is provided to the respondent: they must list names of alters from memory.

Opportunity Phenomenon where the formation of one tie leads to another.

OR (Union) Rule In the context of symmetrization, a rule that considers that there is a tie between two actors as long as at least one of them mentions the other; less strict than the AND (intersection) rule.

Ordination An algorithm that lays out the points of a network in two- or three-dimensional space such that nodes with greater distance (or dissimilarity) between them would be far apart in the diagram, and the points corresponding to nodes with shorter distance (or similarity) would be close together.

Outdegree The number of outgoing ties sent by a node. The row sums of a non-symmetric adjacency matrix.

Outflow When something is distributed from one node to others throughout the network.

P

Partition The product of fragmenting the network into exclusive groups.

Path A sequence of adjacent vertices and edges that may not revisit a vertex or edge.

Pendant A node with only a single tie.

Perceptual Tie A tie that represents one actor's perception of another.

Permutation Test Also known as randomization tests, it is a type of statistical significance test that builds a sampling distribution by resampling the observed data.

Personal Network A network design that is centered around one focal node (ego) and its alters, or that ego's knowledge of their own network.

Pile-sort A data collection method for eliciting respondents' perception of the similarities among items in a domain.

P* Models Another name for an Exponential Random Graph Model (ERGM).

Point An actor or entity that make up the system or network; another name for node.

Popularity When a node has a high indegree.

Position Placement within the network in relation to all other nodes.

Position Generator Elicits types of positions (e.g., occupations) for alters in an ego network.

Preference A type of mechanism that drives social theory, stating that an actor's preferences affect their behavior and networks (i.e., homophily).

Productivity The attainment of an actor's goals as well as the accumulation of resources.

Profile The rows and columns of the adjacency matrix of the relation that contain all the relevant information that can be used to determine the sets of alters.

Profile Similarity A means of comparing two profiles (rows and/or columns) to determine structural equivalence.

Proximity Matrix A valued matrix that indicates proximity or similarity between each dyad.

Q

QAP Correlation A technique designed to correlate whole matrices using simulations to determine statistical significance.

QAP Regression A technique that allows you to model the values of a dyadic dependent variable using one or more dyadic independent variables.

Quasi-experimental Research A research design where there is usually a pre-post design, along with manipulation of the independent variable, but the units of analysis are not randomly assigned to treatments.

R

Random Sample A probability sample where units are selected at random from a population.

Rank-order A data collection method used for discerning the importance of certain items where the respondent is asked to rank the items in a specified order.

Raw Score Refers to measurements before alteration occurs, such as normalization.

Reciprocal Swapping A process for comparing the structural equivalence of two vectors.

Reciprocity In directed networks, it is when an actor receives a tie from another actor and returns a tie to that same actor.

Reflexive Graph If a graph is reflexive it has self-loops and it will have values down the main diagonal.

REGE Algorithm An algorithm for calculating the degree of regular equivalence between two nodes.

Regular Equivalence Two nodes are regularly equivalent if they are connected to equivalent others (not necessarily the same others and not necessarily in the same quantity). It captures the notion of role counterparts.

Relational Cognition Thoughts and feelings people have about one another.

Relational Event Referring to a discrete event that two actors share.

Relational Role Includes relationships such as 'friend of' or 'mother of.'

Relational State Continuously persistent relationships between nodes.

Repeated Roster A network data collection format where the same list of network members is repeated following each network question.

Review Boards/IRBs Institutional Review Boards designed to regulate experimentation and observational research and ensure that ethical standards are being followed.

Robustness A measurement of how difficult it is to disconnect the network by removing nodes or edges.

S

Scale-free Network Networks with a degree distribution that follows a power law.

Secondary Data Collection Refers to archival sources or databases.

Selection A category of hypothesized social processes.

Self-loop When a tie is sent from an actor to itself. This is the main diagonal in an adjacency matrix.

Simmelian Tie A tie that exists between nodes A and B if both A and B have a tie to each other, and both have a reciprocated tie to at least one third party in common.

Single-Link Clustering Where the distance between one cluster and another is equal to the shortest distance from any member of one cluster to any member of the other cluster; also referred to as the nearest neighbor, the connectedness method, and the minimum method.

Small-world Network The phenomenon where social systems tend to be clustered and compact.

Snowball Sample A type of network sampling where additional actors are extracted from existing ties to an original group. This step is repeated until no new members are found or the cost limit is reached.

Social Circuit Configuration Network configurations that include edges that do not necessarily share a node, but are dependent in the sense that the probability of a tie between A and B affects the probability of a tie between C and D.

Social Homogeneity A field of research on ego networks that is interested in how ego's ties determine ego's attitudes and behavior.

Social Media Data A transitional form of data between primary and secondary sources; includes sources such as Facebook, Twitter, and email.

Social Resource Theory The idea that a node's achievement is in part a function of the resources that their social ties enable them to access.

Sparseness Opposite notion of density; a measure of how disconnected the network is.

Stress A measure of the amount of distortion in a multiple dimensional scaling map.

Strong Component The maximal set of nodes that are reachable to each other, accounting for edge direction in directed networks.

Structural Equivalence Two actors are structurally equivalent if they send ties to the same third parties, and receive the same ties from third parties (they have the same in-neighborhoods and out-neighborhoods). These actors do not need to have a direct tie to each other to be equivalent.

Structural Equivalence Matrix A matrix recording the extent of structural equivalence between all pairs of nodes.

Structural Holes The lack of a tie between two alters within an ego network. The number of structural holes in an ego network is often viewed as a form of social capital.

Style A node-level attribute typically seen as an outcome to be predicted. Style outcomes are associated with choices (e.g., what to eat, how to behave) rather than achievement or success.

Subgraph The graph resulting from a subset of vertices and edges derived from the original graph.

Subset Only a portion of the original graph, matrix, or data.

Symmetrize To make the top right half of the matrix (above the diagonal) the mirror image of the bottom half of the matrix.

T

Three-mode Refers to three distinct entities.

Three-way Matrix A matrix that has rows, columns, and levels.

Tie A connection between two vertices. Also known as an edge.

Tie Analysis: Central Tendency A statistical summary of the types and magnitudes of ties an ego has.

Tie Analysis: Dispersion The extent to which a node's ties are equally distributed across types.

Tie Strength Refers to the weight of a tie often describing the strength of the tie or the quantity of flow.

Trail A sequence of adjacent vertices and edges that may revisit a vertex, but not an edge.

Transitive A closed structure so that if A is related to B and B is related to C then A is related to C.

Transitivity The phenomenon where two nodes that share a common tie to a third node will be more likely to be connected themselves, thus closing the triangle.

Transpose A transformation process that interchanges a matrix's rows and columns.

Triad Census A measure of the prevalence of triadic configurations in the network. For directed non-reflexive graphs there are 16 possible configurations.

Two-mode Refers to two entities. In a two-mode matrix the rows and the columns are different entities (e.g., people by events).

U

Undirected A tie between two nodes with no implication of direction; neither node sends or receives the tie, but they are both connected to one another through the tie.

Univariate Analysis on a single variable.

Utopian Stage The initial period of group formation filled with optimism, where there is a general perception that everyone would get along and be friends.

V

Value (of a Tie/valued data) Represent the strength of a tie, the frequency of interaction, or even a probability.

Vector Referring to rows and columns of data (e.g., row vector and column vector).

Vertex (Vertices) Node or point in the network.

Vertex Betweenness The number of shortest paths that pass through a given vertex.

W

Walk Any unrestricted sequence of adjacent vertices and edges.

Way Refers to the dimensions of a matrix (i.e., rows, columns, levels).

Weak Component The maximal set of nodes that can reach each other, not accounting for edge direction in a directed network.

Whole Network A network that focuses on a single group or set of actors (e.g., a classroom, the accounting department in a company)

Y

Yule's Q A standard measure of association used as a measure of alter–ego similarity that is invariant under changes of category sizes.

References

Allen, T J. (1977) *Managing the Flow of Technology: Technology Transfer and the Dissemination of Technological Information within the R and D Organization.* Cambridge, MA: MIT Press.

Athanassiou, N. and Nigh, D. (2000) Internationalization, tacit knowledge and the top management teams of MNCs. *Journal of International Business Studies,* 31(3): 471–488.

Atkin, R.H. (1977) *Combinatorial Connectivities in Social Systems: An Application of Simplicial Complex Structures to the Study of Large Organizations.* Basel and Stuttgart: Birkhäuser.

Avenarius, C.B. and Johnson, J.C. (2012) Adaptation to legal structures in rural China: Integrating survey and ethnographic data. In B. Hollstein and S. Dominguez (eds), *Mixed-Methods in Studying Social Networks.* Cambridge: Cambridge University Press.

Backstrom, L. and Kleinberg, J. (2011) Network bucket testing. *Proc. 20th International World Wide Web Conference.*

Baird, D. and Ulanowicz, R.E. (1989) The seasonal dynamics of the Chesapeake Bay ecosystem. *Ecological Monographs,* 59: 329–364.

Baker, D.R. (1992) A structural analysis of the social work journal network: 1985–1986. *Journal of Social Service Research,* 15: 153–168.

Barber, M.J. (2007) Modularity and community detection in bipartite networks. *Physical Review E.,* 76(6): 066102.

Barr, A., Ensminger, J. and Johnson, J.C. (2009) Social networks and trust in cross-cultural economic experiments. In K. Cook, R. Hardin and M. Levi (eds), *Whom Can We Trust? How Groups, Networks, and Institutions Make Trust Possible.* New York: Russell Sage Foundation.

Batagelj, V. and Mrvar, A. (1998) *Pajek. Program for Large Network Analysis.* Available at: http://vlado.fmf.uni-lj.si/pub/networks/pajek (accessed 29 August 2012).

Batagelj, V., Doreian, P. and Ferligoj, A. (1992a) An optimization approach to regular equivalence. *Social Networks,* 14: 63–90.

Batagelj, V., Ferligoj, A. and Doreian, P. (1992b) Direct and indirect methods for structural equivalence. *Social Networks,* 14: 121–135.

Bearman, P. (1993) *Relations into Rhetorics: Local Elite Social Structure in Norfolk, England: 1540–1640.* American Sociological Association, Rose Monograph Series. New Brunswick, NJ: Rutgers University Press.

Bernard, H.R. and Killworth, P.D. (1973) On the social structure of an ocean-going research vessel and other important things. *Social Science Research,* 2: 145–184.

Bernard, H.R. and Killworth, P.D. (1977) Informant accuracy in social network data II. *Human Communications Research*, 4: 3–18.

Bernard, H.R., Killworth, P.D. and Sailer, L. (1980) Informant accuracy in social network research IV: A comparison of clique-level structure in behavioral and cognitive data. *Social Networks*, 2: 191–218.

Bernard, H.R., Killworth, P.D. and Sailer, L. (1982) Informant accuracy in social network data V. *Social Science Research*, 5: 30–66.

Blondel, V.D., Guillaume, J.L., Lambiotte, R. and Lefebvre, E. (2008) Fast unfolding of communities in large networks. *Journal of Statistical Mechanics: Theory and Experiment*, 10: 10008.

Bonacich, P. (1972) Factoring and weighting approaches to status scores and clique identification. *Journal of Mathematical Sociology*, 2: 113–120.

Bonacich, P. (1987) Power and centrality: A family of measures. *American Journal of Sociology*, 92: 1170–1182.

Borgatti, S.P. (1994) Cultural domain analysis. *Journal of Quantitative Anthropology*, 4: 261–278.

Borgatti, S.P. (2005) Centrality and network flow. *Social Networks*, 27: 55–71.

Borgatti, S.P. (2006a) *E-Net Software for the Analysis of Ego-Network Data*. Needham: Analytic Technologies.

Borgatti, S.P. (2006b) Identifying sets of key players in a network. *Computational, Mathematical and Organizational Theory*, 12(1): 21–34.

Borgatti, S.P. and Everett, M.G. (1992) Regular blockmodels of multiway multi-mode matrices. *Social Networks*, 14: 91–120.

Borgatti, S.P. and Everett, M.G. (1997) Network analysis of 2-mode data. *Social Networks*, 19: 243–269.

Borgatti, S.P. and Everett, M.G. (2000) Models of core/periphery structures. *Social Networks*, 21: 375–395.

Borgatti, S.P. and Halgin, D.S. (2011) On network theory. *Organization Science*, 22(5): 1168–1181.

Borgatti, S.P. and Molina, J-L. (2003) Ethical and strategic issues in organizational network analysis. *Journal of Applied Behavioral Science*, 39(3): 337–350.

Borgatti, S.P. and Molina, J.L. (2005) Toward ethical guidelines for network research in organizations. *Social Networks*, 27(2): 107–117.

Borgatti, S.P., Carley, K. and Krackhardt, D. (2006) Robustness of centrality measures under conditions of imperfect data. *Social Networks*, 28: 124–136.

Borgatti, S.P., Everett, M.G. and Freeman, LC (2002) *UCINET for Windows: Software for Social Network Analysis*. Harvard, MA: Analytic Technologies.

Borgatti, S.P., Bernard, R., Ryan, G., Pelto, P. and DeJordy, R. (2012) The 'Camp '92' dataset. *Connections*, 43(1): 43–44.

Brandes, U. (2008) On variants of shortest-path betweenness centrality and their generic computation. *Social Networks*, 30: 136–145.

Brass, D.J. (1984) Being in the right place: A structural analysis of individual influence in an organization. *Administrative Science Quarterly*, 29: 518–539.

Breiger, R.L. (1974) The duality of persons and groups. *Social Forces*, 53: 181–190.

Breiger, R.L., Boorman, S. and Arabie, P. (1975) An algorithm for clustering relational data with applications to social network analysis and comparison with multidimensional scaling. *Journal of Mathematical Psychology*, 12: 328–383.

Brewer, D.D. (1995a) The social structural basis of the organization of persons in memory. *Human Nature*, 6: 379–403.

Brewer, D.D. (1995b) Patterns in the recall of persons in a department of a formal organization. *Journal of Quantitative Anthropology*, 5: 255–284.

Brewer, D.D. (2000) Forgetting in the recall-based elicitation of personal and social networks. *Social Networks*, 22: 29–43.

Burkhardt, M.E. and Brass, D.J. (1990) Changing patterns or patterns of change: The effects of a change in technology on social network structure and power. *Administrative Science Quarterly*, 35: 104–127.

Burt, R.S. (1976) Positions in networks. *Social Forces*, 55: 93–122.

Burt, R.S. (1980) Innovation as a structural interest: Rethinking the impact of network position on innovation adoption. *Social Networks*, 2: 327–355.

Burt, R.S. (1985) General social survey network items. *Connections*, 8: 119–123.

Burt, R.S. (1995) *Structural Holes: The Social Structure of Competition*. Cambridge, MA: Harvard University Press.

Burt, R.S. (2004) Structural holes and good ideas. *American Journal of Sociology*, 110(2): 349–399.

Butts, C.T. (2003) Network inference, error, and informant (in)accuracy: A Bayesian approach. *Social Networks*, 25(2): 103–140.

Candès, E. and Recht, B. (2012) Exact matrix completion via convex optimization. *Communications of the ACM*, 55: 111–119.

Casciaro, T. (1998) Seeing things clearly: Social structure personality, and accuracy in social network perception. *Social Networks*, 20: 331–351.

Casciaro, T. and Lobo, M.S. (2005) Competent jerks, lovable fools and the formation of social networks. *Harvard Business Review*, June: 92–99.

Christakis, N.A. and Fowler, J.H. (2007) The spread of obesity in a large social network over 32 years. *New England Journal of Medicine*, 357(4): 370–379.

Church, A.H. (2001) Is there a method to our madness? The impact of data collection methodology on organizational survey results. *Personnel Psychology*, 54: 937–969.

Cliff, A.D. and Ord, J.K. (1973) *Spatial Autocorrelation*. London: Pion.

Cohen, J. (1960) A coefficient of agreement for nominal scales. *Education and Psychological Measurement*, 20: 37–48.

Costenbader, E. and Valente, T.W. (2003) The stability of centrality measures when networks are sampled. *Social Networks*, 25: 283–307.

Davis, A., Gardner, B. and Gardner, M.R. (1941) *Deep South*. Chicago: University of Chicago Press.

Derefeldt, U. and Marmolin, H. (1981) Search time: Color coding and color code size. Paper presented to First Annual Conference on Human Decision Making and Manual Control.

Dillman, D.A. (1977) Our new tools need not be used in the same old way. *Journal of the Community Development Society*, 8(1): 32–43.

Doreian, P., Batagelj, V. and Ferligoj, A. (2004) Generalized block modelling of two-mode network data. *Social Networks*, 26: 29–53.

Doreian P., Batagelj, V. and Ferligoj, A. (2005) *Generalized Blockmodelling*. New York: Cambridge University Press.

Erickson, B. (1988) The relational basis of attitudes. In B. Wellman and S. Berkowitz (eds), *Social Structures: A Network Approach*, pp. 99–121. New York: Cambridge University Press.

Everett, M.G. and Borgatti, S.P. (1998) Analyzing clique overlap. *Connections*, 21(1): 49–61.

Everett, M.G. and Borgatti, S.P. (1999) The centrality of groups and classes. *Journal of Mathematical Sociology*, 23: 181–202.

Everett, M.G. and Borgatti, S.P. (2005) Ego-network betweenness. *Social Networks*, 27(1): 31–38.

Everett, M.G. and Borgatti, S.P. (2013) The dual projection approach for 2-mode networks. *Social Networks*, 34(2): 204–210.

Everett, M.G. and Borgatti, S.P. (2014) Networks containing negative ties. *Social Networks*, 38: 111–120.

Festinger, L. (1957) *A Theory of Cognitive Dissonance*. Stanford, CA: Stanford University Press.

Fischer, C.S. (2006) The 2004 GSS finding of shrunken social networks: An artifact? *American Sociological Review*, 74: 657–669.

Fortunato, S. and Barthelemy, M. (2007) Resolution limit in community detection. *Proceedings of the National Academy of Sciences*, 104(1): 36–41.

Freeman, L.C. (1978) Segregation in social networks. *Sociological Methods and Research*, 6: 411–429.

Freeman, L.C. (1979) Centrality in social networks: Conceptual clarification. *Social Networks*, 1: 215–239.

Freeman, L.C. (2000) Visualizing social networks. *Journal of Social Structure*, 1(1).

Freeman, L.C. and Romney, A.K. (1987) Words, deeds and social structure: A preliminary study of the reliability of informants. *Human Organization*, 46: 330–334.

Freeman, L.C. and Thompson, C.R. (1989) Estimating acquaintanceship volume. In M. Kochen (ed.), *The Small World*, pp. 147–158. Norwood, NJ: Ablex.

Freeman, L.C., Romney, A.K. and Freeman, S.C. (1987) Cognitive structure and informant accuracy. *American Anthropologist*, 89: 311–325.

Freeman, S.C. and Freeman, L.C. (1979) *The Networkers Network: A Study of the Impact of a New Communications Medium on Sociometric Structure*. Social Science Research Reports No 46, University of California, Irvine.

Friedman, S.R., Curtis, R., Neaigus, A., Jose, B. and Des Jarlais, D.C. (1999) *Social Networks, Drug Injectors' Lives, and HIV/AIDS*. New York: Springer.

Gamper, M., Schönhuth, M. and Kronenwett, M. (2012) Bringing qualitative and quantitative data together: Collecting network data with the help of the software tool VennMaker. In M. Safar and K.A. Mahdi (eds), *Social Networking and Community Behavior Modeling: Qualitative and Quantitative Measures*, pp. 193–213. Hershey, PA: Information Science Reference.

Girvan, M. and Newman, M.E.J. (2002) Community structure in social and biological networks. *Proceedings of the National Academy of Sciences of the USA*, 99: 7821–7826.

Greenacre, M.J. (1984) *Theory and Applications of Correspondence Analysis*. London: Academic Press.

Guimerà, R., Sales-Pardo, M. and Amaral, L.A. (2007) Module identification in bipartite and directed networks. *Physical Review E.*, 76(3): 036102.

Halgin, D.S. and Borgatti, S.P. (2012) An introduction to personal network analysis and tie churn statistics using E-NET. *Connections*, 32(1): 37–48.

Handcock, M., Hunter, D., Butts, C., Goodreau, S., Krivitsky, P. and Morris, M. (2017) ergm: A Package to Fit, Simulate and Diagnose Exponential-Family

Models for Networks. Available at: http://europepmc.org/articles/PMC2743438 (accessed 25 May 2017).

Hansen, D., Shneiderman, B. and Smith, M. (2010) *Analyzing Social Media Networks with NodeXL: Insights from a Connected World*. Burlington, MA: Elsevier Morgan Kaufmann.

Harary, F. (1969) *Graph Theory*. Reading, MA: Addison-Wesley.

Heider, F. (1958) *The Psychology of Interpersonal Relations*. New York: Wiley.

Holland, P.W. and Leinhardt, S. (1976) Local structure in social networks. *Sociological Methodology*, 7: 1–45.

Johnson, J.C. (1986) Social networks and innovation adoption: A look at Burt's use of structural equivalence. *Social Networks*, 8: 343–364.

Johnson, J.C. (1990) *Selecting Ethnographic Informants*. Newbury Park, CA: Sage.

Johnson, J.C. and Griffith, D.C. (1998) Visual date: Collection, analysis, and representation. In V. de Munck and E. Sabo (eds), *Using Methods in the Field*. Walnut Creek, CA: Altamira Press.

Johnson, J.C. and Griffith, D. (2010a) Linking human and natural systems: Social networks, environment and ecology. In I. Vaccaro, E.A. Smith and S. Aswani (eds), *Environmental Social Sciences: Methods and Research Design*. Cambridge University Press: Cambridge.

Johnson, J.C. and Griffith, D.C. (2010b) Finding common ground in the commons: Intra-cultural variation in users' conceptions of coastal fisheries issues. *Society and Natural Resources*, 23: 1–19.

Johnson, J.C. and Miller, M.L. (1983) Deviant social positions in small groups: The relation between role and individual. *Social Networks*, 5: 51–69.

Johnson J.C. and Orbach, M.K. (2002) Perceiving the political landscape: Ego biases in cognitive political networks. *Social Networks*, 24: 291–310.

Johnson, J.C. and Weller, S. (2002) Elicitation techniques in interviewing. In J. Gubrium and J. Holstein (eds), *Handbook of Interview Research*, pp. 491–514. Newbury Park, CA: Sage.

Johnson, J.C., Boster, J.S. and Holbert, D. (1989) Estimating relational attributes from snowball samples through simulation. *Social Networks*, 11: 135–158.

Johnson, J.C., Boster, J.S. and Palinkas, L. (2003) Social roles and the evolution of networks in isolated and extreme environments. *Journal of Mathematical Sociology*, 27(2–3): 89–122.

Johnson, S.C. (1967) Hierarchical clustering schemes. *Psychometrika*, 2: 241–254.

Kapferer, B. (1972) *Strategy and Transaction in an African Factory*. Manchester: Manchester University Press.

Kent, D. (1978) *The Rise of the Medici: Faction in Florence, 1426–1434*. Oxford: Oxford University Press.

Kernighan, B.W. and Lin, S. (1970) An efficient heuristic procedure for partitioning graphs. *Bell Systems Technical Journal*, 49: 291–307.

Killworth, P.D. and Bernard, H.R. (1976) Informant accuracy in social network data. *Human Organization*, 35: 269–286.

Killworth, P.D. and Bernard, H.R. (1979) Informant accuracy in social network data III: A comparison of triadic structures in behavioral and cognitive data. *Social Networks*, 2: 19–46.

Killworth, P.D., Johnsen, E.C., Bernard, H.R., Shelley, G.A. and McCarty, C. (1990) Estimating the size of personal networks. *Social Networks*, 12(4): 289–312.

Knecht, A. (2008) Friendship selection and friends' influence: Dynamics of networks and actor attributes in early adolescence. Doctoral dissertation, University of Utrecht.

Krackhardt, D. (1984) A social network analysis of the effects of employee turnover: A longitudinal field study. PhD dissertation, University of California, Irvine.

Krackhardt, D. (1987) Cognitive social structures. *Social Networks*, 9: 109–134.

Krackhardt, D. (1990) Assessing the political landscape: Structure, cognition, and power in organizations. *Administrative Science Quarterly*, 35: 342–369.

Krackhardt, D. (1992) The strength of strong ties: The importance of Philos in organizations. In N. Nohria and R. Eccles (eds), *Networks and Organisations: Structure, Form, and Action*, pp. 216–239. Boston, MA: Harvard Business School.

Krackhardt, D. (1994) Graph theoretical dimensions of informal organizations. In K. Carley and M. Prietula (eds), *Computational Organizational Theory*, pp. 89–111, 89(112), 123–140. Hillsdale, NJ: Lawrence Erlbaum Associates, Inc.

Krackhardt, D. (1999) The ties that torture: Simmelian tie analysis in organizations. *Research in the Sociology of Organizations*, (16): 183–210.

Krackhardt, D. and Porter, L.W. (1986) The snowball effect: Turnover embedded in communication networks. *Journal of Applied Psychology*, 71: 50–55.

Krackhardt, D. and Stern, R.N. (1988) Informal networks and organizational crises: An experimental simulation. *Social Psychology Quarterly*, 51(2): 123–140.

Krempel, L. (2002) Netzwerkvisualisierung: Prinzipien und Elemente einer graphischen Technologie zur multidimensionalen Exploration sozialer Strukturen. Habilitation Thesis, Gerhard-Mercator-Universität – Gesamthochschule Duisburg, Duisburg.

Kruskal, J.B. (1964) Multidimensional scaling by optimizing a goodness-of-fit to a non-metric hypothesis. *Psychometrika*, 29: 1–27.

Kumbasar, E., Romney, A.K. and Batchelder, W.H. (1994) Systematic biases in social perception. *American Journal of Sociology*, 100: 477–500.

Laumann, E.O., Marsden, P. and Pensky, D. (1983) The boundary specification problem in network analysis. In R. Burt and E. Minor (eds), *Applied Network Analysis: A Methodological Introduction*, pp. 18–87. Beverly Hills, CA: Sage.

Lin, N. (2001) *Social Capital: A Theory of Social Structure and Action*. Cambridge: Cambridge University Press.

Lin, N. and Dumin, M. (1986) Access to occupations through social ties. *Social Networks*, 8: 365–385.

Lorrain, F. and White, H.C. (1971) Structural equivalence of individuals in social networks. *Journal of Mathematical Sociology*, 1: 49–80.

Luce, R.D. and Perry, A.D. (1949) A method of matrix analysis of group structure. *Psychometrika*, 14: 95–116.

Lusher, D., Koskinen, J. and Robins, G. (eds) (2013) *Exponential Random Graph Models for Social Networks: Theory, Methods and Applications*. New York: Cambridge University Press.

Maiolo, J. and Johnson, J.C. (1992) Determining and utilizing communication networks in marine fisheries: A management tool. *Proceedings of the Gulf and Caribbean Fisheries Institute*, 41: 274–296.

Marin, A. and Hampton, K. (2007) Simplifying the personal network name generator: An alternative to traditional multiple and single name generators. *Field Methods*, 19(2): 163–193.

Marsden, P.V. (1990) Network data and measurement. *Annual Review of Sociology*, 16: 435–463.

McCallister, L. and Fischer, C. (1978) A procedure for surveying personal networks. *Sociological Methods and Research*, 7: 131–148.

McCarty, C., Killworth, P. and Rennell, J. (2007) Impact of methods for reducing respondent burden on personal network structural measures. *Social Networks*, 29: 300–315.

McGrath, C., Blythe, J. and Krackhardt, D. (1997) The effects of spatial arrangements on perceptions of graphs. *Social Networks*, 19(2): 223–242.

McPherson, M., Smith-Lovin, L. and Brashears, M. (2006) Social isolation in America: Changes in core discussion networks over two decades. *American Sociological Review*, 71: 353–375.

Milgram, S. (1967) The small world problem. *Psychology Today*, 1(1): 60–67.

Munzner, T. (2000) Interactive visualization of large graphs and networks. PhD dissertation, Computer Science Department, Stanford University.

Nadel, S.F. (1957) *The Theory of Social Structure*. Melbourne: Melbourne University Press.

Newcomb, T.M. (1961) *The Acquaintance Process*. New York: Holt, Rinehart & Winston.

Newman, M.E.J. (2004) Fast algorithm for detecting community structure in networks. *Physical Review E*, 69: 066133.

Opsahl, T. (2012) Triadic closure in two-mode networks: Redefining the global and local clustering coefficients. *Social Networks*, 35(2): 159–167.

Padgett, J.F. and Ansell, C.K. (1993) Robust action and the rise of the Medici, 1400–1434. *American Journal of Sociology*, 98(6): 1259–1319.

Panning, W. (1982) Fitting blockmodels to data. *Social Networks*, 4: 81–101.

Perry, B.L., Pescosolido, B.A. and Borgatti, S. (2017) *Egocentric Social Network Analysis: Foundations, Methods, and Models*. New York, NY: Cambridge University Press.

Pitts, F. (1979) The medieval trade network revisited. *Social Networks*, 1: 285–292.

Rand, D.G., Arbesman, S. and Christakis, N.A. (2011) Dynamic networks promote cooperation in experiments with humans. *Proceedings of the National Academy of Sciences of the USA*, 108: 19193–19198.

Robins, G. (2011) Exponential random graph models for social networks. In P. Carrington and J. Scott (eds), *Sage Handbook of Social Network Analysis*, pp. 484–500. Thousand Oaks, CA: Sage.

Robins, G., Pattison, P., Kalish, Y. and Lusher, D. (2007) An introduction to exponential random graph (p*) models for social networks. *Social Networks*, 29: 173–191.

Roethlisberger, F. and Dickson, W. (1939) *Management and the Worker*. Cambridge: Cambridge University Press.

Romney, A.K., Weller, S. and Batchelder, W.H. (1986) Culture as consensus: A theory of culture and informant accuracy. *American Anthropologist*, 88: 313–338.

Rushmore, J., Caillaud, D., Matamba, L., Stumpf, R.M., Borgatti, S.P. and Altizer, S. (2013) Social network analysis of wild chimpanzees provides insights for predicting infectious disease risk. *Journal of Animal Ecology*, 82: 976–986.

Sampson, S. (1969) Crisis in a cloister. Unpublished doctoral dissertation, Cornell University.

Schnettler, S. (2009) A structured overview of 50 years of small-world research. *Social Networks*, 31(3): 165–178.

Schwimmer, E. (1973) *Exchange in the Social Structure of the Orokaiva*. New York: St Martin's Press.

Seidman, S. (1983) Network structure and minimum degree. *Social Networks*, 5: 269–287.

Seidman, S.B. and Foster, B.L. (1978) A graph-theoretic generalization of the clique concept. *Journal of Mathematical Sociology*, 6: 139–154.

Smallman, H. and Boynton, R. (1990) Segregation of basic colors in an information display. *Journal of the Optical Society of America A*, 10: 1985–1994.

Smith, D. and White, D. (1992) Structure and dynamics of the global economy: Network analysis of international trade 1965–1980. *Social Forces*, 70(4): 857–893.

Snijders, T.A.B. (2001) The statistical evaluation of social network dynamics. In M.E. Sobel and M.P. Becker (eds), *Sociological Methodology 2001*, pp. 361–395. Boston and London: Basil Blackwell.

Snijders, T.A.B., Pattison, P., Robins, G.L. and Handcock, M. (2006) New specifications for exponential random graph models. *Sociological Methodology*, 36: 99–153.

Snijders, T.A.B., Steglich, C.E.G. and van de Bunt, G.G. (2010) Introduction to actor-based models for network dynamics. *Social Networks*, 32: 44–60.

Sosdian, C.P. and Sharp, L.M. (1980) Nonresponse in mail surveys: Access failure or respondent resistance. *Public Opinion Quarterly*, 44(3): 396–402.

Soyez, V., De Leon, G., Rosseel, Y. and Broekaert, E. (2006) Motivation and readiness for therapeutic community treatment: Psychometric evaluation of the Dutch translation of the Circumstances, Motivation, Readiness, and Suitability scales. *Journal of Substance Abuse Treatment*, 30(4): 297–308.

Van der Gaag, M.P.J. and Snijders, T.A.B. (2005) The Resource Generator: Measurement of individual social capital with concrete items. *Social Networks*, 27: 1–29.

Van der Gaag, M.P.J. and Webber, M. (2008) Measurement of individual social capital: Questions, instruments, and measures. In I. Kawachi, S.V. Subramanian and D. Kim (eds), *Social Capital and Health*. New York: Springer.

Wang, D.J., Shi, X., McFarland, D.A. and Leskovec, J. (2012) Measurement error in network data: A re-classification. *Social Networks*, 34(4): 396–409.

Watts, D.J. and Strogatz, S.H. (1998) Collective dynamics of 'small-world' networks. *Nature*, 393(6684): 409–410.

Weeks, M.R., Clair, S., Borgatti, S.P., Radda, K. and Schensul, J.J. (2002) Social networks of drug users in high risk sites: Finding the connections. *AIDS and Behavior*, 6(2): 193–206.

White, D.R. and Reitz, K.P. (1983) Graph and semi-group homomorphisms on networks of relations. *Social Networks*, 6: 193–235.

White, H.C., Boorman, S.A. and Breiger, R.L. (1976) Social structure from multiple networks. I. Blockmodels of roles and positions. *American Journal of Sociology*, 81(4): 730–780.

Zachary, W. (1977) An information flow model for conflict and fission in small groups. *Journal of Anthropological Research*, 33: 452–473.

Index

Tables and Figures are indicated by page numbers in bold print.